CO-CFW-879

DISCOURSES OF POVERTY:
SOCIAL REFORM AND THE PICARESQUE
NOVEL IN EARLY MODERN SPAIN

ANNE J. CRUZ

Discourses of Poverty:
Social Reform and the Picaresque
Novel in Early Modern Spain

CABRINI COLLEGE LIBRARY
610 King of Prussia Road
Radnor, PA 19087

UNIVERSITY OF TORONTO PRESS
Toronto Buffalo London

PQ
6147
.P5
C78
1999

41174302

© University of Toronto Press Incorporated 1999
Toronto Buffalo London
Printed in Canada

ISBN 0-8020-4439-5

Printed on acid-free paper

University of Toronto Romance Series

Canadian Cataloguing in Publication Data

Cruz, Anne J., 1941–
  Discourses of poverty : social reform and the picaresque novel in early
  modern Spain

  (University of Toronto romance series)
  Includes bibliographical references and index.
  ISBN 0-8020-4439-5

  1. Picaresque literature, Spanish – History and Criticism.   2. Spanish fiction –
  Classical period, 1500–1700 – History and criticism.   3. Poverty in literature.   I. Title.   II. Series.

  PQ6147.P5C78 1999   863'.309355   C99-930684-7

University of Toronto Press acknowledges the financial assistance to its
publishing program of the Canada Council for the Arts and the Ontario Arts
Council.

This book has been published with the help of a grant from the University of
Illinois at Chicago's Office of the Vice-Chancellor for Research.

A Ricardo, que sabe de pícaros.

Contents

Acknowledgments

Cuando me paro a contemplar mi estado
y ver los pasos por do me ha traído ...

– Garcilaso de la Vega

In writing this book, I owe much to my good fortune. Many friends and colleagues shared their expertise with me on issues of genre, history, and gender, and while I cannot name them all here, most are acknowledged in my notes; others will recognize their influence. Susan Tax Freeman, Carroll B. Johnson, Angus MacKay, Mary Elizabeth Perry (*prima inter pares*), and Harry Sieber kindly took the time to read early versions of the manuscript. My thanks to them and to the Society for Spanish and Portuguese Historical Studies for willingly welcoming a literary critic to its fold. Whatever insights this book contains are due to the resourceful scholarship of my colleagues in history and literature; the errors are mine alone.

I wish to acknowledge the University of California–Irvine for generously granting me a research leave and several sabbaticals that released me from the pressure of schedules, and the University of Illinois, Chicago, for supplying moral and material support for the book's publication. My gratitude, also, to my Irvine *ex-colegas* Ana Paula Ferreira, Lucía Guerra Cunningham, and María Herrera-Sobek for their constant encouragement and the good times, and to my Illinois colleagues for their warm reception. Dr Rosilie Hernández-Pecoraro, my UCI graduate assistant and now UIUC colleague, and UIC students Chi-Yoon Young and Danila Miranda saved me much time in the pursuit of obscure sources. Special recognition is due Dr Susan Isabel Stein, who first assisted me on this project and continues to counsel me on many more. I am indebted to Mario J. Valdés for his initial interest in the manuscript, and to Ron Schoeffel and Anne Forte for their care and kindness in seeing it through to print.

The book includes revised and expanded versions of the following previously published essays: 'The Picaresque as Discourse of Poverty,' *Ideologies & Literature* 3 (1985): 75–87; 'Lazarillo de Tormes as Social Redemptor,' in *Marginated Groups in Spanish and Portuguese History: Proceedings of the Seventeenth Annual Meeting of the Society for Spanish and Portuguese Historical Studies*, ed. William D. Phillips and Carla Rahn Phillips (Minneapolis: Society for Spanish and Portuguese Historical Studies, 1989), 61–70; and 'Sexual Enclosure, Textual Escape: The *Pícara* as Prostitute in the Female Spanish Picaresque,' in *Reading Women: Feminist Contextual Criticism of Medieval and Renaissance Texts*, ed. Sheila J. Fisher and Janet E. Halley (Knoxville: University of Tennessee Press, 1989), 135–59. I thank the editors for their permission to incorporate parts of the essays.

For his unflagging devotion, his inimitable sense of play – fair and otherwise – and the morning coffee, I dedicate this book to my husband.

Introduction

The complex dislocations, both symbolic and social, that propelled Spain into the early modern period generated divergent discourses in response to the increasing numbers of marginalized poor that emerged in the early sixteenth century. In this study, which focuses on the articulations of poverty and its relief through charity and social reform in both the picaresque and non-fictional texts, I employ the term 'discourse' in its broadest sense, encompassing its Renaissance and modern definitions as the ideological expressions that circulate within a cultural field. We have learned from such philosophers of culture as Mikhail Bakhtin, Jacques Derrida, and Michel Foucault that discursive practices cannot be formally categorized or limited to historical specificities but must be assessed as they intersect and become textualized. Unique among the many discourses on the issues of poverty, charity, and state welfare – royal *cédulas*, *pragmáticas*, synods, sermons, and other normative writings – the picaresque genre verbalizes its concerns through its unprecedented protagonist, the *pícaro*, who speaks directly to the reader.

This study intends to demonstrate that this new kind of fiction, while accounting for diverse matters of historical, social, and literary import, also discloses the authors' preoccupations with the increasing disenfranchisement of the poor. From Lazarillo de Tormes, who arrives in Toledo when the Poor Laws are enforced, to Estebanillo González, whose hunger compels him to join the Hapsburg armies, the *pícaros* contend daily with both social disenfranchisement and physical deprivation. In my reading of picaresque narratives, I do not mean to give an explicit 'voice' to the poor, the delinquent, or the prostitute of early modern Spain. As I discuss more fully in the text, just as the authors of the picaresque should not be confused with their narrators, neither should the historical *pícaro* be made completely synonymous with the genre's fictional protagonists. Homology, as I use it, signifies an exchange function based on historical factors; while it exceeds mere literary analogy, it cannot and does not denote exactitude. That the authors ground their fictions in the stark realities that surround them does not, in the end, ensure the authenticity of the narratives; where they succeed, however, is in expanding our awareness of the cultural foundations of social reform.

By descanting on the 'life' of the *pícaro*, the picaresque novels raise significant questions regarding the ethos of poverty and the efficacy of poor relief that remain lamentably valid to this day. By stating this, I in no way suggest an uninterrupted progression from early modern Spain's endeavours at eradicating poverty to the modern welfare imperative. Rather, my study attempts to explain the failure of social reform as proposed in the seventeenth century. Nevertheless, it is historically significant that the controversies inhering in welfare to this day – the vision of a social order that not merely alleviates poverty but fosters communal ties, for example, or the establishment of ethical categories – insistently evoke the Soto–Robles debates, discussed in chapter 1, that contrast individual responsibility with social entitlement. Indeed, Norman Barry reminds us that the nineteenth-century English Poor Law discouraged indiscriminate welfare 'because its attractions would cause people to become dependent.' It was countered by an equally influential welfare tradition arguing that 'people were entitled to relief precisely because they could not be held (morally) responsible for the predicaments in which they might find themselves' (Barry 12).

Spanish polemics on social reform followed an earlier chronology than that established by Foucault for France, yet, despite the two countries' different histories, I find the Foucauldian social paradigms useful in that they afford us an effective, albeit provisional, overview and grasp of seemingly contingent events. For this reason, my use of Foucault's theses remains, I believe, valid in that, by focusing on the social constraints imposed, they allow us to reconfigure the picaresque response to their controls as both historical discourse and literary text. Moreover, Foucault's notion of the multiple discursive elements that come into play in various texts enlists a polyphony of responses that runs counter to his purported obsession with vertical power. This concept, as theoretically cogent as Bakhtin's heteroglossia, challenges us to move beyond the strictly formalist parameters that have too often delimited critical investigations of the genre, pointing instead to a reading that requires the narratives' contextualization.

On the other extreme of a purely aesthetic approach, scholars who focus exclusively on the picaresque as social critique draw too direct and transparent a correlation between social and literary histories. From Frank W. Chandler's *Romances of Roguery* to José Antonio Maravall's magisterial *La literatura picaresca desde la historia social*, studies informed mainly by sociological criteria have attributed the genre's origins to the economic conditions prevalent in early modern Spain while ignoring their literary function. To be sure, moralist approaches, counteracting materialist analyses, have also tended to underscore the genre's so-called realism. Alexander Parker's *Literature and the Delinquent*, although a seminal statement on the picaresque's historical groundings, nonetheless restricts the genre to a theological exposition of the thematics of freedom owing to the religious reforms set in motion before and after the Council of Trent (24).

Yet the literary and religious parameters against which Parker posits the genre's emergence cannot be divorced from what he claims are the less satisfactory explanations of economic conditions or the increase of cultural minorities. The very conditions specified by Parker as discrete categories remain undivided in the period. What these studies all fail to consider is that the literary figure of the *pícaro* – and of the *pícara* – did not develop in apposition to their historical avatars, but instead responded dialectically to the multiple conditions that produced them. The picaresque's adeptness in addressing so-called extra-literary issues, therefore, derives from its dialogic relations with those other discourses of poverty – social, religious, and economic – produced in early modern Spain.

In rereading the picaresque novels through historicist, gender, and reader-response theories, I acknowledge the material and symbolic bases on which the complex 'meaning' of a particular cultural community is founded. This meaning is accrued from the community's articulation of its social and political unconscious, as well as of its cultural imaginary. By analysing the narratives as cultural discourses rather than as solely literary artefacts, my study realigns the conventional picaresque canon with religious writings, reformist treatises, and state documents in order to foreground the pressing questions of poverty, delinquency, vagrancy, and prostitution embedded in the novels. To this effect, the study encompasses not only the canonical eponymous anti-heroes of the *Lazarillo de Tormes*, the *Buscón*, and the *Guzmán de Alfarache*, but the more marginalized female picaresque such as the *Lozana andaluza*, the *Pícara Justina*, and *Teresa de Manzanares*. And, since I

believe the genre also to be a penetrating statement on Hapsburg imperialist policies of military conscription, my study incorporates the soldiers' tales still only peripherally assigned to the picaresque genre:
Jerónimo de Pasamonte, Miguel de Castro, Alonso de Contreras, and *Estebanillo González.*

Assuming a role played out as much on the historical as on the literary
scene, the numbers of *pícaros* that appeared in print and on the streets
corresponded in turn to the poor's diminished ability to provide for their
own welfare. Increasingly denounced as an uncontainable social plague,
the impoverished early on replaced the Medieval leper in his ritual role
of *pharmakos*, considered as at once the cause of and the solution to social
malaise. In *The Political Unconscious*, Fredric Jameson identifies the
literary text's strategy to rewrite or restructure a previous historical or
ideological subtext, one that articulates the text's relations with its surrounding reality in order to resolve or dispel intolerable social contradictions (81). The birth of the *pícaro*, in his perceived degeneration from
impoverished to immoral, may be understood in part as a symbolic
means of satisfying the social need for a new mythical figure incarnating
the major ills that afflicted sixteenth-century Spain.

In a country where homogeneity was desired at any price, such marginalized subalterns as the poor, criminals, *conversos*, *moriscos*, and prostitutes shifted easily into the position of the Other, filling the void left by
the leper. In considering the reception of the genre by its readers, I also
hope to demonstrate how the authors' critical thrust is nevertheless
thwarted when the public, in order to insulate itself against social
change, converts the *pícaro* to the risible category of clown. Like the narratives' protagonists, their historical avatars are rejected as a social
force, repressed and transformed into the liminal position of scapegoat
through the symbolic unconscious of the new nation-state.

Yet this new cultural myth could not have taken shape were it not for
the need created by interrelated social, economic, and historical factors.
Precipitated by the rupture of the feudal system, urban development,
and the intermittent plagues, price increases, and food shortages that
vexed Spain throughout the century, the spiralling numbers of disenfranchised could no longer be contained through individual gifts of
charity. As anthropologist Marcel Mauss has explained, economic
imbalance creates a surplus of recipients that ultimately overwhelms the
religio-anthropological pattern of exchange. It is this imbalance that
prompted reformers such as Juan Luis Vives, whose writings introduced the secularization of poor relief in Northern Europe, to question

the effectiveness of private charitable acts as a means of succouring the impoverished. Transposed as protagonists in the novels, these marginalized groups function as highly ambivalent signs of conflicting ideologies on social reform. Whether unable or unwilling to secure an honest livelihood, in their psychological and social mutability the *pícaros* embody the changing perceptions of the poor and of poor relief.

In reviewing the debate of theologians Domingo de Soto and Juan de Robles and the subsequent literature of *arbitrismo* as they relate dialogically to the picaresque, my study aims both to insert the controversy within the discourses of poverty that circulated in the period, and to historicize more thoroughly the genre's aesthetic continuum delineated by its critics. Foreseeing the failure of the Spanish economy, reformers and *arbitristas* joined forces with the unknown author of the *Lazarillo* and Mateo Alemán in their harsh critique of government and its mismanagement of economic and social capital. Quevedo's *buscón*, Pablos, whose cynical rejection of the work ethic parodies aristocratic attitudes, censures the growing aristocratization of the state. Since the *pícaros* are forced to remain at the basest socio-economic level, they function as ominous reminders of the precariousness of economic and social positions.

The novels' profoundly ironic message in no way detracted from their popularity; as we know, the *Guzmán de Alfarache* became the first Spanish 'best-seller.' Nonetheless, the genre's appeal to aristocratic and bourgeois readers confirms its wilful misreading by the bulk of the public. Having the most to lose through historical change, these readers interpreted the novels not as normative social criticism, but as literary diversions that granted them distance from the imminent threat of social reform. In his devaluation from social menace to harmless jester, the *pícaro* registers the paranoia felt by the dominant classes towards the poor and those of impure blood. The role of *pharmakos* is one that I extend to the narratives themselves as sacrificial texts offered to the burgeoning bureaucratic interests of the state. My study thus construes the picaresque primarily as a complex mimetic discourse that performs a cultural leap from fictive text to historical reality, obliquely uncovering the author's underlying social critique through the narrator's autobiographical confession. Yet the novels also serve to assuage the fears of its reading public; their ironic discourse both allows a critical reading based on authorial dissent and proposes a socially pragmatic, or functional, interpretation that reasserts aristocratic values.

This is equally as true of the *Lazarillo* and the *Guzmán de Alfarache* as it is of the *Buscón* and the female picaresque, since the genre increasingly envisages the protagonists, no longer as liminal anti-heroes, but as integrated into the underclass of Spanish culture. As I argue in chapter 4, in Quevedo's novel and in female picaresque narratives like Francisco Delicado's *La lozana andaluza*, Francisco de Ubeda's *La pícara Justina*, and Alonso de Salas Barbadillo's *La hija de la Celestina*, the abjected protagonist becomes the 'other' who is gazed on by and gazes back at the cultural hierarchy. If, in his position of *atalaya*, society's watchtower, Guzmán only partially embodies the ever-seeing Foucauldian panopticon, the *pícaras*, whose every move is controlled by their male authors, testify to the regulations imposed on the physical, social, and textual body. Although generally excluded from the picaresque canon, these female protagonists offer an ideal case study of how literary discourses often implicitly conform to an ideology they seemingly attempt to subvert. While the literary *pícaras* are granted social mobility and appear to celebrate their freedom and linguistic ability, their libertine attitudes in actuality bespeak the male author's prejudice against unconstrained female sexuality: accorded the same low social rank as prostitutes, the *pícaras* are ultimately condemned by the texts.

Closing with an investigation of the *pícaro* as soldier, I conclude in chapter 5 that the proliferating soldiers' tales in the first half of the seventeenth century effectively recuperate the *pícaro* from his delinquent status by conscripting him into the military. These narratives recast both the literary *pícaro* and the historical impoverished as a malleable commodity within the Hapsburg military machine. The end of the picaresque genre, therefore, coincides with the chaotic and amoral decline of Hapsburg Imperial rule. Like its protagonist, who at once indicts the system and profits from it, *Estebanillo González* is neither wholly a picaresque tale nor merely a soldier's tale of fortune. Through its veiled critique of Spain's ruthless military system, the novel extends the social criticism in the *Lazarillo* and the *Guzmán de Alfarache*, circumscribed to Spain and to the Mediterranean, to the theatre of the Thirty Years War. Its depiction of the *pícaro* as a failed rogue and soldier clearly shows that the novel was intended to be read, not solely as an ambiguously subversive literature desensitizing the reader, but as an ideological response to the real issues of poverty and the insolvent military operations of war.

Estebanillo González develops to the fullest the cultural transformations of *pícaros* and the poor envisaged in the earlier picaresque novels. Ironically, the soldier-*pícaro* escapes from the hostilities surrounding him by writing his 'life' in payment for his freedom. The fact that, to denounce his participation in war, he must reinscribe it as fiction, shows how his story records both failed history and the failure of history. Like the rest of the picaresque genre to which it belongs, Estebanillo's story is also, in a conventional sense, a fallacy of fiction. Neither true autobiography nor entirely fictive narrative, in its multiple and protean forms the picaresque novel remains instead a project whose readings are never completely explored nor ever totally exhausted. My study means to draw these ambivalent texts closer to their historical grounding so they intersect with equally significant extra-literary discourses. By performing a dialectical redescription of picaresque novels and social treatises, therefore, my aim is to simultaneously recover the picaresque genre's materialist base and to examine the profound implications of poverty and social reform for the culture of early modern Spain.

DISCOURSES OF POVERTY:
SOCIAL REFORM AND THE PICARESQUE
NOVEL IN EARLY MODERN SPAIN

1

Charity, Poverty, and Liminality in the *Lazarillo*

If it is true that the leper gave rise to rituals of exclusion ... then the plague gave rise to disciplinary projects ... the first is marked; the second analysed and distributed.

Michel Foucault, *Discipline and Punish*

As a result, I had to bring forth strength from my weakness and, little by little, succoured by the good townfolk, I ended up in this noble city of Toledo. Here, with God's mercy, after a fortnight my wound healed. While I was ill I was always given a hand-out, but when I got better everybody said: 'You, you're nothing but a scoundrel and a loafer. Go on, go and find somebody and get a job.'

[Desta manera me fue forzado sacar fuerzas de flaqueza, y poco a poco, con ayuda de las buenas gentes, di comigo en esta insigne ciudad de Toledo, adonde, con la merced de Dios, dende a quince días se me cerró la herida. Y mientras estaba malo siempre me daban alguna limosna; mas después que estuve sano todos me decían: «Tú bellaco y gallofero eres ... Busca, busca un amo a quien sirvas.» (*Lazarillo de Tormes*, III: 71)][1]

The *Lazarillo de Tormes* begins its third *tratado* by describing young Lázaro's hasty exit from the house of his second master, the uncharitable priest of Maqueda, and his inglorious entrance into the noble city of Toledo. Starved by the skinflint priest's total disregard for his physical nourishment and deprived by him of any spiritual support, Lazarillo is expelled from the 'breadly paradise' when the priest discovers him stealing bread rolls to quell his gnawing hunger. As in his previous escapades with the blind man, he is again assisted by the good towns-people, who feel sorry for the poor boy who has fallen into the hands of such miserly masters. Yet once the wounds from the priest's beating are healed, Lazarillo finds that the townspeople no longer offer him alms. No one shows any interest in caring for him, and all goad him to go find work. Describing the penurious situation in which he finds himself as he goes from door to door, Lazarillo gives the readers a clue with which to interpret the social meaning of his life story: 'As I was walking down the street, calling at every door and getting most of them shut in my face, because charity had already gone to heaven' (Andando así discur-riendo de puerta en puerta, con harto poco remedio, porque ya la car-idad se subió al cielo [III: 72]).

Charity has indeed gone to heaven, and it is this departure, so pain-fully felt by Lazarillo and carefully recorded in his childhood recollec-tions, that contributes not only to the moral ambivalence and textual ambiguities of the narrative, but to its historical verisimilitude.[2] Among the many topics mined from this slim novel, one in particular has gar-nered continued interest: the *Lazarillo* is a tale of poverty, not merely of Lazarillo's, but of poverty itself, of the relationship between society and its poor, and of the changing ideologies that leave the two groups no longer beneficently interrelated, but in conflict with each other. Despite its provisional 'happy ending' – since in conforming to the debased val-ues of the society around him, the adult Lázaro eats often and well – Lazarillo's story, as it recalls the hunger pangs that provoked the boy's performance, also remarks on the beginnings of an alienated social force that will not be contained.

Most likely written about 1551, close to its publication date of 1554 and during the Council of Trent's Period II on clergy reform, the *Lazarillo* has challenged historically-minded critics to scrutinize the text for direct ref-erences and allusions to Spain's religious and social upheavals in the mid-sixteenth century.[3] Yet, although they have often been pointed out as coincidental with the narrative, such historical events as Charles V's welfare reforms, the Soto and Robles debates on the poor, and the decrees against clerical concubinage have still to be justified critically, not merely as factors contributing to the narrative's realism, but as informing both the textual and the social origins of a genre that has been perceived far too often solely from an aesthetic or taxonomic perspec-tive.[4] Trapped within the 'vicious circularity' of generic theory, as Ulrich

Wicks puts it, critics attempting to force the picaresque into generic categories continue to debate whether the *Lazarillo*'s fictional autobiography
of its lowly protagonist sufficiently characterizes the genre known as
picaresque.[5] Antonio Gómez-Moriana's recent theorizations on the text's
social nature are helpful in that they compel us instead to question Lazarillo's proposed universality, his archetypal function as 'cosmic orphan'
(Wicks 231–2).[6] The *Lazarillo*'s historical specificity, therefore, configures
both its anonymity and its ambiguity. And as the anonymous novel's
ironically ambiguous discourse exposes the increasing social and economic tensions of early modern Spain, it presages the genre's explosive
development in the literature, which in turn parallels, even as the novels
chronicle, the appearance and proliferation of vagabonds and beggars in
the country's emerging urban centres.[7]

The historical process thus engages the writers of the genre with the
growing numbers of vagrants overrunning sixteenth-century Spain, a
social phenomenon described by contemporary historiographers as a
plague that descended on the country. Their profusion, as the century
wore on, would convince an anxious populace that the disenfranchised
were to blame for the rise in criminality. Indeed, the identification of
delinquency as a trait of the disenfranchised accountable to an ethical
order was, as we shall see, a result of the epistemic changes in mid-century that transformed the country's social conditions and unremittingly
altered traditional perceptions of the poor. As the first Spanish narrative
to elevate an itinerant beggar to the status of a major protagonist, the *Lazarillo* literally identifies from the start with its fictive character's increasingly undesirable historical analogue. The ill and the lame, previously
accepted as requisite figures of the medieval landscape, now took on a
darker shade as they became associated with the impoverished who
streamed into towns and cities. While the episode draws on folklore, it is
significant that Lazarillo is given over first to a blind beggar, anticipating
through their amorally symbiotic relationship the later conflation of the
poor with the delinquent. Paradoxically, then, the text's popularity con-
firmed that the contemporary public delighted in reading about what it
took pains to avoid in the street. This irony was surely not lost on the
reader who, as we discuss more fully in chapter 3, would recognize in
Lazarillo the many street urchins found begging in Spain's expanding
urban centres. Thus, although the term *pícaro* – specifically referring to a
lowly rogue living by his wits and bending, if not breaking, social laws –
did not appear in any literary text until Mateo Alemán's *Guzmán de
Alfarache*, the various editions which were published together with the

Lazarillo ensured that readers would relate the two texts and apply the derogatory term to the earlier text's young protagonist as well.[8]

The social difference beween the lowly letter-writer, Lázaro, and his inquisitorial correspondent, known only by the title 'Vuestra merced,' underscores the contrast between the boy's disgraceful appearance in Toledo and the joyous entry celebrations accorded a victorious Charles V, the 'regocijos' of which presumably reached the selective ears of 'Vuestra merced,' as Lázaro is quick to inform him (VII: 135). By assuming the narrator's voice, Lazarillo obtains on a literary level an importance far exceeding his apparent social worth. In this regard, the text's singularity has inspired critics, as readers conditioned to mimetic practices, to search for similar fictional situations and to propose possible typologies, as well as to seek differences countering previous and coexisting genres. Lázaro's letter to 'Vuestra merced' has so far been identified with, or considered a self-conscious response to, numerous exemplars that make up the broad discursive field of the sixteenth and seventeenth centuries, including such literary and extra-literary narratives as chivalric romances, saints' lives, inquisitional records, confessional narratives, and the epistolary literature currently in vogue in Spain and Italy.[9]

In a thoughtful restatement of his previous studies on the picaresque, Peter N. Dunn is the latest in a distinguished critical line to reject the genre's systematicity, as well as its critique of poverty. Rather, he regards the picaresque's origins as harking back to a miscellany of traditional storytelling, anecdotes, folklore, and literary jests, and considers its individual differences far too great to allow for generic stability.[10] What, for him, does constitute novelty is the first-person narration. He states that the protagonist's 'identity of consciousness,' claimed by Ian Watt in his *Rise of the Novel* to be grounded in the linguistic and epistemological systems of the period, comprises the genre's 'formal realism.'[11] Dunn adds that the self, constituted through recollection, the awareness of identity in a sequence of acts seen as events in a causal chain, has already found imaginative representation in outline in *Lazarillo de Tormes* and, more elaborately, in *Guzmán de Alfarache*, which draws explicitly on a philosophical tradition (Dunn, *Spanish Picaresque Fiction*, 37).

Despite whatever ambiguities the genre may evince, however, its self-awareness remains for Dunn an aestheticizing concept deriving solely from the genre's writerly attributes. Certainly, he is right to assert that the myriad readings engendered by the *Lazarillo*, like the different interpretations of the *Guzmán*, are due as much to its 'openness' and ambiguity as to the diverse interests and preoccupations of its many interpreters (39–40).[12] Nevertheless, the earlier text's ambivalence (like the *Guzmán's* ambiguities, as I note in chapter 3) itself at once relies on and draws from the historical moment. If its autobiographical form may be traced as far back as Apuleius's *Golden Ass*, as numerous critics have averred, its new 'perspective of consciousness,' to quote Alexander Blackburn, works to set the *Lazarillo* apart from classical narratives, separating this new narrative from any notion of universal truth. Instead, its protagonist 'relentlessly act[s] in and interact[s] with a world in which all meanings and values were disintegrating – in which the flux of mutual consciousness was that society' (12).[13]

Spain's feudal disintegration, ruthlessly brought to bear on those whose disenfranchisement would be its end result, conforms with the ironized and distanced position manifested by the picaresque narrator. Intrinsically divided, it is a position that nonetheless struggles to sustain subjective coherence.[14] In this, the newly emergent picaresque genre resembles its contemporaneous narratives far more than it reacts against them. José Antonio Maravall has amply documented the incipient 'individualism' recorded by Renaissance texts in their use of the first person, not from an idealist sense of humanist progress, but as a philosophical critique of self-knowledge and self-determination.[15] These autobiographical writings, whether taken as historically 'real' or as fictive renderings of the life of an 'other,' simultaneously conceal and disclose the growing unease with which early modern writers perceived themselves. The abundant examples during the period help to situate other seemingly unrelated genres.[16] Stephen Greenblatt was among the first to note that treatises like Pico della Mirandola's *On the Dignity of Man*, Castiglione's *Il Cortegiano*, and Montaigne's *Essais* document the Renaissance compulsion for self-fashioning.[17] The profuse writings by Spanish explorers retelling their adventures through *relaciones de Indias* and *verdaderas historias*, if dictated by the historical necessity of communicating between the dominant culture and its other, also speak eloquently to the desire for self-discovery, self-recognition, and, ultimately, self-historicizing.[18] Since the compulsion to fashion one's self as a socially individuated being corresponds to an acute awareness of social alienation, the picaresque genre cannot fail to parody the autobiographical mode or mimic the canonical discourses that invariably aimed to anchor their authors in increasingly evanescent realms, whether as courtiers, intellectuals, or explorers of new worlds.[19]

While admittedly fictional, Lazarillo's tale, therefore, continues to be reconsidered in light of the character's situatedness in history, from the emphasis placed by its early translators on the protagonist's distinctive 'Spanishness' to, some four centuries later, Maravall's monumental *La literatura picaresca desde la historia social*, whose insistence upon the genre's historical beginnings, however, in no way denies the literary *pícaro*'s uniqueness.[20] That Maravall, a social historian, does not hesitate to address the issue in 1986, after so many books and articles have variously asserted and denied the picaresque's social origins, would seem to reaffirm current critical anxieties that post-positivist literary theories tread perilously on ever-shifting, postmodernist grounds. Yet the continual discoveries of new historical data and the consequent reconsideration of received information, not to mention the application of novel critical theories and the rethinking of different critical emphases, constantly contest the validity of all interpretive readings, even those taken as definitive. This is not, however, to claim the text's indeterminacy, but to reclaim the social determinations that, in the words of one cultural critic, 'establish the conditions within which reading can take place.'[21] And, we might add, the conditions that allow for writing. In that it is intellectually inadvisable and, in any case, functionally impossible to maintain as separate entities any sort of Neo-Aristotelian categorizations such as 'history' and 'literature,' not only what Dunn calls the textual 'gaps,' but our own critical perceptions of what comprises literary and extra-literary discursive formations remain always provisional and open to challenge.

In its multiple meanings of travel, speech, thought, motion, and process, the Spanish term *discurso*, as it was employed during the Renaissance, holds analogous meaning to the Foucauldian notion of 'discourse.' Foucault's definition supplants the 'knowing subject' with various subjective positions, conceiving discourse as a 'space of exteriority in which a network of distinct sites is deployed.'[22] Yet his purpose – to reveal the governing systems of formation that reside within discourse itself – necessarily elides not only the reception by readers of the texts' discursive strategies, but these same texts' performative nature. As part of the discourse on the pervasive poverty of the times, whose condition informs the narrative's autobiographical premise, the *Lazarillo* transgresses its literary bounds even before its prologue proves their impermeability a fiction. However, the *Lazarillo*'s recourse to historicity neither reflects strictly upon, nor is reflected directly in, its protagonists.[23] Despite any compassion Lazarillo's mistreatment might elicit from the reader, the young boy cannot, after all, be confused with the author. The text's moral ambiguities instead chart the tensions between the novel's so-called verisimilitude and the surrounding cultural field, even as they blur its fictional and historical parameters.[24]

Lepers and Liminality

Lázaro's pride in having written of 'important events which quite accidentally have never seen the light of day' (de cosas tan señaladas y por ventura nunca oídas ni vistas [23]), as he assures his anonymous inquisitorial addressee in the prologue, at once disguises and engages in the narrative any feelings of shame the recalcitrant Lazarillo may have had about his precarious existence. Indeed, his narrative, which ironically counterposes his 'negra fortuna' to his ability to better his social and economic situation, repeatedly emphasizes the orphaned childhood visited upon him.[25] Yet, just as the adult Lázaro's cynical acceptance of his cuckolded status becomes evident as we read through his lies, so, too, do we doubt the child's ignorance of his parents' degradation when he endorses his childhood fable. In his recollected narrative, the adult Lázaro cunningly exploits the likelihood of the youth's mortification over his parents' ignominious behaviour. Lazarillo would certainly be most humiliated by his mother's prostitution for the family's benefit, which the young boy ingenuously ascribes to the Moor's 'love,' but whose unlawful liaison would be perceived as inappropriate even by a child.

Instead, with an eye towards excusing his current ménage-à-trois with the Archpriest of San Salvador, Lázaro sardonically proffers his mother's illicit relationship as justification for the clergy's immorally misapplied *caritas*, since they steal from the church poorbox to support their concubines:

Seeing that love forces a poor slave to do this we ought not to be surprised that a priest robs from the poor and a friar from his convent for the benefit of his female devotees and others.

[No nos maravillemos de un clérigo ni fraile porque el uno hurta de los pobres y el otro de casa para sus devotas y para ayuda de otro tanto, cuando a un pobre esclavo el amor le animaba a esto. (I: 19)]

The young Lazarillo's humiliation over his despicable origins, ambiguously presented by Lázaro's manipulative narrative, never achieves the rhetorical significance openly manifested in the shameful emotions of Quevedo's *pícaro*, Pablos. Nevertheless, it constitutes an essential element within the narrative's symbolic economy. As Lazarillo absorbs the social evils surrounding him through the lessons learned from his corrupt masters, his role in the text assumes the figure of scapegoat, a propitiatory offering that will be sacrificed for the collective good of that same debased society he so willingly defends.

As the carrier of collective guilt, Lazarillo's literary persona is again identified with the historical *pícaro* who increasingly shouldered the blame for the numerous ills that plagued sixteenth-century Spain. At the historical moment in question, however, the bonds that, no matter how tenuously, continued to unite the marginalized with society had yet to be completely severed. Unlike the *pícaros* of the later picaresque narratives, Lazarillo is not accused of committing socially contagious crimes such as parricide, blasphemy, or sacrilege, or other acts that undermine the social order.[26] His function, akin to the emergent role of the *pícaros* in society, conforms to one of liminality, an ambiguous state combining baseness and the sacred, wavering between established religious and sociopolitical structures, and synonymous with Arnold Van Gennep's term *marge*.[27] Ever on the margins, Lazarillo moves from one unstable familial and social situation to another: abandoned by his biological father, his stepfather, and his mother, he is exploited by the patriarchal figures of his masters until he, too, becomes one of them. The geographical sites he must traverse in his trajectory through the Spanish countryside – the Salamanca bridge, the Maqueda priest's threshold, the Toledo city gates – are also the sites where he experiences his liminal rites of passage, each of which propel him to sustain increasingly dangerous subject positions.[28]

The liminal spaces trespassed by Lazarillo thus correspond to both the symbolic and the material realms. Transgressing the boundaries of Spain's walled towns and open fields, the young boy's errant figure recalls the sacralized infirmity of the medieval *pauperes Christi* even as it prefigures the rogues' perceived abject and aggressive immorality. Lazarillo's liminal position in a society whose dubious feelings towards the poor fluctuated between reverence and disdain is reflected both in the narrative's indeterminate chronology and in the narrator's double vision of himself as inhabiting an uncertain psychic space between child and adult. Yet Lazarillo never once refers to himself in the diminutive, but always as 'Lázaro,' even when he clearly assumes a child's perspective.[29] The recognition of a split subjectivity calls attention to the double significance of his name, echoing the multiple literary and oral traditions from which the text issues forth. Although Marcel Bataillon has attributed its origins to a pre-existing folkloric homonym which eventually becomes entwined with the European tale of the *garçon et l'aveugle*, and whose only published source appears to be Francisco Delicado's *La lozana andaluza*, the more obvious connection is to the two Lazaruses mentioned in the Bible (28).[30]

Underscoring the text's thematics, the correlation between the biblical figures named Lazarus and the *pícaro*–narrator Lázaro de Tormes engages the reader directly in the poverty, suffering, and contagion featured so emphatically in the biblical allusions (Bataillon, *Novedad y fecundidad*, 28). Furthermore, Lázaro's Hebrew variant, Eleazar, which translates to 'helped by God,' lends an unexpectedly ironic twist, for the Spanish namesake finds himself at considerable distance from divine providence. Bataillon notes that the cognates *lazrar, lazdrar,* the modernized *lacerar* and *laceria*, denoting material deprivation, all relate onomastically to St Lazarus, the patron of lepers and leprosariums. This association is recorded in the numerous popular sayings such as 'poorer than Lazarus' (más pobre que Lázaro) and 'We suffer on [St] Lazarus's Day, but we're fine by Palm Sunday' (Por Lázaro laceramos y por los Ramos bien andamos) (*Novedad* 27–8). Lazarillo employs the term metonymically when he calls the bread scraps the blind man tosses him 'laceria,' thus addressing both his sufferings and the blind man's stinginess: '[B]ut I used to take the miserable scrap of food he gave me and gobble it up in two mouthfuls' (mas yo tomaba aquella laceria que él me daba, la cual en menos de dos bocados era despachada [I: 28]). Similarly, he describes the priest as 'lacerado,' meaning avaricious, and thereby extending his condition to that of an emotional and moral cripple: 'But the miser lied in his teeth' (Mas el lacerado mentía falsamente [II: 52]). Lazarillo's lament, 'Oh, miserable me' (lacerado de mí [I: 39]), when the blind man accuses him of stealing the sausage, not only echoes his name, but synthesizes his physical and moral condition.

The text's complex wordplay on the etymological connections of Lazarillo's name with *laceria* compels an exploration of Lazarillo's synecdochical relations to his biblical namesake. As Alan Deyermond, among others, has recognized, the boy's starved existence replicates the sufferings of Lazarus, the beggar in the Bible who barely sustained himself with the crumbs from the rich man's table.[31] Another ironic connection is set in place when Lazarillo finally reaches what he calls 'the height of all good fortune' (la cumbre de toda buena fortuna [VII: 135]). Unlike his Hebrew cognate, Eleazar, Lázaro tells us he has received no help from anyone; instead, he becomes as complacent and morally insensitive as the rich man of the parable. The narrative's motifs of death and resurrection further recall the other biblical Lazarus, the brother of Mary and Martha resurrected by Christ at Bethany. Lazarillo's first episode with the blind man parodies the biblical story in its inversion of Lazarus's restoration to life: through the blind man's teachings, Lazarillo degenerates from moral life to moral death (Deyermond 30).

   At issue for us here, however, is that the biblical resonances in Lazarillo's name reveal a keen awareness of the symbolic role that the poor play within the social structure. The conflation of the two Lazaruses in the Bible into the literary persona of Lazarillo is coextensive with the term applied to those suffering from the disease of leprosy, whose medieval synonym was *lazar*. In his study of medieval lepers, Peter Richards comments on the confusion that arose between the two:

Use of the name lazar for leper is symptomatic of the deep confusion upon which the Church based its attitude towards leprosy and those who suffered from it. Lazarus, the beggar covered with sores, who in the parable lay at the rich man's gate was apocryphally considered to have been a leper ... By some strange and tortuous thinking, Lazarus the beggar became identified with Lazarus of Bethany, whom Jesus raised from the dead, conveniently perhaps, for it may have seemed to promise certain resurrection to the lepers.[32]

During the Middle Ages, the Catholic Church followed Levitical laws on impurity by requiring that lepers be isolated. When, in reaction to increased hostility towards the afflicted, the Lateran Council of 1179 required their segregation, there followed a marked increase in the construction of lazarhouses throughout Europe.[33] The leper was not initially obligated to enter the lazarhouse, but since he was required to separate himself from society, he was usually forced to seek shelter in a hospital through his own personal circumstances (Richards 49). The spiritual favours bestowed by the Church on donors for charitable contributions further encouraged the building of leper hospitals. The benefactors of these foundations contributed to them mainly as a means of attaining their own spiritual salvation, since they garnered the fruits of long-term charity as well as constant prayer (Richards 11).

   The institutionalization of the leper's isolation from social contact was apparently based not nearly so much on fear of infection as on the religious implications of defilement: 'Nothing in the rules needs to be explained on any other grounds than the avoidance of defilement by an outcast, a concept unfamiliar today but very real then. The company of men, water, pathways, goods for sale, posts and gates, the air itself must not be polluted; even the burial place of the dead must not be defiled' (Richards 53). Saul Brody explains that a thirteenth-century German sermon identifies the leper healed by Christ as 'defiled by deadly sins,' and a sermon by Maurice de Sully lists the sins symbolized by leprosy: 'The leper signifies sinners, and the leprosy the sins ... the great damnable sins, such as fornication, adultery, usury, robbery, theft, gluttony, drunkenness, and all those sins by which a man is damned ... Through leprosy a man is cut off from the company of people, and through deadly sins a man is cut off from the company of God.'[34] Most hospitals had strict regulations which were primarily concerned with improving the souls of the lepers, not with containing the disease. Richards points out that lepers admitted to St Julian's hospital in England were required to promise 'to be satisfied without complaint or murmur with the food and drink and other things given me by the master.'

The emphasis placed on the leper's acceptance of his condition and its treatment suggests that society assigned a symbolic value to him that far outweighed the concerns for his welfare. Not only were lepers expected to accept a meek and humble role in society, they were required to wear distinctive clothing which marked them as religious and social outcasts. The regulations of St Julian's, for example, addressed the lepers' value as moral spectacle: 'Since amongst all infirmities the disease of leprosy is held in contempt, those who are struck down with such a disease ought to show themselves only at special times and places, and in their manner and dress more contemptible than other men' (Richards 70). Since the leper's sores were considered the external manifestations of the evils that beset the human race, they were a graphic reminder that God's word should be heeded. As the embodiment of evil, they were to remain marginalized; however, as an example to the people of their need for salvation, it was important that the lepers remain visible to them.

Medieval literature inherited a tradition that branded the leper a pariah, accusing him of immorality, and separating him from society (Brody 146). Lepers were often associated with heretics, their poisoned breath believed to spread the disease (Moore 63). Yet their social presence, like their appearance in literature, served as a warning to others.[35] Robert I. Moore claims that, since the leper was allowed to atone for his sins on earth and could look forward to an early redemption, his status was not only feared, but paradoxically revered and envied by society (Moore 60). This attitude was reflected in the social treatment given the lepers. Richards has recorded the curious ambivalence with which, in opposition to the Lateran Council mandates, hospitals allowed some lepers to visit towns, to participate in town activities, and even to spend a night away from the hospital:

At St. Julian's ... the leper brothers were forbidden to loiter on the path outside the hospital or to converse with others there, yet one at least of their number was permitted to visit the mill and brewery, another supervised the farm work, for which outside labourers were hired, and all were entitled to seek leave from the master to visit St. Albans and even to spend a night away from the hospital. (Richards 51)

Despite the insistence by Church authorities that the lepers be segregated, their presence in society, arranged with the tacit approval of the institutions in control, indicates that they fulfilled a religious and social function by remaining visible to the people. Long considered a normative sight, the leper, according to one new historicist, 'was the figure of a death beyond dying, the image of a mortality that did not even need death to make its message known' (Mullaney 33).

In assuming the role of suffering and poverty, as well as of death and miraculous resurrection, the leper functioned within the nebulous areas where life and death overlap and mingle. The lepers shared many of the qualities attributed to liminal groups, such as uniform clothing, sacredness, and submission to social authority. Anthropologist Victor Turner has affirmed that in increasingly complex societies with divisions of labour, the transitive state of liminal groups becomes a permanent condition.[36] The leper's position in society, then, was neither that of separation nor that of aggregation, but that of maintained liminality. Certainly, one of the most significant reasons that the leper was consigned to such an integral social function was the opportunity he provided to the people to practise charitable acts. If he was taken to be the incarnation of the biblical beggar Lazarus, then those who contributed to his welfare – thus assuring their own spiritual resurrection – were also heirs to the other biblical Lazarus who was brought back from the dead. The leper's presence in society, then, symbolized the constant of spiritual illness of which humans were always victims. By accepting charity to attenuate the physical disease, the same lepers provided the potential cure for sin as well.

In a closed, feudal society such as medieval Spain's, the leper per-

formed an exemplary function, his care dependent on private donations. Wealthy nobles with an avocation towards charity joined a
brotherhood significantly named the Order of St Lazarus, and visited
the hospitals to help in the treatment of the lepers.[37] In the sixteenth century, however, the Catholic monarchs instituted a ministry of medicine
(*tribunal supremo de medicina*) that shifted the care of the lepers from the
exclusive responsibility of the Church to newly created positions based
on secular institutions. These appointed posts, *alcaldes de la lepra* and
proto-médicos del tribunal, as they were called, were filled by physicians
who specialized in the identification of lepers and their confinement to
the lazarhouses (Contreras Dueñas *et al.* 87–8). Demonstrating a social
commitment distinct from religious responsibility, and long before the
Council of Trent, Charles V asserted his right to supervise Castilian leprosariums.[38] However, while the transfer of care from the religious to
the secular realm was done for the purpose of improving the lepers'
treatment, it also resulted in their desacralization. The prevailing perception, in the medieval and early modern periods, that lepers were special members of society whose presence served to strengthen its social
and religious bonds, and therefore permitted to circulate among society,
instead gave way to sanctions against those who refused marginalization and containment.[39]

The issues raised by the treatment of lepers in medieval Europe repli-
cated those which the poor posed to Spanish society in the early sixteenth century. During the height of the disease, lepers mingled easily
with the poor; in France, Louis VI founded a leper house at Compiègne
to keep them from wandering in the street like beggars (R.I. Moore 57).[40]
Like the lepers, the impoverished formed a subculture that demanded
increasing attention, and as the numbers of lepers ebbed towards the
end of the Middle Ages, the poor gradually took on the role of a liminal
group.[41] The relief felt socially by the lepers' disappearance was countermanded by a far greater need for their symbolic function as sacramentalized and demonized scapegoat.[42] As early as 1342, the numbers
of lepers had fallen sufficiently at Ripon, France, to permit the assign-
ment of the lazarhouse property to the poor (Moore 60). And in fifteenth-century France, Michel Foucault notes, lazarhouses were
emptied of their charges, and at least one, Saint-Germain, was converted
to a reformatory for young criminals (*Madness* 3–5). As the lepers before
them had functioned as scapegoats, so the poor were now called upon
to atone for societal ills.

Brody's study of medieval literature mentions Robert Henryson's *The*

Testament of Cresseid, the sequel to Chaucer's *Troilus and Criseyde*, as one
of the few literary examples of a female leper, linking the protagonist's
debauchery to venereal disease (177). Since the accepted cure in these
narratives, he states, was the blood of innocent children, lepers and Jews
were presumed to share the heterodox practices that fuelled popular
fears of child-murders.[43] In tracing the growth of social persecution in
the Middle Ages, Moore postulates that the common thread binding
heretics, lepers, and Jews was their victimization by the persecuting zeal
that seized European society at that time, reacting to its fear of the
'other' as a threat to Christian order (67). This victimization, however,
did not allow the members of these groups to redeem themselves
through individual free will. He concludes that society did not place
blame on the number, quality, or nature of the victims, but rather that it
forced them into certain roles: 'The behaviour and social demeanour of
Jews, as of lepers and heretics, were inextricably entangled with the way
in which they were perceived and treated ... The characteristics of the
part then became those of the actor. The distinction between reality and
perception is hard to maintain if reality only has one form' (Moore 89).
By the sixteenth century, the role of the leper had been taken over by
those social groups that would be denominated as 'other.' Despite the
many real differences among them, such marginalized groups as *conversos*, *moriscos*, 'loose' women, and the poor played out the social roles
imposed by dominant society that had been left vacant by the diminish-
ing numbers of lepers. Even the term *pícaro* was sometimes conjectur-
ed to derive from the rogues' presumed Jewish origins, since the
Hebrew root *pkr* gives the verb *pakar*, meaning irreligious, licentious, or
wanton.[44]

Because control of the impoverished signified the purification of the
social body and its spiritual redemption, their treatment involved not
only religious, but economic and social concerns. All three types of concerns are manifest in the proliferating discourses on poverty – sociological treatises, religious writings, and literary narratives – that circulated
during the century. Despite its seeming simplicity and hilarity, therefore, the *Lazarillo* encodes the serious issues that materially affected sixteenth-century Spain. Derek Lomax has argued that the novel was
written during a period of economic growth fuelled by Charles V's
political expansionism:

[T]he *Lazarillo* was written in a period of boom; and instead of reflecting a ludi-
crously mis-dated decline, it seems more plausible to consider that it reflects this

boom ... The *Lazarillo*, in short, reflects not the disillusion of a decline miracu-
lously foreseen fifty years before it happened; it represents rather a revolution of
rising expectations ... The new interest in poverty appears in literature when a
possibility of freeing men from poverty appears in reality.[45]

Yet, as I argue in the following chapter, the price rise that resulted from
the stimulus of the American demand for goods and the broader European market, while benefiting merchants, caused great anxiety among
consumers. These economic problems most affected the Crown of
Castile, an area that in the sixteenth century comprised two-thirds of
the Iberian peninsula and included Galicia, Asturias, León, Old and
New Castile, Extremadura, Murcia, and Andalucía.[46] Marjorie Grice-
Hutchinson states that 'protests began to be made against the import of
foreign manufactures ... the balance of trade was turning against Castile,
and the hard-won American treasure beginning to melt away.'[47] Even
before 1550, there were already signs of an impending recession, and
historians are agreed that the cost of living rose sharply at mid-century
throughout sixteenth-century Europe. According to Henry Kamen, the
price of wheat increased an unprecedented 376 per cent in Castile
between 1500 and 1600. Kamen considers the term 'price revolution' justified, which he attributes to the inflation caused by bullion imports
from the New World, first documented in 1556 by Martín de Azpilcueta
and in 1558 by Francisco López de Gómara.[48] At the time, Kamen
remarks, it was extremely difficult to adapt to economic change: 'if
bread doubled in price, people starved' (53). We should, therefore, take
seriously Lázaro's bitter protest against the poverty and hunger he is
made to experience, even if the *pícaro* blames them only on his masters'
mistreatment.

Indeed, the stigma of poverty is pervasive throughout the novel, aptly
described by Javier Herrero as 'the story of a starving family' (876).
From Lazarillo's early years at the side of his mother, through his tute-
lage with the blind man, on to his later apprenticeship with the squire
and the priest, he gains knowledge first-hand of the desperation
brought about by near-starvation. Lazarillo's constant hunger is, of
course, only one of the narrative's many motifs, as its abundantly
diverse criticism amply confirms. The tale itself, however, tells us that
hunger is indeed the young boy's prime motivation: it is the reason for
which he lies and steals from his masters, negating whatever feelings of
charity he may once have harboured, and the force which ultimately
drives him to ignore his wife's behaviour in order to forestall the loss of

the material benefits he enjoys from her illicit relations.[49] Francisco Rico remarks that, instead of closing with the expected jokes about cuckolded husbands typical of folktales and Italian *novelle*, Lázaro's ambiguous story of his wife's relations with the Archpriest leaves the reader with the sensation that the situation as it stands is of no great importance.[50] Nonetheless, we should not overlook its rhetorical strategy: because he does not directly admit to any misdeed, but merely assumes the attitude of a helpful servant, Lázaro's clever defence of his adulterous 'case' deflects all blame from him.

What most likely holds far more interest for the anonymous 'Vuestra merced' is not the living arrangements of a poor town crier, but the amoral behaviour of his 'friend,' the Archpriest of San Salvador ('servidor y amigo de Vuestra merced' [VII: 130]). It is significant, therefore, that the narrative clears Lazarillo of any wrongdoing by slyly accusing his religious benefactor of violating the decrees issued by Juan Tavera, Inquisitor-General and Archbishop of Toledo. The eminent reformer had not only warned the faithful against fraudulent pilgrims devising false signs (in whose company one could easily find a deceitful pardoner), but also decreed that no clergy should allow women in their home for any sort of company, whether licit or illicit.[51] His *Constituciones synodales del arzobispado de Toledo*, which were read at the Toledan Synod in April 1536, and published in Alcalá de Henares on 8 July of the same year, intended to correct an immoral situation still common among the clergy despite the 1503 laws against such behaviour:

[F]rom today hence no secular or religious clergy, of any rank or state, who has taken Holy Orders or holds any benefice in our Holy Church or any other within our archbishopric may reside or keep company with any woman suspected of such behavior or reputation, or one who is the cause of such slander, no matter what her age; and those who live in this fashion, are warned and obliged by this decree, within thirty days following its publication, to give the woman due notice and dismiss her from their house or company under penalty, if they disobey, of punishment and discipline for public concubinage

[q[ue] ni[n]gu[n] clerigo ni religioso constituydo en orden sacro o beneficiado en n[ues]tra sancta Iglesia o en otra qualquiera de n[ues]tro arçobispado de qualquier dignidad o co[n]dicio[n] que sea de aqui adela[n]te no tenga muger en su casa o co[m]pañia que segun la disposicio[n] del derecho sea tenida o reputada por sospechosa ni co[n] quie[n] en algun tie[m]po aya sido infamado de qualquier edad que sean; y si alguno al presente las tienen; les requerimos y amonestamos por la presente constitucio[n]: que dentro de treynta dias despues de la publicacion destas nuestras constituciones; los quales les damos y assignamos por tres terminos las aparen y echen con effecto de su casa o compañia; so pena que si assi no lo hizieren ni cumplieren dende en adelante sean auidos por publicos co[n]cubinarios; y como tales sean punidos y castigados. (fol. xvii)][52]

An imposing political as well as religious figure, Cardinal Tavera has been unaccountably ignored by most historians, despite his close ties to Charles V and his secretary, Francisco de los Cobos.[53] Surprisingly, no one has noticed the uncanny similarities between Tavera and 'Vuestra merced' to draw a connection between them. The Cardinal's main social concerns – his efforts to reform the clergy, his defence of *conversos*, and his involvement with the poor – could very well have inspired the *Lazarillo*'s author to utilize Tavera, who had already died before the book was published, as the principal model for the shadowy figure of Lázaro's inquisitor.[54]

Besides being apprised of Tavera's injunctions, *Lazarillo*'s anonymous author, as an educated reader, was surely aware that other contemporary moralists like Francisco de Osuna, one of the most widely read religious writers of the century, held the unmarried state iniquitous for the non-religious. Following Augustine, Ambrose, and Paul, the Franciscan reformer exalted religious orders as the ideal vocation, but considered marriage an essential state for all others: 'In great disarray is the life of all those who have not taken one of the three principal states in Christendom: which are religious, secular clergy, and marriage' (Desco[m]puesta tienen la vida todos los q[ue] no han tomado algun stado delos tres principales q[ue] ay enla cristiandad: q[ue] son religion y clerezia y casamiento).[55] The reader is thus made cognizant of the hypocrisy that structures Lázaro's 'explanation' of his case to 'Vuestra merced' when he praises the Archpriest's efforts to find him a suitable marriage partner. Both men stand to gain in the transaction; the Archpriest's success in marrying Lázaro to his concubine resolves the young man's unsettled state while it allows for the cleric's own immoral activities:

At that time, the Archpriest of St Salvador, my lord and your Honour's servant and friend, heard about me and saw how sharp and ready-witted I was, because I used to announce that his wines were for sale, and he arranged a marriage for me with a maid of his. And since I saw that only good could come from such a person, I agreed to marry the girl.

[En este tiempo, viendo mi habilidad y buen vivir, teniendo noticia de mi persona el señor arcipreste de Sant Salvador, mi señor, y servidor y amigo de Vuestra Merced, porque le pregonaba sus vinos, procuró casarme con una criada suya. Y visto por mí que de tal persona no podía venir sino bien a favor, acordé de lo hacer (VII: 130–1)]

In his appeal to 'Vuestra merced''s sympathy and sense of justice by dwelling on the suffering he endured at the hands of his cruel masters, Lazarillo selectively remembers and recounts their most damning uncharitable deeds. Yet, since he knows that the Archpriest maintains some sort of relations with 'Vuestra merced,' his complaint against the cleric is disguised by the grateful tone with which Lázaro relates the seemingly favourable treatment the Archpriest accords him. However, by blaming others for his misconduct, he implicates all of society in his mistreatment. Through his criticism of his first three archetypal masters, the adult Lázaro condemns the three estates for his inability to escape the cycle of poverty by any means other than becoming a foil for their hypocrisy, even as he purports to share their debased values: 'As a result nobody says anything to me and there is peace at home' (Desta manera no me dicen nada, y yo tengo paz en mi casa [VII: 135]).

Whether or not we believe him, Lázaro's life story mediates between the textualized deformation of the historical poor and the historicized textuality of a new literary genre defined and delimited by its protagonist-*pícaro*.[56] While the concurrent themes of poverty and hunger provide the narrative with a unifying structural force, we must not lose sight of the fact that they also serve as indices to the social realities faced by the subculture of the poor and, equally as important, to the increasingly complex interrelations of the impoverished with other social groups. Dunn conjectures that the picaresque's early reader would not have 'taken the protagonist seriously as a human being' (39). Admittedly, it is difficult, if not altogether impossible, to determine whether, in early modern Spain, Lázaro's human essence would have prevailed over his fictional self. As I discuss more at length in my section on reader response in chapter 3, the picaresque text's ludic intent cannot be divorced from the *pícaro*'s function as *pharmakos*. Nevertheless, despite Lázaro's ambiguous position, and no matter how diminished the figure of the *pícaro*, my study intends to prove that the issues of poverty and mistreatment of the poor that inhere in his narrative assuredly condition the reader's own humanity.

Mid-Sixteenth-Century Debates on Poverty: Soto versus Robles

The definition of poverty at any historical moment is in itself a matter of social and economic relativity. By the sixteenth century, economic status in Europe was a function of source and level of income, with land taking precedence over personal property.[57] Historians have discussed and debated Spain's failure to develop an industrial infrastructure that would offer employment to the disenfranchised, a topic I expand upon in chapter 2. For the moment, however, I wish to emphasize that, as food became scarce, disease spread, and the population of disenfranchised swelled, the poor were defined as those in need of public assistance, their indigence impelling the movement from one location to another in search of labour and sustenance. The 1550 recession, Grice-Hutchinson tells us, gave way to the first of many financial crises; although prices were raised and credit expanded after 1560, relieving some of the pressure, by 1580 the uncompetitive prices, rises in wages, crushing taxation, and absence of productive enterprise had again brought about severe economic stagnation (*Early Economic Thought* 125; 133).

These crises not only propelled Spain's feudalistic society to the beginnings of capitalist enterprise, but demanded a redefinition of the poor based on a new apperception of their role in that changing society.[58] As the poor filled the void left by the lepers, they were subject to the same changing perceptions and hostilities, and their status in society came increasingly into question. Commenting on the confusion that arose during the century regarding poor relief and who constituted the so-called poor, José Antonio Maravall states that much attention was focused on distinguishing between the 'true' or legitimate poor, and the fraudulent beggars who, while physically able to work, preferred to produce lesions and mutilate their bodies in order to exploit the charitable (Maravall, *La literatura picaresca*, 218). The distinctions, as we shall see, reflect upon the new social conditions brought about by the ideological changes first espoused by sixteenth-century religious and secular writers concerned with Spain's increasing poverty. Anticipating the arguments adduced by Foucault for social control, the Spanish reformers that I discuss in this and the next chapter generated a polyphony of discourses inflected by their differing ideologies. Their contributions on diverse means to resolve poverty profoundly influenced the authors of the picaresque.

Despite the enlightened attempts by such humanists as Juan Luis

Vives to address poor relief from the perspective of secularized social reform, the early sixteenth century had formalized a vision of the disenfranchised according to the traditional Christian concept of charity, as representatives of Christ who provided the wealthy an opportune means of salvation in their need for alms and charitable works. Vives's *De subventione pauperum*, written in 1526 and dedicated to his adopted city, Bruges, is the first treatise to remark on the failure of Christian charity, and to propose radically new solutions.[59] Yet Vives also adhered to the conventional belief that poverty offered a hidden advantage to the poor in that it eliminated the occasion of sin and gave them the opportunity to practise virtue. He exhorted them, as lepers had been told earlier, to remain humble and grateful always to their donors:

[The poor] should not be satisfied to mouth their thanks for the benefits they received, but should maintain a grateful spirit, that is, they should remember the benefit received; they should not misspend wastefully or dishonestly what has been given them, nor hoard callously or stingily, since they cannot take it with them when they die.

[No se contenten con haber dado gracias de palabra por los beneficios que recibieron, sino conserven un espíritu agradecido, esto es, que se acuerde del beneficio; no malgasten pródiga y torpemente lo que les han dado, ni lo guarden sucia y ruinmente, que no se lo han de llevar á la otra vida.][60]

The poor thus remained central to a social order that perceived poverty as a natural given. The corollary to this feudalistic tenet was that wealth in the hands of a few was also natural and, therefore, God-given. The nobility thus incurred the responsibility of acting within moral bounds. The impoverished could demand that their rights be observed, and medieval society often witnessed rebellions against abusive lords, so paupers remained fully integrated within the traditional estates.[61] The social balance was maintained through the established system of material exchange for spiritual welfare, which served to diffuse tensions between the two groups. Moreover, the complex structure of ritualized compensation consolidated into the Catholic liturgical calendar, such as the celebrations promoted during Carnival, Easter, and Christmas, offered the poor a temporary release from any potentially dissident feelings they might harbour (Maravall, *La literatura*, 195). The poor's condition, therefore, was considered blameless since it was necessary for the social good.[62]

Nonetheless, the continuing economic crises alerted social reformers like Vives to the responsibility of the state for what had formerly been left to individual conscience. In the mid-sixteenth century, the relatively uniform perception of the poor as part of the natural order soon split into two conflicting positions. One comprised the earlier view of paupers as the redemptors of the rich, meekly accepting their lot in much the same way as the lepers who had no choice but to be stigmatized by their disease; the other position considered the disenfranchised potentially antisocial reprobates, and advocated for their social reform (Maravall, *La literatura*, 196–7). In Spain, the two main protagonists of the debates were the Dominican Domingo de Soto, professor of theology at the University of Salamanca, and the Benedictine Juan de Robles (alias de Medina), abbot of the Monastery of St Vincent in Salamanca. A brilliant scholar who was sent by Charles V as imperial theologian to the Council of Trent, and later authored a monumental work on justice and the law, Soto maintained the traditional medieval criterion of the poor that granted them the right to beg and opposed any form of means test or confinement.[63] He strongly disputed the recent 1540 Poor Laws that attempted to curb alms-giving by first examining whether beggars were truly poor and licensed, and then restricting them to their place of origin. He also did not agree with the pragmatic, recently published in Medina del Campo in 1544, that ordered hospital reforms to feed and cure the ailing poor so they would not have to beg in the street. His treatise, *Deliberación en la causa de los pobres* (Salamanca, 1545), is addressed to the young Prince Philip in both Latin and Castilian ('since this should also be said in a language that all can understand' [es necesario decirse también en lengua que todos entiendan]).[64] Soto's *Deliberación* echoes Thomas Aquinas in asserting that those who are economically able have the moral and religious obligation to succour the poor:

And no one will make a dent in his purse by giving some help to the poor, of which they have great need ... Rich and poor are all admonished to give to those who have naught.

[Y no hay nadie que sin hacer mella en su hacienda no pueda hacer ningún socorro a los pobres, de que ellos tienen gran necesidad ... Al rico y al pobre, a todos se amonesta que den al que no tiene. [55–6]

In arguing that the poor should be physically restricted to a particular town only if the townspeople are enjoined to maintain them, Soto is responding to the petitions to the *cortes* that had complained about the problems brought about by the wandering poor. As early as 1518, the Crown concurred that the poor should remain in their place of birth and that they be given a licence to beg. If sick, they should be confined to a hospital (Martz 14). The numerous petitions that followed in 1523, 1528, and 1534, and the promulgation of the Poor Laws in 1540, clearly speak to the difficulties in imposing these restrictions.[65] Although historian Linda Martz considers the drought and subsequent bad harvests in Castile the main reasons for the Poor Laws' promulgation, popular sentiment against the growing numbers of poor was documented by Pedro Simón Abril, who warned of the social dangers posed by those having nothing to lose (Maravall, *La literatura*, 12).

Soto grounds his arguments that the poor should beg freely on the belief in the Christian obligation to practise the cardinal virtue of charity that, as a Dominican, he shared with the mendicant orders. Founded by the Castilian Domingo de Guzmán in 1216, the Dominicans or Order of Preachers (Orden de Predicadores), along with the Franciscans, valued the disenfranchised for their intrinsic humanity, not merely as instruments for salvation of the wealthy.[66] Nonetheless, the two orders were often criticized; when, in the Middle Ages, these mendicant convents assumed the role of intermediaries between the poor and the rest of society previously entrusted to the Benedictines, they were accused of usurping the place of the genuine poor (Mollat 126–7). Basing his views on the mendicants' perception of the poor as *pauperes Christi*, as imitators of Christ, Soto contends that, if the poor are physically restricted to a particular town without the townspeople's support, they will be condemned to suffer (37). Emphasizing *caritas* over rational ethics and charity over justice, he asserts that there is no harm in succouring the fraudulent poor, since it is preferable to give alms to them rather than to withhold from the truly needy:

When in doubt if some one is truly poor, it is better to be charitable and accept him as such, than to side with justice and rebuke his feigned poverty. For surely it is more cruel and harmful to withhold [charity] from four true paupers because of twenty false poor than it is unjust to help twenty false beggars so as not to harm the four legitimate paupers.

[[Q]ue en duda si uno es pobre o no, antes en favor de la pobreza se ha de aprobar por pobre que en favor de la justicia reprobarse por no pobre. Porque mayor daño y mayor crueldad será que a vuelta de veinte fingidos pobres se excluyesen cuatro verdaderos, que será injusticia por no hacer injuria a cuatro verdaderos sufrir que hubiese veinte fingidos. (75)]

Soto again privileges charity over justice when asserting that charitable acts should not be contingent upon the recipient's moral behaviour. Stating that such an attitude actually allows the rich to forgo their responsibilities towards the poor, he cites from John Chrysostom's second sermon on the biblical figure of Lazarus: 'It is one thing to judge an evil man, and quite another to give alms to the poor. That is why it is called almsgiving, which means compassion, since it is done to the undeserving' (Otra cosa es ser juez del malo y otra cosa es ser limosnero del pobre. Por eso se llama limosna, que quiere decir misericordia, porque se hace a los indignos [87]). Furthermore, to expect the poor to confess to their begging before they could receive alms, as required by the Poor Laws, would effectively condemn them not only to immediate punishment, but to death by starvation, since no one would be willing to aid them for fear of breaking the law. Soto's treatise thus draws on the fundamental principles of charity that acted as a unifying force within the Church, reminding the faithful that, as the representatives of Christ on earth, the poor should be succoured not merely with regard to the spiritual concerns of the donors, but in light of their own immediate needs.

Soto's treatise was published 30 January 1545 by Juan de Junta, nine years before the famous press published the Burgos edition of the *Lazarillo*. Robles's response, *De la orden que en algunos pueblos de España se ha puesto en la limosna para remedio de los verdaderos pobres*, published less than two months after Soto's by the same press, heeds Cardinal Tavera's directive that the reformer write Prince Philip in reply to Soto.[67] Defending the implementation of these laws in Zamora, Robles's preface to his seven chapters reads remarkably like the 'respuesta' to 'Vuestra merced' in the *Lazarillo*'s prologue:

I think the situation is such that it is necessary to address the whole matter, since Your Highness has received so many diverse opinions on the subject. And, therefore, to comply with what you have asked of me, I convey to Your Highness my reasons for having the orders implemented in Zamora.

[[P]aréceme que la cosa ha venido ya a términos que es menester hablar de todo, pues cerca de todo se han dicho diversos pareceres a Vuestra Alteza. Ansí que por cumplir lo que me fué mandado y lo que debo, envío aquí a

Vuestra Alteza los fundamentos que se ofrecieron para comenzar esta orden en Zamora. (150–1)]

The treatise agreed with the conventional view that the fraudulent poor should be punished. Citing as examples the edicts against begging propounded by Vives in Bruges and the Pope in Rome (228–9), however, it emphasized the alternative of improving the conditions of the poor through organized donations rather than through individual charitable acts. Humanists had long believed that begging was beneath man's dignity; for Robles, begging was proof that the poor were not receiving proper care:

> The charity that most aids our fellow man is that which offers him the most benefits and advantages; and since the pauper benefits far more if we relieve his poverty and cure his illnesses than if, for our own personal gain, we allow him to suffer on the streets, then the former is doubtless what is best for him ... And so, no reasonable man will deny that it is better to cure the sick than to toss them a daily coin, and to offer the poor a means of sustenance than to give them money on a daily basis.

> [[L]as obras de caridad que se enderezan a bien del prójimo, tanto son mejores cuanto el prójimo recibe más beneficio y provecho dellas; y pues el pobre recibe mayor beneficio de que le remediemos sus pobrezas y enfermedades que no que con achaque de nuestros aprovechamientos particulares le dejemos andar con ellas por las calles, ninguno dudará, sino que esto es lo mejor ... Y ansí no debe dudar ningún hombre que tenga juicio, que es mejor curar al plagado que darle cada día una blanca, y mantener al pobre que darle cada día un maravedí. (176)]

Insisting that the individual contributions that had previously been given voluntarily would not be diminished, Robles specifies two ways to collect alms: through public collections by prelates, and through secret donations in special collection boxes, a method employed by the ancient Jews (214–19). This money, he stipulates, should be administered by one person, preferably a religious, elected to the office and observed by a prelate and a *corregidor*, or judge (222–3).

Although Robles's response was meant to counter Soto's treatise, it is important to note that not all members of the mendicant orders agreed with Soto and opposed Robles's reform efforts. Francisco de Osuna's *Quinta parte del abecedario espiritual* was published in 1542 by Juan de Junta only three years before the publication of Soto's and Robles's trea-

tises. Although he stresses the role of the poor as *pauperes Christi*, Osuna
nevertheless anticipates Robles in his contention, based on early Franciscan teachings, that the impoverished should make an effort to find
employment. The Franciscan preacher thus complements his order's
mendicant tradition with his belief in the work ethic and women's place
in the home:

> The pauper who earns his food is more blessed than he who begs for it in God's
> name ... and our Holy Father, St Francis [of Assisi] gives first place to the poor
> who work, and then adds, 'When we are not reimbursed the fruits of our labour,
> then let us rely on the Lord's table and beg for alms door to door.' And since the
> poor man who works inspires his family to do likewise, David adds, 'May your
> wife be like the plentiful vine growing on your walls.' The poor man's wife
> should work within the home, and he should work outside.

> [Es mas bendicto el pobre que por su trabajo gana de comer que no el que lo
> pide por Dios ... y nuestro padre Sant Fra[n]cisco en el primer lugar pone al
> pobre que trabaja y luego añade Quando no nos dieren el precio de nuestro tra-
> bajo socorramonos a la mesa del Señor pidiendo limosna de puerta en puerta. Y
> porquel pobre trabajador a de induzir tambien su familia al trabajo añade luego
> David Tu mujer sea como parra abundosa en los lados de tu casa. El trabajo de la
> muger a de ser delas puertas a dentro y el marido pobre ha de trabajar fuera.
> {fol. lxv–x r)][68]

In his 'Avisos de ricos,' Osuna gives several reasons for the poverty then
afflicting Spain: he blames the wealthy for their lack of charity and
excessive spending, for hiring insufficient numbers of servants, thus
limiting the workforce, and for appropriating and enclosing farmland
for cattle grazing. But, in observing the numbers of thieves plaguing the
country, he also condemns the soldiers who loot, rather than do battle,
for survival (fols. ccviii–ccx).

The connections that Osuna makes between soldiering and the poor is
one that I take up in a later chapter. For now, I wish to note that Osuna,
who was well aware that the mendicant orders had been accused of
'robbing' the poor, again defends their position by pointing out that the
brothers were already indigent before joining the order; by choosing to
follow Christ's example, they then dedicated themselves to others (fols.
ccxi–ccxiii). Therefore, in the prologue to his *Quinta parte*, he justifies
mendicant poverty only if the brothers remain spiritually active. The
religious purpose that, for Osuna, must be retained for poverty to con-

tinue to exist has already disappeared in the *Lazarillo*. Anticipating the Toledo townfolks' reproach to the jobless *pícaro*, Osuna condemns, not poverty, but idleness:

If you are poor because of idleness you do not deserve to be consoled but reprehended, nor should you be called poor, but a slacker, because just as man calls himself according to his highest virtue, so he should be called after his worst vice.

[De manera que quando eres pobre porque eres ocioso no eres digno de consolacion sino de reprehension, ni te deven llamar pobre sino holgazan; porque assi como en las cosas de virtud toma hombre nombre de la mejor que tiene, assi enlas cosas de vicio ha de resceuir nombre dela peor que se hallare enel.]

As Robles was to affirm shortly after, moreover, Osuna believed that ecclesiastics had the obligation to distribute funds to the poor. Consequently, he urges the order's council to divide its monies among the poor and view charity as its major expense.

   The administration of alms, collected from public contributions of no more than two *maravedís* and no less than one *blanca* daily per person, and from voluntary donations placed in church collection boxes, was the responsibility of elected government officials. Robles, however, insisted that these funds should remain in the hands of the Church:

I admit that it would look better if [the collection monies] are in the hands of ecclesiastics since, as they say, this is their business and the Prelates's especially ... and I hope it pleases God that the clergy are so affronted and envious to see God's business in secular hands, that they will justly take it away from them.

[Yo confieso que parecería muy mejor en manos de personas eclesiásticas y que es negocio propio dellas y más de los Prelados, como dicho es ... Y plega a Dios que tanta afrenta reciban los eclesiásticos y tanta envidia de ver este negocio de Dios en manos de personas seglares que por justicia se lo saquen de entre las manos. (225–6)]

While the Council of Trent would later attempt to recuperate the principles established by municipal magistrates, it was no secret that many prelates were effectively enriching themselves and their families with the monies from poor relief.

   Tireless in his efforts to effect religious reform, Cardinal Tavera again takes part in the deliberations on poverty that occurred at mid-century.

Concerned about the moral implications of administering poor relief, he had discussed the need for reform with Soto and with Robles, urging the Benedictine to write to Prince Philip in response to Soto.[69] Tavera's apprehensions coincided with those of the municipal representatives. When asked by the Cardinal to air their grievances at a synod he planned to hold, the representatives complained bitterly about the manner in which the clergy were handling the poor. Yet, perhaps influenced by Tavera's belief in the need to effect reform, these same representatives ultimately refrained from requesting the secularization of poor relief (Redondo, 'Pauperismo,' 707–8). It is not surprising, then, that Tavera's hopes for ecclesiastical revision would be echoed in the strong reformist spirit of the *Lazarillo*.

Textual Tensions: The *Lazarillo*'s Ambiguity

Cardinal Tavera died the year Soto's and Robles's treatises were published, and although he had envisioned a lasting reform that would eliminate the need for begging by the poor, by 1552 Toledo again necessitated some secular form of control over vagabonds. The *Pragmática* of that year dispatched all vagrants to the galleys; any unlicensed beggar was ordered to four years' galley service for the first offence, eight years for the second, and life sentence for the third (Martz 30). It is in this increasingly conflictive atmosphere, with its unresolved questions regarding the role of the poor in society, that the *Lazarillo* first appears as published text. Although we can be certain of the intent of *Lazarillo*'s author to formulate a criticism of society, his targets are not at all clear. Critics have long pondered over the author's exact position on the Church and the nobility, and have variously considered Lazarillo's author a *converso*, an Erasmian, and an Illuminist (Deyermond, *Lazarillo*, 11 ff). They have also read picaresque literature as a protest against the treatment of *conversos*. The latest to do so is Colbert Nepaulsingh, who ascribes a hidden *converso* code to the *Lazarillo*, a text he believes written by a *converso* for the crypto-Jewish community.[70]

Together with this authorial ambiguity, it is important to observe the marked ambivalence with which the author presents his concerns regarding poverty and its treatment. It is not insisting too much to repeat that the treatment of the poor is one of the *Lazarillo*'s main themes. Márquez Villanueva affirms that '*Lazarillo*'s deepest religious concern is centered on a complex obsession with the theological virtue of charity' (la más honda procupación religiosa del *Lazarillo de Tormes* se centra en torno a un complejo obsesivo con la virtud teologal de la caridad' [*Espiritualidad y literatura*, 110]). Maravall, for his part, isolates it as one of the main focuses of the picaresque novel in general: 'The picaresque novel emerges to combat, this time from the side of the poor, those forces that insist on restricting people to the old order' (La novela picaresca se levanta para combatir, desde el lado más bien de los pobres, las fuerzas que se empeñan en mantener sujetas a las gentes al viejo orden ['Pobres y pobreza' 215]). While this may not be so evident in other picaresque novels, such as the *Buscón*, it is certainly so for the *Lazarillo*. Yet Maravall also claims the novel resists the medieval view of the poor as a liminal group that serves the spiritual welfare of the rich by accepting their charity:

The fact that Lazarillo tells us ... that he finds himself at the height of his prosperity converted into a cynical individual, patently testifies that, from the first, the picaresque abandons the medieval Christian ideal of the poor.

[El hecho de que Lazarillo nos diga ... que se encuentra en la cumbre de su prosperidad convertido en un sujeto cínico, es un patente testimonio de que la picaresca parte, desde el primer momento, del abandono del ideal cristiano-medieval del pobre. ('Pobres y pobreza' 215–16)]

Although he goes on to prove this to be the case for the *Guzmán de Alfarache*, whose author, Mateo Alemán, was a friend of the reformer Cristóbal Pérez de Herrera, the issue is not nearly so clear cut in the *Lazarillo*, since the abandonment of the Christian ideal of charity is precisely what is at stake in the novel.

The text's ambiguity is especially apparent in its depiction of Lazarillo's immediate family. Lazarillo's hidden shame over his origins is manipulated by the adult Lázaro's project to blame society for his ills, and his less-than-honest portrayal of his family's dysfunctionality serves the narrator's – if not the author's – intentions. As with the polyvalent significance of Lazarillo's given name, those of his parents, mentioned in Lázaro's first chapter, contain multiple meanings. Indeed, the apparently simple names of Tomé and Antona assume an overdeterminism that reflects on Lazarillo's own self. Their multiple symbolism again underscores the impossibility of ascribing monovalent qualities to a fragmented self, one that paradoxically emerges through the realization that he can never become whole, but is seen (and created) solely through his textual self-reflection.[71]

For Augustin Redondo, the father's first name, Tomé, calls to mind the many antithetical allusions of the phrase 'give and take' (dar y *tomar*), such as 'it is better to take than to give' (más vale tomar que dar). The name resonates playfully with the folkloric allusions to millers as thieves found scattered throughout Golden Age literature, and the interconnections are documented besides in numerous proverbs, as in 'one hundred tailors, one hundred millers, and one hundred weavers add up to three hundred thieves' (cient sastres y cient molineros y cient texedores son trezientos ladrones).[72] Similarly, Lazarillo's mother shares her name with a notorious host of sexually promiscuous Antonas, whose proclivities are recorded in various proverbs, especially one that puns with the first names of both parents: 'My daughter Antona, one discards her and another takes her' (Mi hija Antona, uno la dexa y otro la toma [Redondo, 'Folklore' 87]).

Moreover, the linguistic family of *molino* (mill), *molinero/a* (miller), and *moler* (to grind), through its metaphorical equivalences with female genitalia and the sexual act, has conventionally been associated with immoral sexual behaviour and the demonic.[73] That the mill remains always in an isolated place, *extramuros*, distanced from the bustle of city life, and that through its cyclical motions it first crushes the grain with great gnashing and noise, then transforms it into a life-giving substance, presupposes as well the mill's symbolic association with death and resurrection. As part of a metonymic chain of signifiers, the mill connotes both the beginnings of a new life and sexual initiation (Redondo, 'Molinos.' 114–15). Extending the onomastics of the biblical Lazaruses and Lazarillo's given name to include those of his parents, the author places the novel's – and the *pícaro*'s – beginnings in relation to the parents' metaphoric and real occupations. As we soon learn, Lazarillo's mother and father are at once millers, thieves, and sexual miscreants. Their ominous trade situates them far from the respectable areas of Salamanca, downstream on the banks of the Tormes, where they inhabit a demonic world of crime and concupiscence. In their anti-Christian behaviour, then, Lazarillo's parents prefigure the young boy's cruel parental substitutes, from the blind man to the Archpriest, and the mistreatment he will receive from them.

The parents' marginalized position as members of an increasingly feared class also accords with their probable *converso* background. Their names, for all their folkloric value, are cut from such ordinary cloth as might be used to cover up less than Old Christian beginnings. Lázaro's liminal condition, inherited from the unnatural parents who abandon him, recalls Francisco de Osuna's warning to Christian husbands:

Do not approach a woman with her menses, because if a man has marital relations then, or does not wish to abstain on Sundays or other holy days, the children they engender will either be born lepers or with gout or possibly possessed by the devil. In short, lepers are not usually born to wise men who practise chastity on the above-mentioned days, but to rustics and, in particular, to those who cannot control or discipline themselves.

[No allegues a la muger q[ue] esta con su costumbre: porq[ue] si alguno entonces tiene accesso a su muger o no se quiere abstener en domingo o en otra qualquier festividad los infantes q[ue] entonces engendraren o nascera[n] leprosos o con gota coral o ta[m]bien por ventura endemoniados. Finalmente q[ue] todos los que son leprosos no suelen nascer de sabios hombres que guardan castidad los dias ya dichos sino de rusticos y mayormente de aquellos que no se saben contener ni suffrir. (*Norte de los estados*, fol. lxxxv)]

Further, among the polysemic configurations informing the humble origins of Lazarillo's family romance, the father's occupational choice gains importance in that, by bleeding the sacks of grain, he effectively steals (and spills) another's seed.[74] Since the mother's lascivious behaviour is implied by the *molino* metaphor, and the mill known as a place frequented by prostitutes, we may assume that her whoring did not wait until after the father's forced exile, and we are left wondering whether Lazarillo's little brother might not be the only *hideputa* in the family. Tomé's dubious paternity thus signals the picaresque's doubtful origins as much as it anticipates Guzmán de Alfarache's multiple fathers (of the text, pirated and plagiarized, as well as of its protagonist) and the *pícara* Justina's receptivity to textual production and sexual reproduction. It is no coincidence, then, that just as the swelling numbers of anonymous *pícaros* begin to swarm through the town squares, their literary homologue first makes his appearance in print. Lázaro's father's final disappearance, ironically heralded by the narrator as voluntary service in the Hapsburg armies, confirms Osuna's judgment of war as one of the main causes of poverty. As such, it presages the seventeenth-century stories of fortune that both conflate and contrast picaresque narratives and pseudo-biographical soldiers' tales as their picaresque anti-heroes are sent off to war.

Abandoned by his father, Lazarillo becomes an added burden to the mother who, without the husband's theft to support the family, looks desperately for other means of survival and quickly settles on Zaide. The lessons he learns from his mother's experience – that as the 'poor

widow' of a condemned thief she can make life a bit better for herself
only by sleeping with another thief, and an infidel, at that – is brought
home to the young boy every time he attempts to find a better master
than his first. Javier Herrero condemns the remote ecclesiastical aristo-
crat who owns the stables for exploiting Lazarillo's stepfather, stating
that Zaide is 'the strongest moral character of the book' because the
Moor steals to feed his brood (881). Yet Herrero takes at face value Lazarillo's glowing depiction of his family, which presents his stepfather as
a loving paternal figure.[75] What bleeds through instead is the unforgiv-
ing *pentimento* of an unholy family comprising a whore/mother, a thief/
father, and an ingrate son who denounces them both.

It is significant that the text's contradictory characterization of the
family reveals yet another ambivalent view of the poor and their entitlement. Zaide is punished for his lasciviousness and larceny, the same
crimes committed by those ecclesiastics who illegitimately supported
their bastard sons with Church income. The mother's advice to Lazarillo
that the child take care of himself is ironically juxtaposed to her comment that he has gained a good master in the blind man, since Lazarillo
is neither able to care for himself, nor will he find a charitable master to
look after him.[76] Lázaro's narrative begins with the clear intent of persuading 'Vuestra merced' of Lazarillo's 'bad luck' from the start, relieving the boy of his moral responsibility with regard to his future
behaviour. As I have indicated previously, by strategically recounting
the mistreatment he receives from his masters, Lazarillo sheds any
blame for his actions. If anything, the surrogate father figures have
taught him too well, for from them he learns to dissemble, cheat, and
steal in order to improve his lot. In accusing society of his ills, Lázaro
places himself in the role of victim, yet the narrative also points to the
double bind in which the poor, like Lazarillo, find themselves from
birth: the only means available to them of escaping poverty is by breaking God's law. If the poor are to behave according to Christian principles, then they must *remain* poor, since any attempt on their part to
relieve the situation constitutes both social and religious transgression.

The mid-century crisis that produced the Soto–Robles debate also
determines the narrative's ambiguity, as traditional Catholic belief in
charitable acts as a means of salvation came increasingly under attack.
Unsurprisingly, Lazarillo's masters all demonstrate a distorted view of
charity. The mother is the first to cast off the child, separating him from
what little familial *caritas* he enjoyed. The blind man introduces him to
the self-serving almsgiving of the townswomen, who toss the couple a

coin solely for their benefit. This first master reveals his own greed when, dissatisfied with these donations, he takes Lazarillo with him on the road in search of wealthier prospects. In teaching the boy his trade, the blind man cautions: 'I cannot give you any gold or silver, but I can teach you many ways to earn a living' (Yo oro ni plata no te lo puedo dar; mas avisos para vivir, muchos te mostraré [I: 23]). He is, of course, literally truthful in that he withholds any form of payment to Lazarillo: what the young boy vividly learns instead through his apprenticeship to his teachers are the ruthless economic lessons of exchange value. The blind man serves as an immediate precursor to the priest in part because he teaches only those prayers that are rewarded with alms, just as the priest brings him along to pray when the boy stands to gain for them both. When he is apprenticed to the blind man, the young boy's continuing education in survival pays off in that it teaches him to hoard in his mouth the few *blancas* he is able to hide from his master. By spitting out coins worth half their value, in the process he makes a neat – and nominally illegal – profit (Rico, 'Resolutorios'). Lazarillo metaphorically transmutes the *blancas* into devalued hosts in the same way that, in chapter 2, he sacrilegiously transforms the bread rolls at Maqueda into a parody of Holy Communion. Lazarillo simultaneously 'eats' the blind man's earnings and 'receives communion' by ingesting the white coins. Through its symbolic commercialization of the Eucharist, the first chapter also prepares us for the second chapter's blasphemous discourse.

However, no matter how well he learns his lessons at the blind man's side, Lazarillo does not criticize his master for begging since, by praying for the needy, he fulfils his religious avocation and works for his pay. Instead, he rebukes him for approaching the *wrong sort* of almsgivers – who, by cynically expecting a reward in return, do not benefit spiritually from their donations – and for cheating even these in his prayers. Despite his poverty, the blind man is still better off than Lazarillo, and therefore responsible for his charge's welfare. The young boy justifies his resentment by portraying his master, not only as uncharitable, but as an ungrateful cheat interested only in his economic gain. Lazarillo's cheerful revenge when the blind man hits the post must surely have elicited laughter from the novel's contemporary reader. Yet the amusement undoubtedly stems as much from the moral indignation stirred by the old man's refusal to accept his poverty meekly and act accordingly, as from the adult Lázaro's manipulative depiction of the poor, abused child who finally wins one over his master.

But while Lazarillo censures those who do not adhere to the principles of Christian charity towards the poor and the sick, he is also quick to learn that he must behave like them to survive. His experience with the priest reinforces the lessons gleaned from the blind man:

> And when we brought the sacraments to the sick, especially the last rites, and the priest ordered those present to pray, you can be sure that I wasn't the last to begin, and that with all my heart and goodwill I prayed to the Lord not that He should do His will but that He should take the sick man from this world.

> [[Y] cuando dábamos sacramento a los enfermos, especialmente la Extremaunción, como manda el clérigo rezar a los que están allí, yo cierto no era el postrero de la oración, y con todo mi corazón y buena voluntad rogaba al Señor, no que le echase a la parte que más servido fuese, como se suele decir; mas que le llevase de aqueste mundo. (II: 53)]

Given the second master's priestly vocation, the chapter's religious symbolism assumes thematic and structural significance within the narrative (Deyermond, *Lazarillo*, 27). Yet its parody of the holy sacraments also exemplifies the various intratextual tensions as well as those of contemporary society since, by demythologizing Catholic ritual, religious parody serves to uncover the contest between sacramental and secular values. Lazarillo's adoration of the bread as if it were actually the sacred Host when he has the luck to come across a piece underscores its scarcity, and thus its holiness for the boy ('I opened the chest. When I saw the holy bread, I began to worship it, although I knew I could not receive it' [Yo ... abro el arca, y como vi el pan, comencelo de adorar, no osando rescebillo (I: 58)]). But this bread, while figuratively the Holy Eucharist, is never truly consecrated by the priest, despite Lazarillo's pun on the 'cara de Dios.' As a re-enactment of the death of Christ, the sacrament confers upon the faithful the redemption of sin. At the chapter's end, however, Lazarillo is not saved, but condemned. In an inversion of the Fall, the young boy is forced by the ungodly priest to leave the 'breadly paradise,' which we know can hardly be considered an Edenic site. Crossing himself to ward off evil, the priest expels the demonized young boy from his house: 'And warding me off with the sign of the Cross, as if I were bewitched by the devil, he went into his house and shut the door' (Y santiguándose de mi, como si yo estuviera endemoniado, tórnase a meter en casa y cierra su puerta [II: 71]). With his expulsion, the Christian concept of sacrifice as expiation for man's sins remains blocked, and Lazarillo, who is rejected once again as the agent of redemption of an uncharitable master, is thrust back into an increasingly secularized society.

When he is cast out from the priest's care, therefore, Lazarillo finds that the townspeople give him a hand-out only while he is recuperating from his wounds. As soon as he is well, he is labelled a lazy good-for-nothing, and exhorted to look for work. Echoing the incident of the biblical Lazarus who begged for crumbs, the townspeople call him *gallofero*, from the term for crumbs, *gallofa*, chastising him for expecting to receive even this minuscule form of bread. The townspeople's charity conflicts with their incipient belief in a work ethic; it is precisely at this point that Lázaro relates the neighbours' rebuff, as the battered boy goes from door to door receiving precious little succour, 'because charity had already gone to heaven ('porque ya la caridad se subió al cielo' [III: 72]).[77] Since the narrative states that the Poor Laws were in force in Toledo when Lazarillo joins the squire, the question arises if the episode is meant as a critique against the decrees, and if the author indeed desires a Lazarus-like resurrection of religious charity.[78] The third *tratado* signals the double bind in which Lazarillo is caught: he takes the only job available, but still has to beg not only for himself, but now also for his new master, the squire, who is too ashamed to beg for himself.

Midway through this inverted *Bildungsroman*, when Lazarillo has yet to lose all his innocence and can empathize with another's pain, we are introduced to the only other character in the text who feels shame and mortification. Although the squire goes to great lengths to hide them, Lazarillo and his new master recognize each other's feelings and symbolically exchange roles. The emotional transference between the two takes place when Lazarillo acknowledges the squire's impoverished existence. For if the young boy is a poor beggar, his master is a *pobre envergonzante*, or one of the 'shamefaced poor,' a social category that permitted destitute members of the lower nobility to accept humiliating charitable donations in private. Despite his having been employed by the squire, Lazarillo realizes that he still needs to beg to survive; yet if he is caught begging, he will be whipped and thrown out of town. He thus finds he has complied with changing societal expectations for the poor, only to be in a worse situation than when he was allowed to beg with the blind man.

After the squire's furtive departure, the boy finally discerns that his master had been resorting to lies and fraud in order to conceal his disgraceful poverty from the outside world. In another failed attempt to reflect an integrated self, Lazarillo has again chosen a fragmented image with whom to identify. This is not so unusual if we remember that the squire, like the poor, formed part of a changing society whose function within that society had also been recently devalued. At the bottom rung of the social hierarchy, occupying an increasingly archaic and useless position, squires were the first to suffer the consequences of the new mercenary armies reliant on firearms, armies that soon were to consume the very *pícaros* the *Lazarillo* privileges as its major protagonist.[79] The thin line separating the tax-exempt *hidalgo* from the long-suffering *pechero* was stretched even further by the former's likely *converso* origins. Lest he be found out and lose his rights as a nobleman, Lazarillo's third master must give the appearance of nobility and cleanliness of blood at all costs, even if this means endangering his young servant's life.

Lazarillo's identification with the squire comes full circle in the sixth *tratado* when, with the monies saved from selling water, Lázaro dresses in second-hand clothes to emulate the squire's illusionary honour. However, his loss of status from his sacramentalized position as a member of a liminal group is, if we are to believe his letter to 'Vuestra merced,' the adult Lázaro's gain. No longer a member of a society that required him to remain poor for its spiritual benefit, Lázaro finds that he must assume instead the secularized values that relegate him to an unwanted surplus population. From his river birth, he has become a truly marginalized entity, lacking any semblance of religious significance. His only mode of existence, then, as John Beverley has well noted, is 'a tradeoff between moral integrity and material wellbeing.'[80]

The tensions of the mid-sixteenth century regarding the poor and poor relief are clearly manifest in the ultimately untenable position in which Lázaro finds himself. In an attempt to escape from the circle of poverty into which he is born, he accepts the despicable job of town crier in the growing bureaucracy of the Court. Lázaro's ironic narrative intends to convince 'Vuestra merced' that his good work as a wine vendor has drawn the attention of the Archpriest, who rewards him by marrying him to his servant. Leaving in doubt whether Lázaro unwittingly enters into the ménage-à-trois conveniently arranged for the Archpriest's own benefit, or whether this liaison is but evil gossip spread by his enemies, the narrative ends in moral and economic paradox. Lazarillo both is and is *not* 'at the height of all good fortune' (en la cumbre de toda buena fortuna), as Francisco Rico has suggested (*La novela picaresca* 50 ff.) The text's ambiguity stems as much from the confusion of changing social values as it does from the narrator's duplicitous double voice. Lázaro's narration of Lazarillo's adventures fails to account for a complete transition of the protagonist's sacramentalized social role to his position as secularized outsider who becomes his own commodity in order to survive within the system. This transition can be fully apprehended only if the narrative is taken as forming part of the proliferating discourses on poverty then circulating in Spain. What Grice-Hutchinson calls 'the movement towards centralization,' though opposed by Soto on both religious and moral principles, would eventually prevail as an essential characteristic of mercantilism and thus inform the next major picaresque narrative, the *Guzmán de Alfarache* (Grice-Hutchinson, *Early Economic Thought*, 133). At the time of its publication, however, by documenting the *pícaro*'s literary birth, his role as social *pharmakos*, and his prefigurement of the increasingly marginalized poor, the *Lazarillo de Tormes* at once textualizes and engages in the historical conflicts prevalent in the mid-sixteenth century. No matter how dissembling the *pícaro*'s discourse or ambiguous the author's attitude, the picaresque narrative exposes to the reader the complex tensions that arose at the time between religious and secular values and the ensuing divergent ideologies on the impoverished and methods of poor relief.

2

The Poor in Spain:
Confinement and Control

Confinement was a gross error, and an economic mistake: poverty was to be suppressed by removing and maintaining by charity a *poor population*. Actually, it was *poverty* that was being artificially masked; and a part of the *population* was really being suppressed, wealth being always constant. Was the intention to help the poor escape their provisional indigence? They were kept from doing so; the labor market was limited, which was all the more dangerous in that this was precisely a period of crisis.

Michel Foucault, *Madness and Civilization*

In *Madness and Civilization*, Michel Foucault has written of 'inalienable poverty,' of a 'Christian tradition for which the Poor Man had had a real and concrete existence' (230). He explains, however, that in a mercantilist society, the pauper, since he is neither producer nor consumer, has no place: idle, vagabond, and unemployed, he belongs nowhere and is therefore destined to confinement. Limiting himself to the containment of the poor, the criminal, and the insane in Classical France, Foucault focuses most extensively on madness, whose displacement from its previous tragic significance in the Middle Ages and early Renaissance, he asserts, authorizes 'the return of reason' (32).

Claiming similar 'reason,' early modern Spain devalued the religious worth earlier accorded the poor as symbolic spectacle.[1] This chapter considers mid-sixteenth-century economic treatises as discourses that profoundly influenced contemporary thinking on the poor, It attempts to demonstrate how the growing pressures to solve the grievous problems of poverty led to the confusion of the impoverished with the infirm and the criminal, and ultimately resulted in efforts to confine them through secular means. As Foucault explains, however, such measures merely masked the problems without attacking their source. No longer conceding any individual spiritual gain to succouring the poor through charity, the secularized judgment passed on the impoverished in early sixteenth-century Europe was based on the new rationalist concept of an ethically free and employable workforce.

Historians continue to debate the reasons why Spain, unlike countries that encouraged industrial development such as Belgium, Germany, and England, failed to develop an infrastructure that would help absorb its excess population of disenfranchised. Some have questioned E.J. Hamilton's explanation that the influx of gold and silver from the New World was the primary cause of inflation in sixteenth-century Spain.[2] Most historians, however, are in agreement that the country's mercantilist interests, best represented by its textile industry in such cities as Burgos, Segovia, Soria, Avila, and Toledo, clashed with and finally capitulated to the interests of investors like the Mesta, the association of sheep growers, whose revenues came from the exportation of raw materials and taxes on grazing lands.[3] Charles V's control of wheat prices had discouraged peasants from raising unprofitable crops, and his support of the Mesta further blocked agricultural production by forbidding the enclosure of arable lands.[4] Small farmers eventually sold out to latifundist nobles whose land investments, with the concomitant privileging of primogeniture, anticipated what Maravall has called the 'aristocratization' of the Baroque.[5]

For Michel Cavillac, the failure of the urban *comunero* revolts was symptomatic of the opposition that, as early as 1521, arose between a stymied nationalist capitalism based on local industry and the international capitalism successfully supported by the Emperor.[6] Already by the latter half of the sixteenth century, these events had led to such interrelated factors as the chronic lack of employment in both agriculture and industry, heavy taxation, and the general rise in prices, all of which contributed to make the number of vagabonds in Spain the highest in Europe.[7] The various Poor Laws decreed in Valladolid in 1523, Toledo in 1525, Madrid in 1528 and 1534, and in Zamora, Salamanca, and Valladolid in 1540, had failed to stem the flow of paupers circulating from one urban centre to another.[8] The economic crisis in turn spelled a crisis in social redefinitions: pauperism, like leprosy, had been dealt with principally as a moral problem, and its accepted solution, charity, was religiously inspired and vertically distributed. But as the numbers of poor multiplied uncontrollably, the positions illustrated by the Soto–Robles debate discussed in chapter 1, which claimed dissenting views on the Church's role in the matter, soon crystallized into opposing political ideologies with irreconcilable responses to the challenges posed by poverty. Individualized assistance through charitable means thus became identified with aristocratic values, whereas organized systems of donations concurred with the incipient bourgeois rationalism of poor-relief reform.

The differing attitudes towards the disenfranchised were dictated by the break that ensued between a primarily feudal society in whose symbolic economy lepers and other unprivileged retained religious significance, and the early capitalist mentality secularized under new social conditions allowing for freedom of choice. Increasingly frustrated by the growth in pauperism, and no longer perceiving the poor as Christocentric reminders of redemption and resurrection, economists no less than ordinary townsfolk angrily accused them of refusing to work and of preferring a life of beggary and vagabondage. Those blaming the impoverished imposed an ethical judgment that effectively held these same poor responsible for differentiating between rightful and wrong behaviour. Critics have deemed this a puritanical attitude that invited harsh judgment on the disenfranchised, harking to Vives's rational ordering of a mercantilist society in constant need of labour.[9] Yet this ethical view, which predominated by the end of the sixteenth century, led religious writers and economists alike to investigate the larger social causes of poverty and to propose diverse solutions by the government (Maza Zorrilla 78).

At midcentury, Spain's first political economist, Luis de Ortiz, had weighed external factors when examining the probable causes of increased pauperism. In a 1558 *memorial* to Philip II, the Burgos mercantilist and controller of royal finances boldly attributed the rise in prices in Spain to excessive exports to the New World, to the cities' desire to keep prices high, and to the bad organization of Spanish commerce (Grice-Hutchinson, *Early Economic Thought*, 128–9). He further blamed the flight of hard currency on the Spanish rejection of the work ethic and on the country's resultant lack of industrialization.[10] Echoing the criticism of the *hidalgo* class voiced by the anonymous author of the *Lazarillo* – three of whose four extant 1554 editions had recently been published in the mercantilist centres of Antwerp, Medina del Campo, and Burgos – Ortiz argued that the material production required for economic development conflicted with the unsound ideals of a nation peopled by the indolent, the unlettered, and those unskilled in mechanical crafts or trade.[11] Moreover, he stressed that it made little economic sense for Spain to have 'so many noblemen, monastics, clerics, and other members of religious orders exempt [from taxes' (hay gran suma de hijosdalgo, monasterios, clérigos y otras personas de orden que son libres [de impuestos]). He recommended that all laws limiting artisans be eliminated and their status instead elevated through various honours: 'artisans are belittled and disparaged by these laws, and others should be instituted and enforced in their favor, honouring and offering them jobs' (por las cuales [leyes] están los oficiales mecánicos aniquilados y despreciados, y se promulguen y hagan otras en favor dellos, dándoles honras y oficios [qtd. in Michel Cavillac, 'Introducción,' cxi]).

With the sole exception of Segovia, where the textile weaving industry prompted a population expansion in the 1590s, most urban demographic growth did not coincide with an equivalent rise in economic prosperity.[12] John Lynch affirms that the dislocations of heavily taxed unemployed artisans and landless peasants from the countryside to the urban areas were barely contained by the growing need for manpower in the New World and in the various European theatres of war:

> In the first half of the century, when industry appeared to be flourishing, the peasants tried to find a way of escape from the destitution of the countryside by flocking to the cities in search of work. But once this brief boom had passed and the middle classes were beginning their exodus from trade and industry, there was nothing in the cities for them either, so the number of unemployed increased, wandering from one monastery to another in search of free soup. In these conditions the only solutions open to them were to enrol in the army, to enter the religious orders, or to resign themselves to a life on the margin of society. (Lynch 116–17)[13]

The interrelated problems of vagrancy and lack of employment first arose in the sixteenth century under Charles V's monarchy; they worsened substantially during Philip II's reign, and were further complicated by the religious dissensions that sprang up throughout the Spanish Empire and which gave rise to other marginalized groups. Following his father's abdication not long after the publication of the *Lazarillo*, the new monarch had scarcely begun to build Spain's strength in the Mediterranean against the Turks when he found himself having to face discontent in the Netherlands as Calvinists, in 1566, rioted and sacked the churches. Pressured by heresy from beyond his borders, Philip was also alert to the dangers of Protestant revolt in Catalonia, since its unstable border with France provided easy access into Spain to Huguenot heretics, whose long-standing hatred of Castile could easily convert the area into a second Netherlands (Elliott, *Imperial Spain*, 232–4). The *morisco* rebellion in the Alpujarras, as much a response to increased taxation of the silk industry as an anguished outcry of a conquered minority against enforced acculturation, was also viewed by Philip as a serious threat to the country's religious and political stability. After crushing the uprising, he ordered the dispersion of the *moriscos* throughout Castile (Elliott, *Imperial Spain*, 240; Lynch 264–5).

Perceived by most Spaniards as a threatening alien force unrestrained by national boundaries and unchecked by Old Christian morality, these displaced and marginalized 'others' were soon blamed for the disorder and chaos enveloping the country. Together with the poor, such heterodox elements as Protestants, *conversos*, *moriscos*, and gypsies were judged deleterious to the social well-being and therefore requiring of increased distribution and control by the state. Foucault comments that the two social projects are not incompatible, since distribution aspires to a pure community, while control ensures a more disciplined society.[14] As we shall see, however, in Spain, as the century wore on, the tendency towards discipline gained primacy over distribution. Seemingly isolated acts of social control such as the promulgation of the 1559 Inquisition Index, the inspection of public and private libraries, the *autos de fe* in Valladolid and Seville, the dispersal of the *moriscos*, and the reformation of convents, were, in fact, correlated manifestations of the intensifying fear of religious and cultural subversion that took hold during the latter half of the sixteenth century.

Philip II's public support of the Inquisition, manifested by his royal presence at five *autos de fe*, contributed to the Holy Office's authority and its expansion to a total of twenty-one tribunals, fifteen on the peninsula and another six throughout the Spanish Empire.[15] Both church and state reacted swiftly and with harsh measures to the national anxiety fuelled by the social awareness of difference, of the dangers represented by the 'other' so insistently present despite the institutional objectives promulgated on behalf of cultural homogeneity. In their contradictory stance of representatives of Christ and social deviants, the poor oscillated precariously between their roles as sacramentalized *pharmakos* figures and completely disenfranchised miscreants. Prefigured by the vulnerable Lazarillo's metamorphosis into a cynical Lázaro, the earlier redemptive image of the medieval leper was ineluctably transformed, by the latter decades of the century, into the socially perceived threat of the potential criminal.

As the leper's symbolic heir, the *pícaro*'s lacerated body gave rise to exclusionary tactics on the part of the state in order to ensure social purity. Increasingly denounced for their self-mutilation, the 'false' poor were forced to undergo examinations given at beggars' hospitals. The anxieties instigating their public condemnation spilled over to the *pícaro*'s manifold representations in literature. Despite their authors' ideological differences, the seventeenth-century novels that soon formed the picaresque genre – Mateo Alemán's *Guzmán de Alfarache*, Quevedo's *Buscón*, the *Estebanillo González*, as well as the numerous narratives that focus on the figure of the female *pícara* – all register the increasing paranoia felt by the population at large towards the growing groups of subaltern 'other.'

The Inquisitional censorship enacted against the *Lazarillo* and the conspicuous absence of other picaresque narratives during the almost fifty years that separate the anonymous 1554 *Lazarillo* and its equally anonymous *Part II* from the *Guzmán de Alfarache*'s appearance in 1599, not only signal the strictures imposed on this newly invented genre, but remark significantly on the conflictive social attitudes towards the poor and poor relief. Although exhaustive efforts were made to confine the disenfranchised, as I discuss in subsequent sections of this chapter, it is instructive to keep in mind that the historical *pícaro*'s fate, similarly to that of the leper, never resulted in complete confinement. This would have effectively eradicated his normative value to the public as a moral spectacle, a value that the authors of picaresque narratives appropriated for their purposes in depicting their literary characters. And while Foucault rightly asserts that, as the lepers vanished, their symbolic function was assumed by the disenfranchised, we should take note that the rigorous division that occurred in France between the poor (as well as the mad and the criminal) and the rest of society was actually reversed in Spain, not only due to fluctuating boundaries between workers and unemployed, but, as I argue in chapter 4, because Spain's 'other' was ineradicably contained within the social body.[16]

Maravall explains that the divisions between the medieval Spanish urban elite (distinguished by their power, wealth, and nobility) and such socially excluded groups as manual labourers served to further split the latter into two positions categorized by their assumed ability to change their situation. There were those whose professed anomie clearly labelled them as deviants, vagrants, or heretics; others were disqualified socially because of their menial occupations, their infirm condition (such as the sick, the mad, the aged), or their 'foreignness' in terms of their national, religious, or legal status.[17] While these divisions were strictly enforced during the Middle Ages, the boundaries between them eventually became more flexible, resulting in the groups' inclusionary status. Labourers oscillated between periods of employment and unemployment, for example, their status easily slipping from a social group disqualified for its menial employment, to that of criminals and vagrants.

Nonetheless, as we discern in the *Lazarillo*'s mention of the Toledan Poor Laws, rules governing the behaviour of the disenfranchised were motivated by the state's conviction that, if left to themselves, the poor would purposefully misbehave. The new rational precepts encouraged the public to distance themselves – emotionally, rationally, and physically – from the poor. By admonishing Lazarillo not to become a 'good for nothing' and instead go find work, the townfolk articulate the confusion between the legitimate pauper and the delinquent that soon transformed into the collective fear and abhorrence of all marginalized groups intimated by the later picaresque narratives. Yet despite the multiplying attempts to exclude vagabonds from cities and to enclose the local poor, Lazarillo's historical avatars, like his literary siblings, continued to circulate freely as unbounded signs of social unrest throughout the vast expanse of the Habsburg Empire until their final recruitment into the Imperial armies. Indeed, it is no coincidence that their military adventures are recuperated, fictionalized, and hybridized with the picaresque through such soldiers' tales as *Alonso de Contreras*, *Jerónimo de Pasamonte*, and the last exemplar of the picaresque genre, *Estebanillo González*.

In their generic hybridity, the soldiers' narratives, which I discuss more fully in chapter 5, reject once and for all the exhausted Renaissance *topos* of arms and letters which aimed to ennoble military exploits by their assimilation of humanist ideals.[18] Again, the *Lazarillo* offers a point of departure for investigating the radical changes undergone by the military in the early modern period. In the prologue, the author/narrator compares himself to a soldier, whose desire for fame outstrips his fear of death:

Who thinks that the soldier who first reaches the top of the ladder hates life the most? No, of course he doesn't. It's desire for praise that makes him expose himself to danger and it is the same in the arts and in literature.

[¿Quién piensa que el soldado que es primero del escala tiene más aborrescido el vivir? No, por cierto; mas el deseo de alabanza le [el soldado] hace ponerse al peligro; y así, en las artes y letras es lo mesmo. (8)]

The irony, of course, is that the authorial voice of the prologue – which ends by imperceptively assuming the narrational persona of Lázaro himself – cannot, in this case (and particularly in Lázaro's *caso*) aspire to literary greatness because he chooses to remain anonymous to the reader.

   Does the author, then, really believe, as he states, that the soldier risks his life for fame? In keeping with the prologue's ironic stance, an equally ambivalent response may, in fact, be found in what we are told of Lazarillo's father's final exploits. Serving as a nobleman's muleteer, he participates in an expedition against the Moors, emphasizing his 'loyalty' to his master. But the phrase is grammatically unclear: we do not know whether he fought against the Moors or – since, historically, most muleteers were Moors – he was on their side, having renounced his Christian faith after escaping from jail:

About this time there was an expedition against the Moors and my father went with them, exiled for the disaster I mentioned earlier. He served as a mule driver for a knight who went along with it, and ended his life with his master, like a loyal servant.

[En este tiempo se hizo cierta armada contra moros, entre los cuales fue mi padre, que a la sazón estaba desterrado por el desastre ya dicho, con cargo de acemilero de un caballero que allá fue; y con su señor, como leal criado, feneció su vida. (I: 14)][19]

What becomes apparent is that Lázaro's father intends to take part in the expedition, not because of any desire for glory, but because he has been found out a thief.

   Rather than reproducing the heroic exploits ascribed to the literary knights of the *Libro de Alexandre* and *Tirant lo Blanc*, as Rico posits, or mimicking historical ventures such as the soldier/poet, Garcilaso de la Vega's premature demise in battle two decades earlier, the father's tribulations prefigure soldiers' tales by suggesting the radical changes that eventuate in the military, from an army led by nobles to mercenary forces. In contrast to the prologue's exemplary soldier, whose desire for fame impels him to be the first in line, the reasons given by Tomé

González for volunteering to serve are far less heroic and much more pragmatic. But if Lazarillo's father attempts to dodge his punishment by joining, albeit reluctantly, a military expedition of his own choosing, the *pícaros* of the later picaresque tales, like the groups of poor to which they belong and with which they identify, will find themselves dragged unwillingly into the armies. As Foucault has said of the classical age, the Hapsburg soldiers' bodies will be disciplined, controlled, and, ultimately, sacrificed for a 'common' good that has, ultimately, little to do with their welfare.[20]

Secularization and Social Containment

The Poor Laws decreed at mid-century illustrate the state's concern over the church's inability to curb vagabondage by appealing to moral law. Traditionalists and reformers alike were baffled by a growing problem whose regulation no longer responded to religious tenets. As early as 1534, the Córdoba *procuradores* had requested that the poor and sick be enclosed in hospitals, and vagrants punished by law.[21] Such a suggestion makes clear that that the poor were becoming not solely a moral and religious concern, but were increasingly looked on as a social disease. As we shall see, the compulsion to confine the poor, which, as Foucault admonishes in this chapter's epigraph, resulted only in masking poverty itself, would lead to an irreconcilable double bind that trapped the impoverished in its vicious circle.

As the century wore on, the Crown's attempts to eliminate vagrancy supported the building of hospitals to house the poor, a plan carried out under the advice of Robles in Zamora but strongly attacked by Soto, who believed that, without the pauper's undeterred circulation as a visual reminder to society, most people would neglect to carry out good works:

The limits on almsgiving have been going on for at least three years ... Your Majesty should mandate that the results be fully investigated ... if, since we no longer see any poor calling door to door who touch our hearts, then [find out] if the hospitals are fuller or if new ones have been built with sufficient room for the poor who previously roamed the streets.

[Tres años ha o más que esta razón de limosnas se ha comenzado a platicar. El fruto que della se ha seguido ... Vuestra Alteza mande que diligentemente se sepa el fruto que se hace ... si ya que no vemos andar pobre ninguno por las casas que nos ablande los corazones, si están más llenos los hospitales o se han erigido otros nuevos, donde quepan los que andaban por las calles. (*Deliberación* 139–40)]

Numerous organized methods of containing the poor had already been implemented in several cities, however, depending on sufficient local interest and support. One unusual example of a wealthy noble couple's dedication to the poor was the establishment by Luis de Antezana and Isabel de Guzmán, in 1483, of the Hospital de Nuestra Señora de la Misericordia, still known and functioning today as the Hospital de Antezana, in Alcalá de Henares. A member of the Council of the Toledan Archbishop, Alonso Carrillo de Acuña, and a staunch defender of Queen Isabel, Antezana, together with his wife, donated the front part of their house to the hospital, bequeathing, for its maintenance, 30,000 *maravedís* yearly collected from *juros* or government bonds, and taxes from slaughterhouses and Toledan silk and species markets. The hospital was to receive 150 *fanegas* of wheat yearly and the rent from several properties in Guadalajara (Fernández Majolero 57). The will included the donation of twelve equipped beds with the proviso that the hospital house and care for at least two sick poor at all times.[22] Although ostensibly a secular establishment managed by a town chapter and confraternity, a papal bull issued by Adrian VI at its founding granted plenary indulgences to those supporting the hospital and permission for its confraternity members to be buried on its premises.[23] The hospital's founding thus obeyed the traditional notion that charity bestowed spiritual advantages upon the donors while ministering to the poor's spiritual, not merely physical, health. As late as 1650, the hospital rules stipulated that

a visiting nurse will be charged with ensuring that [the sick] confess at the start of their illness and that they not receive a second food ration until they do so, as this confraternity's principal goal is to foster spiritual over temporal care.

[Encárguesele a un visitador enfermero que les haga confesar al principio de la enfermedad y no se les dé segunda ración sin que lo ayan hecho, porque el fin principal desta hermandad es el cuidado con lo espiritual antes que lo temporal. (Fernández Majolero 77)]

However, hospitals of such modest size, no matter how well funded, could do little to stem the growing tide of ill poor that flocked to urban centres. The *protomédicos* and *alcaldes de la lepra* instituted by the Catholic

Monarchs for the care of lepers had formed part of the hospital-reform movement that spread across fifteenth-century Europe. Responding to the need for change, Isabel and Ferdinand founded hospitals in Santiago de Compostela and Granada, and converted the royal hospital in Seville into a retirement hospital for poor and injured soldiers (Martz 36). Granada's most famous hospital was founded in 1537 by the Castilian saint Juan de Dios. Accepting everyone who requested admittance, its wards soon filled with all sorts of marginal types: beggars, vagrants, pilgrims, lepers, syphilitics, the aged, and – a scandal for the times – prostitutes.[24] Often numbering close to 200, hospital inmates were encouraged to work, probably to help pay for expenses, despite the many donations received from patrons. Smaller hospitals were consolidated into larger units; in Toledo, Cardinal Tavera, who had been named governor of the realm in 1542, merged several small hospitals to found a grand edifice, named San Juan Bautista but which soon became known as the Hospital de Tavera in recognition of its founder's concern for the needy. An ironic result of its lavishness, given its primary purpose, was that people criticized its appropriateness as a hospital for the poor.[25]

Regardless of its excess, the hospital represented Tavera's contribution to his diocese as much as it remains to this day a monument to its founder. The Cardinal's sepulchre, housed in the hospital chapel and carved in Carrara marble by Alonso de Berruguete, epitomizes Tavera's main virtue by depicting the figure of Charity in one of its *tondos* (Garnica 119–20). Unlike the Hospital de Santa Cruz, which it replaced, the Hospital de Tavera did not depend on the cathedral chapter's administration; after the Cardinal's death in 1545, his nephew Arias Pardo de Saavedra, marshal of Castile, assumed its management (Salazar, qtd. in Garnica 204). Supported mainly by income received from its ecclesiastical benefices, rents, and interest from *juros*, Tavera's hospital operated as a general hospital, admitting only those afflicted with non-contagious diseases and rejecting lepers and syphilitics.[26]

Shortly after Tavera's death, a committee for relief of the poor, composed of both secular and cathedral authorities, was formed to publicize the poor's situation in Toledo. The newly appointed Archbishop of Toledo, Cardinal Juan Martínez Silíceo, contributed generously to the committee, which had specified that the donations be distributed to the poor and to beggars, who included the disabled and peasants from the countryside besides the professional mendicants seeking alms. Martz notes that this relief effort was unique in its solicitous treatment of beggars, as they were accepted in unlimited numbers and welcomed in private houses. The new method of caring for the poor, in fact, eschewed all rhetoric that associated them with contagious disease or its moral equivalent, social disorder. Significantly, it demonstrated that Cardinal Silíceo, unlike Tavera, preferred Soto's unlimited approach to poverty relief, but it also implied that he would be far less amenable to applying social reforms such as those recommended earlier by Robles and his predecessor.

The Sevillian Hospital de las Cinco Llagas was endowed in 1539 by Fadrique Enríquez de Ribera, the son of Catalina de Ribera, known as Seville's 'mother of the poor,' who herself had converted a house into a small hospital for women. The Hospital de las Cinco Llagas continued its founder's legacy in sharing Juan de Dios's concerns about poor women.[27] The hospital was famous for its architectural splendour, the edifice's luxuriousness contrasting markedly with the condition of its inmates, as well as with the spirit of charity that inspired its construction (Perry, *Gender*, 156). Citing the *cortes'* criticism of hospital consolidations, since large general hospitals no longer appealed to moderately wealthy donors, Martz remarks that donors were presumably more interested in their own spiritual well-being than in that of the hospitals or the poor (84–5). Nevertheless, the hospitals' liberal admittance policies anticipated Soto's claim that charity was meant to succour all those in need. Yet, in recalling the methods for enclosure of lepers undertaken during the Middle Ages, the policies also suggested to some reformers that hospitals might ideally serve specifically to enclose the poor, thereby eliminating begging and vagrancy. In 1581, Philip II consolidated several hospitals in one edifice, known as San Jerónimo, which was later moved to a general hospital divided by gender.[28]

The prospect of hospital enclosure as an institutionalized solution to the problems brought on by vagabondage was first introduced in 1560 in an anonymous manuscript that circulated fifteen years after the Soto–Robles debate.[29] Although not explicitly addressed in the manuscript, the social disease of poverty became analogous with corporal infirmity, which now needed to be not only cured, but enclosed, so as to be hidden from public view. Recommending that the poor be relegated to general hospitals supported by the state, the manuscript was most revolutionary in its insistence that such hospitals be limited to beggars, and that the state accept full responsibility for its maintenance through taxation:

Assuming as a given the obligation to succour the poor, and since, as we know, this cannot be carried out with coins and bread crumbs alone, and having determined that hospitals cannot be maintained solely by the devotion of a fickle public ... all future [hospitals] should be self-supporting since, just as natural law obliges mothers to feed their families, and the church requires fasting and confession of those unwilling to comply freely, all cities and nations should be publicly apprised that they must subsidize their poor, and what is not done willingly through charity must be demanded of them.

[Puesta por sin duda la obligación de acudir al remedio de los pobres, y dado por ninguno de que proviene de blancas y mendrugos de pan, y averiguado que el sustento de los hospitales no está bien situado en sola la devoción del pueblo antojadizo ... los que se fundaren se sustenten, que así como las leyes apremian a las madres de familias que alimenten a los suyos, y la iglesia a que ayunen y confiesen los que no lo hicieren de su grado, se provea públicamente que cada república y ciudad se encargue del sustento de sus pobres, y que lo que no hace de caridad como debiera, se haga de necesidad. (qtd. in Soubeyroux 122)]

Internment of the poor depended on state provisions, yet despite a complex system of subsidies, hospitals continued to rely as much on private charities as on public donations. With the exception of those under royal patrimony, which included the numerous San Lázaro hospitals previously dedicated to the treatment of leprosy, most hospitals came under ecclesiastical control (Martz 47, 54–7).

The anonymous manuscript's recommendations went unheeded and had little if any impact on the elimination of vagrancy. What they pointed to, however, was another means of succouring the poor. The manuscript recommended that, in the spirit of *hermandad*, or brotherhood, different provinces join in the redistribution of the disenfranchised and the alms collected for them:

[S]ince there will be fewer poor, there will finally be no need to exile them and return them to their lands. Rather, they will be welcome everywhere, and this way, different provinces and kingdoms can unite in brotherhood to redistribute among themselves alms and the poor wherever there are too many or too few.

[[A]l fin no habrá necesidad habiendo pocos pobres de desterrarlos para volverlos a sus tierras, antes se desearán en todas partes, y por este medio podrá haber unión y hermandad entre provincias y reinos diferentes para ayudarse con limosnas y con pobres cuando sobren o falten en algunos. (qtd. in Soubeyroux 123)]

The term *hermandad*, here employed in the sense of 'community,' alludes also to another primary source of poor relief institutionalized in Spain: the brotherhoods or confraternities, founded as private charitable organizations dedicated to pious works.[30] Acting against the recent efforts to secularize the the treatment of the impoverished, these quasi-religious organizations were rooted in and conserved the traditional medieval belief in charitable works and the spiritual value of the poor.[31] The Burgos *hermandades*, for example, were organized as early as 1400; formed around the parish churches, they celebrated religious holidays, ensured proper burial and funeral masses for the dead, and were in charge of the network of hospitals that stretched across the Burgos *comarca*.[32] At times, however, church and confraternities also clashed, as when the Alcalá Confraternity of the Hospital de la Misericordia was forced to resort to Cardinal Cisneros in their efforts to recover property donated by Isabel de Guzmán from the Santa María parish chapter.[33]

While they cut across occupational lines, confraternities maintained class differences, relying instead on religious practices to inspire and nurture a sense of community. Popular saints – in particular, the many apparitions of the Virgin Mary – were chosen as spiritual guides for the members. In her study of the Zamora confraternities, Maureen Flynn points out that the Virgin was an especially apt patroness, since, as a most compassionate intercessor between the world and her Son, she personified the spirit of an all-encompassing charity (28). Generally organized to perform various works of benefaction, the majority of confraternities chose to manage hospitals; Flynn counts at least thirteen Zamora confraternities operating their own hospitals. The hospital of St Ildefonso gave preference to local paupers, providing them with daily food rations and 'general cures' for those wishing to be purged and housed for a month during May and September (Flynn 50–2).

In contrast, by 1550, although Toledo's confraternities had grown to a total of 143, only about 20 openly practised charity, and only 4 operated either hospitals, hospices, or home relief. The pathetic figures of Lazarillo and his third master, the impoverished squire from Valladolid, as they seek shelter within the Toledan city gates, are but slight literary exaggerations of the urban immigrants that flooded into the Imperial city. Indeed, the young beggar and the *pobre envergonzante*, the shame-faced squire too embarrassed to show his poverty, typify many of foreign poor drawn by the city's munificence towards its impoverished citizens, who were cared for not only by the hospitals, but by the cathedral's daily bread rations for a minimum of thirty poor, and by the mendicant orders' disbursement of 1,000 ducats granted for this purpose by the Counts of Ribagorza (Garnica 186). An unexpected and unwelcome outcome of Toledo's preoccupation with the poor was that the confraternities ended up competing with the beggars, who were required by the Poor Laws to obtain licences to receive alms. Although discouraged from doing so by the Council of Trent, the confraternities also solicited licences for the *domandores*, persons appointed to beg for alms. In 1600, the Confraternity of the Santa Caridad received permission from the diocesan authorities to be the first to beg during Holy Week (Martz 163–8).[34]

In its system of poor relief, which obeyed the biblical directives to visit the sick and the poor in their homes, in jail, or on the streets, the Confraternity of the Santa Caridad exemplified how the majority of *hermandades* treated the poor. Yet confraternities rejected enclosure not only on religious grounds, but because of their own unstable financial status and the rising costs of operating hospitals. The profusion of confraternities during the period confirms the fact that, despite the recommendations to the Crown by *memoriales* and treatises, the efforts made to institutionalize and secularize the care of the impoverished continued to prove largely unsuccessful. The impact of the *hermandades* on the public may be gauged by the numerous parodies staged by picaresque narratives of these religious groups.[35] The fictional upside-down worlds of good and evil depicted by the *Buscón's* criminal squad, the *Guzmán's* Roman confraternity, and Monipodio's brotherhood of thieves in *Rinconete y Cortadillo* take playful yet critical aim at the organizational strictures enjoined by their real–life models. Those wishing to join the Antezana hospital confraternity in Alcalá de Henares, for example, were required to adhere to statutes containing more than forty laws, expanded in 1525, 1526, 1530, and 1535. Members were to be of a peaceful nature and not libel others or spread gossip; until 1650, applicants had to prove their Old Christian background on all sides ('que sea cristiano viejo de todas partes y buen hombre pacífico y no reboltoso ni calunioso' [Fernández Majolero 74–7]). As enclosure of the poor gained precedence over licensed vagabondage in the various solutions proffered by political economists, the picaresque subtext of individual freedom, while at times an ambiguous and contradictory position independent of the author's convictions, resulted in making a mockery of the *hermandades'* hierarchical pattern by uncovering their conservative nature.

In their unwillingness to enclose the impoverished, confraternities reaffirmed the Counter-reformational doctrines championed by Philip

II. Once he became king, he zealously enforced traditional Catholic beliefs, encouraging the practice of charitable acts, while at the same time imposing severe social controls on other marginalized groups such as criminals and prostitutes.[36] His sacralized view of the poor as blameless *pauperes Christi* was evident in that, although he resisted policies for the containment of beggars, Philip considered enclosure the best solution to the frightening rise in criminal population. This increment was itself due to the monarch's insistence on strict law enforcement: although Parker asserts that Seville's royal prison, built in 1563, held between 500 and 1,000 criminals (*Philip II* 55–60), a contemporary source, Cristóbal de Chaves's *Relación de lo que pasa en la Cárcel de Sevilla*, estimates its capacity at more than 1,800 prisoners.[37] In part, this proved that Philip was unable to visualize the relation between poverty and criminality. It is not until reformers address the connection specifically that the monarch seems finally convinced of the correlation.[38] Accepting poverty as an integral part of the Medievo-Christian tradition, his opposition to state welfare extended to the Netherlands: the king's extreme devotion to Catholicism, combined with his desire to crush Dutch resistance, accounted for his edict to a Flemish town restoring the poor's right to beg. He made certain that his mandate would be carried out by sending the Augustinian friar Lorenzo de Villavicencio, author of the influential treatise *De aeconomia sacra circa pauperum curam a Christo institutam* (1564), as his secret agent to defend traditional Christian views on charity.[39] Ironically, and undoubtedly as a symbolic act, the town Philip chose to 'liberate' from social beneficence was Bruges, where Vives, some forty years earlier, had published his revolutionary *De subventione pauperum*.

Miguel de Giginta's Synchretic Reform Movement

As we have seen, the many attempts, both secular and religious, to reduce poverty and vagrancy during the second half of the sixteenth century proved increasingly futile. Following the closure of the Council of Trent in 1563, the 1565 revision of the Poor Laws admitted to their failure, and again instituted begging, albeit with various conditions. Each parish was instructed to record its infirm poor before issuing them an annual licence, signed by the parish priest and the local justice, limiting their begging solely within city limits.[40] This permission, also extended to students and mendicant friars, sought to reconcile the opposing views represented by Robles and Soto by allowing the town's true poor to beg freely, thus distinguishing them from vagabonds and those who refused to work. Like the prior laws, however, it was unable to counter the incessant migration of poor from town to town.

Proposals by religious and secular authorities urging solutions to what appeared to be an unresolvable dilemma, therefore, continued to circulate often in manuscript and in print. In 1579, the Catalonian canon Miguel de Giginta, known for his reform work in Portugal, published his *Tractado de remedio de pobres*, which he had written at the behest of the Castilian *procuradores* who thought that his plans for Portuguese hospitals should be applied throughout Spain.[41] The author himself believed the situation to be a matter of state concerns, asserting that 'poverty relief goes beyond the Church's attributions' (la asistencia de los menesterosos sobrepasa la atribuciones de la Iglesia), and becomes the 'responsibility of those who govern' (obligación del cargo de los que gobiernan).[42]

The Biblioteca Nacional in Madrid houses an undated *memorial* that briefly sums up Giginta's *Remedio de pobres*, stating that its proposal meets with what is required by Poor Laws 19, 24, and 25 of the *Nueva Recopilación*. Addressed to Philip II, the unsigned manuscript presents Giginta's recommendations as a novel means of protecting children from a life of poverty and of redirecting the false poor from stealing alms without eliminating charity, but by 'organizing' (*ordenar*) the disorderly poor:

Discussing the possible solutions to [poverty], [Giginta] believes he has found a means of succinctly addressing poverty relief that would easily provide a remedy without eliminating the goals of charity solely by organizing begging.

[Discurriendo sobre el remedio q[ue] para esto podria auer piensa hauer hallado un modo hasta aqui no aduertido tan compendioso en materia de remediar pobres con el qual sin quitar el objecto de la caridad y solo hordenando la mendicidad se remediaria facilmente.][43]

Giginta's treatise, however, reprints another *memorial*, one he dedicated in 1576 to the president of the Council of Castile, Antonio Mauriño de Pazos y Figueroa, in which he outlines his basic plan for the Lisbon hospitals or *casas de misericordia*, recommending that similar ones be built or reconverted in Spanish cities. The buildings, which were also to house pilgrims on the route to Santiago de Compostela as well as the unemployed looking for work, were an idea he conceived, he tells us, when he saw so many poor turned away from a royal hospital (*Memorial* 1).

In her study of Spanish social welfare, Elena Maza Zorrilla has accurately characterized Giginta's reform movement as synchretic, since it attempts to combine his endorsement of social containment with the freedom that Soto had believed was the right of the poor, together with Vives's and Robles's sharp critique of the rich's indifference to their social duty. Giginta's treatise, therefore, significantly redirects the prevailing perceptions that poverty relief should remain an exclusively religious concern, to a broader, secularizing view that intends its expansion along socio-economic lines (*Remedio* 89).

Anticipating the English workhouses for the poor by more than a century, Giginta's plan for his *casas de misericordia* shows that treatment for the sick poor was, at best, an inefficient method of caring for the generally impoverished. No longer referring to those suffering from curable illnesses, the plan specifies that the residents be given licence to beg food from markets and alms from the monasteries, from the wealthy, and from regular townfolk. Although their clothing was to be marked with the hospital insignia, the poor should be allowed to enter and leave at will. Besides carrying out their daily chores, they would be trained in the manufacture of wool, silk, reed, or other material, and in basic trades from hospital officers. Women and young girls would learn to weave and do fine needlework to make a living or find husbands (Cap. iij.15). All were required to obey the Church Commandments, and attend mass and sermons in the hospital chapel, whose main *retablo* should depict the parable of Lazarus and the rich man.

The painting's topic, allowed to be viewed only by the inmates, was meant to serve as a visual lesson that poverty, in contrast to the rich man's indifference, warrants spiritual recompense in the hereafter. The proposed *retablo*, depicting the Last Judgment and Lazarus, the archetypal recipient of charity, is yet another vivid reminder that Giginta's tolerant attitude towards begging remained closer in spirit to Soto than to Robles. Yet Giginta was highly critical of incompetent and self-interested religious alms collectors and hospital administrators. He stipulated that the hospitals should be administered without charge by a secular *cofradía*, supported by town aldermen and the Council of State, with building funds collected through the church in the improbable event that no rich donor had offered to subsidize at least the chapel (*Memorial* 8r).

Giginta's *memorial* introduces his main text, the *Remedio de pobres*, a lengthy fictional discourse on poverty employing the rhetorical strategies of the Renaissance dialogue. Its three interlocutors, Valerio, Mario, and Flaminio, function as defendant, respondent, and witness, respectively, of the benefits of his plan (Cap.j.9r). Martz has pointed out the many contradictions contained in the treatise; for instance, that the poor were to beg in pairs at the local churches and monasteries, but that they must also occupy their time weaving or otherwise working, keeping one-sixth of the proceeds for themselves and the rest for other poor and hospital expenses (*Memorial* 7r). Giginta's design envisioned the hospitals to be sufficiently self-supporting so as to be able to accept all those in need. What he leaves out, Martz claims, is a practical plan explicitly detailing the hospital's maintenance and how it meant to deal with the vagabonds that managed to elude entering the hospital (69). However, it is clear that the reformer was cognizant of at least some of the contradictions in his proposed solutions, as his *tractado* exposes and attempts to respond to many of the problems left unresolved in the earlier reformers' treatises.

Indeed, Giginta's dialectical strategy, which effectively internalizes the Soto–Robles debate in its synchretic resolution, allows him to foresee and reply to any lingering doubts that its intended readers, Philip II and the council president, may still have harboured.[44] The interlocutor Mario asks his counterpart Valerio whether, in seeking an easier life, the ill, the poor, and those employed as servants might desire to fill the hospital wards, thereby reducing the number of available workers. The latter responds that, on the contrary, the hospitals will furnish even more workers by identifying the false beggars, curing the truly ill, and teaching trades to mendicant children. Furthermore, he states, no one will be allowed to stay in the hospital if there are jobs they can fill (Cap.jx 37r). To Mario's continuing apprehensions that the idle poor and false beggars, fearing exposure, will leave the cities and resort to banditry, Valerio replies that few become criminals when their needs are met, and that those naturally inclined towards crime will not change their ways even under threat of hanging (Cap.jx 38r).

Valerio's faith that man's natural goodness always prevails over evil, which encapsulates a moral philosophy more in touch with the universal categories of good and evil characteristic of and maintained by restricted feudal societies, is thus reminiscent of Soto's inspired defence of the poor as *pauperes Christi*. The concerns expressed by Mario, however, mirror the growing social fears over the disenfranchised's latent delinquency typically evinced in the modern period, with its emphasis on rationalism and human freedom. By the end of the century, the social perception of the poor had hardened from the medieval notion of their magico-ritual function as sacramentalized *pharmakos* to an increasingly secularized perception of the disenfranchised as social deviants. Despite Giginta's seemingly contradictory position, the change in ideology, which, on a practical level, registers the state's urgent interest in augmenting the labour force, is revealed in his proposal to abolish the circumstances that induce delinquency:

Rid the many false poor of their free time, as they ruin themselves and the nation by feeding from others' labour ... This will eliminate the many dissolute actions that our present disorderly state allows the false beggars ... They will stop lacerating themselves and punishing their flesh, as is the custom among many false and true beggars ... Many who would otherwise never be found out will abandon their crutches, their tricks, and all their false inventions ... Neither false nor true beggars will continue to use their children in their vile business ... Parents will not harm or blind their children to gain profit from them ... Mendicant women will no longer shun the complications of pregnancy, labour and child-rearing by seeking abortions because the mother lacks the funds necessary for her and her child's survival, their deaths thus lying on the city aldermen's conscience for taking no heed in relieving the poor ... There will therefore be more people available to cultivate the soil and to work, and besides ... there will be more male and female servants at more moderate salaries.

[Quitar el ocio de tantos fingidos como ay, dañosos a si mesmos y a la republica, comie[n]do de trabajo ageno ... Se quitaran tantas y tan grandes dissoluciones, como muchos destos fingidos hazen con la desorden presente ... Cessara el llargarse y martyrizarse sus proprias carnes, como se entiende que hazen muchos fingidos ... Dexara[n] las muletas, los embustes, y todas las inuenciones fingidas ... No pondran mas los vnos ni los otros los hijos a su vicioso officio ... No estropearan ni cegaran ningunos padres a sus criaturas ... Cessara[n] ... algunas mendigas que para escusarse el embaraço de la preñez, y el trabajo del parto, y la occupacion del criar procuran de parir mal ... por falta del recaudo que vna parida ha menester ... para que no se muera en dos palabras con la criatura, en tanto daño de sus consciencias y cargo de los regidores, que no se curan del conueniente remedio de los pobres ... Aura con esto mas gente que cultiue las tierras y que trabajen ... demas de que ... se hallaran mas criados y criadas por mas moderados precios. (Cap.x 42r, 43r)]

In his efforts to convince his readers of the *Remedio de pobres*' pertinence,

Giginta dwells pragmatically on the economic advantages that accrue
from aiding the poor as much as on the moral benefits. That the measures he recommends advocate self-reform fully as much as they feature
assistance by the wealthy signals the move away from a 'natural' concept of human goodness towards a deliberate choice of action, controlled by disciplinary procedures, but governed above all by ethical
responsibility.[45]

Further, by claiming that abortion would be abolished, he appeals to
social anxieties generated by the supposed sexual excess of poor
women, many of whom, as I argue more fully in chapter 4, had no
recourse but to practise prostitution. Abortion and abandonment were
often the only methods available to women to free themselves of the
economic burdens of childrearing; they also allowed the women to
remain sexually active as a means of survival. This social problem is
reflected early on in the *Lazarillo de Tormes*, where Lazarillo's tearful
farewell from his mother belies her urgency in turning over the child to
his first master, the blind man.[46] Giginta's opinion on the subject is that,
if more children were born and nurtured, society would reap the benefits of a larger and cheaper workforce. In this, Giginta was likely influenced by contemporary European political treatises, which considered
the lack of manpower an ongoing and serious concern for all states in
that it seriously affected economic development. Giovanni Botero's
widely circulated *Ragioni di Stato* clearly correlates the needs of the state
with its treatment of the poor and the current depletion of manpower:
the impoverished represent a danger to the nation, while depopulation
weakens it.[47] Botero speaks directly to Spain's depleted manpower:

And if Spain is deemed a sterile province, it is not because of defect in the land,
but for the lack of inhabitants ... The inhabitants are fewer than anciently, first
from the war in which the Moors imposed themselves on Spain ... The Spaniards
no sooner saw themselves freed from this war than they turned their arms to the
undertakings in Africa, Naples, Milan, the New World, and lastly to the recov-
ery of the Low Countries; and in these undertakings there perished innumerable
of their people both from the sword and want. (155–6)

The country's reduced manpower resulted as much from continuing
conscription in Castile, the main source for Habsburg military manpower, and from urban decline due to recurring famines and plagues, as
from the notion that the fraudulent poor refused to work.[48] By identifying the false beggars and withholding alms and shelter from them, Gig-

inta saw an opportunity to require them to join the workforce in order to strengthen the economy.

Yet Giginta nonetheless recognizes the social imperative to succour the truly poor, an economic challenge that individual donors, no matter how charitable, were no longer able to meet. The dialogue anticipates the excuses the town aldermen may offer in rejecting the proposal by having them admit that, if the expense does not fit in their original plans, they are in no rush to accommodate the poor (Cap. xx 78). To Mario's defensive comment that a large part of city funds had been spent on repairing streets, fountains, and bridges, because these were necessary for the public good, Valerio answers that the people themselves should be a government's first priority (Cap.xxi 79, 80r). However, in his conclusion, Giginta discloses his fundamentally religious bias towards poor relief. His ultimate reliance on an orthodox argument illustrates the fact that, in Spain, secular and religious approaches to poverty relief often intersected for both ideological and practical reasons.

In contrast to Soto's views that the poor should not be enclosed, Robles had complained about the abandonment of the poor throughout the countryside, not only because this served as an example of man's basic inhumanity to man, but also because the poor, out of the sight of priests, were negligent in following church commandments, especially in attending Mass, saying Confession, and receiving Communion (Soto 157). Following Cardinal Tavera's 1536 synod, which itself prefigured Tridentine measures by requiring mass Christianization as a system of spiritual control, Robles believed that poverty led inevitably to religious indifference, which then opened the doors to heresy and apostasy.[49] Decrying Spain's shameful record in spiritual care for the poor in comparison with non-Christian nations, Giginta concurred with Robles that the impoverished needed both spiritual sustenance and material nourishment. Ultimately, then, the reformer's final reasoning centres as much on Spain's nationalist concerns as a Catholic state as on its moral obligation to assist the poor:

Why is it that Gentiles, Greeks, Romans, Indians, Americans, Chinese, ... Jews, Apostates, Manicheans, Turks, Moors, and old and modern heretics give so much consideration to what should concern us, given that we have more reason and obligation.

[Que es esto q[ue] los ge[n]tiles, Griegos, Romanos, Indios, Americos, Chinos ... Iudios, Apostatas, Manicheos, Turcos, moros, y hereges antiguos y modernos,

sean tan cuydadosos de lo q[ue] a nosotros conuiene, con mayor razon y mayor
obligacio[n]. (Cap.xxvii 99 r)]

Giginta's rhetorical question seemed answered in Toledo in 1581, two
years after the publication of his treatise, with the establishment of its
first beggars' hospital. Unlike those of other *arbitristas*, his project also
received government approval and support in Madrid, Granada, and
Barcelona (Martz 72–3). Toledo's situation was exacerbated by the influx
of thousands of forcibly resettled *moriscos* and starving peasants who
required more hospital beds and a greater distribution of alms and food,
but it counted with a strong economy.[50] The refusal of other cities to follow suit indicates that they foresaw what Toledo was soon to find out:
that such hospitals were economically unsound. As Martz reasons, if
they functioned as Giginta proposed, the hospitals would be overrun
with thousands of poor: 'The primary difficulty of the Spanish beggars'
hospitals was the discrepancy between the theory, which promised so
much to so many, and actual practice, which frequently was unable to
offer more than a small amount of bread to only the most destitute of
society' (72–6).

The debates on whether the poor should be allowed to beg in the
streets thus persisted throughout the century. Reinforced by the
Counter-Reformation, the paupers' visual impact continued to be
emphasized in the doctrine of salvation through good works. It was
only one year after Trent, after all, that Villavicencio had responded to
Vives's earlier treatise with his virulent *De oeconomia sacra circa pauperum
curam*, in which he labelled efforts to secularize charity 'pestilential, pernicious, and injurious to the dignity of the Catholic church' (qtd. in Cavillac, 'Introducción,' cvii). Enclosure of the poor continued to come
under the attack of many church prelates, who felt that the pauper's
absence from society weakened people's desire to perform charitable
acts. They also took the prohibition of begging to be a heretical manifes-
tation of Erasmian and Lutheran policies. This overtly Christian discourse constitutes a case of what Raymond Williams explains as a
'residual' element, in conjunction with dominant and emergent elements of a given cultural field.[51] As secular measures proved ineffective
in dealing with the social issues of poverty, the renewed recourse to religious beliefs, recently institutionalized and reimposed by the Council of
Trent, lent itself as well to a discourse of xenophobic nationalism. Dove-
tailing with the neo-aristocracy that ensues in the seventeenth century,
this conservative religious movement reactivated the reliance on charity

that had previously marked – and would continue to inform – Spanish political thought on poverty. In contrast to the changes that the Foucauldian narrative spells out in industrialized France, it is not until the liberalism of the mid-eighteenth century that poverty is again taken up as a concern of the state.[52]

Cristóbal Pérez de Herrera: Beyond Centralized Confinement

Severely affected by the bad harvests, droughts, and plagues in Castile as well as by uncompetitive prices, rise in wages, and heavy taxation, the Spanish economy continued its decline during the last decades of the sixteenth century.[53] The fall of the Armada and the raids on Cádiz further fostered a defeatist attitude that reinforced strong feelings against the impoverished and destitute. It is in this despondent atmosphere that another reformer, the brilliant physician, economist, and soldier Cristóbal Pérez de Herrera, first proposes his 1595 treatise *Del amparo y reformación de los fingidos vagabundos*. In 1598, he publishes, at his own expense, ten of his revised essays on poverty and vagabondage in a collection titled *Discursos del amparo de los legítimos pobres y reducción de los fingidos*.[54] Pérez de Herrera's status as a *protomédico* and non-religious, unlike the majority of reformers we have seen, is of considerable significance, since it demonstrates that, by the seventeenth century, the issues of poverty and vagrancy had failed to be resolved by local religious and legislative means, therefore eliciting more forceful responses from state government.[55]

The country's declining economy contributed to the increased perception of the poor as a social threat due to their presumed abandonment of the work ethic. Although the term *arbitrista* has been villified, Pérez de Herrera belongs to the loose group of political economists who disapproved, as religious thinkers such as Soto and Robles had earlier, of the consequences brought about by increasing and uncontrolled poverty, and who offered sundry solutions, called *arbitrios* or 'projects,' to Spain's economic problems.[56] Criticized by writers of such different ideological stripes as Cervantes, Quevedo, and Vélez de Guevara, their abundant writings nevertheless give voice to the mounting frustrations on the state's incapacity to govern.[57] Together with the previous treatises and the poor laws, the *arbitristas'* projects form part of an expanding discourse of political protest that joined with the fictional picaresque narratives in expressing various and often contradictory positions on poverty and poor relief. Although these treatises and *memoriales* had a relatively limited readership and did not circulate as freely as the far more popular fictional narratives such as the picaresque, exemplary novels and courtesan short stories, their subject matter permeated the literature, affected discussions at court, and set the tone for religious sermons.[58]

Despite his reliance on previous treatises, what differentiates Pérez de Herrera from earlier writers on poor relief is his project's comprehensiveness. Resuming Vives's unprecedented thought that poverty was of no benefit whatsoever to either the poor or society, but instead constituted grievous social injustice, Pérez de Herrera's *Amparo de pobres* responds not merely to the immediate historical circumstances, but to the more extensive need to forestall poverty and to transform the poor into productive members of society. Conflating the earlier tenets that attributed poverty to external causes with those that condemned the disenfranchised, Pérez de Herrera deemed the causes of poverty at once diverse and inseparable. For him, destitution resulted as much from the moral issue of idleness as it did from the economic conditions due to lack of circulating capital (Maza Zorrilla 91). His solution, which makes use of many aspects of Giginta's *casas de misericordia*, proposes a centralized program of *albergues* or hostels built systematically throughout Castile. He thus advances a totalizing view that encompasses aid to the truly poor and the elimination of false beggars as not merely a spiritual and moral necessity, but an economic and political one as well.

As a direct observer of Spain's foreign policies, Pérez de Herrera was in an excellent position to gauge the country's declining economy on the international scene; in 1580, when he was twenty-five years old, he was named *protomédico* of the Spanish galleys. Assigned from 1585 to 1592 to Martín de Padilla, Captain General of the Spanish fleet, he docked in Barcelona in 1588, where he witnessed the riots protesting the economic devastation brought upon the city by the export rights granted by the viceroy, Manrique de Lara, to Genoese merchant ships (Cavillac, 'Introducción,' xxix). On the death in 1592 of Francisco de Vallés, Philip II's physician, Pérez de Herrera was appointed court physician, whereupon he founded the Royal Pharmacy in 1594.[59] He was to serve in a far broader capacity, however, since his experiences at sea as galley doctor and his observation of the Barcelona rebellion had afforded him a unique opportunity to envisage a connection between the exploitation and abuse of galley slaves and the threat of social unrest. His new position at court and his friendship with Rodrigo Vázquez Arce, then president of the Council of Castile, gave him entry into a political arena that, he expected, would allow him to transform his opinions into state policy (Cavillac, 'Introducción,' xlviii). Fittingly, the *Amparo de pobres* includes eleven *respuestas* or responses to objections raised by several of his detractors. Philip II, hardly an advocate of secular reform, nevertheless recognized the weakness of the country's metallurgical and munitions industries, as the loss of the Spanish Armada had so graphically illustrated; his approval of Pérez de Herrera's *Amparo de pobres* may very well have been due to its recommendations for preparing a skilled workforce.[60] Certainly, the *cortes*'s two requests in 1595 and 1596 that he implement the treatise helped to further persuade the King. Acutely aware that Philip II was nearing death, as a strategy for calling continued attention to the treatise, Pérez de Herrera addressed the *Amparo de pobres* to him but made sure to dedicate it to Philip III, although the twenty-year-old prince had yet to assume the monarchy.

The urgency with which Pérez de Herrera sought a resolution for Spain's internal dilemmas was not shared by the young prince, whose approaching reign was already overwhelmed by Spain's transnational conflicts. Although Cavillac believes 1598 a propitious year for broad social reforms, given its uneventfulness, the peace aspired to by an exhausted Spain had been made imperative by the Crown's bankruptcy two years earlier (Elliott, *Imperial Spain*, 290). Still, Pérez de Herrera had good reason to be optimistic: just one month before the publication of his *Amparo de pobres*, the unfinished Madrid *hospitium pauperum* initially endorsed by him and approved by the *cortes* in 1595 had received two donations from Philip II amounting to 54,000 ducats.[61] Despite earlier attacks, Pérez de Herrera's unprecedented projects finally won support from the King, the *cortes*, and Vásquez Arce, and the intellectual atmosphere at court seemed most receptive. Indeed, several important public figures, including Lope de Vega, who contributed two sonnets for the collection, composed laudatory poems prefacing each of the *Amparo*'s ten discourses, illustrating that the treatise was familiar to and championed by a large cross-section of secular and religious writers.[62]

Demonstrating the level of secularization intended by the revision, Pérez de Herrera eliminated the following from the *Amparo de pobre*'s earlier prologue, which emulated Giginta's treatise in that it proffered a religious motivation for his reforms:

[S]o that we may live in a Spain free of immoral or indolent people, unlike the many barbarous and unlawful nations whose obligations are fewer than ours, and which we justly surpass, since we profess the Catholic faith of our Lord, Jesus Christ.

[[P]ara que de esta manera vivamos en España sin gente perdida ni ociosa, como lo hacen muchas naciones bárbaras y sin ley que no tienen tantas obligaciones como nosotros, a los cuales es bien llevemos mucha ventaja, pues profesamos la fe católica de Jesucristo Nuestro Señor. (*Amparo* 16, n.23)]

Pérez de Herrera's revised treatise, dedicated to the as yet uncrowned Philip III in 1598, the year of his father's death, instead cites reasons of state and emphasizes public welfare as essential to the conservation and expansion of the monarchy.[63] Cavillac has rightly pointed out that Pérez de Herrera's worries regarding the many deaths occasioned by bull-fighting and his stake in collecting a surtax of two *maravedís* on theatre tickets to help fund the *albergues* stem from an interest in regulating popular entertainment according to rational principles ('Introducción xliii). We should note, however, that the surtax on theatrical productions functions as another example of Raymond Williams's residual element, in that it tends to revert to the Christian notion of individuals contributing to charitable causes, since charity remains a means to simultaneously awaken and assuage the donor's guilt for indulging in recreational pleasures.[64]

By dedicating the *discursos* to Philip III before his accession to the throne, Pérez de Herrera aims to apprise the young prince of his kingly mission to provide 'poor relief which includes the abolishment of vagabonds and aid to the soldiers who return maimed or otherwise disabled from the wars, or who have aged so much as to be useless to carry on in battle' (el remedio de los pobres, en que está inclusa la estirpación de los vagabundos, y el amparo de los soldados que salen mancos y estropeados de la guerra, o han llegado a tanta edad en ella, que están ya inútiles para proseguirla). This, he assures the future king, will no doubt result in his 'eternal fame and universal prestige' (*Amparo* 11). Such a means of drawing the future Philip III's attention to his enterprise follows upon Botero's 1598 supplement to his *Razón de estado*, 'On the Reputation of the Prince,' in which the Italian stresses the ideal ruler's need to temper sternness with prudence: '[P]rudent will be he who with little harshness and few executions holds his subjects to their duties ... Because in truth today there is no greater need of anything than men for war, for the galleys, and for other affairs, it is fitting to take care of their lives as far as possible' (*Practical Politics* 241–2). In Book VIII of his *Razón de estado*, Botero had addressed the issue of population: '[t]he population and the forces are augmented in two ways – by propagation and by adding others; propagation takes place through agriculture, the arts, by favoring the education of offspring, and by colonies' (*Practical Politics* 157). Likely influenced by the Italian, Pérez de Herrera was also aware of the devastation to the economy caused by depopulation; however, he had only to look around him to see the damages caused by the recent epidemics. The loss of labourers in turn raised the price of foodstuffs and manufactured goods, forcing Spanish merchants to rely heavily on credit and into the hands of Genoese merchants and bankers, as I discuss in the next chapter. By the end of the century, along with depopulation, Spain's increased unemployment among the poor fostered higher rates of vagrancy. Pérez de Herrera's *albergues* intended to isolate the 'legitimate' or true poor from the vast numbers of vagabonds and false poor, whose many vices, according to the reformer, set a bad example and discredited all the disenfranchised by marking them as potential criminals. Only the true poor, the sick, and the elderly were to be allowed to reside at the *albergues*; in keeping with the reformer's strong disapproval of idleness, those sufficiently able-bodied were required to register for a beggar's licence and expected to find food outside the shelter.

According to Cavillac, Pérez de Herrera's determined efforts to differentiate the legitimate from the false poor followed Soto's arguments against confinement (*Amparo* 54, n.18). Nevertheless, as Williams's theory of residual actions explains, the treatise, while still manifesting vestiges of his interest in individual charitable donations as a sign of its author's religious concern, clearly exhibits his centralizing views on poor relief:

Your Majesty should mandate that, in all cities, towns and locations within these kingdoms ... all the poor begging at peoples' doors and along the roads should come, on the same day and at the same time at all locations, to the aforementioned houses or shelters, or to those nearest where they first hear the proclamation.

[Mandando V.M. que se pregone en todas las ciudades, villas y lugares destos reinos ... que, en un día señalado, a un mismo tiempo en todas partes, acudan todos los pobres que piden limosna por las puertas y caminos a las dichas casas y albergues ... o los más cercanos, donde les cogiere la voz y pregón. (*Amparo* 53-4)]

The time, he notes, should be next year, 1599, on the Day of Our Lady of the Incarnation, 25 March, allowing for the completion of the Madrid hospital (*Amparo* 183). Convening on the same date, in different specified locations, ensures that the unmotivated poor not claim ignorance of the event and vanish to another town.

Pérez de Herrera's advice to the King that the poor's confinement be orchestrated simultaneously throughout the country is startling only if we fail to note that this call represents an appeal to a king – overtly Philip II but in reality the youthful Philip III – preoccupied with strengthening his political position at home as well as abroad. As Cavillac suggests ('L'enfermement' 56), the measure demonstrates the growing tendency towards a bourgeois national consciousness whose organizational efforts offered a rational approach to social problems. Despite their ultimate failure, the sweeping reforms proposed by Pérez de Herrera not only aimed to improve the poor's living conditions and to arbitrate moral behaviour following Giginta, but, extending far beyond what other *arbitristas* had suggested previously, meant to profoundly reorganize and redirect national interests.

For this reason alone, the *Amparo de pobres'* scope proves both more broad and complex as well as more engaged in the slippage from hierarchical values to rational structures of control than Giginta's treatise. Although it begins, like the others, with the need to eliminate vagabondage, the *Amparo* is the first to propose institutionalized means to care for the legitimate poor unable or unwilling to enter an *albergue*, as well as to protect the population from loss. His plan, then, anticipates by close to a century the control mechanisms first adopted in France to contain plagues, strategies that extended into the panopticism of nineteenth-century asylums, penitentiaries, hospitals, and reformatories (*Discipline* 195–9). Moving from the 'great confinement' as a means of treating the leper – but which, as we have seen, did not preclude the leper's ritual circulation in society – the plague and what it stood for, confusion and disorder, gave rise to 'disciplinary projects' that, among other things, interpellated the socially marginalized for service to the state. Once the relation between surveillant and observed was set in place through the field of visibility, the panopticon provided a space for social experiment in that it penetrated into human behaviour (*Discipline* 204).[65]

The recommendations spelled out by Pérez de Herrera approximate the levels of control that led to the change from a ritualized society of spectacle to one of surveillance (*Discipline* 217). As we shall see in chapter 4, women were no strangers to enclosure, from their enforced stays in houses of prostitution, to their recruitment in Magdalen houses and imprisonment in the *Galera*, or women's prison. While far less punitive than the measures imposed on women by the latter, the *Amparo*, no doubt due to the damages against moral and social health generated by gender disorder, treats women accused of vagabondage, robbery, witchcraft, or procuring more harshly than their male counterparts. Segregating the inmates by gender, it relegates women to containment in separate houses, locked in at night, and occupied in menial tasks to cover the cost of their meals (*Amparo* 120–5). Yet, in keeping with its emphasis on social reform, the *Amparo de pobres* stipulates that the poor who reside in the *albergues* are all expected to learn a trade; the handicapped should not let their infirmities get in the way of work, 'since those without feet who learn to sew can still practice their trade' (Que el que no tiene pies, sabiendo coser puede ejercitar su oficio [*Amparo* 59]). The contagious are to be hospitalized, while the *pobres vergonzantes*, or shame-faced poor, whose good name prevents them from begging publicly, and the poor in prison will require special brotherhoods founded to administer to their individual needs. Indeed, the Madrid Hermandad de San Martín to which Pérez de Herrera belonged, dedicated to these poor and founded in 1594, was organized along the *Amparo's* recommendations.

Pérez de Herrera's stint as physician to the royal jails in Madrid and Valladolid made him especially conscious of the ill treatment to which the incarcerated poor were subjected. Perhaps as a reproach to Philip II's prison expansion with no attention given to the inmates' care, he specifically asks Philip to 'come to their aid as most Christian and compassionate King, God's representative in his kingdoms, and responsible for their temporal governance' (lo que más importa es que de V.M. venga el amparo desta gente, como de Rey tan cristiano y misericordioso, que está en lugar de Dios en sus reinos, y remedio para el gobierno dellos en lo temporal [77]).

Both to offer better care to the prisoners and to save operating expenses as much as to avoid recidivism, Pérez de Herrera recommends that convicted criminals be consigned to the galleys:

[I]t is better that they carry out their sentence as soon as possible in galleys or in exile, so that the labour will be over quicker, since in jail they are of no use other than to deplete the alms assigned to incoming prisoners, from whom they learn evil and depraved customs and new methods of becoming even more infamous thieves; and as the length of stay and the jail's corrupt air makes them ill, the sea air of the galleys is much better for them.

[Y a los que necesariamente han de ser castigados, está mejor que cumplan desde luego su penitencia en las galeras o destierros, porque el trabajo se les acabe más presto, pues en las cárceles no son de más provecho que para consumir las limosnas de los otros que suceden, y deprender dellos malas y depravadas costumbres, y nuevas liciones para ser más famosos ladrones; y enfermando ellos con la largueza del tiempo y corrupción de aires que allí hay, de los cuales gozan mejor en la mar cuando estuvieren en galeras. (79)]

Asserting that the young are important to the national welfare, Pérez de Herrera thoughtfully incorporates the care of children in his project: abandoned infants are to be placed in homes, in orphanages, or to stay at the *albergues* with the poor women. Healthy girls are to be married or placed in convents, while boys are to be placed as servants, sent to the galleys as sailors, or taught a trade in the armories or in the tapestry factories that compete with their European counterparts:

So that others, taking as they do our wool and other resources from us in Spain, do not sell and profit from our material what can be manufactured in Spain by Your Majesty's orders, since we have metals and materials for everything, and there will be enough to occupy part of those who otherwise would be well on their way to becoming vagabonds and incorrigibles.

[Porque, llevándonos de España la lana y otras cosas, como nos la llevan, no nos vendan y ganen con nuestros materiales lo que puede V.M., siendo servido, mandar se haga en España, pues tenemos metales y materiales para todo; y habrá disposición con esto para ocupar parte de los que habían de ser vagabundos y perdidos por el camino que iban. (*Amparo* 106)]

Most important, Pérez de Herrera's interest in developing a national military industry was aimed at utilizing Spain's raw materials; his treatise recognized the country's youth itself as an essential component of those materials. His expanded concerns envisioned a centralized economic program that would, in the process, serve to redeem young boys from a life of vagabondage not only as a means of eliminating poverty, but in order to make significant contributions to the nation-state. His reforms proposed to employ the youth as resources for the much-needed development of Spanish military technology, all the while ensuring their loyalty to the Crown and the church:

[A]nd so that [the most apt boys] may become machinists, levellers, and renowned gunners, so in need on land and sea ... and [learn to] make clocks, maps, globes, spheres, and navigational instruments, and other needed technology ... and Your Majesty will no longer have occasion to employ for these purposes people of different nations, subjects and vassals of other kings and governments, or of lands rebelling against your Majesty, brought over at much expense and lacking our faith and loyalty.

[Y para ser maquinistas, niveladores, y artilleros famosos, tan necesarios en mar y tierra ... y hacer relojes, mapas, globos, esferas e instrumentos para la navegación, y otros muy necesarios artificios ... Y no tendrá V.M., en tiempo de ocasiones, necesidad de servirse para este efeto de gentes de diferentes naciones, sujetos y vasallos de otros reyes y repúblicas, o de tierras rebeldes a V.M., traídos con mucha costa, y con falta de fe y fidelidad. (*Amparo* 107–8)]

Cavillac notes that Pérez de Herrera's 'mercantilist project' exhorting Spain's industrialization synthesizes the calls from other *arbitristas* such as Giginta for the local fabrication of artillery.[66]

Commercial operations had expanded sufficiently to make use of manuals teaching accounting skills, such as Pérez de Moya's *Tratado de Mathemáticas* (1573) and Juan de Timoneda's *Timón de tratantes* (1574), that followed earlier 'artes' in the vernacular.[67] It was customary for poor children to enter a training period soon after the age of six, when they were sent out as servants, domestics, or apprentices, while the *colegios mayores* taught grammar to older, impoverished students.[68] This practice is integrated into the picaresque's episodic structure, as the young *pícaro* passes from his parents to begin his education: Lazarillo is apprenticed to the blind man, and Pablos, the *buscón*, accompanies his wealthy *converso* friend, Don Diego Coronel, to school as his servant. According to Cavillac, the schooling of young boys in trades and mathematics, as well as letters, would build an intermediate stratum of artisans and merchants revalorizing these activities, looked down upon by the aristocracy for being practised by the lower classes and the *conversos* (*Amparo de pobres* cxxiv).[69]

Pérez de Herrera's concern about Spain's economy as a nation-state points to the growing preoccupation for the country's weakened position vis-à-vis other European communities. Following Jean Bodin, Botero had already called attention to its lack of industry:

[A]nd not only are the Spaniards negligent in the culture of their lands but also in the practice of the manual arts, for there is no province more stripped of artisans and industries. Therefore the wool and silk and the other materials in great part go out of the country, and what remains there for the most part is worked up by the Italians, as in some places are the fields and vineyards by the French. (*Practical Politics* 156)[70]

Pérez de Herrera's resolution to broaden and improve Spain's social and material bases is nowhere more evident than in his liberal endorsement of university fellowships for the most intelligent of the poor, an unprecedented directive that builds on the blueprint for social ascendance first drawn by Vives and far surpasses all other political treatises. Given its importance, fully acknowledged by the author, I quote the entire passage:

[T]he most competent [youths] may be chosen from the seminars to form four or five more of two dozen [youths] each, *as this is the most important issue of all those we have been discussing.* And these [seminars] can be held in this Court, in Seville, Valladolid and Salamanca, and administered through the University, since these are rich and populated locations, where [the youths] will be taught to read Mathematics, a subject of great benefit to the nation, and these seminars may be taught in Latin in Salamanca and Valladolid, and in Castilian in other locations. And another eight or ten [youths] may be added to each [seminar] held in Salamanca and Valladolid, to teach [them] Anatomy and Surgery in addition to Mathematics – this last being very important, since the navigational arts are ideally taught in the latter [seminar], and since Your Majesty rules many kingdoms reached by sea and from which many riches are shipped, it makes sense to insure them with good pilots – and Architecture, which includes Geometry, to construct buildings and holy churches to celebrate Mass and to adorn cities and large areas.

[Se podrán escoger los que parecieren más hábiles destos seminarios, para hacerse en estos reinos otros cuatro o cinco, de dos docenas dellos en cada uno, *que es negocio de más importancia que todo cuanto se ha dicho acerca desto*; y éstos se podrán hacer en esta Corte, Sevilla, Valladolid, Salamanca, por razón de la Universidad, y por ser lugares más populosos y ricos, adonde se les enseñasen y leyesen matemáticas, cosa de gran utilidad para la república, y podrían leerse en latín en Salamanca y Valladolid, y en las demás partes en castellano. Y aun, en los que se hicieren en Salamanca y Valladolid, se podrían añadir otros ocho o diez en cada uno, para que se les enseñase anatomía y cirugía, fuera de los que han de aprender las matemáticas dichas pues se sabe perfectamente con ellas el arte de navegar, que es de mucha consideración, teniendo V.M. tantos reinos para donde se navega, y de adonde por mar se traen tantas riquezas que es bien asegurarlas con buenos pilotos); y arquitectura – sabiendo geometría – para fabricar edificios y templos solenes para el culto divino, y ornato de las ciudades y lugares grandes. (*Amparo* 107; my emphasis)]

Pérez de Herrera adds that these youths should take up these critical fields, as well as engineering and other military arts, in order to, in his words, produce 'eminent engineers' whose technological and military proficiency would serve to strengthen and otherwise fortify the Spanish dominions and to conquer others ('y ser famosos ingenieros—tan necesarios en el uso y ejercicio militar –, haciendo fuerzas inexpugnables y otras industrias necesarias para la fortificación destos reinos, y conquistas de otros' [107]). Cavillac has drawn attention to the preference for teaching in the vernacular, noting its Erasmian tendencies and its implications for social reform ('Introducción' clxii). Instruction in Castilian of mathematics, the most 'inclusive' of rational subjects, makes sure to privilege intellectual superiority over noble birth.[71]

The value of Pérez de Herrera's treatise is that it extends far beyond the scope of poverty relief to search for global solutions to state welfare. Unlike Giginta, whose *casas de misericordia* proposed a static reform still preoccupied with and grounded on the polarization between rich and poor, Pérez de Herrera subscribes to a rationalist economic theory that transcends the alleviation of poverty by sheltering the disenfranchised through a distributive housing program. His prominence as a social scientist lies instead in presaging the utilization, not only of physical labour, but of intellectual capital, in what would come to be known, for better or for worse, as a welfare society. Foucault's analysis of Bentham's *Panopticon* serves as a valuable means of understanding Pérez de Herrera's sweeping reform project; it is especially useful in comparing the former's structural function with the *Amparo de pobre*'s potential for observation and social change. Foucault states that Bentham's program made it possible to differentiate among the various enclosed groups: to observe hospital patients' symptoms, to assess students, and to distinguish workers' aptitudes (*Discipline* 203). Yet, the fact that such a mechanism constitutes, in Foucault's words, a 'new physics of power' that functions outside the realm of the king's body could not help but threaten the principles of absolute monarchy, as indeed happened in eighteenth-century France when panopticism displaced royal control: '[p]anopticism is the general principle of a new "political anatomy" whose object and end are not the relations of sovereignty but the relations of discipline' (*Discipline* 209).

For all purposes, then, Pérez de Herrera's vision was decidedly ahead of its time; as I discuss in the next chapter, the *Amparo's* recommendations came at a critical turning point for the Spanish economy and were sharply curtailed after Philip II's death.[72] The *Amparo de pobres* was notably more advanced than other sixteenth-century treatises in that it promoted a coherent welfare reform no less attainable for the thoroughness with which it approached social problems. Most important, its recommendations made certain that, once the ill were cured, the legitimate poor educated, and the false poor reformed, they would no longer require even this minimal containment but instead contribute to the needs of the state, expanding its material base through agricultural labour, increased technology and industry, and military manpower. According to Cavillac, the *albergues* would allow the country to extract itself from the colonialist exploitation imposed by foreign capital through manufacturing instead of the exportation of its raw materials. Indeed, the *Amparo de pobres* proposed to expand and mobilize a workforce dependent on productive enterprise rather than on a rentier economy whose material goods and technology remained dependent on foreign imports.

Moreover, the social paradigm envisioned in Pérez de Herrera's *Amparo de pobres*, as Cavillac notes, reinforces the possibility of class mobility in that its recommendations create the conditions for social advancement through education and skilled labour ('L'enfermement' 54–5). Yet, although Cavillac situates the reforms clearly within the bourgeois model of a growing national consciousness, the progress that seemed so imminently within reach to *arbitristas* such as Pérez de Herrera became, after Philip II's death, a utopian ideal. Its final failure, which closed the lengthy chapter on poverty relief through individual charitable acts practised in the hope of spiritual salvation, also documented the state's inability to resolve poverty through solely secular measures. In the end, the absolutist legacy of Philip II, the most Catholic of Habsburg rulers, remained too potent to eliminate its traces entirely through state reform. The residual religious element that viewed charity as part of the Christian ritual of salvation, and that continued to coexist with secular measures of poverty relief supported by Philip II's administrative monarchy, weighed too heavily on the social fabric to yield to revisionary methods of social welfare that sought resolution not through conventional moral means, but by rational procedures.

This is not to say, however, that Philip II's advisers could not have convinced him of promoting at least some of Pérez de Herrera's reforms. As we have seen, their aims concurred in principle with traditional Catholic ideals; certainly, Pérez de Herrera did not foresee the latent threat to royal authority that later inhered in Bentham's disciplinary mechanisms. Instead, following Philip II's death, his young son's ineffectual monarchy ensured that neither the church nor the state would strive again for rational or pragmatic solutions to poverty and poor relief. Dedicated to pleasure and surrounding himself with nobles, courtiers, and servants of the Duke of Lerma's choosing, Philip III was kept isolated from the country's tribulations.

Thus it is that, in contrast to the lepers, whose presence had diminished since the late Middle Ages almost to the point of disappearing altogether, and whose enclosure had guaranteed some degree of separation from society, the impoverished grew in number to remain steadfastly and permanently visible to the public. Harkening to the medieval view that conflated the poor, as *pauperes Christi*, with lepers and heretics, the dominant society once again appropriated the impoverished's function for conservative, non-rationalist objectives.[73] Consequently, as the sixteenth century drew to a close, the poor were recast from their initial sacralized role as scapegoat into the increasingly demonic figure of the social outcast.

3

The Picaresque as *Pharmakos*

The ceremony of the *pharmakos* is thus played out on the boundary line between the inside and the outside, which has as its function to trace and retrace repeatedly. *Intra muros/extra muros*. Origin of difference and division, the *pharmakos* represents evil both introjected and projected.

Jacques Derrida, *Dissemination*

Although I'm a Moor, I well know, by my association with Christians, that holiness consists of charity, humility, faith, obedience, and poverty; despite this, I say that he who is content with being poor has much Godliness.

[Yo, aunque como moro, bien sé por la comunión que he tenido con cristianos, que la santidad consiste en la caridad, humildad, fee, obediencia y pobreza; pero, con todo eso, digo que ha de tener mucho de Dios el que se viniere a contentar con ser pobre.]

Cide Hamete Benengeli, *Don Quixote de la Mancha*

As Ginés de Pasamonte's sly critique of autobiography in *Don Quixote* unwittingly conceded, the popularity of the *Guzmán de Alfarache* gave new life to the genre initiated by the *Lazarillo*. Very few editions of the latter, and only two sequels, were published after 1554 before a picaresque narrative again took on the fictional life writings of an orphaned boy exposed to mistreatment, poverty, and hunger.[1] Despite the genre's oft-noted lack of realism, the *Guzmán*'s engagement with these issues, in accordance with its specific historical circumstances, substantiates the author's, Mateo Alemán's, concern to comment on contemporary social problems. For the first time, the picaresque novel's eponymous protagonist is recognized as a *pícaro*, a discredited epithet that, by the end of the sixteenth century, held ideological force as well as literary significance. The misfortunes visited on Guzmán, a *pícaro* less impoverished and far more informed and worldly wise than his literary precursor, Lazarillo, while replicating the country's anxieties towards the economy's decline internationally, also continued to implicate the views on poverty that circulated at the national level.

From the moment he assumed the throne, Philip III proved too inaccessible a monarch to endorse any drastic solutions to poor relief, despite the efforts of numerous *arbitristas* and the generally auspicious atmosphere that anteceded his father's death. Although construction of several hospitals was under way, and although, in 1597, council president Vásquez Arce had instructed religious and secular administrators in fifty towns and villages to put in motion Pérez de Herrera's recommendations, one year later the reformer was still reminding a moribund Philip II that the mandates needed to be published and carried out (*Amparo* 182). Once the young prince became king, his father's advisers were abruptly banished from court, leaving Philip III in the hands of the ambitious Duke of Lerma.[2]

Nonetheless, efforts to relieve poverty were not completely stymied by the new government, as documented by a fourteen-page royal *cédula* drafted for approval by Philip III in 1599, synthesizing most of the recommendations submitted by Pérez de Herrera.[3] Indeed, the *cédula*'s circulation so soon after Philip III's accession to the throne confirms that some of the young king's more enlightened advisers hoped he would continue his father's endeavours in favour of poor reform. In its elimination of key areas introduced in Pérez de Herrera's *Amparo de pobres*, however, the draft also reveals that the state's concern for the poor was already regressing to the earlier conservative position that deemed poverty a primarily religious and moral issue.

Rather than follow Pérez de Herrera's revolutionary recommendations for eliminating the basic causes of poverty through education and national self-sufficiency, the *cédula* limits itself to licensing beggars and mandating their nightly shelter in *albergues* cared for by religious. Addressed by the king to town magistrates and justices, it begins by criticizing the inefficacy of the earlier poor laws, but returns to the long-debated issue of who constituted the true poor:

Don Felipe, d.g. Know ye that, despite the numerous laws and pragmatics passed by the Kings our predecessors for relief and aid to beggars and other poor ... it has not been possible to accomplish their goals. And considering that, with his Catholic piety and zeal, the King my Lord and father whose glorious memory we conserve wished to see the true poor relieved and the number of vagabonds reduced ... all the legitimate poor, whether beggars, shame-faced, prisoners, orphaned, and the rest, shall be succoured and aided, as Christ our Lord commanded us. And the lazy and the fraudulent among them, together with their children and descendents, [will be] reprimanded and occupied in labour of import to the nation, particularly the cultivation of land, which is most needed at present.

[Sabed que por las muchas y diversas leyes y prematicas que por los Reyes nuestros antecessores en estos Reynos se han hecho acerca del remedio y amparo de los mendigantes y los demas pobres dellos ... no se ha podido conseguir el efecto que con ellas se pretendia y considerando lo mucho que deseo el Rey mi Señor y padre de gloriosa memoria con su catholico y piadoso zelo ver remediados los verdaderos pobres y reduzidos los vagabundos ... que los pobres legitimos assi mendigantes, como vergonçantes, encarcelados, huerfanos, y todos los demas, sean socorridos y amparados, como Christo nuestro Se[ño]r nos lo dexo mandado y los ociosos y fingidos que andan entre ellos y sus hijos y decendientes, sean corregidos y ocupados en oficios y ministerios importantes a la Republica particularmente en cultivar y labrar la tierra, de que tan notoria falta ay al presente en ella. (fol.1r)]

Following Giginta's and Pérez de Herrera's repeated counsel to grant beggars' licences solely to the legitimate poor and to build *albergues* in cities and large towns, the *cédula* declares the exact date that the poor are to convene at the appointed houses, specifying the action that should be taken by each town magistrate and officer of the peace:

In the following year, 1600, on the Monday after Quasimodo Sunday, the *justicia*, aided by the [*albergue*'s] administrator, will review and examine at designated locations all the poor who beg in these kingdoms. And those who can prove need and legitimate cause to beg due to weakness or ill health, or are younger than eight years old or sixty years or older, and unpropertied besides, or blind, crippled, or maimed, will receive written licence to beg, signed by the *justicia* or the administrator, stating their first and last name, birthplace, age, and physical characteristics. This licence will be good for one year until revalidation on the same date the following year. And you will forbid begging for those who, upon examination, do not demonstrate legitimate cause, under punishment of law as vagabonds, giving those who more or less appear as such thirty days' leave to find a livelihood.

[Que la jus[tici]a con asistencia y examen del administrador ... haga visita general y examen de todos los pobres que mendigan enestos Reynos el Lunes despues del Domingo de Quasimodo del año que viene de mil y seiscientos, en todos los lugares de consideracion y a los que pareciere que tienen necessidad y causa legitima de pedir limosna por concurrir en ellos falta de salud y fuerças o edad por ser de ocho años abaxo o por vejez, de sesenta arriba, y junto esto con falta de hazienda notable, o ser ciego, ma[n]co de los bracos o tullido, seles de licencia por escrito, firmada de la just[ici]a y administrador poniendo en ella el nombre propio y apelativo, naturaleza, edad y señas de su persona y que esta licencia valga por un año hasta que se revalide el siguiente enel mismo dia. Y los que en este examen paresciere que no tienen causa legitima de mendigar, mandareisles ha que no lo hagan, so pena de ser castigados por vagabundos; dandoles treinta dias de termino para buscar manera de vivir mas o menos el q[ue] paresciere. (fol.1r)]

Although the *cédula* follows Pérez de Herrera's *Amparo de pobres*, it recalls the earlier perceptions of poverty as always forming part of the social fabric even as it manifests the need to respond through a more modern version of traditional charity than that earlier espoused by Soto.

In restructuring Pérez de Herrera's goals, the *cédula* has as its main interest the maintenance of control over marginalized groups. Emphasis is placed on restricting the poor to the towns where they are licensed:

Once examined and approved, the poor may not leave the place and the *albergue* where they reside without permission from the Officer of the Peace and the Administrator.

[Que ninguno de los pobres examinados y aprouados se pueda ausentar del lugar y albergue donde fuere recibido, sin licencia de la Justicia y Administrador. (fol.3)]

While encouraging the reformation of vagabonds, it restricted them to menial work as servants and day labourers (fol.11r). Delinquent and incorrigible women were to be enclosed in houses of reclusion to be built in Madrid, Seville, and other cities with chancellories, where they would learn to weave and carry out other household tasks (fol.11). The *cédula*'s most controversial order concerns its treatment of impoverished delinquent youths; it mandates that, after submitting to reform measures, all boys in good health between the ages of ten and eighteen or twenty are to be transferred to the galleys according to their age and size, without permission to leave the ship:

And we order all magistrates from now on to send to the galleys and navies, for this purpose, all the vagabonds too young to serve as oarsmen, and those not needed in the navy are to be sentenced to public works in the armies and military expeditions.

[Y mandamos a todos los corregidores que de aqui adelante embien a las galeras y armadas para este efeto, a los vagabundos que no tuvieren edad para remeros, y a los que destos no fueren menester para los dichas armadas, los condena ser ocupados en oficios de gastadores de nuestros exercitos y jornadas. (fol.14r)]

To my knowledge, the draft of the royal *cédula* was never approved by Philip III. However, its numerous cross-outs and corrections document the shift from Pérez de Herrera's unprecedented position regarding education to the retrenchment on poverty and poor relief after Philip III took office, with a corresponding return to stricter regulation of the poor as a means of social control. In light of Pérez de Herrera's recommendation that young boys between ten and fourteen be sent to the Spanish navies as cabin boys to learn navigational skills, the *cédula*'s orders for the care of young vagabonds seems harsh, and even cruel. And yet, as we will see, it is the same sentence that Mateo Alemán visits upon the seasoned protagonist of the *Guzmán de Alfarache* as punishment for his picaresque life. Alemán's narrative thus posits its fictional narrator in the role of *pharmakos*: at once responsible for and sacrificed to the country's social and economic degradation, Guzmán the *pícaro* assumes the guilt for the woes befalling Spain, while Guzmán the narrator renders a devastating critique of its social and economic situation.

Alemán's Critique of State, Cellorigo's *Restauración de Estado* and the Doctrine of Free Will

The distance between Pérez de Herrera's aspirations for poor youths by means of education and the newly delimited possibilities outlined in the *cédula* draft apparently did not go unnoticed by Alemán, whose devastating portrayal of galley life – which the *pícaro*-narrator would have us believe contributed to his moral conversion – corroborates the ultimate futility of the punishment. His description of the galley slaves' wretched existence in the *Guzmán*'s ending chapters raises serious doubts about both the ethical and the pragmatic value of condemning criminals to the galleys as the king's 'slaves,' a practice also craftily censured by Cervantes in *Don Quixote*'s political parody of the Don's liberation of the *galeotes*.[4] Alemán's critique of state policies, like his novel's distinctly disillusioned tenor, has often been ascribed to the author's *converso* origins.[5] His angry routing of convicts from the Usagre jail and his imprisonment of its sheriff and jailer when he audited that town's royal accounts as visiting judge in 1583 have been characterized by Claudio Guillén as the pessimistic actions of an outsider, defrauded by a society that rejects him.[6] Certainly, Alemán's inspection, ten years later, of the Almadén mercury mines, whose lessees, the German Fuggers, had notoriously abused the galley slaves sent to labour in the mines, seems to have increased his cynicism with regard to state control.

On this second occasion as visiting judge, however, Alemán gives no signs of the angry temperament that marred his official visit to Usagre; instead, he diligently interrogates the workers, placing the mine administrators under house arrest only when documents are not forthcoming. His actions at this time seem guided by renewed hope that he could effect change by exposing injustice through his written efforts. Rather than letting his frustration get out of hand, he dedicates his time to gathering incriminating evidence of the miners' exploitation. After interrogating the working populace of gypsies, *moriscos*, ruffians, one or two religious fornicators, thieves, and other criminals, as well as numerous free workers, he compiles a secret report that, despite the administrators' contradictory testimony, paints a dire portrait of the galley slaves' treatment.[7] The workers uniformly describe hellish scenes of backbreaking labour cruelly enforced by the overseers' whippings and aggravated by lack of food, clothing, and medicine. These conditions were hastily remedied only when the Fuggers, warned of the impending investigation, managed to delay it for two years.[8] Yet the prisoners' painful body sores and extensive brain damage inflicted by mercury poisoning gave vivid testimony of their abuse: their sorry condition, and the shocking fact that nothing came of his inquiry, surely influenced Alemán's perception of a corrupt justice system easily manipulated by the wealthy and powerful. For Germán Bleiberg, who first published the author's secret report, the episode reflects the complex struggle between the incipient capitalism represented by the Fuggers and those oppressed by the system, among whom he includes Alemán for having had to capitulate to the bankers (*El 'secreto'* 31). It is not surprising, then, that Cavillac, deeming Guzmán a 'failed bourgeois,' concludes his thoughts on Pérez de Herrera's *Amparo de pobres* by stating that Alemán's *converso* conscience led him to reject such reform efforts, abetted by the Jesuits, for ultimately endorsing the poor's exploitation by a capitalist plutocracy like the Fuggers' that was the principal cause of their impoverishment ('Introducción' clxxxix).

Tellingly, Alemán's own life story recounts the social repudiation suffered by those whose family lines were not easily assimilated into the Old Christian hegemony.[9] Son of a physician, the author studied medicine at the University of Seville and Alcalá de Henares; rather than continuing his education, however, he joined the many investors who borrowed notes against high interest rates. Unable to repay his loans with his bride's dowry, he was thrown in debtor's prison. From early on, then, Alemán participated in and was victimized by the investment craze that swept Spain in the late sixteenth century.[10] Despite the fact that the *Guzmán* was Spain's first 'best-seller,' the author's poor investments caused him economic hardship throughout his life, forcing him to sell the rights to his books.[11] Most critics agree that his departure to New Spain, in all probability due to his penurious condition, was arranged by the only means available to *conversos* for securing permission to travel to the New World; like numerous others before him, he concealed his Jewish origins and bribed officials (Guillén, 'Los pleitos,' 179; McGrady 36).[12]

While his plausible *converso* background cannot be proved to have fostered his reformist ideals, Alemán developed close ideological ties to a group of *arbitristas* that included, among others, Alonso de Barros and Pérez de Herrera.[13] The author's friendship with the latter definitely influenced his ironic narration of a *pícaro*'s life, which reasserts the reformer's objectives and laments their final collapse. The numbers of abandoned poor children and those abused by so-called idle women, who employed the youngsters as bait for alms, were considered a serious threat in that they soon matured into full-fledged delinquents.[14] Again, Alemán did not confine his comments to fiction; his protests against these and the many other indolent beggars who congregated on the streets echo Pérez de Herrera's anxieties about their future, not merely their unsavoury presence in the towns.

In his *Amparo de pobres*, Pérez de Herrera traces the *galeotes*' circular criminal life, noting that many were condemned to the galleys as thieves after having refused to work and begging for alms as false poor. Alemán's experience with the galley slaves shipped to the Almadén mines alerted him to the exploitation that, as with the poor, often befell criminals. Just as destitute youth required some sort of education to escape from poverty, the 'false' poor who chose a life of crime would benefit from rehabilitation rather than punishment, protecting them from abuse by the law. But it would also eliminate the need to join false beggars' 'cofradías' or 'hermandades' similar to those formed by criminals both in and outside jail, and riotously ridiculed in Cervantes's *Rinconete y Cortadillo*.[15] The nefarious influence of these mendicant brotherhoods is soon noted by Guzmán; when he encounters such an organization in Rome, he learns that its rules serve to promote the criminal lifestyle by teaching him to simulate leprosy (1a,III,3.366–75). A veritable inversion of the religio-military orders such as that of the Knights of Santiago, which discriminated against 'tainted' lineage, the underworld fraternity, with its Rabelaisian Micer Morcón, or Master Blood Sausage, at its head, prescribes a hilarious catalogue of hierarchically organized ordinances. The parody prepares Guzmán for his fraudulent encounter with a cardinal who, in practising the charity espoused by the narrator in one of his seemingly solemn *consejos*, is in turn bilked by the increasingly cynical *pícaro*. The episode reflects on Alemán's doubts as to the value of Christian charity over secular welfare, but also stresses its failure in leaving the poor to their own resolve. Despite Maravall's insistence that the impoverished have little or nothing to do with the *pícaro*, it is clear that the novel wishes to underscore the strong links between the two groups.[16] Indeed, the narrative warns against the bonds between *pícaros* and criminals precisely through the lessons learned from the thieves' society. Edmond Cros further draws attention to the connection when he notes that, after his sojourn in Rome, Guzmán is no longer a *pícaro*, but a criminal ('Guzmán no es ya un pícaro, sino un criminal' [*Mateo Alemán* 179]).

It is no coincidence, therefore, that the *Guzmán de Alfarache* follows the criminal's life trajectory of cause and effect when narrating Guzmán's misadventures, from his initial disinheritance as an innocent child, to his rejection of the work ethic, on to his condemnation to the galleys as a full-fledged criminal.[17] In effect, in 1597, Alemán writes to his reformer friend expressing his concerns about the fraudulent poor in response to one of Pérez de Herrera's treatises on vagabondage:

If, just as you propose, your intended goal indeed becomes reality, I shall certainly feel relieved and at peace, since that has also been my main purpose in writing the first part of the *Pícaro* [*Guzmán*], where, by disclosing a number of strategies and tricks utilized by the fraudulent [poor], I appeal and entreat the care of those who are truly as materially poor as they say, so that, in our feeling compassion for them, they may readily be succoured.

[[Q]ue si, como lo escribiste, tuviera tu intención verdadero efecto, sin duda me dejara el ánimo con apasible sosiego, por haber sido ese mi principal intento en la primera parte del pícaro que compuse, donde dando a conoser algunas estratagemas y cautelas de los fingidos, encargo y suplico por el cuidado de los que se pueden llamar y son sin duda corporalmente pobres, para que, compadesidos dellos, fuesen de veras remediados. (cited by Rico in his 'Introducción,' *Guzmán de Alfarache*, 46,n.57)]

Alemán's correspondence with Pérez de Herrera dates the *Guzmán's* composition at least two years before its publication, when Pérez de Herrera's reforms had gained strong support from Philip II and the council president, Vázquez Arce. The novel's Part One joins forces with the *arbitristas* in its optimism that the legitimate poor will soon receive assistance in government-supported hospitals and that the false poor will learn to assume responsibility for their behaviour. Alemán makes sure to criticize the insufficiency of individual charitable contributions. In an aside after his father's death, Guzmán comments on the dangers of donating food directly to the sick, rather than contributing to the institutions' maintenance:

And as [proof of] charity poorly disbursed, doled out [to the sick] with no thought to its usefulness or potential harm, the season or the illness, and whether warranted or not, it is stuffed down their throat like capons being fattened, and ends up killing them. Let it be recorded that, from now on, [any charitable contribution] should be turned over to the administrators, who will know how to distribute it, or its monetary value given instead, to allay [the hospital's] greater needs.

[Y en cuanto a caridad mal dispensada, no considerando el útil ni el daño, el tiempo ni la enfermedad, si conviene, o no conviene, los engargantan como a capones en cebadero, con que los matan. De aquí quede asentado que lo tal se dé a los que administran, que lo sabrán repartir, o en dineros para socorrer otras mayores necesidades. (1a,I,2.139)][18]

Although the *pícaro's* authority is undercut by the narrator's ironic concession immediately following that he is no Juan de Dios, the Granada hospital's saintly founder, and thus has exceeded his expertise, the observation corroborates Alemán's full agreement with Pérez de Herrera's assessment of the misuse of private charity and the advantages of institutionalized beneficence.

Even so, Alemán's social philosophy, so close to Pérez de Herrera's, cannot always be taken to be that of Guzmán the narrator. The *pícaro* learns the hard way – if he learns at all – that the poor may overcome poverty and hunger only by applying themselves and learning a trade. Foreshadowing his fate, on his entrance to Madrid he calls himself a 'gentil galeote,' a gentleman oarsman, although his filthy and tattered clothes belie this description. Guzmán believes that his brief education at cards and his newly sharpened wit will ensure him a life of leisure and unbounded pleasure:

What a fine kind of life and how leisurely! To have a position and a benefice without a thimble, thread or needle, pliers, hammer, or drill, or any tool other than a solitary basket, like the brothers of Antón Martín – although without their good life and seclusion. It was meat without gristle, shoulders without burden, a merry occupation and free from all vexation.

[¡Qué linda cosa era y qué regalada! Sin dedal, hilo ni aguja, tenaza, martillo ni barrena ni otro algún instrumento más de una sola capacha, como los hermanos de Antón Martín—aunque no con su buena vida y recogimiento—tener oficio y beneficio ... era bocado sin hueso, lomo descargado, holgada ocupación y libre de todo género de pesadumbre. (1a,II,2.261)]

Guzmán's first appraisal of picaresque life is thus grounded on the 'liberation' it affords him from having to maintain family and social honour. The narrative's irony is never far removed from the concerns voiced by Pérez de Herrera, since what Guzmán celebrates, first and foremost, is freedom from the work ethic. It is no accident that the only tools he finds fitting for his trade, the 'florida picardía,' are the baskets used for begging by those same friars of San Juan de Dios, the order that oversees the Antón Martín hospital. Freedom, as Cervantes's young *pícaros*, Rinconete and Cortadillo, soon find out, remains always at one remove from the biological need for food and from the proclivity to exploit the weak and thus remain tied to the social order.

It is much more difficult to accept the *pícaro*'s railings against poverty and its attack on human dignity as forming part of the narrator's ironic discourse. This is an outlook shared, pointedly enough, by a literary outsider, *Don Quixote*'s Moorish historian, Cide Hamete Benengeli, whose wariness of the Christian emphasis on and acceptance of poverty heads this chapter. Although Guzmán attributes these opinions to adulators, for whom no rich man can ever be stupid or stubborn, his tirade echoes the same questions regarding the value of poverty as an essential human condition posed by Vives almost a century before:

Poverty that is not born of the spirit is the mother of dishonour, universal infamy, bias towards all evils, man's enemy, agonizing leprosy, the road to hell, and an ocean where all patience is engulfed, honours annihilated, lives ended and souls lost.

[Pobreza que no es hija del espíritu, es madre del vituperio, infamia general, disposición a todo mal, enemigo del hombre, lepra congojosa, camino del infierno, piélago donde se anega la paciencia, consumen las honras, acaban las vidas y pierden las almas. (1a,III,1.353)]

However, in combatting this 'leprosy,' a term that, significantly, recalls and reinscribes Lazarillo's etymon as a trope for poverty, Guzmán reverts to the same picaresque irony that explains away the honour code. Tracing the inversion of values in picaresque narratives, José Antonio Maravall opines that 'good' came to converge with the bourgeois appreciation of wealth at the moment when the traditional virtuous behaviour associated with feudalism was exchanged for the early modern period's bent on accumulating capital (*Literatura picaresca* 363–5). Maravall's reasoning is most relevant to our study: if, in the Middle Ages, commoners and nobles alike could acquire a comfortable level of existence through servitude, by the sixteenth century there was no longer any guarantee for those taking on the role of servant that such employment equalled good treatment and a satisfactory life. Material gain, as opposed to traditional spiritual values, not only came to signify success and status, but itself assumed a new kind of virtue, one that Maravall associates with the development of individualism (304).[19]

Yet, since higher economic levels remained as difficult to achieve as advancement in social standing, picaresque novels call our attention to the anxieties caused by the elimination of social, as well as economic, opportunities. In this, the *pícaros* serve merely as a literary pretext; through their protagonists, the narratives in reality aim their sights on the challenges posed by the social stagnation that first resulted in the latter half of the sixteenth century, when different groups became more exclusive and closed their doors to outsiders. As Maravall makes clear, *pícaros* had little opportunity to enrich themselves or climb up the social ladder (*Literatura picaresca* 364). In their need to advance, he tells us, the *pícaros* could only resort to the *appearance* of wealth and the usurpation of a social status that guaranteed them the same leisurely lifestyle enjoyed by the indolent (*Literatura picaresca* 371). Although wealth had become the key to well-being across most social spheres, it also created a bind for those commoners and lower nobles who attempted to better their position through their acquired riches. Acclimatizing themselves to a rentier economy, they strove to act the part of the aristocracy, yet the increasing closure of the various social hierarchies placed them in constant danger of losing their new status. The climbers who, like the *pícaros*, repudiated service and managed to scale the social ladder by their accumulation of wealth, enjoyed a precarious success that lasted only until they were found out and rebuffed by the same social forces to which they aspired (Maravall, *Literatura picaresca*, 369).

The anxieties induced by ambitioning diverse social roles are evident in the *Guzmán*'s Part One, which clearly places responsibility on the young boy for his actions: from the first, Guzmán distinguishes his decisions from Lazarillo's presumably forced entry into the picaresque life. Instead, Guzmán's amoral deeds are presented mainly as his own doing, beginning with his voluntary departure from Seville, where, impelled by the poverty that ruins the family after his father's death, he takes the initiative in leaving his family home. Even at this early stage, the narrative seeks to blame the aristocratizing tendencies of the newly wealthy and the middle class. Concurring with the concerns of numerous *arbitristas*, Guzmán blames the family's impoverishment on his Levantine father's having relinquished his fertile farmland for recreational purposes, giving proof yet again of his extravagant spending habits. The novel allegorizes, through the *pícaro*'s genesis in this sinful garden, how Spain's abandonment of agriculture and its squandering of wealth on luxury items contributed to the procreation of its many poor (1a,I,2.141).

Guzmán's volition at this point in the narrative also evinces the tension that builds in the novel's two parts between predestination and free will, as Guzmán understands and applies the theological terms currently being debated. On the one hand, by renaming himself according to his only proven – and provable – maternal birthright, he rejects both his fathers. Yet, on the other, he remains coupled to his picaresque past through his maternal connections. Naming himself after his mother's outrageous claim to the noble Visigothic surname of Guzmán given her by her whorish mother, he adds as his place-name, in the parodic tradition of Lazarillo's *de Tormes*, the sinfully Arabic site of Alfarache, where he was conceived:

The best means I found was to try my hand at abandoning my misery, leaving my mother and homeland. I did so, and so as not to be recognized, I refused to take my father's surname: I took the Guzmán of my mother and Alfarache from the estate where I originated. With this, I left to see the world, roaming around, relying in God and good people, in whom I put my trust.

[El mejor medio que hallé fue probar la mano para salir de miseria, dejando mi madre y tierra. Hícelo así, y para no ser conocido no me quise valer del apellido de mi padre; púseme el Guzmán de mi madre y Alfarache de la heredad adonde tuve mi principio. con esto salí a ver mundo, peregrinando por él, encomendándome a Dios y buenas gentes, en quien hice confianza. (1a,I,2.145)]

In contrast to the *Lazarillo*, which propounds, albeit ironically, the young boy's lack of choice, manipulated and exploited as he is by the system, the *Guzmán*'s Part One – unlike its Part Two – strongly supports the doctrine of free will.[20]

Francisco Rico has rightly pointed out that Alemán was undoubtedly influenced by the debates on divine grace and free will led by the Dominican Domingo Báñez and the Jesuit Luis de Molina.[21] However, his conclusion, that it is difficult to ascribe Guzmán's opinions ultimately to one or the other theological position, since the narrator seems to support predestination as often as not, needs to be re-examined in light of Guzmán's ironizing discourse (*Guzmán*, 'Introducción,' 41–3 n.49).[22] In effect, a careful reading of the text reveals that, in his endeavour to exonerate his picaresque actions by identifying with the poor, the *pícaro* at times reverses the effects of free will and predestination. In Part One, Guzmán takes charity, in the form of compassion for others, to be a sign of preordained nature: 'A true sign of our predestination is compassion for our neighbour' (Una verdadera señal de nuestra predestinación es la compasión del prójimo [1a,III,4.378]). He reasons that, since it is God, as first cause, who instils charity in us, it is God who enables the wealthy to behave in a charitable manner, which then becomes the secondary cause:

He who is charitable will receive our Lord's mercy on Judgment Day. And since, without God, we deserve nothing for ourselves alone, and as [charity] is a gift from heaven, we must beg tearfully that it be granted us and do good acts to deserve it, moistening our scorched souls and hardened hearts ... And although wealth is next to pride, and by weakening virtue, becomes the occasion of vice and endangers its owner as a tyrant who betrays and enslaves him, its nature is like sugar in that, being palatable, it heats with hot foods and cools with cold. For the rich, [wealth] is an instrument with which to purchase saintliness through charity. And charitable and truly wealthy is he who, enriching the poor, impoverishes himself, since by this he becomes a disciple of Christ.

[El que fuere caritativo, el Señor será con él misericordioso en el día de su justicia. Y como sin Dios, nada merezcamos por nosotros y ella [charity] sea don del cielo, es necesario pedir con lágrimas que se nos conceda y hacer obras con que alcanzarla, humedeciendo la sequedad hecha en el alma y durezas del corazón ... Y aunque la riqueza, por ser vecina de la soberbia, es ocasión a los vicios desflaqueciendo las virtudes, a su dueño peligrosa, señor tirano y esclavo traidor, es de la condición del azúcar, que, siendo sabrosa, con las cosas calientes calienta y refresca con las frías. Es al rico instrumento para comprar la bienaventuranza por medios de la caridad. Y aquél será caritativo y verdaderamente rico, que haciendo rico al pobre se hiciere pobre a sí, porque con ello queda hecho dicípulo de Cristo. (1a,III,4.379)]

Yet Guzmán goes on to declare that, since the poor are the recipients and not the givers of charity, in contrast to the wealthy, who aspire to imitate God in their giving, they do not share this fate but are instead 'free' to beg: 'Therefore only the poor are given the freedom to beg' (Así que la libertad en pedir sólo al pobre le es dada [1a,III,4.383]).

By differentiating between the 'predestined' charitable and the 'free' poor, Guzmán immediately equates the latter with the picaresque life. He slyly relates how the freedom given the destitute regales their senses with great pleasures that nevertheless seduce them into delinquency. The *pícaro* enumerates the delights obtained through each sense: Hearing allows the poor, who sleep outdoors, to enjoy street music, but also to listen in on all secrets and to learn flattery. Sight permits them to lust in church after angelic faces on which suitors dare not gaze, while smell draws them to rummage through other people's houses, and to enjoy the scent of luxuries on street corners. Finally, touch enables them to compete with the wealthy for a woman's attentions, and to kiss the hand of a rich man's wife (1a,III,4.384–5). If, therefore, predestination means that we act in God's image when dispensing charity, then the free will that grants the poor licence to beg also results in the *pícaro*'s freedom to behave licentiously. As the inclusionary, universal 'we' of his sermon – that is, reader and narrator alike – shifts to the exclusionary pronoun 'I,' Guzmán the *pícaro*'s support of begging becomes Guzmán the narrator's severe reproach against those not willing to abandon their corrupt behaviour.

To bring home Part One's point that *pícaros* should, by their own volition, change their habits, Guzmán's ironic discourse extends 'free will' beyond those purely sensual pleasures which the poor are at liberty to enjoy. The following passage illustrates just how profoundly, through their free will, the poor have assumed typically picaresque attitudes in Alemán's text. But, even more important, it demonstrates that Alemán makes use of his fictional narrator, as well as of the *pícaro*'s assigned volition, to assail what he believes to be the most serious cause of poverty in Spain. By having Guzmán celebrate monetary accumulation, the author Alemán chastises the poor for exercising their freedom, not to enjoy the free gifts procured through their senses, but to employ their senses to secure currency, which they then permit to lie fallow:

But this is great miserliness and foolishness, since above all else, the real object of the five senses combined – taste, sight, smell, hearing, and touch – was the blonde faces of those blushing doubloons, the beauty of that Castilian royalty, the silver *real*, which we secretly possessed and much enjoyed in abundance. To pay with, or otherwise make use of [these coins], then, is not to enjoy them. Enjoying them means being able to spare them, without needing them for anything more than for bodily comfort. Although others say that money is never enjoyed until it's spent.

[Mas esto es gran miseria y bobería: que sobre todas las cosas, gusto, vista, olfato, oído y tacto, el principal y verdadero de todos los cinco sentidos juntos era el de aquellas rubias caras de los encendidos doblones, aquella hermosura de patacones, realeza de Castilla, que ocultamente teníamos y con secreto gozábamos en abundancia. Que tenerlos para pagarlos o emplearlos no es gozarlos. Gozarlos es tenerlos de sobra, sin haberlos menester más de para confortación de los sentidos. Aunque otros dicen que el dinero nunca se goza hasta que se gasta. (1a,III,4.385)]

In graphically correlating the joy attained through excess monetary accumulation to that of sexual gratification (*goce* as both economic satisfaction and sexual pleasure), Guzmán's sexual symbolism extends radically beyond the simple collection of alms by the poor and the *pícaros'* uncomplicated enjoyment of 'natural' pleasures. In effect, his metaphors strikingly emphasize the dangers brought about by the amassing of money, a warning aimed not, of course, at the poor, whether *pícaros* or not, but at the aristocracy, whose increasing bent for purchasing interest-bearing stocks and bonds left their capital idle.[23] Aleman's critique of Spain's socio-economic situation may thus be inferred at least as much from the abruptly subversive shifts in Guzmán's discourse – at times ironic, as in this case, but at other times fiercely serious – as from the narrative's traditional division into *consejas y consejos*, or tales and their morals (*Guzmán*, 'Introducción,' 9).[24] This rhetorical strategy, wherein the narrator shifts from ironic to straightforward, is exemplified in the paragraph's final sentence, which sharply undermines the exaltation of monetary stockpiling that immediately precedes it. By introjecting a counterpoint from an anonymous 'other'– from those who, like the merchant class, disputed the dubious wisdom of accumulation – the sentence, in opposition to the *pícaro's* opinion, instead serves to remind the reader that, as in sexual pleasure, the most productive benefits from any accumulated wealth ultimately may be gleaned only through its expenditure.

Alemán's advice, which concurred with Pérez de Herrera's belief in the country's need to invest in a market economy, also went unheeded, despite the warnings that continued to sound from numerous *arbitristas*.[25] In 1600, the political economist and lawyer Martín González de Cellorigo published his *Memorial de Política restauración*, known today as *Restauración de estado*.[26] This treatise combines a series of conservative recommendations for strict punishment of the feigned poor with a surprisingly modern 'macroeconomic analysis' transcending the economic theories of fair rates and protectionism upheld by his contemporaries.[27] Reinforcing the ideology that Maravall has called 'refeudalization,' its purpose, as the title indicates, was to restore Spain to its prior glory under the Catholic monarchs, a goal that also meant the re-establishment of rigid social hierarchies.[28] To accomplish this, Cellorigo advocates forcefully for capital and manpower investment in agriculture and industry, supports the middle class and its interest in mercantilism, and calls attention to the three main factors on which he blames Spain's economic woes: 1 / the dwindling population; 2 / the increasing abhorrence towards 'non-noble' occupations, with the corresponding emulation of aristocratic behaviour; and 3 / the investment in *censos*, or state bonds, and *juros,* or mortgage loans, at the expense of agricultural and industrial development.[29]

To Cellorigo, all three factors are necessarily interrelated; while he suggests that the first may be remedied in the long run by encouraging a more respectful attitude towards marriage and its primary function, childbearing, as well as by improved childcare, he also implicitly imputes the lack of manpower to the growing rejection of manual labour, and thus regards slavery as an immediate, if severe, solution:

No one can force our Spaniards into servile occupations, the mechanical arts, or fieldwork and, as everything is being abandoned, some action must be taken.

[[N]o hay quien sujete nuestros Españoles a los oficios serviles, ni a las artes mecánicas, ni a la labor del campo, y que se va todo perdiendo, algún medio se debe tomar. (Cellorigo 66–7)]

The latter two factors to which he assigns the country's decline required far more detailed consideration and make up the greater part of his economic tract. Cellorigo understood that the economy necessitated the investment of working capital, despite the temptation to purchase stocks and bonds for their yield:

States are ruined when wealth is deposited in currency and interest-producing rents, which like a plague has left these reigns in great misery, since all or the majority prefer to live off [these rents] and their interest, without thinking of where what allows for their lifestyle will come from next. This is what has so obviously ruined this state and those who invest in rents, because by depending on the profit, they have abandoned the worthy occupations of agricultural and animal farming, and of all that naturally sustains humankind.

[Destruyen las Repúblicas cuando ponen la riqueza en el dinero y en la renta del que por medio de los censos se adquiere, que como peste general ha puesto estos reinos en suma miseria por haberse inclinado todos o la mayor parte a vivir de ellos y los intereses que causa el dinero, sin ahondar de dónde ha de salir lo que es menester para semejante modo de vivir. Esto es lo que tan al descubierto ha destruido esta República y a los que usan destos censos, porque atenidos a la renta se han dejado de las ocupaciones virtuosas de los oficios de los tratos de labranza y crianza, y de todo aquello que sustenta a los hombres naturalmente. (Cellorigo 20–1)][30]

According to the lawyer's theories, all these factors led to a stagnated economy with a high inflation rate caused by devalued coinage, lack of investment in the production of basic foodstuffs and industry, exportation of primary materials, and rampant consumerism fostered by the aristocratic proclivity for luxury items also imitated by the newly wealthy.

The treatise is remarkable for its far-reaching economic vision: it urges the establishment of an economic infrastructure by the rehauling of state finances through their consolidation with private capital, and proposes a free-market economy and taxation according to one's income, at a time when only the non-nobles (*pecheros*) paid taxes.[31] To a far greater extent than other *arbitrios*, Cellorigo's economic analysis discerned the major causes of Spain's weakness, yet, like his recommendation that slavery be reinvigorated, it often resorted to reactionary solutions, specifically with regard to the lower classes. In keeping with his conservative social ideology, evinced in his support for the Inquisitional *autos de fe* and the expulsion of the *moriscos*, Cellorigo's reproving attitude is nowhere more uncompromising than when dealing with the 'false' poor.[32] In his *Memorial*, he indignantly informs the king that, of the 5,000 poor examined in Valladolid in 1599, fewer than 600 were truly impoverished, as the rest had all covered themselves with rags and lesions, pretending to need assistance. He admonishes that, like the criminals who are sent to the galleys, the reprobates should be forced to work in prisons built specifically for this purpose:

To remedy the situation [of the false poor], houses could be built in cities and large towns to include jacks-of-all-trades [false beggars], where those leading this life would be detained first and sentenced by *justicias* to remain in this kind of prison according to their demerits, making them work for their keep, which would easily be earned by manual labour. And this would ensure that all sorts of unscrupulous people desist in their activities and the legitimate poor garner more relief. And for women vagabonds, there would be a separate house in lieu of the galleys, since, as they cannot serve [at sea], the great harm they cause has no ready means of punishment.

[[A] cuyo remedio se podría acudir con que en las ciudades grandes y villas de mucha vecindad se ordenasen casas, que fuesen capaces de incluir en sí oficiales de todos oficios, en las cuales a los que esta vida siguen se les hiciese estar en forma de prisión los años que sus deméritos pidiesen por orden de las justicias, precediendo condenación sin dejarlos salir fuera, haciéndolos trabajar y merecer el sustento de sus personas, que por cuenta de propios y de la labor de sus manos sería fácil de sustentar. Y sería medio con que todo género de gente perdida se refrenase y los pobres legítimos hallasen más refrigerio, y que para las mujeres vagabundas, a las cuales se ha de hacer casa aparte, sirviese esto de galeras a cuyos daños, con ser muy grandes por no poder servir en ellas, no se halla remedio conveniente. (*Memorial* 75–6)]

Similarly to Cellorigo's treatise, the *Guzmán's* Part Two concentrates on the 'false' poor's threat to the social body. The different reasoning behind the *pícaro's* actions coincides with the strengthened Báñez position supporting predestination at the time of its publication. If, in Part One, Guzmán's 'free will' could not compel him to reverse his picaresque leanings, in Part Two he struggles against his inclinations, only to succumb time and again a Sisyphus who nonetheless blames God for his misfortunes.[33] In attempting to account for Alemán's pessimism, Enrique Moreno Báez has seen in this fall the allegorization of the doctrine of Original Sin.[34] Yet such an interpretation, whereby Guzmán assumes the role of an Everyman whose universality and timelessness incorporate our own, denies the novel's historical specificity. Instead, I argue that it is through the rejection by society of his paternal identity and through the state's ineffectual handling of the poor – both consequences linked to Alemán's historical moment – that Guzmán's hopelessness epitomizes his author's pessimism. The change noted in Alemán's representation of the *pícaro*, by inverting Guzmán's exaltation of 'free will' into his final inability to disconnect with his social origins, discloses the author's disillusion in any likelihood that the state might initiate meaningful social reform. Consonant with his disenchantment – we remember that, by the end of the novel, Guzmán has neither obtained physical release nor attained spiritual redemption – Alemán's sentencing the *pícaro* to the galleys also effects a profound critique of the retrenched moral perception of poverty. Unlike Pérez de Herrera's innovative efforts to avert the criminal consequences of impoverishment, the moral view condemned the 'false' poor to prison and hard labour.

This renewed moral position was predicated on the dubious reasoning that, since the state's prosperity depended on agricultural labour and mercantile exchange, these were 'noble' occupations. The labourers and merchants who had abandoned their occupations for the indolence of a rentier economy, therefore, should be encouraged to return to them. The corollary, of course, was that both labourers and merchants should resign themselves to, and remain in, their inferior social positions.[35] Yet, although Cellorigo promotes these occupations, and resorts to Alfonso X's *Segunda Partida* to give authority to the honour due them, he is far more cautious when attributing to them any kind of nobility.[36] We will discuss Cellorigo's view of the merchant class in the next section; for now, I wish to note his conservative leanings with regard to labourers. Reciting a long list of kings who gave up their reign for agricultural labour, Cellorigo confirms that the occupation is as 'noble' as any other, for both noble and non-noble landowners. However, for tenant farmers who, not being essential to the war effort, take over these tasks from the nobility, Cellorigo is caught in a tautology when he pronounces that, as with the *moriscos*, these labourers' nature is as rustic as their labour:

[O]wing to the great wretchedness in which they are raised and because their character is as rustic as their labour, they are normally timid, dull, and inept, defeated and subdued by their wretched, humble state.

[así respecto a la gran miseria en que se crían como porque tienen los ánimos muy semejantes al rústico trato en que se ocupan, y de ordinario son tímidos, indiscretos y poco expertos, abatidos y sujetos a la miseria de su humilde estado. (*Memorial* 84)]

Guzmán's choice of occupations throughout Part Two reflects Alemán's agreement with Cellorigo's concerns regarding social mobility. The *pícaro*'s attempts to dress up as a noble and, as a gesture towards his paternal inheritance, to swindle others in the guise of a merchant, result only in his continued moral degradation (2a,III,2.756–71). While Guzmán's occupational limits are defined by his inability to escape his debased condition, he again assumes the Báñezian position in abandoning himself to God's omnipotence, implicitly comparing himself to Job:

Ours is an evil nature, we do not help ourselves, we sacrifice nothing, we make no effort; we wait until things come to us. Yet God never forgets or abandons us. He knows well how to divest in a minute the power of evil men gained in a lifetime and to quickly return doubly to Job what He had taken from him little by little.

[Somos de mala naturaleza, nada nos ayudamos, ninguna costa ponemos, no queremos hacer diligencia; todo aguardamos a que se nos venga. Nunca Dios nos olvida ni deja. Sabe muy bien quitar a los malos en un momento muchos grandes poderes adquiridos en largos años, y darle a Job brevemente con el doblo lo que le había quitado poco a poco. (2a,III,4.797)]

After his sentencing, Guzmán tries several methods of escape; failing these, he readily takes up the picaresque activities common to the galleys until he realizes he is again placed in a position of servitude if he wishes to better his position. But when, betrayed by those he had believed were his friends, he is severely beaten by his master for stealing, Guzmán again blames fortune for his change of luck: 'Its nail loosened, the wheel spun me in unfamiliar ways and as never before' (Desclavóse la rueda, dio vuelta comigo por desusado modo nunca visto [2a,III,9.893]). Earlier, he had reconsidered his sufferings not as misery, but as a token of divine providence, since God's works, like an artist's painting placed upside down, are wrongly perceived by humans, yet when viewed correctly they reveal His compassion:

> Our travails seem harsh to us, we are baffled by them, since we are given little knowledge of them. But, when He who sends them to us uncovers the mercy enclosed therein and we see them rightly, we will accept them as delights.

> [Hácensenos ... los trabajos ásperos; desconocémoslos, porque se nos entiende poco dellos. Mas, cuando el que nos los envía enseñe la misericordia que tiene guardada en ellos y los viéremos al derecho, los tendremos por gustos. (2a,III,9.892-3)]

Guzmán's acknowledgment that his afflictions hold a different, transcendental meaning is, according to some critics, itself a sign of Baroque *desengaño* to which he awakens a changed man.[37]

For Rico, Guzmán here conflates his belief in free will with the complex Báñez notion of divine first and secondary causes: God allows not only that humans choose rightly (through His grace), but that they choose at all (*Guzmán*, 'Introducción,' 42 n.49). The *pícaro*'s ambivalent position, imparted through his ironic discourse, functions primarily, however, as a means of capitulating to his preordained fate.[38] It is through the *pícaro*'s rethinking of free will that Alemán's critical discourse comes to the surface, in turn conceding an antithetical explication of the protagonist's redemptive process.

Guzman's 'awakening' alludes to the narrator's morally didactic function in Part One as 'watchtower' (*atalaya de la vida humana*), the title originally given Part One by Alemán in 1598. Even after this experience, and despite his assurances of conversion, the *pícaro*'s decision to expose his galley companions' plans of sedition to the ship's captain just as certainly stems from his desire for vengeance as from his longing to escape punishment.[39] That he ends, as he himself discloses and an entire critical tradition has argued, still a criminal, back on the galley bench, is textual proof of his failure to achieve spiritual redemption, whether through his own volition or God's will, and of his Sisyphean return to his status of *pícaro*.[40]

The doubts Alemán expresses regarding free will in Part Two correlate with the renewed ill feelings harboured against the poor immediately following Philip III's accession to the throne. Increasingly, Guzmán takes on the poor's position, for if the *pícaro* is not only unmoved to change but, given his sinful condition, cannot do so voluntarily, then the 'false' poor – who were then considered the vast majority of the impoverished – become a permanent threat to society. Moreover, for those who followed the Báñez creed, which posited that charity had no bearing on salvation, there was little incentive to assist the poor, whose image as the representatives of Christ had, we have seen, long ago metamorphosed into social reprobates. My study submits that all discourses – theological as well as economic, social, and fictional – remained interconnected and intertextualized in the Renaissance. The belief in predestination, as the dogma was proposed and accepted at the time, must also have contributed to the general mood of hardened feelings towards the poor that, according to Maravall, stemmed from the neo-feudal aristocratization that obtained in the seventeenth century. Cleaving to contemporary opinion, the *Guzmán*'s protagonist rejects the work ethic advocated by the numerous treatises on poor relief for a return to an aristocracy based on *otium*. What the picaresque narrative's ironic tone reveals to us, then, is that despite its undeniably distorted image of social reality, in articulating the general scorn heaped on industrialization and trade as a means of developing the economy, and in underscoring the disbelief in free will, Guzmán's defiance of the work ethic affords an accurate view of the dominant ideology.

The *Guzmán de Alfarache*'s Defence of Mercantilism

The polarized feelings towards the poor and the socioreligious roles attributed to them since the Middle Ages had, by the end of the sixteenth century, collapsed into one of hatred and rejection. This rejection held the utmost significance in a country whose 'other' was internalized within, yet whose banishment was deemed to be essential in order to cleanse the social body. According to Michel Cavillac, by the time the *Guzmán de Alfarache*'s Part One was first published in 1599, the fear of *conversos* had subsided, substituted by ill feelings towards foreigners and *moriscos*. The latter's perceived threat was soon to unleash another xenophobic wave of expulsion.[41] Yet, while many *conversos* had assimilated, their mention in the many discourses circulating in early modern Spain suggests that they were regarded with intensified suspicion and categorized with numerous minority groups as 'other.' Social distrust was thus directed inward to a critical mass that had transformed from its alterity into a powerful internal force that threatened to subvert traditional hierarchies.[42]

Inheriting his father's sinister characteristics of foreignness with the transgressions of the internalized 'other' in his debauched role of usurer, womanizer, and effete, the *pícaro* Guzmán de Alfarache necessarily enacts a more complex social role than Lazarillo's homologue of the impoverished at mid-century. Although he assumes a significantly different social position from that of his precursor Lazarillo, his *figura* is far less morally and generically paradigmatic than has been presumed by critics such as Alexander Parker, who interprets the picaresque primarily as a normative discourse of the Counter-Reformation.[43] Indeed, Guzmán's polymorphism, which earned him the name Proteus from his contemporary readers, has influenced some modern critics to situate his experiences in a debased, teleological and essentialized universe, thus slighting his authentic, albeit ironic, connections with the immediate concerns affecting his historical avatars (Cros, *Mateo Alemán*, 99).[44]

For our purposes, the disparity between Lazarillo and Guzmán is best illustrated by the beginning scene in the *Guzmán de Alfarache*'s third chapter, when the young boy abandons his comfortable maternal home.[45] Although he is a widow's son like Lazarillo before him, Guzmán takes pains to let his readers know how beloved – and well fed – he was:

I was a plump, spoiled lad, bred in Seville, never chided by my father, my mother a widow – as you have heard – myself stuffed with good bacon, the finest bread and creamiest butter, and honeyed toast in rose-water, more admired and adored than a Toledan merchant's son or one like him.

[Era yo muchacho vicioso y regalado, criado en Sevilla sin castigo de padre, la madre viuda – como lo has oído – cebado a torreznos, molletes y mantequillas y sopas de miel rosada, mirado y adorado, más que hijo de mercader de Toledo o tanto. (1a,I,3:146)]

From the novel's inception, the young boy is portrayed as pampered, his every whim indulged to excess, his hunger sated by the rich food with which he is overly nourished. Unlike Lazarillo, who, after a life of starvation, has only begun to benefit from his wife's provident commerce with the Archpriest when he is called to account for his good fortune, Guzmán informs us that he is fattened from birth. Yet the very description of his consuming the costly delicacies as if force-fed ('cebado') submits the young boy's coddling to something akin to animalistic ritual and puts the reader on guard that, no matter how pampered his beginnings, his picaresque persona will come to symbolize a sacrificial offering in a society that must shoulder much of the blame for its own degradation.

The *pícaro's* metaphorical role of scapegoat is seemingly challenged early on in the narrative by Part One's emphasis on free will: although Guzmán ascribes his leaving home to his destitution after his purported fathers' deaths, the distinct sense of guilt that pervades his actions contrasts with Lazarillo's innocent victimization when he is hastily handed over to the blind man. Yet his freedom to determine which actions he will take in no way precludes Guzmán's postlapsarian condition: that his is a fallen nature is indicated from the first by his expulsion from Alfarache, his father's Edenic garden.[46] While he typecasts himself as a wealthy Toledan merchant's son, a cliché also wielded by Cervantes in his novella *El coloquio de los perros* to account for lax living, Guzmán's stated reasons for departing – a burning desire to see the world and meet his 'noble' relatives in Genoa – already implicate him in his circular search for, and inability to escape from his paternal legacy.

The narrative's mention of the conflictive father/son ties also situates the *pícaro* firmly within the historical parameters of the *limpieza de sangre* controversies. The allusion to bacon as a favoured luxury, while an apparent ploy to obscure his *converso* origins, in effect calls attention to them and to the strictures under which *conversos* laboured to adopt Old Christian customs. Further, Guzmán's stopping to rest on the St Lazarus church steps reconstructs the times when the *converso* merchants, his father among them, congregated on the cathedral *gradas* in Seville, desecrating the temple with their trade. Even though Guzmán finds himself near a church, a potential source of spiritual sustenance, he feels only physical craving. The prayer he recites there lacks piety, and the water he drinks from the fountain holds no religious significance:

When I came to St Lazarus, which is a short distance from town, I sat on the stairs or steps leading to the holy hermitage. I felt like having something for dinner but had nothing to put in my mouth, except for some fresh water from a local foun-

tain. I didn't know what to do with myself or which haven to seek ... I was unsure
of what would happen, and decided to leave it in God's hands: I entered the
church, said a brief prayer, but whether devout enough, I don't know; they didn't
allow me more time since it was time to close and retire for the night. The night
closed and with it, my thoughts, but not my copious tears. I cried myself to sleep
outside on the church porch.

[Cuando llegué a San Lázaro, que está de la ciudad poca distancia, sentéme en la
escalera o gradas por donde suben a quella devota ermita ... Vime con ganas de
cenar y sin qué poder llegar a la boca, salvo agua fresca de una fuenta que allí
estaba. No supe qué hacer ni a qué puerto echar ... Anduve vacilando; quise
ponerlo en las manos de Dios: entré en la iglesia, hice mi oración breve, no sé si
devota; no me dieron lugar para más por ser hora de cerrarla y recogerse. Cer-
róse la noche y con ella mis imaginaciones, mas no los manantiales y llanto.
Quedéme con él dormido sobre un poco del portal, acá fuera. (1a,I,3:146–7)]

After his expulsion from Alfarache, Guzmán's banishment from the
church of St Lazarus – appropriately, a name harking back to the medieval notion of religious charity – leaves him doubly an outsider. This
predicament symbolizes his social and religious exile and underscores
his affiliation with those classes rejected by the Old Christian dominant
group. I disagree with Michel Cavillac's standpoint that Guzmán and
his father function as literal embodiments of the merchant class. However, I agree with his situating the *pícaro* as one of the groups who constitute the social 'other.' Cavillac is right in assessing that the narrative
should be contextualized historically within 'the degradation of aristocratic ideals and the crisis of a merchant capitalism that fell victim to its
own untimeliness' (il conviendra ainsi de restituer le *Livre de Gueux* a
son historicité qui l'immerge dans la dégradation des idéaux et la cris
d'un capitalisme marchand victime de sa précocité [*Gueux* 121]).

That Guzmán's parents embody, to the contemporary conservative
majority, what was 'wrong' with Spain permits us to reconstrue,
through Guzmán's ironic discourse, Alemán's affirmative view of the
merchant class to which Guzmán's father belonged. At the same time,
the author illustrates, in the satiric reverse portrayals of both father and
son, the negative concept of this 'other' promoted by the Old Christian
hegemony.[47] Ever since Américo Castro's efforts to explain the multicul-
turism inherent to the Iberian peninsula as one based on a caste system,
critics have been at odds as to which designation – ethnic, economic,
social or religious, or a mixture of any of these – to assign *conversos* and

moriscos.[48] When intending to define and categorize Guzmán's origins, some, Bataillon and Castro among them, take the term applied to his father, *levantisco,* to ensure his Jewish heritage, especially so because of the father's occupation as usurer in Genoa.[49] Cavillac, repudiating Castro's *converso* thesis, stresses that, in contrast to Pablos the *buscón* and the *pícara* Justina, neither Lazarillo nor Guzmán is defined as *converso* ('Force est de reconnaitre ... que ni Lazare ni Guzmán, a l'inverse de Pablos ou de Justine, ne se définissent en tant que *conversos*' [*Gueux* 40]). Maravall, for his part, states unequivocally that there is no *converso* element in the picaresque (*La literatura* 537).[50] Since the picaresque's circular narrative sends the *pícaro* in search of his origins, Guzmán's paternal legacy cannot be lightly dismissed, yet the narrative's ambiguity admits to the possibility of both multiple origins and multiple interpretations of those origins. While Guzmán's heritage may not necessarily verify his *converso* status, his father is nonetheless described in sufficiently pejorative terms to embody those elements most despised in early modern Spain. Morally corrupt, he transgresses all social and religious norms: at once a seducer of women and a homosexual fop, he is a Christian and Muslim renegade as well. Moreover, as a Genoese, he is a reminder of the hated foreign bankers enriching themselves from Spanish spoils. As with his father's equivocal position, therefore, Guzmán's bastard status fails to define an essential or even specific ethnic, social, or economic category. His is, instead, an overdetermined status, one that encompasses all the dubious circumstances of the 'other.'

If the father and son's ambiguous standing fails to identify the *converso* by caste, race, or class, it nevertheless revives the group's presence within seventeenth-century Spain's social and economic hierarchies. At the time the *Lazarillo* was written, there still likely lived a number of *conversos* and *moriscos* born Jews and Moors; the *Guzmán*, printed over a century after the edicts of expulsion, cannot make a similar claim. As early modern Spain clamoured for a scapegoat on which to blame the country's decline, it raised the specter of an amorphous, internalized 'other' personifying the evils it had long striven to eject. While the groups' vanishing corporeality, paradoxically reinforced by their demonization, in no way negates the bases for their historical singularity, the zealous efforts to cleanse the social body at the hands of the Inquisition implies that these groups were far less marginalized than previously thought. The statutes' insistence on documented proof of 'cleanliness of blood' in fact confirms that assimilation, accomplished through numerous means such as religious vocation, marriage, and purchase of titles and land, was often markedly successful.[51] Some five generations after the 1492 edict, the *conversos* were no longer regarded as a 'nationality' distinct from Old Christians. At precisely this time, however, the economic upheavals that had allowed for increased assimilation reached a crisis point that compelled the group's renewed differentiation, but now as members of a newly totalized 'other.' Their difference was soon mythologized into an all-encompassing, monstrous otherness that, as René Girard has argued, becomes so only through arbitrary persecution, which chooses at whim which group to victimize.[52]

Since, as Henry Kamen reminds us, the controversial *limpieza de sangre* statutes had no judicial or legislative basis and were therefore frequently ignored, Spanish *conversos* continued to wield power through the purchase of offices, sinecures, and titles.[53] Supported by strong family ties, wealthy *conversos* ascended to social and political prominence with relative ease.[54] In Seville especially, the artisan and merchant classes swelled with the large numbers of Portuguese, *conversos* in the majority, who immigrated after the union of Spain and Portugal in 1580 (Pike, *Aristocrats*, 17). The port city, which boasted the largest population in Spain by 1599, had always attracted foreigners; Ruth Pike's study of the Genoese immigration explains that, from the early sixteenth century, its rapid economic and demographic growth combined with the capitalistic attitudes of its nobility to create new values that encouraged their integration with wealthy Genoese merchants.[55] In these cases, strong bonds were formed with the church:

Like other wealthy Sevillians, [the Genoese merchants] gave generously to religious and pious foundations, and it was not unusual for children of assimilated and hispanized families to enter the priesthood and religious orders. Moreover, the Sevillian Genoese had a reputation for orthodoxy at a time when the religious loyalties of many Sevillians were being tested ... [N]o members of their community were ever accused or brought up before the Inquisition for heresy during the sixteenth century. (Pike, *Enterprise*, 15)

Although Pike does not specify their religious antecedents, a number of these families were of Jewish origin. In any case, despite their assimilation, the Genoese were singled out by the Old Christian hegemony for possessing the same traits stereotypically applied to *conversos*, who made up the second dominant group of Sevillian merchants. Dedicated to trade, both groups were criticized for their materialism, avariciousness, cupidity, and parsimony (*Enterprise* 11–13).

What is instructive, then, is not that the Genoese merchants were accused of *converso* lineage, but that the negative characteristics ascribed to them by a society increasingly envious of their success intended to essentialize and group them with the 'other' so as to differentiate them from Old Christian Spaniards. It is quite clear that this was not done on religious grounds, but primarily for economic reasons. Most *arbitristas* and numerous modern historians, focusing on the distinction between *otium* and *negotium* as one of indolence versus commerce, have blamed the merchant class's abandonment of the latter on their desire to imitate the aristocratic lifestyle, renouncing their bourgeois beginnings. Pike states that, with few exceptions, second-generation Genoese neglected trade, and by the third generation the commercial background of the family had been forgotten (*Enterprise* 3).[56] Yet she also asserts that those who had ascended into the ranks of the Sevillian nobility did not feel dishonoured because of their trading and believed that commerce and nobility were compatible (*Enterprise* 38). Indeed, if the merchants purchased titles of nobility and political posts, it was because this benefited their business:

The people who try to purchase *hidalguías* and *veinticuatrías* are merchants, and businessmen who do so in order to further their own interests, and to facilitate the shipment of their merchandise, and the activities of their agents ... They pay excessive prices for the said patents [of nobility] and councilmanships in order to use these positions to avoid paying the customs duties [*almojarifazgo*] and to pressure the officials of the latter to pass their shipments without inspecting them. (qtd. in Pike, *Enterprise*, 38)[57]

Among the many business connections established between the Genoese and their Sevillian hosts, Pike notes that the former often influenced the Sevillian economy through their banking practices (*Enterprise* 92–4). Although, by mid-century, most shipping magnates were native Sevillians (Pike, *Aristocrats*, 128), the Genoese had wrested control of Spain's finances from the Germans from as early as the latter half of the century to 1628, a situation that Philip II attempted to check several times and which resulted in the state's bankruptcy in 1597.[58] The Genoese so controlled the Spanish economy, in fact, that *arbitristas* complained of Spain's transformation into the 'Indies of Europe,' since its wealth was plundered by foreign investors.[59]

The resentment against the Genoese by the Spaniards revealed itself in the latter's search for a means to denigrate and segregate the group, as it had become increasingly assimilated and difficult to distinguish from the Sevillian nobility.[60] In a pamphlet attributed to Quevedo, the 'harmful international capitalism' fostered by the Genoese, which was responsible for obstructing the development of national mercantilism and industry, was considered to have been the work of his nemesis, the Count-Duke of Olivares, and of his *marrano* bankers:

In Rouen we hold the purse-strings of France against Spain and at the same time those of Spain against France; and in Spain, under a disguise which conceals our circumcision, we help the monarch [Philip IV] with the wealth we possess in Amsterdam, in the country of his mortal enemies. We do the same in Germany, Italy and Constantinople. We weave the bland web, the source of wars, helping everyone with money taken from the pocket of his greatest enemy, for our help is like that of the banker lending money at huge interest to a gambler who plays and loses, so that he will lose even more.[61]

It should not come as a surprise, therefore, that the insults applied to the Genoese as a group readily derived from the same xenophobic code that, regardless of its historical or genetic inappropriateness, also served to villify and scapegoat the multiple manifestations of an already internalized 'other.' Guzmán himself encourages the practice when he tell us that Genoese merchants were called 'white Moors' by their compatriots because of their lack of charity (1a,III,5.386).

Guzmán's second trip to Genoa vindicates his previous exile from the city, forced by his relatives 'so as not to dishonour them with his poverty' (quisieron desterrarme, porque no los deshonrara mi pobreza [1a,III,2.361]). This time, believing Guzmán rich, his uncle invites him to become a 'naturalized' Genoese through a marriage of convenience to a deceived and dishonoured relative. In his most sophisticated swindle, Guzmán's pretended wealth is offered in exchange for expensive wedding gifts, an inexpensive, gold-filled chain serving as collateral against his gambling debts. In both cases, the dividends gained in the speculative transaction depend on the quantity and the length of time of the deposit. The swindle, therefore, serves also to illustrate Genoese trading methods, since, banking on their cupidity, Guzmán receives a doubled interest rate: revenge for his mistreatment and unwarranted economic profit. Furthermore, by abandoning his proposed bride, Gracia, the personification of the comforts of the Catholic Church, Guzmán claims his heretical inheritance. He re-establishes his paternal legacy by emulating his father, who had stolen and exchanged his Moorish wife's belongings to return, a Moslem renegade, to Spain (Ia,III.1.114). In that Guzmán has by now embraced his father's thieving ways, the passage neatly imitates and closes the *pícaro*'s previous justification, in Part One, of his father's larceny, which Guzmán compares to the profitable merchant strategies commonly practised in Spain ('estratagemas son de mercaderes, que donde quiera se practican, en España especialmente, donde lo han hecho granjería ordinaria' [1a,I,1.115]).

In Part Two, however, since the *pícaro*'s actions allegorize contemporary Genoese merchant practices, the episode instead addresses the decline of the Spanish trade. Sevillian mercantilism flourished, thanks to the opening of the Indies trade. Merchants who sold wholesale, in bulk quantities, or entire cargoes for a fixed price were in no danger of forfeiting their noble rank, as Cellorigo's *Memorial*, which I cite below, makes clear. Recognizing that Spain needed to maintain its trade advantages, the *arbitrista* stipulates three points on which to judge whether mercantilism should be socially acceptable – quality, quantity, and international status:

As to quality, if trade is graded, in bulk and mainly imported from outside the kingdom, with connections handled through fairs and universities chosen for this purpose by all merchants, and the quantity large and destined to a number of exchanges rather than only one, then there is no law stipulating that whoever trades in this manner is not noble or honourable, and he is worthy of all the honours of the state and should be granted as much authority as the most illustrious and distinguished.

[En cuanto a la calidad, si el trato es calificado y en cosas grandes y lo más del fuera del Reino, con correspondencia en las ferias y universidades diputadas por el común de todos los tratantes, y la cantidad es copiosa y en diferentes tratos sin estar atenida a uno solo, no hay ley que diga que el que esto siguiere deje de ser noble y muy honrado, digno de todos los cargos honrosos de la República y merecedor de autoridad en ella, tanta cuanta se debe al que es más ilustre y más aventajado. (*Memorial* 84–5)][62]

Cellorigo's urgings would seem to agree with Cavillac's premise, cited above, that the merchant class was caught in the crisis caused by a loss of ideals and its own untimeliness ('la dégradation des idéaux et la crise d'un capitalisme marchand victime de sa précocité' [*Gueux* 121]). Recently, however, historians have concluded that the decline of Sevillian mercantilism at the end of the sixteenth century was mainly due, not to the lack of interest in trade by ennobled merchants – which, as we have seen, continued strong – but to the crippling of Spanish shipping and the New World trade after the failure of the Spanish Armada.[63] This decline coincided with the entry in Spain of North European shipping interests. Spaniards, believing rightly that they were losing out to the competition, increasingly despised the Genoese foreigners, assigning them the same degraded value they gave to their assimilated, and less threatening, minority groups. Kevin Ingram estimates that, by 1592, foreign ships represented over 20 per cent of the vessels involved in the Indies run; Peruvian traders, the Creole representatives of wealthy Peruvian merchant houses, also threatened the native traders (Ingram 22). We are now better able to understand why the granting of export rights by Barcelona to Genoese ships in 1588, the same year as the defeat of the Spanish Armada, precipitated the riots witnessed by Pérez de Herrera at the Catalonian port.

Ironically, what Alemán, following Cellorigo, offers the *pícaro* is the possibility of bettering his social position precisely through his Genoese merchant origins. Indeed, Alemán has Guzmán express what Pérez de Herrera might very well have thought as the reformer observed the merchant fleets in the Barcelona harbour:

What I found out the first time that I was in Barcelona, and now on my return from Italy in these two days, is that to be a merchant means having dignity.

[Lo que de Barcelona supe la primera vez que allí estuve y agora de vuelta de Italia en estos dos días, es que ser mercader es dignidad. (2a,III,2.771)]

The *pícaro*, however, remains a *pícaro* by following his father's amoral career and the abandonment of his land, emulating him through his own indifference in pursuing any kind of occupation. To *arbitristas* such as Pérez de Herrera and Cellorigo, cognizant as they were of the economic disasters caused by the abandonment of the work ethic and the control of trade by foreign merchants, Guzmán personifies the evils both within and beyond Spain's frontiers. Their treatises, although unread by the majority and disregarded at court, joined with the more popular picaresque narratives in sounding an alarm to the broad readership that hailed the fictional narratives.

Yet the impact of these discourses, which I shall discuss in the next section, may at best be speculated on, since we cannot presume, as Cavillac would have it, that the majority of its contemporary readers embraced the *Guzmán* – or any other picaresque novel, for that matter – as a didactic bourgeois fable, or as a redemptive, collective *mea culpa* of the 'new man' (*Gueux* 174). Nonetheless, while it is difficult to envision the *pícaro* as a positive image of the 'mercader en grueso' as Cavillac portrays him (*Gueux* 312), the despair given voice in Guzmán's narrative reflects, I submit, the yearning for what might have been as much as the frustration over the deplorable conditions in which the country found itself. The *Guzmán de Alfarache*'s overdetermined discourse attributes the negative characteristics of the 'other' to the Genoese merchants, but it also points to the *pícaro* as the expiatory element in the narrative, as the scapegoat that must be sacrificed to safeguard the nation-state.

Rhetoric and the Role of the Reader in the Picaresque

Previously in this chapter, I have attempted to demonstrate that the *Guzmán de Alfarache* should be read at least in part as the author's response to his authentic concern for social justice. If, in accumulating the manifold ills of a debased Spanish society, the historical *pícaro* functions as *pharmakos*, as a means by which the social group may expiate its faults through either his care or his casting out, the ironic discourse of the picaresque also offers a way through which the genre's readership may come to an understanding and a ritual cleansing of social problems. The *pharmakon* operates dialogically, not solely within the text itself or as passive reflection of its social context, but simultaneously through and against the grain of its reading.[64] To posit the picaresque as a kind of *pharmakon*, therefore, requires that we first analyse how these texts are approached by their readers.

The *Guzmán de Alfarache*'s copiousness invariably frustrates our efforts to determine and demarcate its thematic specificity.[65] Critics interested in the novel's formal aspects have observed its narrative structure; while some have focused on its rhetoricity, others have more strongly emphasized its moral and religious dimensions.[66] Yet each aspect is contingent on the other, as the *Guzmán*'s structure obviously intersects with its rhetorical strategies, which in turn cannot be isolated from the novel's religious and ethical concerns. The various roles played by Guzmán, whether *pícaro, converso*, galley slave, or witness to his world, all manifest Alemán's involvement with the social issues confronting early modern Spain. As the protagonist's distinct facets also inform the narrative's teleology, I have addressed several of these dimensions separately without intending to isolate or privilege any particular one.

Just as the *pícaro*'s Protean character gains coherence through his assorted masks, his discourse develops cohesively despite its fragmentation into seemingly unrelated and discrete units. The double image projected (and introjected) by Guzmán, dependent on a bipartite narrative split into picaresque adventures and moral digressions, has been central to the critical apprehension, both of the protagonist's duplicity and of the narrative's rhetoricity. It is also one of the principal blocks in assigning authorial intention. The division has been classified by Edmond Cros as falling into two conventional rhetorical patterns: *argumentación intrínseca* (the narrative's thesis sustained through its intrinsic logic) and *argumentación extrínseca* (the use of examples from outside sources to buttress the argument) (Cros, *Protée et les gueux*, 188–98). The novel relies heavily on the latter, which lends authority to the argument and is often taken from the Bible, from Patristic writings, and from secular sentences, refrains, apothegms, exempla, anecdotes, fables, and moral apologies. By juxtaposing a combination of these, Alemán creates a fractionalization that, Cros suggests, questions the narrative's so-called realism as well as its ideality, and forces the task of unifying the message upon the reader (*Mateo Alemán* 88).

The role of the reader is brought up again by Paul Julian Smith, who claims both the *Lazarillo* and the *Guzmán* as fictions representing not speaking, but writing, subjects (*Writing in the Margin* 99). For Smith, then, Alemán's text is constituted by what he calls a 'rhetoric of representation': the two pictorial anecdotes that, in their apparently marginal positions, not only frame the narrative, but exemplify its heterogeneity, dramatize the illusorily unified nature of the text's aesthetics as well as the narrator's psyche (100). Modern critics, confused by the inconsistency of Guzmán's 'individual and deficient testimony' and the narrator's 'universal and authoritative commentary,' often feel they must choose between them (105). Extending Cros's rhetorical analysis beyond its grammatological limits, Smith proposes instead a deconstructive reading based on the textual contradictions inherent to the writing practice in general and at its historical moment.[67] As Cros proves, however, the text's reliance on conventional rhetoric denies immediate access to the author and his protagonist: with no single, identifiable author and no particular focus, there can be no unified or unifying critical opinion.[68]

But Cros is careful not to ground his interpretation solely on traditional rhetorical premises. Granting Alemán the same freedom that he exercises, Cros asserts that the *Guzmán*'s author 'neutralizes' the *dam-*

nosa heritas evident in other picaresque narratives by maintaining Guzmán's ambiguous origins and his indeterminate ending, and by blaming
the *pícaro*'s hardened attitude on his treacherous friendships (*Mateo Alemán* 93). Yet neither Cros's rhetorical analysis nor Smith's deconstructionist approach, for that matter, fully disengages the text from conventional views of authorial control. While Cros banks on Alemán's
contemporary knowledge of rhetorical topoi, Smith claims that the distinctions between these external and internal loci in themselves account
for the disparity between the fallen character and the high moral precepts that, as narrator and *atalaya de la vida humana*, the *pícaro* propounds
from the privileged perspective of his tower.

The two critics diverge more in their perceptions of the narrative's
reader, inferred and actual. Smith speaks of a reader already projected
and controlled by the text, since it reflects upon its readership the fragmentation suffered by the narrator: 'The *Guzmán* contains within itself a
constant and ever-changing projection and representation of the public
to whom it is addressed. But the readership is shown to be as multiple
and fragmented as the narrator. Divided initially and uncompromis-
ingly into the common and the disabused reader ('vulgar' and 'dis-
creto'), it is unceasingly imaged throughout the narration' (*Writing* 105).
In spite of the narrator's obsession in continuously addressing his
reader, the text, we are reminded, is primarily a written exercise. Following Ong, for whom the reader is always a fiction, Smith asserts that
the circularity created in reading the *Guzmán*, an exercise made end-
lessly deferable by an absent public, refuses to assume the deceptively
naturalized intimacy made possible when rhetor and audience are
present to each other (*Writing* 106).[69]

In contrast, Cros is sensitive to the text's rhetorical ploys on actual,
'historical' readers who remain external to the narrative, and who, while
interpellated and defined by the author, remain ultimately unknowable
to him. The potentiality of the *Guzmán*'s didacticism is, of course, obvious: the discreet reader is advised to sweep up the textual mine dust
and melt it down to recover its lost value. The image just as surely
recalls the toxic gases that Alémán warned were emitted by the mercury
mined at Almadén and is no less highly suspect. Cros asserts that the
author's tone even rings a bit apologetic when emphasizing the trivial-
ity of the picaresque subject matter, since the reader is deemed capable
of distinguishing between subject matter and function:

In reading the sermon you may moralize according to what is offered you; you are given a wide margin. Whatever you find trivial and disorganized is due to the *pícaro*'s being the subject of this book.

[En el discurso podrás moralizar según se te ofreciere; larga margen te queda. Lo que hallares no grave ni compuesto, eso es el ser de un pícaro el sujeto deste libro. (94)]

Cros allows that the discreet reader grasps the text's moral meaning entirely on his own, with the author merely pointing the way. The common reader, in contrast, is reproached from the first for not heeding the novel's lessons and for preferring the picaresque storyline, the *argumentación intrínseca*. The author foretells this reader's expected behaviour through the external exempla of two household pests: the country mouse, who prefers the melon's bitter rind to its sweet pulp, and the irritating fly, who seeks out waste rather than pleasant surroundings:

You are like the country mouse who eats the bitter, tasteless rind of the melon and finds its sweet flesh cloying. You imitate the annoying and bothersome fly that, scorning fragrance, flees from gardens and woods to pursue dungheaps and other filthy areas.

[Eres ratón campestre, comes la dura corteza del melón, amarga y desabrida, y, en llegando a lo dulce, te empalagas. Imitas a la moxca importuna, pesada y enfadosa que, no reparando en oloroso, huye de jardines y florestas por seguir los muladares y partes asquerosas. (92)]

The discriminating reader is expected to know well enough when to invert the novel's pictorialist allegory. The seemingly primary narrative of the *pícaro*'s hilarious misadventures (the *argumentación intrínseca*) turns out to be both the melon rind, the exterior that one discards in order to reach the fruit, and the *muladar*, the place *extramuros*, outside the walls, where the city rids itself of its waste. By reversing their assigned values, the discreet reader transforms the moral digressions (the *argumentación extrínseca*) into the sweet, inner pulp too cloying for the mouse and into the perfumed *hortus conclusus* neglected by the fly. The common reader instead reveals his lack of judgment (and his presumed inability to read correctly) by indulging himself with the narrator's witticisms and the *pícaro*'s fictive escapades, all the while disregarding the text's moral message.

Alemán's bifrontal address to these two kinds of readers, although a literary topos and a rhetorical strategy and thus intrinsic to the text, also intends to guide and control the historical reader's response, as Barry Ife makes clear:

> If [the writer] wishes to retain the dynamism of natural narrative, the give and take that is essential if the reader is to be anything more than a passive and perplexed onlooker, then the writer has to set up a role in which the unknown reader can cast himself, conjure up a fictional person whom he can use as a sounding board and whose anticipated responses can act as a shaping force for the narrative.[70]

But is a reader who accommodates the 'shaping force' of a narrative by assuming the role its author has anticipated for him any less passive than the reader who remains merely at one remove from the plot? Might not a novel form of writing, particularly one whose narrator identifies, not with his intended reader, but with antisocial forces, generate a markedly *different* response from the two programmed in the prologue by its author? Ife's assertion, that in order not to fall victim to the circumstances under which it is read, a text must give its reader a clear sense of its 'point and purpose' (93), intends a response more closely allied with the historical reader. He rejects, through his critique of Neoplatonic essences, Smith's deconstructionist contention that the novel means to repress the absence of the writer's audience by means of its endless extension, its totality subtending its readership. Yet Ife nevertheless overlooks the significance of an actual public engaged in reading who may have distanced itself from the narratives' rhetorical force, in part because it refused to identify with their scruffy narrators. The challenge to authors, particularly those of newly minted genres, to control their readers might offer the most compelling reason for the proliferation of prologue literature in early modern Spain.

In Helen Reed's intertextual approach, the novels' fictitious or hypothetical reader guides the 'real' or historical reader's own interpretation. The *Guzmán*'s antagonistic addressee forces the narrator to defend and exonerate himself, underscoring the 'paranoid mistrust' that the Guzmán, as narrator, feels towards the world. Yet she reminds us that, despite the narrator's attempt to influence his public, 'real' readers also rely on their own attitudes, whether due to differing social experiences or to varying 'horizons of expectations' (Reed 111).[71] What reader-response theorists have made clear, albeit at times unwittingly, is that while a Renaissance text's meaning did not matter so much as its effect on its readers, those readers reacted and responded to the text according to their own subject positions.

The contemporary reader could not help but recognize in the Lazarillos, Guzmáns, and other *pícaro* archetypes the many street urchins populating the growing urban areas. What seems a literary *mise-en-abîme* divorced from its social moorings instead discloses the readers' complex interconnections to the historicity of literature, precisely as mediated through a discursive act.[72] That the *Lazarillo*, placed on the Inquisition's 1559 Index, surfaces castigated, purged of its religious satire in Philip II's court, attests to the readers' fascination with issues other than religious reform. Harry Sieber has recently attributed the novel's publication in 1573 by Juan López de Velasco to the publisher's interest in language and style.[73] But Velasco's prologue reveals that the *Lazarillo*'s vivid language and, most important, its 'charming' descriptions of Spanish life, also appealed to readers outside Spain:

'Even though this short treatise on the life of Lazarillo de Tormes is not, when it comes to language, as worthy of consideration as the works of Christobal de Castillejo and Bartolomé de Torres Naharro, it is such a lively and fitting representation of what it charmingly and wittily imitates, that as a whole it is deserving of esteem; and as such everyone always found it appealing, which is why *despite being prohibited in this kingdom, it was commonly published and read outside of it.*'

[Aunque este tratadillo de la vida de Lazarillo de Tormes, no es de tanta consideración en lo que toca a la lengua, como las obras de Christóbal de Castillejo y Bartolome de Torres Naharro, es una representación tan biva y propria de aquello que imita con tanto donayre y gracia, que en su tanto merece ser estimado, y assi fue siempre a todos muy acepto, de cuya causa *aunque estaba prohibido en estos reynos, se leya, y imprimía de ordinario fuera dellos.* (quote, translation, and emphasis by Sieber, 'Literary Continuity,' 148–9)]

Rather, the amazing popularity of the picaresque in Spain forces us to speculate that, while the genre fulfilled at least one of the enlightened reader's needs – the articulation and attempted resolution of pressing social problems – it must also have satisfied other, repressed desires by the majority of the public. There has been some attempt to define this public: Claudio Guillén has argued that the contemporaneous reader shared the modern view of the picaresque as social critique and deems him to be ideologically in accord with the authors of the *Lazarillo* and the

Guzmán, constituting what he calls 'the discontented middle class.'[74] Yet, on Guillén's own count of twenty-five editions of the first half of the *Guzmán* (and nine of the *Lazarillo*), it seems unlikely that the no fewer than 50,000 copies published would be obtained only by those disagreeing with the system. The early modern reading public had increased considerably when compared with that of the Middle Ages, but it still comprised mainly the aristocracy and the middle classes, who shared the former's hegemonic aristocratic sentiments.

In a more specific study, Maxime Chevalier has categorized the reading groups by social and professional rank: clerics, nobles, and *letrados* such as doctors, lawyers, architects, and public officials, as well as merchants and a small percentage of tradesmen.[75] Besides the limitations imposed by social rank and education, the novels' cost must also be taken into account. He contradicts Guillén in his assessment that the bourgeoisie, made up mostly of merchants, did not demonstrate much interest in fiction.[76] A quantitative study by Sara Nalle instead shows that the lower classes, comprising mostly artisans and labourers, had benefited from the expansion of literacy in the period noted by Kagan (*Students and Society* xvii–xix). Literacy in Castille, at least for males, was as high as that in northern Europe surpassing 50 per cent.[77] This is due, she reasons, to the growth of schools, the impact of the printing press, and, in view of the subject matter of the majority of books sold, what Keith Whinnom termed 'the preoccupation with one's salvation.'[78] Nalle points out that, in Cuenca, a town with more than 3,000 families (*vecinos*) and three printing presses, male literacy rates reached 54 per cent in the period from 1571 to 1590 (Nalle 72).

Yet Nalle's data reveal that only one of ninety-nine readers between 1560 and 1610 was accused by the Inquisition of owning a prohibited book, a distinction that included the *Lazarillo*, if not the *Guzmán* (Nalle 78). The inventory of the Toledan printer-publisher Juan de Ayala confirms that the two most popular categories of books in sixteenth-century Spain were devotional and fictional, called *libros de entretenimiento*, in the main novels of chivalry.[79] Taking her cue from the ninety-one Cuenca readers, Nalle avers that the 'libraries of poorer readers reveal that they especially regarded reading as an extension of their religious lives' (Nalle 86). She also notes, however, that the younger, unmarried defendants, more so than their older cohorts, also read (and likely listened to) novels of chivalry, perhaps drawn by the texts' adventures and fantasies (Nalle 88–9). Most importantly for my own premise, Nalle concludes that the fascination with these elite, idealized fictions demonstrates the neo-aristocratization then taking place, as middle- and lower-class Castilians aspired to nobility and lineage.

Since the picaresque formed part of what was designated as literature of entertainment, it makes sense to assume that, to a public intent on emulating aristocratic values and largely uninterested in reformist concerns, the humble protagonists of the genre appeared as intruders upon the literary scene, belonging to an infrahumanity which it despised.[80] Thus, although the picaresque speaks to the concerns of an otherwise alienated and silent minority, its consumption by the dominant hierarchy and by the *vulgo* results in the displacement of its antiheroes from their historical alliances to the marginal, risible category of literary clowns. While the genre's irony renders its discourse highly ambiguous to the modern reader, thereby accounting for the multiplicity of modern critical interpretations, it is far more likely that, at the time of its publication, the picaresque's deprecative humour distanced the *pícaro* from the reader's empathetic understanding of his social condition. As in the case of the *gracioso* in the *comedia*, literary decorum relegated the lower classes to the function of comedy relief. To the aristocratic reader, and to the reader who identified with the aristocratic ideology, the *pícaro's* bumbling attempts to imitate the nobility, even when motivated by his need to keep body and soul together, serve only as the sources of grotesque jokes. Any compassion that might be evoked by the sufferings of the young Lazarillo would be quickly dispelled by the adult Lázaro's final posturing and debased sense of honour, and the reader is encouraged to laugh gleefully when Guzmán and Pablos are rewarded with physical pain and ridicule for their inept impersonations of noble swains.

When the subversive potential of the texts as social commentary is diluted by its emphasis on the comedic aspects of the *pícaro*, the discourse becomes part of the ruling ideology instead of a disclaimer against it.[81] By this, I do not mean to deny the picaresque narratives their moral and didactic value, whether unintended or as a direct expression of their authors' social concerns, nor their impact on the enlightened readers of the time. That their discourse forms part of the contemporary commentaries on poverty is, after all, the major thrust of my study. And, certainly, modern readers are acutely aware of the social injustices prevailing in the mistreatment of the fictional *pícaros* and of the critical intent of their authors. Yet at least one study has taken the *Lazarillo* and the *Guzmán's* so-called realism as coincident with the dominant ideology:

Progressive criticism has tended to view both picaresque novels, the *Lazarillo* and the *Guzmán*, fundamentally as a critique of the values promulgated by the dominant classes of the 'Golden Age': that the *pícaro* observes society from below, from his position as *lumpen*, then, gives us the key to their demythifying realism. However, whatever truth there is in this does not negate that the *Guzmán*'s dominant ideology *totally* rejects life; its 'realism,' therefore, coincides with a rigidly dogmatic ideology that ferociously opposed any change whatsoever. Lázaro ends his autobiography by 'mixing with respectable people,' that is, with those in power; the *Guzmán* makes absolutely clear that its antihumanist and degrading ideology emanates directly from the power of those same 'respectable people.'

[Desde perspectivas críticas progresistas ha solido verse la novela picaresca, tanto el *Lazarillo* como el *Guzmán*, como fundamentalmente crítica de los valores establecidos de las clases dominantes del 'Siglo de Oro': el que el pícaro vea la sociedad toda desde su posición *lumpen*, desde abajo, será así la clave de su *realismo* desmitificador. Lo que haya de verdad en ello no excluye que la ideología dominante en el *Guzmán* sea un rechazo de la vida *toda*; su 'realismo', por lo tanto, coincide con lo más cerril y dogmático de una ideología que luchaba ferozmente contra todo cambio. Lázaro termina su autobiografía arrimándose 'a los buenos', que son los que mandan; en el *Guzmán*, con absoluta claridad, la ideología antihumanista y degradante emana toda ya desde el poder mismo de 'los buenos.']⁸²

Whether or not the *pícaro* repents, his antisocial character is perceived to be motivated by his own spiritual failures. As we have seen in the *Guzmán*'s Part One, and as Cervantes contests in his reappropriation of picaresque *topoi* in *Rinconete y Cortadillo*, the attribution of free will causes the *pícaro* to be further alienated from society, as his moral downfall is an individual act against God for which he is held accountable. In his alienation, the *pícaro* also transgresses human law: Cervantes again teaches a lesson in voluntarism from a borrowed text when he associates the *pícaro* with the criminal in the Ginés de Pasamonte episode of *Don Quixote*. It comes as no surprise that picaresque narratives have been compared to the criminal biographies of the day.[83]

Not only is the *pícaro* a figure of scorn to the reader in his ineffectual efforts to better himself, but because he chooses to do so through immoral means, he is morally contemptible as well. The picaresque's formal characterization of the *pícaros* as literary characters merely to be laughed at, as undesirable social elements, happens to coincide with the neo-aristocratic values then current, further desensitizing the contemporary reader to the imminent issues of poverty and vagrancy. The reader's self-interest in clearing himself of any social guilt helps to accentuate the role of scapegoat played by the protagonists of the picaresque. The *pícaro*'s humiliations and physical sufferings could be blamed on the *pícaro* himself as a consequence of his moral choices, as in the *Guzmán*'s Book One and the *Buscón*. Others, who condemned the poor for their 'natural' predatory tendencies, would not fail to see their essentializing ideology reflected in the *Guzmán*'s Book Two and in the female picaresque. Unlike the direct discourses of the *arbitristas*, who specifically spelled out their social messages, the picaresque text itself becomes a kind of *pharmakon* to both its contemporary and its modern audience. Guzmán, as narrator, tells his reader that he suffers from hunger so the reader will learn from him and connive and cheat to avoid it ('Mía es la hambre, para ti la industria como no la padezcas' [II,i.36–7]). Aware that the reader prefers fiction to fact, he exclaims:

Either I lie to you or I tell you truths. No, no lies, although I would feign ask God that they were, since I know your inclination and how you would like to hear them, so much that you would froth at the bit. I tell truths that you find bitter.

[O te digo verdades o mentiras. Mentiras no; y a Dios pluguiera que lo fueran, que yo conozco de tu inclinación que holgarás de oírlas y aun hicieras espuma con el freno. Digo verdades y hácensete amargas. (I,i.37)]

But there is good reason for the *pícaro* to sweeten his dissembling tale with humour: it is not only his contemporaries whom Guzmán divides into *lectores discretos* and the *vulgo*. We postmodern critics may opt either to distance ourselves from and dismiss the social problems engaged by the picaresque novel through the *pícaro*'s buffoonish acts, or to acknowledge and acquiesce to its social purpose. Our quandary lies not so much in knowing to what extent these Renaissance storytellers deal in fact or fiction, as William Nelson explains their dilemma, but in discerning how their fictional discourses may serve to instruct us in the cultural practices of early modern Spain.[84]

4

Textualizing the Other's Body

[T]he body becomes a useful force only if it is both a productive body and a subjected body.

Michel Foucault, *Discipline and Punish*

The mass of unemployed beggars, vagabonds, and *pícaros*, scarcely undistinguishable to authorities who viewed them all as delinquents, was increasingly forced into subjection during the reign of Philip III. The neglect by the Crown of the *arbitristas'* many warnings led state policy to coalesce with the prevailing conservative opinion against social reform to the point where, as we have seen, most reformers were removed from public office and became alienated from court.[1] Lerma himself was little interested in public governance: during his tenure as *valido*, he attended only 22 of 739 meetings held by the council, preferring to influence the monarch directly.[2]

Although historian Henry Kamen points out that Philip III's government broke with the absolutism instituted by his father, such a government, left in the hands of his many appointees, nevertheless offered few prospects for the kinds of reform and renovation demanded by the country's predicament (*Sociedad conflictiva* 318–20).[3] As Lerma's corrupt alliances pervaded government policies, his desperate economic measures – which depended on the sale of offices and jurisdictions, the extraction of subsidies from Portuguese Jews, and issuance of devalued coinage – failed to reduce the gross inequalities between wealthy and poor.[4] The lack of control in facing the country's deplorable conditions most affected those who had fought to avert what historians have rightly termed the 'crisis' of the seventeenth century. After publishing the *Guzmán de Alfarache*'s Book Two and travelling to Portugal, Alemán returned to Seville, where, receiving little income from his writings, he resolved to abandon Spain for the New World. The trip, postponed because of bad weather, finally took place in June 1608; once settled in Mexico, he continued to write and publish. His daughter's entrance in an aristocratic convent in Mexico City gives credence to the belief that Alemán found in New Spain the wealth and status he had been denied in the old (McGrady 37–9). The 'third and last part' promised at the end of the *Guzmán*'s Book Two never materialized, and while most critics interpret the statement from the literary perspective of an open text versus a closed one, the narrative's social commitment seems to have waned as its author's position improved.[5]

In ironic contrast to his literary *pícaro*'s fortunes, Alemán's economic problems apparently improved considerably by following the advice of another literary *pícaro*. Pablos's closing caveat, in Francisco de Quevedo's *La vida del buscón llamado don Pablos*, speaks to those wishing to better their lives by leaving the old: 'No one improves his condition by merely moving from one place to another without changing his life or ways' (nunca mejora su estado quien muda solamente de lugar y no de vida y costumbres [256]).[6] From the little we can glean from the latter part of his life, Alemán managed to distance himself geographically and materially from the poverty that hounded him and his *pícaro*–protagonist's real–life models. Despite their satirical intent, Pablos's words had more than a ring of truth: only those able to change their cultural 'customs' to emulate the aristocracy could improve their lot. The *Buscón* proves how difficult this remained for some, as the 'other' in Spain were increasingly marginalized from the centres of power. The reactionary turn that took place under Philip III's reign changed public opinion from its willingness to improve the poor's lot through such social benefaction as education and shelter to a renewed conservatism that condemned the impoverished to public discipline and enclosure in prisons and galleys.

Despite its author's rejection of his juvenilia, the *Buscón* has most often been considered a manifesto of his aristocratic, conservative position.[7] For this reason, critics who view the picaresque as social critique refuse to accept the text, in whole or in part, as belonging to the genre. Paul Julian Smith's succinct guide to Quevedo's novel synthesizes the critical schools of thought that have long clashed over the intent and targets of its satire, led by Alexander Parker's theological interpretation of

Pablos as sinner in contrast to Fernando Lázaro Carreter's aesthetic perception of the text as no more than dazzling literary fireworks.[8] Other critics have attempted to resolve this apparent dichotomy: Gonzalo Díaz Migoyo and Pablo Jauralde Pou, for example, see the narrative's linguistic brilliance as inextricable from the author's moral intent.[9] Although unpublished until 1626, the *Buscón* was most likely written in 1604, when the young Quevedo begins his *Sueño del juico final* (Jauralde, 'Introducción,' 17).[10] Jauralde's edition is based on one of three extant manuscripts, the Juan José Bueno, or B, manuscript, which he considers closest to the original and possibly in Quevedo's own handwriting ('Introducción' 53). Comparing the B version to others, both in manuscript and published, Lázaro Carreter attributes its numerous variants to Quevedo's 'youthful impetus, cheekiness, [and] impudence that, in certain places, were later curbed somewhat' (un ímpetu, una lozanía, un desparpajo juveniles, que, en determinados puntos, fueron relativamente frenados después ['Estudio preliminar' xlviii]).[11] Quevedo's later modifications, he states, have as much to do with improving narrative style as with protecting the text from censure or attack. The latest critical edition, by Fernando Cabo Aseguinolaza, agrees with those who assert that the B manuscript is the author's revision of an earlier text ('Prólogo' 42–51).

Regardless of whether the B manuscript comprises Quevedo's primitive or revised text, its 'impudence' is what most draws us to this version, since it is during Quevedo's stay at court in Valladolid, and very soon after the *Guzmán*'s publication with the *Lazarillo*, that the young writer decides to take up the challenge presented by the new genre.[12] The manuscript's circulation at court is proof that the young Quevedo, eagerly seeking recognition and prestige, intended it as a diversion for a restricted aristocratic audience. He is also acutely aware that his model, the *Lazarillo*, whose popular new form he usurps, meant serious social reform while endeavouring to entertain its readers.[13] In their editions, both Cabo Aguinolaza and Jauralde, as well as Edmond Cros, retain the B manuscript's initial address to a lady: 'I, my lady, come from Segovia' (Yo, *señora*, soy de Segovia (*Buscón* 73; my emphasis).[14] Curiously, so far as I can ascertain, no editor or critic has commented on the implications of the gendered opening sentence, save to suggest that the book was intended as a gift to the Duchess of Medinaceli.[15] Although this could very well have been the case, it is important to note that the address, like that of Lazarillo to Vuestra Merced, forms part of the *Buscón*'s fictional structure. The novel parodies the common practice of seeking a noblewoman's patronage by, at the same time, reversing the gender of Lázaro's anonymous interpellator. Yet when we recall Quevedo's feminized household and his later misogynistic attitude, his spoof of the literary custom poses certain disturbing questions about his treatment of women.[16] Ife notes the text's 'strong sense of exclusiveness,' derived, he states, from a 'code within a code,' since the novel was written for 'those who were like [Quevedo] and thought like him' (151). When Quevedo writes the *Buscón*, however, his social position, if we are to believe Jauralde, was less that of a full-fledged writer seeking a patron than a student dependent on a court functionary ('Introducción' 7–8).

Quevedo's motives for incongruently addressing the grotesque satire to an anonymous noblewoman are grounded, I submit, not merely in the young author's bid to appropriate the new genre through his version's elitist tenor, and as a means of calling the court's attention to his talent, but in his seditious desire to shock that same aristocratic readership with its obscenely macabre depictions. I am in agreement with George Mariscal's assertion that Quevedo manifests his attraction to subversives modes of discourse through his own scatological poems and use of *germanía*.[17] Indeed, by abruptly juxtaposing a lady of the nobility with the despicable *pícaro*, the *Buscón*'s opening address initiates what will prove to be his ongoing fascination with the socially marginalized, represented not only by the protagonists of his satirical poetry, but by Pablos and his cohorts. It also questions the dubious distinction of some so-called ladies at court: if we consider that *cortesana* is an amphibological term meaning both a noblewoman and a *buscona*, or prostitute, then the novel's indecorous address implies little or no moral distance between its feminine reader and a *buscón*.

Quevedo's interest in these marginalized figures need not negate his allegiance to the dominant hierarchy; we should remember that the novel's composition occurred shortly after his having written the famous *letrilla*, 'Poderoso caballero es don Dinero' (Sir Money's a Powerful Lord), long considered an expression of the writer's frustrations on how wealth works to overturn social hierarchies:[18]

> Es tanta su majestad
> Aunque son sus duelos hartos,
> Que aun con estar hecho cuartos
> No pierde su calidad.
> Pero pues da autoridad
> Al gañán y al jornalero,

Poderoso caballero
es don Dinero.[19]

[Money's majesty is such / that despite bringing many woes / and even
when [drawn and] quartered / it loses none of its luster. / Instead, since it
grants authority / to labourer and hired hand, / *Sir Money's a Powerful Lord.*]

If Quevedo creates a poetic space wherein his picaresque characters
may speak with the same freedom he attributes to them, he also wields
his verse as a verbal weapon against what he perceives to be one of the
greatest dangers to the state and the status quo: the unrelenting power
of money to transform and command social positions.

Following Francisco Rico's comment that Quevedo speaks through
Pablos, B.F. Ife's view of the *Buscón* focuses on how the text's language,
while ascribed to the protagonist, remains the author's (155):[20]

[T]here is an extra dimension to our sense of estrangement from the words on
the page, and this results from the fact that the words which are quite obviously
Quevedo's and no one else's are attributed to a character, Pablos, who is nothing
like Quevedo at all ... His voice is constantly out of tune with himself; he abases
himself, betrays himself, willingly allowing his innermost thoughts and motives
to be exposed not just to the light of day but to the vilest ridicule. He humiliates
himself for the benefit of the reader, all to get a laugh and provide, as he puts it,
'some light relief for times when the heart is heavy.' (155)

But Ife also notes, rightly, an uneasy quality to the discourse, the
'constant sense of self-betrayal that makes [for] uncomfortable and
unpleasant reading' (155). As he points out, Quevedo cruelly ridicules
his protagonist, both by imputing grossly blasphemous jokes – a self-
destructive strategy also noted by Henry Ettinghausen – and, as we
shall see, through the *pícaro*'s failures to achieve a measure of social
success, blocked by the 'others' in the narrative.[21] Unlike Lázaro, whose
ironic discourse intends to conceal the *pícaro*'s embarrassment by
portraying his life situation in glowingly hyperbolic terms, Pablos
constantly exhibits his most shameful experiences to the reader's gaze.

While the *pícaro* fails to attain his desire to integrate completely within
the social body, he nonetheless demonstrates his symbolic value by
simultaneously standing for and being rejected by those groups that
remained, menacingly, both within and outside society. My reasoning
here is not quite the same as Mariscal's contention that the *pícaro*'s free-

dom, no matter how provisional, allows for the creation of alternative subjectivities.[22] Although I concur that the genre opens a linguistic space within which to oppose the dominant hierarchy, the historical positioning of the novels' authors remains important to my argument. To my mind, Quevedo's ambivalent critical stance shows that the author himself was none too assured of his social position, an insecurity that insinuates itself through the imperious tone with which he often addressed the 'vulgo.' As Jauralde observes, while Quevedo undoubtedly formed part of Philip III's courtly retinue, he nevertheless kept at a respectable distance ('Introducción' 10).

In satirizing the lower elements of society, Quevedo does not fail to disclose the anxieties and fears of that same class to which he owes allegiance. Rather than serving as literary homologue for the growing numbers of poor in order to address the issues of poverty and vagabondage, the *pícaro* in the *Buscón* takes on the role of an undesirable social climber. Destined, from the text's beginning, to fail repeatedly in his pursuit of social standing, Pablos misfires every time he tries to disguise himself by changing his name and his appearance. Instead, he is exposed time and again for who – and what – he really is. Cros identifies the fictional protagonist, reared in the shadow of Segovia's deserted textile mills, with the historical groups who, like the many *converso* textile workers, aspired to change their status ('Estudio' 71–2). Epitomized by the fabulous fortunes soon amassed by such court favourites as Rodrigo Calderón and Pedro Franqueza, Spain's inflation of honours reached a peak at the time the *Buscón* was first written. Elliott remarks that the court had much to offer younger sons and impoverished *hidalgos*, its draw extending to 'the rootless, the dishonest, and the ambitious' (*Imperial Spain* 315).[23] Pablos himself reports on the court when he and his cohorts arrive in Madrid, falsely attired as noblemen, their outer clothes scarcely concealing their nakedness beneath. Despite attempting a grand entry, what these *pícaros* drag into court is their corporeality, which will be jailed, beaten, and slashed into submission ('dimos con nuestros cuerpos en Madrid' [180]). Significantly, it is a master of disguises, the protean *converso* figure calling himself by the suspect names Don Toribio Rodríguez Vallejo Gómez de Ampuero y Jordán, who defines the court constituency:[24]

[T]he court harbours always the most mulish and the wisest, the richest and the poorest, and the extremes of all things. It shields the evil and obscures the good; and [at court] there are those like myself, whose roots, possessions, or families from whence they came remain unknown.

[en la Corte hay siempre el más necio y el más sabio, más rico y más pobre, y los estremos de todas las cosas; que disimula los malos y esconde los buenos y que en ella hay unos géneros de gentes, como yo, que no se les conoce raíz ni mueble ni otra cepa de la que descienden los tales. (175)]

The episodes leading to the *pícaro*'s downfall have been astutely connected by Cros to the Catholic liturgical calendar, not only demonstrating the text's chronological structure, but correlating its mythical extratextual referent with its ideological referent.[25] One such episode is the hazing event at Alcalá, where the mythical referent, set during Holy Week, harks to Christ's Passion and the parodic title given him – namely, King of the Jews. The title is alluded to in the children's game of *rey de gallos*, played on Fat Thursday, when Pablos is chosen from among twelve schoolboys. Since the rooster holds redemptive value in folklore and its slaughter acts to exorcize demons and death, the symbolic function of the child-rooster becomes that of the ideological referent, the *converso*, whose real hazing is carried out by the Inquisition and the crowd during the *autos de fe*. As in the *auto de fe*, Cros construes this episode as the text's denunciation of both the Jewish nature of Christ in his role of redemptor, distanced from sin, and the *converso* elements in society who, as false Christ figures, must suffer the Passion of their divine model, exorcizing Christ's Jewishness in the process (Cros, 'Estudio,' 12–15). Pablos, the *converso* narrator, acting out the role of scapegoat in scenes that impiously mimic the Last Supper and the Passion, is transformed into a Christological emblem.

Cros's analytical method, which he calls 'textual genetics,' and which brilliantly illuminates the coherence of the text's ostensibly disparate episodes and demythologizes its carnivalesque atmosphere fostered by popular tradition, is undoubtedly the most innovative and penetrating interpretation of the *Buscón* to date. For this very reason, his conclusions are ultimately disappointing in that they seem to revert to the formalist aesthetic reading preferred by Lázaro Carreter. Despite his emphasis on the text's exorcism of social evil, Cros disregards the *Buscón*'s social relevance when he adjudges the theme of hunger in the book as nothing more than a folkloric motif divorced from any socio-economic context. He asserts further that the absence, in the *Buscón*, of the problematics of poverty and vagabondage that form an integral part of the *Guzmán de Alfarache*'s reformist discourse denotes the picaresque genre's first major ideological displacement from such issues ('[e]sta ausencia de toda la problemática de la pobreza y de los vagabundos en que se fundamenta en parte el discurso reformista de *Guzmán de Alfarache* ... representa un primer desplazamiento ideológico significativo dentro de la novela picaresca' ['Estudio' 18–19]). For Cros, the novel's 'semiological void' reflects Quevedo's reactionary position regarding welfare reforms, converting the *Buscón* into a 'counter-picaresque' that then allows us to better understand its two precursors.

Certainly, we would have to agree that concern for the poor is not the main inspiration for the narrative, and that the *Buscón*, unlike the *Guzmán* or the *Lazarillo*, cannot be credited with launching either an explicit or a covert appeal for social reform. Yet Quevedo's negative attitudes towards the poor are more than hinted at by the ease with which the *pícaro* incorporates himself into their midst and becomes one of them.[26] Observing the crafty Valcázar, who cunningly hides his legs to feign lost limbs and employs three small boys as beggars, Pablos decides to similarly refashion himself when he takes off on his last journey to Toledo: 'I determined to leave the court and take the road to Toledo, where I didn't know anyone and no one knew me. In the end, I willed myself' (Determiné de salirme de la Corte y tomar mi camino para Toledo, donde ni conocía ni me conocía nadie. Al fin, yo me determiné [238]). This last phrase, in which Pablos asserts control over his new persona, suggests that the episode serves as a plot device that impels the novel to its close by offering the *pícaro* yet another opportunity to dissemble and 'determine' who he is. But it also demonstrates the aversion Quevedo felt towards the poor, perceived by the author as inextricably linked with his *pícaro*–protagonist, as well as his belief that, unlike Saul, felled from his horse by God's redemptive grace and transformed into the new Christian Paul, our Pablos remains unalterably bound, through his many falls, to his *converso* beginnings. To Quevedo, the false poor and the falsely converted fully deserve the ignominy they bring on society.

By following Cros's own keen insights, therefore, we discern the text's unspoken message that, in contrast to its stated concerns, decisively addresses the marginalized 'other' whose threatening presence subsumes a growing number of the socially despised that includes not only the poor and the vagabonds, but *conversos* and *moriscos* as well. What Quevedo's *pícaro* embodies is not merely early modern Spain's fear of the impoverished – a category, as we have seen, already merged with several 'others'– so much as its fear of all the unwanted elements the social body continuously undertook to cast out. The scatological imagery saturating the *Buscón* with loathsome bodily excreta holds a social function far more powerful even than the carnivalesque readings given the narrative by Cros. In the persona of Pablos, the *buscón*, Quevedo's picaresque text simultaneously re-enacts and reincorporates the polymorphously sinister 'other' within the social body by graphically reinscribing the evilness of the 'other' on the body of the *pícaro* himself.

Scatology and the Social Body in Quevedo's *Buscón*

One benefit in applying Bakhtinian categories to Quevedian scatological imagery has been to save it from wrongful neglect due to critical circumspection.[27] Cros's Bakhtinian analysis of the *Buscón*'s scatological humour posits an organic comicity that is governed by a 'single logic of imagery' in which the carnivalesque elements form the 'comic drama' uniting the death of the old world with the birth of the new ('Estudio' 25). In *Rabelais and His World*, Bakhtin assigns the similarities between these worlds to the particular historical moment, still strongly dependent on medieval folk beliefs:

[A]t the time of folk legends the language of excrement was closely linked with fertility . . . Rabelais did not hesitate to combine the words 'our Lord' and 'our Lord's blessing' with the image of excrement ... He saw no sacrilege in doing so and did not anticipate the stylistic abyss that was to draw the line between the two terms for the men of the seventeenth century.[28]

Cros is only partially correct in attributing Quevedo's scatological excesses to a folkloric subtext akin to the *Lazarillo*'s that transgresses official discourse. However much we may wish to read the two antithetical worlds as forming a continuous whole, we must take into account that Quevedo did not belong to Rabelais's century, one that, in effect, understood these worlds in distinct opposition to each other. Bakhtin makes this quite clear in his directive on how to interpret the French Renaissance author's scatology:

[T]here is nothing grossly cynical in Rabelais' scatological images, nor in the other images of grotesque realism: the slinging of dung, the drenching in urine, the volley of scatological abuse hurled at the old, dying, yet generating world. All these images represent the gay funeral of this old world; they are (in the dimension of laughter) like handfuls of sod gently dropped into the open grave, like seeds sown in the earth's bosom. If the image is applied to the gloomy, disincarnated medieval truth, it symbolizes bringing it 'down to earth' through laughter. *All this should not be forgotten in the analysis of the scatological images that abound in Rabelais' novel.* (178; my emphasis)

Pablos's excremental encounters lack the 'positive element' that, according to the Russian critic, was still alive in Rabelais' time (148). Cros admits just such an absence when he protests that, by privileging its negative imagery, the *Buscón* distorts its carnivalesque perspective ('sufre una evidente perversión' ['Estudio' 33]).

But if the *Buscón*'s scatological episodes are not narrated in triumphalist tones, and reflect no regenerative view of nature, as is obviously the case in Rabelais, their function is no less significant for all their negativity. The text utilizes corporeal waste to create a permeable barrier, or skin-like film, that, just as it provisionally separates the *pícaro*'s outer self from his inner being, intends to isolate the marginalized from the centre. This permeable division permits us to understand the process of social contagion not merely as one from the *pícaro* to the social body, but as a reversible procedure, wherein the social body itself pollutes and contaminates the *pícaro*. Julia Kristeva has called this 'the horror within': 'The body's inside ... shows up in order to compensate for the collapse of the border between inside and outside. It is as if the skin, a fragile container, no longer guaranteed the integrity of one's "own and clean self" but, scraped or transparent, invisible or taut, gave way before the dejection of its contents.'[29] While this barrier allows Pablos to remain temporarily distanced from the dominant centre, therefore, it acts as a transformative device that ultimately converts society's internalized self into the *pícaro*. Once the students and townspeople eject their excretions onto the *pícaro*, he assumes and externalizes the negative values that remain, still, at their core.

Malcolm Read's arresting study on Quevedo's fascination with and fear of the body eloquently describes both what Quevedo perceived as intrinsic to the social body and how he reacted to its corporeality. Echoing Kristeva, Read states that, to Quevedo's dread, not only is the *pícaro*'s tainted lineage equated with dirt, but its filth extends to society in general: 'the horror of horrors for Quevedo was that what is true of the *pícaro* is true of us all: we are all dogged by dirt.'[30] That the author also conceived of wealth as waste, as 'courtly dirt,' explains money's hold over the elite as well as his marginalized characters (Read 6). If we read this bodily filth allegorically, we note that it traces a precariously thin line between the social body and its 'other.' The scapegoat is scapegoated because he externalizes what Spain's dominant hierarchy wished to expel from its interior. The scatological excess discharged on the *pícaro* expresses the disquietude of a xenophobic society that simultaneously acknowledges and rejects the presence of the 'other' in itself.

In attempting to cast out the 'other,' Quevedo conceptualizes the marginalized similarly to the juridical view that, Foucault explains, retained a dissymmetrical rule over life and death wherein sovereign power was exercised as a right of seizure and symbolized by the sword.[31] In such a society, power was wielded through public executions and *autos de fe* in order to make visual the punishment inflicted on the social body, since, according to Foucault, 'one had the right to kill those who represented a kind of biological danger to others' (*History of Sexuality* 138). Just as his *Política de Dios* reacts against Machiavellian pragmatics, the *Buscón* novelizes the sovereign right to control life and death by exercising the author's control over his character. That Pablos, as *pícaro*, can never be expelled, much less eliminated, merely confirms Quevedo's regressive tendencies against the transformations in mechanisms of power, proposed by *arbitristas*, endorsing the *pícaro*'s reinstatement in society through regulatory controls. In this, Quevedo reflects the conservatism of Philip III's reign, which would soon put in motion an act that can only be described as displaced genocide: the expulsion of the *moriscos*.[32] As I have argued of the *Lazarillo*, the *Buscón*'s narrative emplots the ambiguities and contradictions of the historical moment. The tensions in the text between authorial control, representing the dominant hierarchy, and the *pícaro* are manifested in Quevedo's scatological strategy. Scatology serves to highlight chaos, to call attention to the alarming disarray of an uncontrolled social body; its purpose, in the *Buscón*, is to visually place the blame of this contagion on the 'other.'

But by ejecting its threatening interior onto the marginalized, the dominant hierarchy only succeeds in converting the *pícaro* into its mirror image.[33] The *Buscón*'s grotesque imagery not only reflects the fear of pollution by the 'other,' but admits to the fact that, for all purposes, contamination by these despised elements cannot be averted or contained, since they originate precisely from within the social body itself. The contagion, therefore, comes about because of society's unclean blood – not, as Maravall has argued, due simply to the low social standing of the 'other.'[34] Quevedo's strong anti-Semitism needs no corroboration. His recently discovered invective, the *Execración contra los Judíos*, in which he inveighs against Spain's economic transactions with Portuguese *marranos* and against their proponent, the Count-Duke of Olivares, offers further proof of his position.[35] It is this recognition of the 'other' within that makes the *Buscón*, even more than its other picaresque counter-parts, an enclosed, centripetal narrative. The *Buscón*'s lesson to us as readers is that, just as Pablos's circular journey entraps the literary *pícaro* with no hope for an exit, the historical *pícaro* – whose classification as 'other' already entails the *converso*, the *morisco*, the witch, and the prostitute – remains always, for Quevedo, an internalized element within the social body.

Pablos's scatological incidents enact their double function, at once protective and polluting, most explicitly and graphically through his falls. At the beginning of Lent, the young boy, chosen by the teacher as *rey de gallos*, is knocked off his own bestial extension – a skeletal horse of suspected Jewish ancestry – for the animal's stealing and eating a cabbage from the vegetable stalls. The conceit 'batalla nabal' plays on the homonym 'naval'/'nabal,' which opposes the lofty pursuit of maritime glory to the irate sellers' base attack with root vegetables. But its water/earth dichotomy also hints at the contrast between the chivalrous contest between knights on horseback, and the battles then carried out either at sea by sailors and galley slaves, or on land by pikers, troops forcibly composed of the destitute and delinquent. In effect, the debased 'war' waged by the vegetable vendors causes Pablos to tumble unceremoniously off his mount and into a privy, grounding him in human mire.

The episode describes the first of several falls by which Pablos forfeits a new, distinctive social identity. When, on occasion of the *rey de gallos* festival, the *pícaro* specifically denies his *converso* origins by 'confessing' to his noble addressee, he ends up stressing them all the more:

I'd like to confess to Your Ladyship that, as my hat was adorned with feathers, when they started to throw the stalks, turnips, et cetera, I thought they had taken me for my mother and were throwing things at her as they had done before, and foolish child that I was, I began to cry out – Sisters, although I'm wearing feathers I'm not Aldonza de San Pedro, my mother! As if they couldn't tell as much by my size and face.

[Quiero confesar a vuestra merced que, cuando me empezaron a tirar los tronchos, nabos, etcétera, que como yo llevaba plumas en el sombrero, entendiendo que me habían tenido por mi madre y que la tiraban como habían hecho otras veces, como necio y muchacho empecé a decir: –¡Hermanas, aunque llevo plumas no soy Aldonza de San Pedro, mi madre! Como si ellas no lo echaran de ver por el talle y rostro. (88)]

Pablos's *converso* status is revealed precisely by his ironic use of the Catholic sacrament to narrate his denial, since a *converso* who confesses cannot be presumed to tell the truth. Similarly to Inquisition prisoners who 'confess' through torture, Pablos, pummelled by the vegetables, admits to, even while denying, his Jewish origins. Despite his efforts to win over the vendors by calling them his 'sisters,' he reinforces his lineage through his mother by claiming his likeness to her. That she, too, had been pelted by onlookers when, feathered for being a witch, she was paraded through town – and that her lowly first name, Aldonza, and overtly religious surname, de San Pedro, simultaneously call to mind both a common prostitute and Peter, the apostle who thrice denied Christ during the Passion – only serves to highlight what he so insistently endeavours to suppress.

James Iffland also maintains that Pablos's tumble from the horse is the first of many falls that impede the *pícaro*'s success in achieving higher social standing.[36] His shameful origins are visibly exposed to a spiteful public – those within the narrative and the extratextual reader – who will then revel at the *pícaro*'s disgraceful decline. Yet, by dropping into the privy, Pablos is ironically set 'free' to commence his picaresque adventures, since he escapes not only from his jailor, but from his parents' control:

[The sheriff] tried to take me to prison, but didn't because there was no place left to grab me, I was so covered in dung ... I decided I wouldn't ever return to school or to my home, but stay on as Don Diego's servant, that is, as his companion, and my offering my friendship to the boy made his people very happy.

[[el alguacil] quísome llevar a la cárcel, y no me llevó porque no hallaba por dónde asirme, tal me había puesto del lodo ... [D]eterminéme de no volver más a la escuela ni a casa de mis padres, sino de quedarme a servir a don Diego y, por mejor decir, en su compañía, y esto con gran gusto de los suyos, por el que daba mi amistad al niño. (88–9)]

Instead of returning the boy to the oppressive atmosphere of his *converso* parents, the excremental shield gained in the fall not only protects Pablos from the law, but allows him to assume a new subject position from which to advance socially. We know, however, that the freedom gained by the young boy only offers him continued opportunities to voluntarily engage in amoral acts. The text constantly stresses Pablos's 'determination' to lead a picaresque life; unlike Alemán's critique of free will, however, Quevedo's attribution of choice to his *pícaro* functions as an excuse to mete out his rigorous retribution. In one of the many episodes that function as *mise en abîme* in the novel, Pablos's choice of master, the wealthy young *converso* Don Diego Coronel, reiterates the experience of ascendant *converso* families opposed by the *Buscón*'s aristocratic ideology.[37] I will return to the final episode with Don Diego, but for the moment I wish to emphasize that it is no accident that the novel ends with Don Diego disclosing and cruelly reinscribing Pablos's real – and only – identity.[38]

Our reading of the *rey de gallos* episode means to show how, when covered with the town's excrement, Pablos is displaced from the margins to the dominant social structure: sullied, he is 'liberated' to sally forth on his life's journey. Complying with the picaresque genre, the following episodes instruct the young boy in social cruelty by placing him in grotesque parodies of educational institutions. Pablos's first fall thus thrusts him into the *Buscón*'s most famous episode, the boarding-school run by the licentiate Cabra. This miserly, emaciated figure assumes the most repugnant features of the stereotypical *converso*: slovenly dressed, frugal to excess, and, what is worse, a menace to the lives of innocent children.[39] Heretically garbed in clerical gown (the same raiment worn by the abundant *converso letrados*), his skeletal frame sounding like lepers' clappers ('tablillas de san Lázaro'), the demonic Cabra conjures up the sinister myths that fuelled social hatred against all 'others.' By exaggerating the lack of food, the episode magnifies the theme of hunger so prevalent in the previous picaresque narratives. Cleverly elucidating the passage as one of 'inverted scatology,' Iffland explains that '[w]heareas the scatological usually depends on the presence of excrement, here it depends upon its absence' (*Quevedo* II: 93). The episode's occurrence during Lent reinforces the allusions to starvation and depletion, yet, fittingly, the episode ends with another disgusting discharge of bodily waste. The two boys, who had feigned constipation, are forced to empty their bowels as Cabra obliges them to 'reimburse' him. The episode's grotesque humour has the boys instead splattering the licentiate's old aunt – the same old aunt who then, we are told, increases the soup with indigestible detritus (Iffland, *Quevedo and the Grotesque* II: 95–6). The nauseating turn of events uncovers the episode's scatological economy: the *converso* couple, Cabra and his aunt, acting as another set of perverse parents, demand payment from the two *converso* youths, yet withhold food from them until they almost die from starvation.

No matter how similarly repulsive this episode is to Pablos's other

scatological experiences, we need to distinguish it from his fecal fall into
the town privy and the Alcalá episode, where he is spat and shat upon
by the university students. The Cabra episode's difference lies not
merely in its initial absence of excrement, but in the proposition it presents that a member of a marginalized group would mistreat and attack
its own. In the town episode and that at Alcalá, the aggressors are never
identified as *ex illis*, and the precarious dividing line between them and
the *pícaro* is drawn by the corporeal waste matter exchanged. As we
have seen, with Cabra, no real transaction takes place, even after the two
youths spray the degenerate pair, since they return only what was
forced into them. Instead, the two boys' abuse at the hands of the diabolical 'goat' must be judged allegorically as an anti-Baptism, its denial
of redemption and (ex)change vividly illustrating Quevedo's conviction
of the *converso*'s self-hatred and rejection of his own kind.

In Alcalá, the *pícaro*'s abuse and repudiation by his university companions will eventually lead to another act of liberation, as Pablos
decides to separate from Don Diego. The description of the *pícaro*'s
Christ-like passion at Alcalá, where, by denying his role of 'ecce homo,'
he nevertheless again underscores his function as scapegoat, supports
my claim that the students expiate their fears of the 'other' by disgorg-
ing their corporeal waste on their victim, even as they are identified as
forming part of a demonic throng:

You can imagine my anguish! The infernal mob shouted so loud they left me
bewildered, and from what they hurled at me from their stomachs, I thought
they were trying to save on doctors and drugstores by purging themselves on
the new students.

[¡Aquí se han de considerar mis angustias! Levantó la infernal gente una grita
que me aturdieron y yo, según lo que me echaron sobre mí de sus estómagos,
pensé que, por ahorrar de médicos y boticas, aguardan nuevos para purgarse.
(114)]

The episode ends with another excremental experience, but before this
occurs the young boy is so disconsolate that, taking pity, a *morisco* cautions him: 'Look out for yourself, as here you've got no mother or father'
(Mira por ti, que aquí no tienes otro padre ni madre [116]). The ironic
warning, offered by an alienated 'other,' means to distinguish between
the mistreatment received from his various *converso* parent-figures and
that inflicted on him by the general populace, who assign him the role of

pharmakon. Once in bed, he is set upon by students, who beat him unmercifully. After the beating, he awakens to find himself completely covered in dung, never guessing that the students had defecated in his bed. Wondering how he could have soiled himself, he feigns illness until the students, led by Don Diego, remove his covers and expose his shame. Pablos's paradoxical stance perfectly defines his social position of scapegoat: 'In the end, I was both innocent and guilty, and I didn't know how to exonerate myself' (Al fin, yo me hallaba inocente y culpado, y no sabía cómo disculparme [117]). The scatological event imposes on Pablos the role of scapegoat: he at once represents and expiates, through his suffering, the iniquity brought on society by the 'other.'

That Pablos the *pícaro* manifestly functions as scapegoat to his society is not to say, however, that Quevedo, the *Buscón*'s author, consciously accepts or even acknowledges the presence of the 'other' within the social body. The author, so proud of his untainted *montañés* descent, would not likely admit to projecting his fears on his fictional character. Written shortly after the Valladolid plague of 1599, the *Buscón*, through Pablos's constant attempts to deny his tainted lineage, nevertheless articulates the repressed social anxieties of contamination. The *pícaro*'s refusal to consume his father's corpse, in the infamous passage of the meat pies, is clearly meant to suggest an Oedipal rejection of his origins, pointing to Quevedo's view that society should reject its 'other.' It is also a reminder that no matter how hard he tries to separate himself, the *pícaro* is inevitably drawn back to his unreformed roots: like Guzmán before him, Pablos hates and resents his father, but desperately needs to identify with him (Johnson, *Inside Guzmán*, 221). Yet, if Foucault's analysis of the pre-Classical sovereign power to control life by death serves to explain to us Quevedo's intention to control the 'other' by expelling it, the episode confirms that the 'other' responded with another form of power: wealth.

To Quevedo's certain distress, given his own family background, the historical *converso*'s paternal legacy of economic prosperity provides an effective means for social integration. The rich *converso*'s indulgence of his children, his assurance of assimilation, is alluded to in Cervantes's *Coloquio de los perros*, and, in the *Buscón*, in Don Diego's relationship with his father. Parodying the *converso*'s enrichment through family ties, by rejecting his father's quartered remains, Pablos strikes a much better bargain. The meat pies are worth only four *maravedíes*, as the pun on 'quartered' pastries refers as much to their cheap price as to the macabre source of their stuffing.[40] In contrast, the *pícaro*'s inherited capital, which he does not decline, amounts to three hundred ducats. This money allows him to travel to the court in Madrid and purchase new clothes, thereby giving him the opportunity to replace his habits, that is, to change his customs and exchange his clothes: 'There, I intended to hang up my habits as soon as I arrived [at court] and to buy the new short clothes more in style' (Allí propuse de colgar los hábitos en llegando y de sacar vestidos nuevos cortos, al uso [170]).

Although he renounces his father's dispersed body, Pablos's interest in collecting the monies coming to him remarks on the unbroken and unbreakable bond with his *converso* origins, affirmed in his comments to his hangman uncle:

I profess to be a worthy scion of my family, as it is impossible to be two, unless I fall into your hands and you quarter me like you do others. Don't ask for or mention me by name, since it's critical that I deny our shared bloodline.

[Yo pretendo ser uno de mi linaje, porque dos es imposible si no vengo a sus manos, y trinchándome como hace a otros. No pregunte por mí ni me nombre, porque me importa negar la sangre que tenemos. (170)]

That the 'habits' Pablos repeatedly replaces can never be those that, in the end, permit him to escape the picaresque life, is made clear at the novel's conclusion. Wittily punning on the requisite for *conversos* to abandon their Jewish customs, the narrator's final declaration on the apparent need to change one's moral behaviour to improve one's state also gives voice to the author's stoic stand against what, to him, represented unacceptable social mobility. The *Buscón*'s subtext, then, verifies what Quevedo's discourse means to negate: that society's bonds with the 'other,' although repeatedly disavowed, can never be dissolved.

In his last disguise as a nobleman, whose name, Don Filipe Tristán, scandalously suggests royal status, Pablos attempts to marry a young woman who, like him, we find out, pretends to noble and untainted blood. Playing the same game of economic seduction as Pablos, the young woman's procuress aunt tempts the ignoble swain with the promise of an exaggerated dowry downplayed by the aunt to emphasize her nobility: 'She may be poor, as she only has 6,000 ducats for dowry, but she owes no blood to anyone' (Ella pobre es, que no tiene sino seis mil ducados de dote, pero no debe nada a nadie en sangre [221]). Pablos's materialist aspirations to the dowry reveal that Quevedo's anti-Semitism, generally attributed to his religious orthodoxy, was based as much on his belief that *conversos* followed the aristocratic practice of investing their monies in bonds:

I confess that I couldn't sleep all night thinking of what I would do with the dowry. And what I most tossed about was whether I should build a house or invest it in bonds, since I didn't know which would be to my best advantage.

[Yo confieso que no pude dormir en toda la noche con el cuidado de lo que había de hacer con el dote. Y lo que más me tenía en duda era el hacer dél una casa o darlo a censo, que no sabía yo cuál sería mejor y de más provecho. (222)]

The *pícaro*'s agitated state coincides with the criticism aimed at the nobility for failing to invest in agriculture and industry. Perhaps frustrated by their more liberal stance, Quevedo's distorted image of the *arbitristas* marks his opposition to their failed recommendations; the ridiculous means proposed as a solution to the siege of Ostend (136) is but one illustration of his scepticism.[41] Nonetheless, and despite the critics who relegate the *Buscón* to purely literary display, the author's condemnation of the *arbitristas'* projects reminds us that, with all its hilarity, the *Buscón* proffers strong commentary on contemporary social issues.[42]

After the Cabra episode, where Pablos is brutally tormented by a member of his caste, we should not be surprised that it is again a *converso*, significantly reappearing from Pablos's past, who denounces and castigates the *pícaro* for assuming a fictive persona:

May Your Lord forgive me, since until I heard your name, I took you for someone quite different from yourself, as I've never seen a face so like that of a servant I had in Segovia, called Pablillos, son of a barber from that same town.

[Vuestra Merced me perdone, que por Dios que le tenía, hasta que supe su nombre, por bien diferente de lo que es, que no he visto cosa tan parecida a un criado que tuve en Segovia, que se llamaba Pablillos, hijo de un barbero del mismo lugar. (224)]

Equally significant is the method used by Don Diego to accomplish his devastating punishment. From the moment he appropriates Don Diego's identity by wearing his cape, Pablos is condemned to pay for the wealthy *converso*'s successful rise to power, as the cape's exchange reconnects the two men to each other through their unacceptable social goals and their inescapable origins. The slash he receives across the face indelibly stamps Pablos with the sign of the unredeemed, unredemptive 'other,' but its provenance from that same 'other' shows the author's hand in the retribution. Although unable to camouflage his coarse features, Pablos had hidden his lineage by means of his clothes and lavish lifestyle. Recalling his birth from a *converso*–witch mother, the *pícaro* is nursed back to health by a woman whose dubious qualities point to her suspect origins:

She whitened hands and throats like walls, polished teeth and eliminated facial and body hair. She cooked up a potion called Herod with which she killed unborn innocents, causing stillbirths and preventing pregnancies. During my eight days at home, I saw her do all this ... she dealt with drugs, without being a pharmacist and, if her hands were greased, she would grease herself and leave by night through the chimney.

[Enlucía manos y gargantas como paredes, acicalaba dientes, arrancaba el vello. Tenía un bebedizo que llamaba Herodes, porque, con él, mataba los niños en las barrigas y hacía malparir y mal empreñar. En solos ocho días que yo estuve en casa, la vi hacer todo esto ... que trataba en botes, sin ser boticaria, y, si la untaban las manos, se untaba y salía de noche por la puerta del humo. (236)]

The narrative thus returns Pablos to his maternal beginnings, to the witch-womb from which he cannot escape. The gash inflicted by Don Diego, cutting through Pablos's masquerade and leaving him in the care of his surrogate *converso* mother, graphically reinscribes his *converso* status. Despite his dissembling discourse, it is through visible violence to his physical body that he is finally disciplined and controlled. However, if the *pícaro* is rejected as the 'other,' Don Diego, in his role of rich *converso*, is fully integrated into society. Pablos's wound bleeds Don Diego's own tainted blood; yet by turning the social body's feces into gold, Don Diego overturns Quevedo's anti-*converso* diatribe. As text and protagonist, Pablos, the *buscón*, at once emplots and embodies the *pharmakon*.

Pícaras as Prostitutes

While the *pícaro's* lacerated body bears the visible marks of his socially repugnant origins, the picaresque text's ambiguity oftentimes defuses and conceals its social message. Similarly, female picaresque novels advocate women's control and enclosure by exploiting the protagonists' sexuality as a lure to the male reader. Indeed, these apparently amusing tales of sexual escapade establish an ironic homology between the *pícara* and the prostitute on at least two counts: by pandering to readers' prurient interests and by proposing that women utilize their bodies for their social and economic benefit. Foucault's theses on modern surveillance and the discipline of the social body have been rightly criticized for ignoring gender difference.[43] The female picaresque offers an opportune site on which to apply the French philosopher's notions of social control, both to analyse the genre's severe critique of women's corporeality, and to investigate more broadly the Spanish patriarchy's castigation and confinement of early modern prostitutes.

The very conditions of the genre are at stake: the female picaresque is generally relegated to a minor genre, and critics have often debated whether such a term should be applied at all to texts that deal with marginalized women.[44] Critics who acknowledge these narratives as a literary category usually consider them conceived in the image of the male picaresque, a literary *segundona* ancillary to the traditional canon.[45] An exception is Edward Friedman's fine study of female picaresque discursive practices, which asserts that '[t]he incipient psychological realism of the *Lazarillo*, the *Guzmán*, and the *Buscón* counts less in these readings than the re-creation of antisocial events to conform to the female characters.'[46] My own study means not to rehearse the picaresque's well-known formal characteristics, but to question why such a genre – understood broadly, thereby including its variants, the female picaresque and soldiers' tales – emerged and proliferated at this particular historical moment. Only when gender is given equal significance to genre will these novels – which, after all, are the first to depict the lives of marginalized women – reveal their profound insights on early modern culture.

While both the male and female picaresque were written by male authors, those with women as their protagonists share neither the origins of the male picaresque tradition nor its purpose.[47] Although the *Lazarillo* – whose anonymous author is unquestionably male – has long been recognized as the progenitor of the male picaresque, the female picaresque derives from Fernando de Rojas's *Tragicomedia de Calisto y Melibea*, known by the name of its most famous character, the old go-between Celestina.[48] This novel in dialogue form dwells as much on the picaresque lives of the servants as on the ill-starred lovers of its title, and it is this lower-class stratum of the text, inhabited by the lascivious servants and the old bawd, that the female picaresque narratives reconstruct as their social milieu. If, by parodying the exploits of knights-errant, the male picaresque novels invert the image of their archetypal heroes into the amoral *pícaro*, the female picaresque models its literary anti-heroines on the already debased female characters of the *Celestina*. Through these narratives, the picaresque becomes a gender-oriented genre, separated by the sex of the protagonists and differentiated by its distinct literary parentage. Like its protagonists' bodies, the corpus of the female picaresque has been traditionally exploited as much by its masculine readers as by its male authors. Despite the years that separate them, such female picaresque novels as *La Lozana andaluza* (1527), *La pícara Justina* (1605), *La hija de la Celestina* (1614), *La niña de los embustes, Teresa de Manzanares* (1632), and *La Garduña de Sevilla y anzuelo de las bolsas* (1642) all descend from a matriarchy that delimits the heroine's role primarily to her sexual function. Alonso de Castillo Solórzano's last two tales focus more on the *pícaras'* confidence tricks than on their overtly immoral conduct, but both narratives rely on the women's willingness to entice their suitors sexually in order to rob them. Peter Dunn has rightly commented that 'women, in Castillo's novels, are "el flaco sexo" – "the weaker sex", with due emphasis on the "sex".'[49] What is clearly evident is that, in nearly all the picaresque novels, the *pícara* is portrayed either explicitly or ironically as a prostitute.[50]

Such a depiction distinguishes her from her male counterpart, since her marginalized role in society is more complex and deeply embedded than the *pícaro's*: the prostitute historically holds a significant function in society, and her treatment reflects the prevailing consciousness about women and sexuality in general.[51] From the Middle Ages on, the moral ambivalence towards prostitution created an atmosphere of oppression that encouraged society to punish the prostitute while it ignored the reasons for her behaviour – principally, the dreadful poverty and mistreatment suffered by these primarily lower-class women. Historians Angel Galán Sánchez and María Teresa López Beltrán have noted that the times were conditioned by a triple exigency: first, the total repression of prostitution; second, the acceptance of its inevitability and the need to control it as much as possible; and, finally, the fact, no less obvious, that prostitution could bring in substantial revenues.[52] Thus, despite the moral urgency of the issue, prostitution was allowed to remain a practical means of support for many women.

The ambivalence with which prostitution was treated may be noted in that, although the clergy were permitted their concubines, and the *scorta erratica* followed the military expeditions, most prostitution remained illegal in much of medieval Spain. Playing on the relationship between the devotional and the defiled, clandestine houses of prostitution were often called 'monasteries,' with the madames in charged correspondingingly known as abbesses. Penalties for acts of prostitution committed by the 'sisters' consisted of fifty lashes for the first offence, one hundred for the second: a prostitute's nose was cut off for the third. Justice was generally much more lax towards the owners of the houses, who were usually rich noblemen. When such a 'monastery' was discovered, the confiscated property was sold to the highest bidder, only to be reopened by a new owner when the pressure subsided. Despite the many laws, inns frequently harboured prostitutes, as it was quite easy to bribe a judge with the favours of the very prostitutes accused (Henríquez Solís 46–8). While the municipal charters (*fueros*) of the sixteenth and seventeenth centuries in part liberated the third estate from the abuses of the nobility, protecting women from the accustomed *droit du seigneur*, they also severely punished the prostitute. The Sepulveda *fuero* 235, for example, which governed the whole of the Extremaduran province, provided for the injury, and even death, of a prostitute who insulted an honest man or woman (Rodríguez Solís 50–1). Alfonso el Sabio's *Siete Partidas* permitted concubinage, but ruled that procurers and their whores should be driven out of town. In an attempt to effect a restitution of sorts, the seventh *partida* also specified that, where procurers had lured women to a life of sin, they were responsible for the prostitutes' rehabilitation under penalty of death, and should provide for their dowries and marriage.[53]

Although prohibited within the cities, prostitution *extra muros* was legally allowed. As early as 1321, the city of Valencia decreed that a series of small houses outside of the city and rented by *hostalers*, or procurers, who then furnished supplies to their wards at exorbitant prices, should be turned into a public brothel. To protect the prostitutes from exploitation by these procurers, the city fathers imposed several laws forbidding the *hostalers* to live among the women or to hire them for immoral acts. Their treatment under this system, while decidedly more humane than the punishment meted out under the various *fueros*, nonetheless reveals the moral condemnation implicit in their segregation. All prostitutes found practising within the city were relegated to the brothel and, in order to distinguish them from 'decent' women, were forbidden to enter the city wearing a cape. They were also forbidden to enter dancing or to dance while in the city, activities deemed too seductive to engage in outside the brothel.[54] The Valencian brothel, for instance, remained protected by law through the sixteenth century; similar arrangements were allowed in other cities under Philip II's 1571 law, which regulated the brothels.[55]

From 1470 through 1473, any prostitute caught working outside the designated brothels was heavily fined by the town council of Seville, which served as model for many of the town councils in the recently incorporated kingdom of Granada. After the kingdom's conquest in 1492, the Catholic Monarchs granted the monopoly of all houses of prostitution in the area to Alonso Yáñez Fajardo, a local noble known, disparagingly enough, as 'el putero,' the 'whoremonger.' All prostitutes were legally required to work only in Yáñez's brothels, or *mancebías*, which he in turn rented to third parties called *padres*, who looked after the prostitutes and established the rates to be charged.[56] Despite prohibitions against loans, prostitutes often incurred heavy debts to the padres, resulting in their forced stay (López Beltrán, *La prostitución*, 125). While the desired outcome of the Monarchs' organizing efforts was to restrict and control the prostitutes' activity, there remained a considerable number of unregulated prostitutes who acted as free agents (Galán and López Beltrán 163).

Although Foucault's scheme does not account for gender difference, the control of prostitutes would seem to fall under the 'power to *foster* life or *disallow* it,' which, Foucault explains, replaced the traditional sovereign right to take life (*History of Sexuality* 138). For him, however, this control starts in the seventeenth century, as he observes power following two complementary forms, both focusing on the human body. The first kind of power, which he calls 'anatomo-politics,' is characterized by discipline: taking the individual body as a machine, increasing its usefulness and 'integrating it into systems of efficient and economic controls' such as armies, schools, and workshops. Once these systems are set up, it then becomes imperative to regulate the 'species body': such issues as birth rate, housing, and public health respond to what Foucault calls 'bio-power' (*History of Sexuality* 139). For Foucault, then, these ungendered bodies were first introduced to the various production machines, which in turn necessitated the growth and care of both bodies and machines; the resultant 'institutions' of state power were not fully developed or theorized until the eighteenth century (*History of Sexuality* 141).

In Spain, control of the body required that attention be paid to gender, as the country continued its attempts to regulate prostitution throughout the sixteenth century. The 1568 syphilis epidemic forced Seville's city government to redouble its efforts to control the spread of the disease:

Rumors of an epidemic so frightened city residents that they were willing to accept greatly expanded government regulations. These regulations were directed particularly against prostitutes, who were commonly suspected of passing on plagues. Clients of prostitutes, after all, often entered the city from a ship that had arrived in port, and prostitutes could easily contact any diseases they carried and pass them on into the city. Prostitutes were more susceptible to illness, too, if they were the poorer women who were undernourished and used secondhand clothing and bedding, both of which frequently carried disease in this period.[57]

Legalized prostitution not only prevented diseases by ensuring routine medical examinations, it also provided for those young girls who were unable to find employment and who were too poor to marry. If prostitution was an evil, it was one accepted by society as necessary in order to respond pragmatically to the economic hardships suffered by so many women. As Perry points out, not only was it profitable for city officials and churchmen, many of whom owned the property leased to the brothels, it was 'even a form of public assistance, providing jobs for women who would otherwise starve. It strengthened the moral attitudes that supported the city's hierarchy of authority, and it permitted the city oligarchy to demonstrate its authority to define and confine evil' (*Crime and Society* 233).

From the Middle Ages on, Spanish society had attempted to circumscribe both the libertine actions of its prostitutes and the everyday lives of its 'decent' women. In 1527, Vives, in his *Instrucción de la mujer cristiana*, urged young girls to remain indoors as much as possible. However, if they had good reason to venture out, they were to protect their reputations by covering their breasts, throat, and face, looking straight ahead with only one eye exposed, and avoiding all eye contact so as not to see nor be seen by anyone. Although 'decent' women followed his precepts by covering their faces with a cloak when going outdoors, it was not long before prostitutes and other women of questionable virtue began to take advantage of the anonymity afforded by such a garment. The two groups were finally differentiated by the public's naming the first group of women *cubiertas*, and calling the second group *tapadas* – both synonyms meaning 'covered,' but establishing a moral distinction between them. To end the prostitutes' abuse of the cloak, which permitted them to mingle freely in society, its use by all women was finally prohibited in 1639.[58]

Comments by several contemporary foreign travellers to Spain attest

to the enforced confinement of most Spanish women by their male relatives in order to protect the family honour, a reclusion which condemned them besides to a life of ignorance and childish frivolity
(Deleito y Piñuela 17 ff.). The zealous overprotection of wives by their
husbands had the ironic effect of allowing the prostitutes far greater
freedom on the streets, creating a division of internal and external space
for women along behavioural lines – the 'good' women were literally
locked indoors, while the 'bad' had the run of the outdoors. The prostitutes' relative mobility also resulted in their easy availability as companions to the majority of men who valued their wives mainly for their
domestic and maternal functions.

Increasingly, the role of prostitution in society extended beyond its
marginalization in the criminal underworld to its broader consequences
for all women within the social order. The literary characterization of
the *pícara* as a prostitute thus provides a means of understanding the
social and historical attitudes towards women held by the male authors
of the female picaresque. By portraying the character as a whore, the
novels allow us to view her as transgressor, freely moving within a society whose moral and legal boundaries no longer deter or confine her.
This release from the hypocritical constraints of Spanish society affords
the *pícara* an apparent honesty in her actions and thoughts: just as she is
free to behave as she wishes, she is able to state openly what she thinks,
with no regard for the consequences, since she has already violated the
strict social standards required of women. The freedom with which the
pícara expresses herself is most evident in the narratives that are structured autobiographically, such as *La pícara Justina* and, at least partially,
La hija de la Celestina. Here, the male author not only creates a female
character, but, by narrating her life in the first person, also assumes a
feminine voice. Given the freedom he ostensibly allows her, the author
would seem to partake of the character's unfettered outlook. Instead,
the *pícara*'s discourse serves to reveal his manipulation and control, disclosing a relationship of repression between author and narrator.[59]

The female picaresque novels expose their authors' perceptions of
prostitutes and prostitution, but, even more important, they illustrate
the manner in which the male authors themselves are re-created by their
texts, speaking to other men from their privileged place in a society separated by gender and delimited by their own definitions of virtue and
vice. Thus, a homologous situation arises between the prostitutes of
early modern Spain and their literary counterparts. As the prostitutes
become socialized by royal decree and their activities increasingly regu-

lated for the benefit of the male population, so the language of the female picaresque is both generated and controlled by the male point of view. The licentiousness of the *pícara* does not give her licence to break away from authorial control: the protagonist remains at the service of the author, a seductive figure of speech ready to lure the reader into a male-dominated and male-oriented discourse.

As I shall argue, then, the female picaresque differs from the majority of picaresque novels whose aim is to criticize social attitudes towards the poor. Instead, by restricting the *pícaras* to their role as prostitutes, the texts are in collusion with a society that views them as performing a necessary and vital service. Since female sexuality historically has been deemed threatening to the social order, its containment guarantees the health and morality of the existing society, thereby contributing to its preservation (Perry, 'Deviant Insiders,' 141). The constant attempts to enclose the prostitute as a social 'other' are thus a means of protecting both men and women, inasmuch as confinement of prostitution within approved urban zones neutralizes the dangers its practitioners pose to the social order. Ironically, then, in their description of the *pícaras* as wanderers and pilgrims, generally free to cross the different social-class boundaries, the female picaresque novels ultimately disclose a severe critique of those prostitutes who remain unconstrained.

The criticism implicit in the female picaresque reveals a polarized view of woman as either entirely 'good' or 'bad' held by its male authors – a view that helped to shape social reality for all women. The male perception of women's morality in turn reflects the symbiotic relations between purity and pollution delineated by anthropologist Mary Douglas: 'Where sexual purity is concerned it is obvious that if sexual purity is to imply no contact between the sexes it is not only a denial of sex, but must be literally barren. It also leads to contradiction. To wish all women to be chaste at all times goes contrary to other wishes and if followed consistently leads to inconveniences.'[60] In Spain, this contradiction was resolved through the purity of those young women who would remain chaste until marriage. As Perry has noted, for the *Siete Partidas* marriage was a means 'to avoid quarrels, homicides, insolence, violence, and many other very wrongful acts which would take place on account of women if marriage did not exist' (Perry, 'Deviant Insiders,' 141). Yet those who did not marry also contributed to the social order. By servicing the sexual demands of men, regulated prostitutes protected the purity of marriageable women and the morality of the matriarchs: 'Women who did not marry ran the risk of losing their respectability,

but even "bad women" could be tolerated if they were carefully distinguished from "good women"' (Perry, 'Deviant Insiders,' 141).

As we have seen, then, prostitution was not only tolerated by Spanish
society, it was considered necessary to its welfare. The polarization of
virgins and whores was based on a social infrastructure that required
both, so long as each remained readily identifiable. The rampant poverty among women contributed to the maintenance of the status quo.
While the religious life was an alternative to marriage for women with
dowries, poor women who did not marry could enter relatively few
nunneries, and by the middle of the sixteenth century even these were
further restricted by royal decree. For an increasingly large number of
poor women, then, the option remaining required a different form of
social enclosure – the public brothel.

The social spaces assigned women admit one more attempt to com-
partmentalize and enclose and reform Spain's 'lost' women.[61] Houses
sheltering prostitutes had been established as early as 1345; Seville's
Convent of the Sweet Name of Jesus gathered repentant women and, by
1581, had been converted into a convent housing more than 100
inmates.[62] Pérez de Herrera's *Amparo de pobres* contains a chapter on the
need to 'restrain and punish vagabond and delinquent women.'[63] The
reformer protests that the public punishments given 'loose' women –
who, like Pablos's mother, were feathered and exhibited through town –
not only failed to elicit remorse, but actually advertised the women's
sexual availability to future clients (120). He recommends instead that
workhouses be built in Madrid, Valladolid, Granada, Seville, and other
large cities to enclose 'indolent vagabonds, or those accused of thievery,
witchcraft, fraud or other crimes, for one, two, three or more years, and
even ten, according to the offence, and for life, if she comes close to
deserving the death penalty' (vagabundas ociosas, o delincuentes de
hurtos, hchicerías, o embustes o de otros delitos, por uno, dos, tres o
más años, y aun por diez, conforme a sus culpas, y de por vida a la que
mereciere casi pena de muerte [121]). The women were to be dressed
and fed simply, and taught 'women's work' such as spinning, knitting,
and button making to pay for their food, medical expenses, and salaries
for their guardians, who should be older, married and of strong moral
character. Foucault's 'anatomo-politics,' the control of the human body
through discipline and enclosure, gave way to what he terms 'a bio-pol-
itics of the population,' directed towards the processes of life (*History of
Sexuality* 139). Reflecting the need for these regulatory controls, Pérez de
Herrera expected that the prostitutes' enclosure would reduce abor-

tions, child abuse and abandonment, and control venereal disease, freeing hospitals to treat other ailments. If treated well, he argued, these women could be rehabilitated for the good of the state by learning a trade or being hired as servants, thereby eliminating the prevalent custom whereby, for a fee, poor parents placed their daughters in households and then forced them to quit to continue collecting fees.

Cavillac reckons that Pérez de Herrera's reformatory was built next to the Atocha Hospital in Madrid, known as the 'galera' in an ironic reference to the punishment given male criminals.[64] An earlier 'galley,' Santa Isabel in Madrid, had been commissioned by Philip II, who asked the redoubtable nun Magdalena de San Jerónimo to oversee its construction (Pérez Baltasar 30).[65] In 1608, the nun wrote a *memorial* to Philip III outlining the *galera*'s goals as a prison for women, but before this plan, in 1588, she already directed one of the numerous Magdalen houses founded after the Council of Trent. This Casa Pía de Arrepentidas de Santa Magdalena, established in Valladolid, most likely served as blueprint for the *galera*, as the nun successfully lobbied for the Casa's expansion and endowment (Barbeito 42–55). The nun's chosen religious name, Magdalena, reflects on the redemptive quality of her social work: as with Lázaro, the name conflates several biblical women who are assigned the role of repentant prostitute.[66] For Sor Magdalena, redemption of her charges must be exacted through prayer, humiliation, and sacrifice, since the women – whom she compares to wild beasts who nightly leave their caves to hunt – are to blame for Spain's depravity: 'A great part (if not the greatest) of the havoc wreaked on moral customs throughout Spain's kingdoms is caused by the liberty, dissolution, and debauchery of many women' (gran parte [si no es la mayor] del daño y estrago que hay en las costumbres en estos reinos de España, nacía de la libertad, disolución y rotura de muchas mujeres).[67]

The continuing national discontent in 1608 precipitated extremely retrograde measures to control the 'other': although Parliament saw fit to reissue Pérez de Herrera's *Amparo de pobres*, the expulsion of the *moriscos* was already being planned. Sor Magdalena's *memorial* that same year thus reintroduces a highly moralistic view of women's behaviour that believed in apportioning stern punishments rather than opportunities for conversion. While Pérez de Herrera also advocated stricter enclosure for women, Sor Magdalena's proposal exhibits both the regressive tendencies of public spectacle and far more rigorous gender control through incarceration. She stresses that, although orphaned girls should be confined to designated quarters to protect them from evil, those women already fallen needed to be severely punished and enclosed in the *galera* to safeguard others from their influence (*Galera* 75).[68] The galley was intended to function as nothing less than a jail; the women's hair was to be shaved, and their belongings confiscated; ropes were not allowed so women could not escape or commit suicide. A separate room was assigned for the solitary confinement of incorrigibles; all sorts of chains, handcuffs, and disciplinary artefacts should be visible to frighten the women into good behaviour (*Galera* 78–9). On completing their sentence, they should be warned against recidivism, as their sentence would be doubled, and they would be branded on the right shoulder with the town arms. On their fourth offence, they would be hanged at the galley door, a death sentence urged for notorious criminals, so others would take heed and not follow suit (*Galera* 81).

Sor Magdalena's proposal, which encourages work only as a means of avoiding idleness, contrasts with Pérez de Herrera's earlier plans for a workhouse that would train women in various occupations. Since the *galera* was meant to be run by town officials, it was primarily a secular institution, its rigour and discipline harking to the severe measures recommended for vagabonds and false poor. In this, it fully relies on the public function of punishment as spectacle, whether by exhibiting women's bodies as warnings to others, or by inscribing those warnings directly on women's bodies. Rather than solely reproaching Sor Magdalena's austerity as patriarchal, therefore, we should take the *galera* as an example, not only of the reactionary changes that were taking place in the strategies towards the poor and poor relief, but of the escalating strictures against women who, as we shall see in the female picaresque, were increasingly perceived, not as the givers of life, but as the embodiment of evil.

Misogyny, Male Voice-Over, and Female Enclosure in the Female Picaresque

As the female picaresque relegates its protagonists to a primarily sexualized role, there is no doubt that they belong to the category 'bad women.' The poor, lower-class origins of the *pícara*, her early promiscuity, and her social marginalization are literary commonplaces that assign the genre different formal characteristics from those of the male picaresque. In particular, it is the female picaresque's separation of the *pícara* from 'decent' society that underscores its male-authored critique of women's sexual freedom. By doing so, the female picaresque acknowledges its debt to the *Celestina* as the novel that first redirected the focus of the picaresque genre from its male protagonists to the *pícara*. Indeed, the dangers of the wicked intermingling with the virtuous are spelled out clearly in the *Celestina*. Here, servants and masters come into contact with each other with easy familiarity. Areúsa and Elicia, the servants of the old bawd, lead carefree lifestyles markedly different from the other servants' cloistered dependency on their vigilant mistresses. Because their actions have yet to be socially constrained, Areúsa and Elicia not only work for Celestina, they also function interchangeably as lovers of Calisto's manservants and of Celestina's young relatives and wards.

This interaction, marked in the text by the servants' many comings and goings from Melibea's residence to Celestina's shack, creates a network of relationships which ultimately leads to Melibea's seduction and consequent downfall. Since the servants have followed Celestina's lead in preferring their own economic interest to their mistress's honour, critics have viewed Melibea's fall as symbolic of the destabilization of the closed, structured society. Maravall has rightfully attributed the breakdown of *Celestina*'s feudal world to the substitution of money for the mutual respect that had previously existed between the servants and Calisto and Melibea.[69] Alan Deyermond notes perceptively that the exchange of money for respect has caused the rupture of the social order, thereby permitting Calisto's servant Sempronio to fall in love with Melibea, and Lucrecia, Melibea's most trusted servant, with Calisto. He asks: 'How must we interpret those sexual bonds between members of different social classes? They surely indicate that lust is contagious, and that Calisto's obsessive desire for Melibea's body influences both their servants' (¿Cómo interpretar estos nexos sexuales entre miembros de clases distintas? Seguramente indican que la lujuria es contagiosa, y que el deseo obsesionado de Calisto por el cuerpo de Melibea influye en los criados de ambos).[70] While it is true that Calisto and Melibea's furtive trysts have served as an incentive to the immoral desires of their servants, it is also evident that the constant interrelationship of Melibea with Celestina and the servants has precipitated their loss of respect for her, to the extent that Lucrecia can now emulate her mistress's desire for Calisto, and Sempronio fantasize possessing Melibea, his own master's lover.

The *Celestina* exposes the dangers young women face who are insufficiently protected from the immorality which surrounds them. The novel's dramatic irony is evident in its choice of punishment for the two lovers' illicit passion: leaving Melibea's side to investigate a noise outside, Calisto accidentally falls to his death from the garden wall; mourning his death, Melibea throws herself from a tower, dying at the feet of her bereaved father. The *Celestina*'s moral point is well taken by the female picaresque novels, which measure their heroines' moral downfall by the physical freedom the novels allow them, yet which are careful to restrict the *pícara* to her own social milieu. This is not, however, to agree with those who see in the first exemplar of the female picaresque, Francisco Delicado's *La lozana andaluza*, a realistic portrayal of its protagonist or its time.[71] Rather, the dissembling discourse of the *pícara* should be measured against her author's increasing didacticism, from its beginning carnivalesque blitheness to its final global significance (Bubnova 152).

The *Celestina*'s tragic ending, as well as its portentous first act, in which Calisto meets Melibea when he rashly enters her walled garden while hawking, are vividly recalled in the first chapter of *La Lozana andaluza*. The sexual symbolism of the hunt and the lover's intrusion into the *hortus conclusus* are echoed in the later work by Lozana's significant loss of blood when she scales a wall without her mother's consent:

[W]hile scaling a wall without her mother's permission, she spilled the first blood from her sex.

[Saltando una pared sin licencia de su madre, se le derramó la primera sangre que del natural tenía. (*LA*, I.176)]

Lozana's 'escaped' menstrual blood, a metaphor for her early loss of virginity, signifies her attempt to escape her mother's example, whose *pleitos*, or money squabbles, like the father's contested will over his whoring and gambling, point to the young girl's picaresque legacy. She leaves Seville with her Italian merchant lover for Marseille, where the lover's father abandons her with only a ring hidden in her mouth, a folkloric motif of the sexual economy she will engage in. Once in Rome, she heads to the Pozo Blanco district known for its Spanish prostitutes, setting up housekeeping with Rampín, a *pícaro* who will act as her pimp, servant, and lover. Although Lozana is most successful in her new occupation, her social position has already been determined both by birth and by her loss of virginity. The blood spilled in the garden symbolizes besides the social rupture she experiences in Rome: as a procuress and as a prostitute, she remains always with her own kind.

In *La Lozana andaluza*, the polarity between 'good' women and those of little virtue is textually noted by the comparison between the two Roman matrons whom Lozana encounters during her first outing in the city:

LOZANA: Oh, those two women are so beautiful! By my life, they look like matrons; I've never seen anything so honest, nor so decent.
RAMPÍN: They are Roman nobles.
LOZANA: Then why are they walking so alone?
RAMPÍN: That is their custom. When they go out, they accompany each other, unless one goes out by herself, and then she takes a servant, but she never goes out with a man, nor with more than one woman, even though she is the noblest in Rome. And notice that they walk quietly, and although they might see someone they know, they do not speak to him on the street, but instead, the others become silent and move aside, and the matrons do not bow their heads nor change their stride, even if the others are their fathers or husbands.

[LOZANA: ... Oh ¡qué lindas son aquellas dos mujeres! Por mi vida, que son como matronas; no he visto en mi vida cosa más honrada, ni más honesta.
RAMPÍN: Son romanas principales.
LOZANA: Pues ¿cómo van tan solas?
RAMPÍN: Porque ansí lo usan. Cuando van ellas fuera, unas a otras se acompañan, salvo cuando va una sola, que lleva una sierva, mas no hombres, ni más mujeres, aunque sea la mejor de Roma. Y mirá que van sesgas; y aunque vean a uno que conozcan, no le hablan en la calle, sino que se apartan ellos y callan, y ellas no abajan cabeza ni hacen mudanzas, aunque sea su padre ni su marido. (*LA*, XVIII: 257)]

The contrast between Lozana, recently arrived in Rome, and already walking the streets busily chatting with her future lover, and the aloof Roman matrons, silently going about their business, is striking. Unlike the rest of the characters who populate the novel, the noblewomen never interact with Lozana, and are only mentioned once. Treated with uncommon respect by the author, they signify his concern with maintaining order among the different social classes, and exemplify besides his own beliefs as to how matrons should behave.

In contrast, Delicado humorously relates Lozana's sexual encounters in scurrilous detail. *La pícara Justina* was to emphasize that the picaresque genre should be viewed solely as entertainment, and most of the female picaresque novels gloss over the weighty social issues of poverty and criminality central to the male picaresque tradition. Although Delicado had revised his earlier version of *La Lozana andaluza* to incorporate the sack of Rome in 1527 as divine punishment for the city's wickedness, he deceptively casts a benevolent eye on his protagonist's sinful business – so much so that the ending, which carries out the motif of separation first indicated by her literal and moral fall, is primarily a happy one. We find Lozana tired of her life as whore and procuress: 'I'm tired of fixing whores to pass as virgins' (estoy harta de meter barboquejos a putas [*LA*, LXVI: 481]). She is wealthy and ready to isolate herself willingly from society by retiring with the faithful Rampín.

Yet Lozana's carefree life, which culminates with the couple on the island of Lipari – a well-known literary *locus* for lovers – barely conceals the many tensions within the text.[72] Delicado proudly proclaims the mimetic excellence of his novel, whose earthy language and vivid descriptions, he claims, accurately capture the amoral ambiance of the Roman underworld. Lozana's experiences as a whore fittingly take place in the Roman districts known for prostitution; indeed, while the text clearly exaggerates the numbers of prostitutes in Rome at the time as 30,000, the 1526 census attests to 4,900 prostitutes among a total population of 55,035 spread throughout the city's districts – an alarming ratio of one prostitute to every ten residents.[73] However, Lozana can hardly be considered a real woman, since her life is far too idealized to be taken as a realistic representation. Delicado's romantic depiction of the *pícara*'s adventures skilfully disguises the actual conditions in which she lives. A careful reading of the text, however, reveals that, while Lozana appears to take advantage of her customers, it is she who must be constantly on her guard to protect herself from her customers, who would not hesitate to leave without paying for her services. Lozana cannot allow herself to trust anyone: her relations with Rampín disclose her need for human contact as much as they celebrate Lozana's voracious sexual appetite. And although she is insistently described as graceful and lovely, her small nose and the scars on her forehead are not physical manifestations of beauty, as she would have us believe, but the ravages of venereal disease. Lozana's beauty, her shrewd business sense, and her keen enjoyment of sex, then, are qualities wilfully exaggerated by the author to delight his male audience.

Clearly overrating Lozana's qualities as a vivacious free spirit, Delicado restricts the *pícara* to her profession. Although the young Lozana ardently desires financial independence, she can obtain it only by moving up from whore to procuress; both occupations, however, require that she remain in the low-life milieu of Roman prostitution. When she is compared to the legendary pimp Zoppino, known for his corruption of young girls, Lozana retorts that she has never abused her expertise as a procuress for anyone evil enough to harm an innocent person. In her own version of thieves' honour, she proudly notes that she has limited her activities to those already in the trade:

I can go everywhere with my face uncovered, as I have not committed any vile deed, or acted as go-between or given a message to an evil person ... And if anyone wants to write about me, he may say this of me: Lozana had much more wisdom than she revealed.

[Yo puedo ir con mi cara descubierta por todo, que no hice jamás vileza, ni alcaguetería ni mensaje a persona vil ... Y esto se dirá de mí, si alguno me querrá poner en fábula: muncho supo la Lozana, más que no demostraba. (LA, XV.366–7)]

Lozana is further constrained by her Jewish origins, as she joins other *conversas* in the Pozo Blanco district who recognize their common religious background: 'By your life, she's one of us!' (Por tu vida, que es *de nostris*! [LA, VIII: 200]). Yet Delicado does not blame Lozana's lifestyle on religious persecution: she did not leave Spain for religious reasons, and her ties to Judaism imply as well her 'otherness' as woman and as prostitute.[74] Since it is most unlikely that the percentage of Spanish prostitutes of either Moorish or Jewish descent was any higher than those of Old Christian stock, the author portrays Lozana as a *conversa* to further isolate her from society. The text makes use of the literary archetype of the 'dark woman' to highlight Lozana's sensual nature, thereby justifying her choice of profession. Both her social class and her inherent sensuality collude to separate her from 'decent' society: though a Cordoban by birth, Lozana sets up trade in Rome, a city whose reputation as Babylon, as city of whores, reflects upon her own choice of action and confirms her segregation.

Neither does the female picaresque recognize the consequences to women of their restricted social roles; it signals instead the the dangers that women pose to society as conceptualized by the genre's male authors. Writing before the Counter-Reformation, Delicado confirms his liberality in his apology: 'How the author apologizes at the end of the Portrait of the Lozana, lauding women' (Como se escusa el autor en la fin del Retrato de la Lozana, en laude de las mujeres) by recommending reasonable moderation to both men and women in their sexual relationships. Nevertheless, he should be taken at his word when he states that only the fear of God differentiates good women from wicked:

And since women know they are men's solace and their recreation, they think and do what they would not if only they had the principle of wisdom, which is to fear the Lord, and whoever achieves this wisdom or intelligence is more precious than any diamond, and therefore, whoever does not, is very wicked.

[Y como las mujeres conocen ser solacio a los hombres y ser su recreación común, piensan y hacen lo que no harían si tuviesen el principio de la sapiencia, que es temer al Señor, y la que alcanza esta sapiencia o inteligencia es más preciosa que ningún diamante, y ansí por el contrario muy vil. (*LA*, 484)]

Lozana's three names trace her development from the young, lower-class prostitute, Aldonza, to one who lives from her looks, Lozana (or beautiful), to, finally, Vellida (or long-haired), a pointed reference to the Magdalen. Rather than interpret Lozana's last name as a sacrilegious parody of Mary Magdalen, as Allaigre does, we may see it as Delicado's ironic commentary on her sinful life ('Introducción' 152).

Thomas Hanrahan points out that the anti-feminism of the female picaresque stems more from the genre's role as an ascetic and didactic literature of the Counter-Reformation than from medieval misogynist writings. He rightly concludes that, while the medieval tradition and the female picaresque both ultimately view women as 'seductive, lascivious, and avaricious,' the female picaresque's anti-feminism was meant to have a far more serious purpose than to censure women. It was directed instead towards the instruction and reformation of the most important member of society – the male (Hanrahan 1.85ff.). In its warning against women, *La Lozana andaluza* anticipates the shift in focus from the medieval reprobation of women's moral weakness to the later female picaresque novels' emphasis on virtue as a uniquely male quality.

In seeming contradiction to the *Lozana* yet, as Bruno Damiani has suggested, surely influenced by it, López de Ubeda's heroine, the *pícara* Justina, plays to the reader's sympathies by relating her adventures as a virginal peasant girl who constantly foils her suitors' attempts to seduce her.[75] But all the puns and euphemisms she coyly uses when referring to herself belie her innocence and point to her role as that of the prostitute she undoubtedly represents. Ironically naming her for the inviolable virgin, Saint Justina, a name neatly conflating Seville's virgin martyrs, Justa and Rufina, the author pointedly assigns Justina such picaresque characteristics as her probable *converso* origins, and her childhood experiences at her parents' inn, where she first learns to steal from the customers. The novel, which follows Justina's rise as a rogue, her travels to several Spanish towns, and her marriages, imitates the format of the *Guzmán de Alfarache* with its picaresque chapters followed by a moral coda, or *aprovechamiento*, of little relevance. Given its contrived plot, critics have long debated whether *La pícara Justina* should even be considered a picaresque novel, rather than a parody of the *Guzmán de Alfarache* or a roman-à-clef of the court of Philip III. Marcel Bataillon, for example, views the novel as a sarcastic reply to the seriousness of the picaresque, appropriating its format in order to satirize the concerns of the privileged classes.[76] Bataillon accurately points out that, in the chapter on Justina's so-called pilgrimage to León, López de Ubeda is less interested in realistically depicting the peasant girl's misadventures than in parodying Philip III's recent visit to that city, in which López de Ubeda most likely took part (125 ff.). Another critic, José Miguel Oltra Tomás, accepting Francisco Márquez Villanueva's identification of Perlícaro as a veiled reference to Mateo Alemán, sees the narrative both as an anti-picaresque novel, mocking Alemán and Cristóbal Pérez de Herrera's social concerns, and as an attack on Rodrigo Calderón.[77] Yet, although López de Ubeda may intend the novel to comment on the immediate realities of the Spanish court, his views of women must be seen in the context of its patriarchal system. Even though he appropriates long-standing misogynist values, by breaking with the male picaresque tradition and casting a woman as the protagonist, *La pícara Justina*'s author reveals his own concerns about women's role in society.

While Delicado blames Lozana's faults on her lowly social origins, López de Ubeda is quick to condemn Justina's feminine nature as well. In Justina's constant defence of her equivocal virtue, López de Ubeda establishes a parallel between all 'good' women and the whore, since she argues that her weaknesses are common to all women, and openly warns the reader of their perfidy:

Note the false tears of a woman; the astuteness of a virgin; the greed of a young girl, her deceptions and lies, and everything will be a lesson and a warning to you.

[Nota las falsas lágrimas de una muger: la astucia de una doncella, la codicia de una mozuela, sus embustes y mentiras y todo te servirá de escarmiento y de aviso. (*PJ*, II: 670)]

López de Ubeda's ironic depiction of the poor, innocent Justina, therefore, results in a much stronger condemnation of women than Delicado's comparatively candid admission of a prostitute's experiences.
Uneasily conflating the prostitute and the virgin, the author at times
blames Justina's weaknesses on her legacy from Eve, as the first woman,
and other times on the direct picaresque inheritance from her mother; in
both cases, constantly undermining Justina's seeming virtuousness.
Thus, while at the last Justina refuses to continue the narrative ostensibly so as not to bore the reader with her virginal tale ('I'm right in
believing that the long story of my virginal state will bore you' [justo es
que piense que la larga historia de mi virginal estado te dará fastidio: *PJ*
II: 739]), she has conveniently forgotten the double-entendre at the
beginning of her story, where she describes her dubious family origins:

Don't be horrified – I had a drummer grandfather whose members were never
still; you'll see me lean towards the fluted many times; this shouldn't come as
anything new, since I had a flutist grandfather and it seems like I was born with
the flute inserted in me – I enjoy it so much.

[No te espantes, que tuve abuelo tamboritero a quien no le holgava miembro;
verásme echar muchas veces por lo flautado; no se te haga nuevo, que tuve
abuelo flautista y parece nací con la flauta inserta en el cuerpo según gusto de
ella (*PJ*, I: 184)]

Justina's picaresque beginnings, her life as a whore, and her future as a
go-between are all borne out in the various sexual meanings of the term
'flute,' which represents both the phallus and the sexual act arranged by
a go-between, as well as the go-between herself. As a literary *pícara*, Justina cannot escape from her lowly origins; neither, as a woman, can she
run away from masculine control. By blaming Justina's moral frailty on
both her mother and Eve – on her social and natural conditions – the
author reveals his own uncertain attitudes towards all women. But,
most important, by admitting his belief in man's 'higher' nature, he
attempts to justify the need for masculine control of the 'weaker' sex not
only to himself, but to society as well.

López de Ubeda discloses his perception of male superiority by continually ascribing Justina's talkative nature and her constant movement
both to her maternal legacy and to her inherently feminine condition. As
a *pícara*, Justina traces her lineage from a long line of *pícaros* on her
mother's side whose shady occupations of puppeteer, mask vendor,

musician, and barber have all contributed to her gadabout and gossipy character:

Oh, brother reader! I meant to persuade you not to be surprised if in the narrative you not only find me a gabber in keeping with the inheritance you saw in the previous chapter, but also a frenzied jumper, skipper, dancer, jigger, since, as you'll see in the present chapter, this too I inherited from my mother.

[¡Ay hermano lector! Iba a persuadirte que no te admires si en el discurso de mi historia me vieres, no sólo parlona, en cumplimiento de la herencia que viste en el número pasado, pero loca saltadera, brincadera, bailadera, gaitera, porque, como verás en el número presente, es también herencia de madre (I: 183)]

To substantiate his claim that Justina, as a woman, comes to this inheritance naturally, López de Ubeda bases himself on biblical authority. Slyly parodying Genesis, he insists that women owe their loudness and their footloose nature to Eve's having been created from Adam's rib. In her own version of the biblical story, Justina assures us that, since Adam begged Eve not to rest until she found his missing rib, Eve's descendants are obliged to continue her futile search:

And for this reason, since the first woman went about clamouring, all women sound their horns, and as they can never find anyone with a rib to spare, they are naturally inclined to wander about in search of Adam's rib, looking for men with an extra one.

[Y de aquí les vino a las mujeres que, como la primera iba pregonando ellas salen vocineras, y como nunca acaban de hallar quien tenga una costilla de más, nacen inclinadas a andar en busca de la costilla y viendo si hallan hombres con alguna costilla de sobra. (PJ I: 247)]

The burlesque tone of the narrative does nothing to conceal the text's seriousness; rather, it confirms an anti-feminism so entrenched that it would allow a comical reading of the Bible, despite Justina's disclaimer that the anecdote is 'blasphemy only for those who believe it' (PJ, I: 247).

La pícara Justina resolves the problem of woman's freedom through marriage; according to the author, her motivation, like all women's, is not love but greed. Since she marries only men of her own station, Justina does not represent all women: she maintains the social separation seen earlier in La Lozana andaluza. Justina's three marriages therefore underscore López de Ubeda's hesitation in unequivocally condemning all women, whether 'decent' or not. However, by plotting these repeated marriages – the last to the infamous *pícaro* Guzmán de Alfarache – the author doubts the effectiveness of marriage to reform the protagonist, and by implication, questions its power as a social institution to protect society fully from the moral weaknesses of all women.

Justina's several marriages may indeed restrain the *pícara* from her compulsive wandering, at least for a time. Her talkative and gossipy nature, however, appears uncontrollable and undiminished throughout the narrative. Since the power of language as a means of self-expression and self-determination is central to the issue of authorial control, *La pícara Justina* must somehow account for women's talkative nature while delimiting its use by Justina. Both Vives and Fray Luis de León had earlier stressed silence as a cardinal virtue of the Christian woman, with the latter cleverly drawing an analogy between her closed mouth and the enclosed state in which she should ideally remain:

Because, as nature ... determined that women should remain enclosed, guarding the home, so it required them to keep their mouth closed.

[Porque, así como la naturaleza ... hizo a las mujeres para que encerradas guardasen la casa, así las obligó a que cerrasen la boca.][78]

Justina, however, is never at a loss for words; her loquacious nature becomes a part of the female condition which the author consciously parodies in his garrulous tale.[79] He discounts Justina's extraordinary verbal ability by attributing it yet again to her legacy from Eve, in the process imputing man's fall to Eve's purported abuse of language ('[D]el cuerpo de Eva heredamos las mujeres ... parlar de gana, aunque sea con serpientes ...' – From the body of Eve we women inherit our ... incessant chatter, if only with serpents ... [*PJ*, I: 181–2]). Ironically, since the author speaks through Justina's persona, he cannot silence his heroine without rendering mute his own voice. López de Ubeda appropriates Justina's language by superimposing his own discourse upon the prostitute's unlearned speech. The author's control of his protagonist's language is demonstrated in the puns, amphibologies, and complex conceits Justina delights in, yet which are hardly consonant with her illiterate village background.

Thus, while appearing to celebrate Justina's freedom and her linguistic ability, *La pícara Justina* decries women's attempts to liberate themselves from male control. Whether by regulating women's voice or actions, the authors of the picaresque impose male standards upon women, using their female literary characters as illustrations of their own social prejudices. Like Lozana's, Justina's questionable ancestry may be 'tainted' with Jewish blood, but her author is not so concerned with presenting Justina's dark sensuality as he is with satirizing the Spanish obsession with proving one's *limpieza de sangre* (cleanliness of blood). The Counter-Reformation, with its insistence upon the determinism of sin and the moral frailty of all women, provides the backdrop for *La pícara Justina*. In the paranoid atmosphere of a Spain rigorously controlled by the Inquisition, Justina stands, not for a marginalized group of conversos or *moriscos*, but for everyone's social fears of the 'other' (Bataillon 215–43). Similarly, her assumed virginity is an invisible symbol whose precariousness marks all women; her freedom, a literary ruse by which the author again condemns them all. Yet, like *La Lozana andaluza*, *La pícara Justina* also maintains the separation of the *pícara* from the rest of society by setting her as an example of how women ought not to behave (and by pointing out the fate in store for the unmindful):

In this book the virgin will come to know the cause of her perdition, the dangers a libertine woman exposes herself to when she does not accept the advice of others.

[En este libro hallará la doncella el conocimiento de su perdición, los peligros en que se pone una libre mujer que no se rinde al consejo de otros. (*PJ*, I: 76]

The more liberated the protagonist of a female picaresque novel, therefore, the stronger the condemnation by its author of women in general, and the more insistent the warnings of the potential hazards in permitting both 'decent' and 'indecent' women to interact without any differentiation.

The hazards of unconstrained prostitution are illustrated most forcefully in *La hija de la Celestina* by Alonso Jerónimo de Salas Barbadillo. Narrated in the third person, the novel assumes the pretense of a woman's discourse only when Elena relates her genealogy. Otherwise, her story is told from its inception by a stern moralist who passes swift and certain judgment on his literary creation. The narrative begins with the wedding of a young and dissolute nobleman, Don Sancho, hastily arranged by his rich uncle to put an end to the youth's scandalous behaviour. Elena, the *pícara* of the story, together with her pimp and lover, Montúfar, proceeds to bilk the rich old man by accusing Don Sancho of raping her, convincing the old man by showing him a dagger Elena had previously taken from a servant, who in turn had stolen it from the nephew. The picaresque plot can unfold only when Elena flaunts her beauty in complete freedom and mobility, since she must pass herself off as a wronged virtuous noblewoman to the uncle. Upon seeing Elena in Toledo, the young nobleman falls desperately in love in her, destroying the social stability sought by the uncle through the arranged marriage. Yet what at first seems a *caveat* against arranged marriages turns out to be a strongly worded directive against prostitution:

The other Don Sancho's wife's previous suitor pined for the new spouse, she, for the ingrate by her side – whom she loved truly, and whose moral weakness she had found out – and he, for the fleeing Elena; and of the three, the one who truly deserved his grave suffering was the sad, the sorrowful don Sancho since, although he lay in the decent and beautiful arms of his wife, he desired those of a wicked whore, who had been and was common fodder to all, giving herself cheaply to all those who showed the slightest interest.

[El otro suspiraba por la desposada, ella por el ingrato que tenía al lado—a quien amaba con verdad de corazón, y le había conocido la tibieza de la voluntad – y él por la fugitiva Elena; y entre los tres, quien justamente merecía grave pena, era el triste, el infeliz don Sancho pues pudiendo descansar en los honestos y hermosos brazos de su mujer, codiciaba los de una vil ramera que había sido y era pasto común, entregándose por bajos precios a todos aquellos que con medianas diligencias la pretendían. (*HC*, 70)]

Don Sancho's untimely desire for Elena is clearly to blame for the disruption of a potentially happy marriage between two social equals. Yet, while male desire sets the narrative in motion, it is Elena, as the untrammelled prostitute fleeing with Montúfar through the countryside, who propels the novel to its close. Although Don Sancho at first chases after Elena, he eventually returns repentant to his forgiving wife and wealthy uncle. Elena, desirous of reaching Madrid where she can earn more money on her own, attempts to escape from Montúfar's control. He catches her, ties her to a tree, beats her, and releases her only when he is certain that she will not try to escape again. Significantly, the male author shifts his focus from a critique of male desire as the cause of social destabilization, to the condemnation of the prostitute. The actions of the four main characters in the novel are to be read normatively, since each character represents a particular social position. Thus, the differences between Don Sancho and Montúfar are mainly of social class; their actions are eminently acceptable under the male code of behaviour for each social group. Don Sancho's lack of resolve is presented as an unintentional slip brought about by Elena's diabolical beauty, while Montúfar's violent behaviour is a direct result of Elena's treachery. The two women, Don Sancho's wife and Elena, are also of different social class, but Don Sancho's wife conforms to her role of the patiently suffering wife, whereas Elena undertakes to lead her own life. While the wife is rewarded with her husband's love, Elena must endure Montúfar's wrath as punishment for her short-lived independence. Despite the difference in their roles – the virtuous wife in opposition to the wily whore – both are defined by male expectations of women, and their behaviour is condoned or condemned accordingly.

The violent denouement of the narrative is Salas Barbadillo's final and most devastating criticism of Elena's attempts to liberate herself from masculine control. Montúfar, after marrying Elena and pandering her to wealthy men in order to support the two in style, again beats her unmercifully when she refuses to ignore the attentions of a young street tough. When he realizes she has served him a dish of poisoned cherries in revenge, Montúfar threatens her with his sword but is stabbed through the heart instead by the young tough. The youth is hanged for his troubles, and Elena garrotted, placed in a wooden barrel, and tossed into the river Manzanares. Elena's punishment is Salas Barbadillo's eloquent commentary not only on the picaresque life, but, more specifically, on the *pícara*'s endeavours to interact freely with all levels of society.

The female picaresque novels all acknowledge their debt to the *Celestina* by making repeated references to the primary text. Lozana's house is extolled as the place where 'Calisto worshipped, ... Melibea is not valued, ... Celestina counts for nothing' (idolatró Calisto, ... no se estima Melibea, ... poco vale Celestina), while Justina exhorts the reader to listen to her story: 'listen and you'll hear the exploits of another Celestina' (escucha y oyrás las hazañas de otra Celestina) – and *La hija de la Celestina* is most obvious in its title, which names Elena the 'daughter' of Celestina. These three novels, however, have learned the social lesson taught by the older narrative. Despite the licentiousness of their language, both *La Lozana andaluza* and *La pícara Justina* portray only the illusion of liber-

ated discourse. The authors reveal their power by their implicit judgment of the circumstances in which they place the female protagonists.
While *La hija de la Celestina* is the most explicitly punitive of the novels
discussed, even *La Lozana andaluza*, with its reminder of the sack of
Rome, pressures Lozana to flee from Rome and give up her sinful life. *La
pícara Justina* ends with Justina's dubious marriage to the more significant literary *pícaro* Guzmán de Alfarache, who, as Justina's author well
knew, narrates his own life from a watchtower where he espies everyone's vices and foibles. All three *pícaras*, then, are forced to delimit their
range of action in accordance with male-defined boundaries.

By taking the *Celestina* as their model, the authors of the female picaresque accept its premise that unrestrained immorality poses a serious
threat to society. The *pícara*'s ironic homology to the prostitute becomes
especially evident as woman's domination is attempted through containment. As Perry makes clear, prostitution ritualized the confrontation
of 'money and morals, purity and evil, rich and poor, Church and
state.' The ongoing dialogue, she explains, 'led to an evolution from
toleration of sexual commerce to institutionalization and then on to
intensification of control' (*Gender and Control* 143–4). As I have argued of
the male picaresque and the various discourses of poverty, these dia-
logues on prostitution – which also inform the ideologies on poverty –
included the female picaresque. The solution they adopt not only illustrates their awareness of the social importance of legalized prostitution
as a means of maintaining the status quo, but also reveals to the reader
the authors' own historically conditioned prejudices against women,
and the strategies through which these prejudices become ideology. The
trajectory of the female picaresque moves from the dangerously inte-
ractive society of the *Celestina* to the enclosure of the prostitute and her
separation from the rest of society, to the final erasure of differences
between all women, whether virgins or whores. Either as pure or
defiled, the woman is viewed by the male-dominated society as a necessary evil who must be controlled by the governing institutions. The sexual specificity of that control signifies the danger she presents to society
– woman's sexuality threatens constantly to disrupt the male order.

As such, women's sexuality is a social factor to be repressed, bartered,
and controlled by the male structures of power. In like manner,
woman's voice is suppressed, dominated, and exchanged for the male's.
In its mimicry of what the authors construe as female discourse, the
female picaresque, while claiming to assume a feminine voice, in actuality bespeaks male prejudice, formulating a cultural strategy through

which sexual and social reality is created and maintained. By implicitly condemning the purported freedom of the *pícara*, the genre sanctions only such legally constrained sexual behaviour as benefits the social order – but it also succeeds in continually defining that order to male specifications. The authors of the female picaresque fabricate their own male identity as surely as they create the persona of the *pícara*. Moreover, in repressing and controlling the female picaresque as literary corpus, they demonstrate that women's bodies must be dominated and disciplined for the public good.

5

From *Pícaro* to Soldier

The soldier was someone who could be recognized from afar; he bore certain signs: the natural signs of his strength and his courage, the marks, too, of his pride; his body was the blazon of strength and valour; and although it is true that he had to learn the profession of arms little by little – generally in actual fighting – movements like marching and attitudes like the bearing of the head belonged for the most part to a bodily rhetoric of honour.

Michel Foucault, *Discipline and Punish*

I'm off to the wars for the want of pence;
If I had any money I'd have more sense.

[A la guerra me lleva mi necesidad;
Si tuviera dineros, no fuera, en verdad.]

Don Quixote de la Mancha

As but one instance of the 'refeudalization' that obtains at the beginning of the seventeenth century, Sor Magdalena's stern measures for the women's *galera* contributed to the re-establishment of a conservative social order based primarily on hierarchy and privilege. The discipline imposed on prostitutes adhered to an archaic pattern of control endorsing renunciation of the body over its utility (Foucault, *Discipline*, 137). The return, in disciplining the social body, to violent and ritualistic systems of power that countermanded proposals such as Pérez de

Herrera's *Amparo de pobres*, which admitted some measure of class mobility, would also signal the failure of emergent capitalism in early modern Spain. Classical France, Foucault claims, transformed its previous 'economy of visibility' into a new 'bio-power' combining disciplinary techniques with regulative methods that, among other consequences, normalized society by training bodies and controlling populations (*History of Sexuality* 140–1). In Spain, however, since the numerous state apparatuses (educational, military, industrial, or medical) remained either stymied or restricted, new systems of power were thwarted early on.[1]

The Spanish war machine, while arguably the most imposing of the state apparatuses, attempted control of its recruits' physical bodies without, however, intending their improvement and transformation through 'projects of docility.' The *pícaros* and the poor enslaved in Spanish *galeras* are thus enjoined from developing into the 'docile' bodies manipulated and mechanicized by the subtly coercive disciplinary institutions that, according to Foucault, led to greater mastery over life processes (*Discipline* 136–8; *History* 142–5). Neither did the impoverished recruits resemble the warrior's elegant figure described by him in this chapter's epigraph; the pikers and other infantrymen conscripted into the Hapsburg armies usually march off bedraggled and, if they do not desert or perish in battle, return to civilian life maimed and embittered. Warfare, then as now, provided the nation-state with an unparalleled opportunity to rid itself of the unwanted even as its armies exploited the poor to sustain and expand its dominions.[2]

Spain's renowned *tercios*, or troops of 3,000 soldiers apiece, were dependent on their size to retain and exercise their strength. Gonzalo de Córdoba, the Great Captain, had revolutionized the Spanish army by fortifying the infantry and reorganizing their formation. Equipping the soldiers with better armour and offensive weapons, Elliott states, made them superior to the feared Swiss, creating a professional army whose skill would rebound to Spain's military glory (*Imperial Spain* 133). By 1534, the army was composed of heavy and light brigades, artillery, and an infantry of pikers and harquebusiers. The infantry in particular relied heavily on soldiers from the Empire's diverse regions, as well as on German mercenaries. The bulk of the fighting was carried out by the *tercios*, divided into 12 companies of 250 soldiers led by captains.[3] Foucault concludes that this formation, which had gained Spain considerable fame in the early Renaissance, became outdated and ineffectual in the seventeenth century:

In an army of pikes and muskets – low, imprecise, practically incapable of select-ing a target and taking aim – troops were used as a projectile, a wall or a fortress: 'the formidable infantry of the army of Spain'; the distribution of soldiers in this mass was carried out above all according to their seniority and volume, of giv-ing density to the body, were the least experienced; in front, at the angles and on the flanks, were the bravest or reputedly most skillful soldiers. (*Discipline* 162)

Although artillery and firearms soon transformed the methods of con-ducting war, military technology had still not advanced sufficiently to eliminate the pike as the main weapon, since the unwieldy harquebuses and muskets took too much time to load. The harquebus, greatly improved in the early 1500s, ensured the battle of Pavia's success and Francis I's imprisonment.[4] Nonetheless, the Spanish *tercios*, which, unlike the artillery, received their armaments directly from Spain, relied on two pikers for every harquebusier until the Duke of Alba established parity among the two groups (Fernández Alvarez and Díaz Medina 247). Braudel estimates that it was not until the end of the seventeenth century, when muskets were replaced by rifles and bayonets adopted, that the double nature of the infantry was finally eliminated.[5]

It was due precisely to the *tercio*'s continued need for footsoldiers and pikers – a term often given as the etymological root of *pícaro* – that the poor were coerced into service. The soldiers flanking the *tercios* personi-fied the *miles gloriosus* who made his colourful appearance provoca-tively dressed in bright clothes and plumed hat, his sword at the ready, in the literature of the period. Ridiculed for their exaggerated dress at a time when Philip II had imposed black as the leading court colour, Spanish soldiers were often called by the Italian word for parrot, 'papa-gallo.'[6] But if the soldiers in the Duke of Alba's 1567 expedition to the Netherlands flaunted their princely attire, Geoffrey Parker cites the Duke of Parma's complaint, ten years later, decrying the shameful spec-tacle of a Spanish *tercio* recently arrived from Italy, 'not only without arms but also without proper clothes.'[7] The following comment, by an observer in Turin of a 1620 contingent of recruits, is worth quoting in full:

Those in the first two ranks were good enough, with a martial spirit about them, but the rest were poor boys between 16 and 20 years old, sickly and ill-clothed, the majority without hats or shoes. Their carts are already full of sick men, although they have only been on the march five days, and I firmly believe that ... before they reach Burgundy half of them will fall by the wayside.[8]

The distinction drawn between the officers who continued the medieval code of chivalry and the professional soldiers prideful of their military status called *particulares*, versus conscripted pikers and other footsoldiers, became an issue heatedly debated by *arbitristas*.[9] By 1647, Diego Henríquez de Villegas had written of the lassitude of the Spanish nobility:

How few imitate today their brave progenitors! How few occupy themselves in worthy efforts! How few gfive themselves to glorious battles! How few strive for immortality through memorble exploits! If noble blood obliges one to execute glorious acts, what do nobles do at court? How can the illustrious blood that gave invincibler life to the body of Spain now amuse itself going for walks?

[Que pocos imitan oy a los esclarecidos varones de que proceden? Que pocos se emplean en honrosos sudores? Que pocos se entregan a gloriosas fatigas? Que pocos solicitan con memorables hechos la inmortalidad de sus nombres? Si la obligacion de buena sangre induce a acciones glorioss, Que hazen en la Corte los hombres generosos? La ilustre sangre, que animo el cuerpo de España con vida invencible, como se diuierte en el passeo? (Henríquez de Villegas 4–5)]

He divides soldiers into *naturales* (those from the same province as their lord), *no-naturales* (from the same country, but different kingdoms), and the *extranjeros*, or foreigners. He states that since the *extranjero* is 'forced to serve, involuntarily, and obeys despite himself and not for love, he hates to leave his home, [and] finds it bothersome to spend too much time in the military' [sirue forçado, y no voluntario, obedece violentado y no por amor, aborrece el alexarse de su casa; tiene por molesto perseverar mucho tiempo en la milicia (Henríquez de Villegas 44)].

Pérez de Herrera proposes that the poor be trained for military service:

By removing [the poor] from the indolence and sloth in which they live, and training them in the use of arms, they can serve in the military, at least as sailors and labourers ... and when [young boys] become of age, according to their ability, they can be assigned to duty on land or sea ... and if reared with virtue and honour, they will make very good soldiers and sailors.

[[Q]ue, quitándoles [a los pobres] de aquel ocio y pereza en que viven, y ejercitándoles en las armas, puedan servir en la milicia alguna parte della, por lo menos de marineros y gastadores y ... [los niños] en llegando a edad de muchachos, los pongan a oficios, y, conforme al talento que cada uno mostrare, se podrán escoger de allí para ejercicios de mar y tierra ... pues déstos podrá haber adelante muy buenos soldados y marineros, criándose con virtud y honra. (*Amparo* 173)]

Pérez de Herrera's utilitarian connection between the poor and the military may be discerned by tracing the picaresque narratives' enlarging focus, which takes the *pícaro* from begging and swindling throughout the Spanish countryside to the greater expanse of the Hapsburg theatres of war. Lazarillo's desire to remain in the good graces of the Archpriest so he might live comfortably in Toledo contrasts markedly with the bellicose attitudes of the mercenary soldier Estebanillo González, who is not averse to turning his back on Spain and fighting with the enemy when it suits him. The *pícaro*'s struggle for daily subsistence, initially confined to Castile, then delimited by Spain's borders and the Mediterranean basin, extends to his need to survive in the chaotic expanses of the broader Hapsburg Empire.

The homology between *pícaros* and soldiers becomes manifest in the situation that unfolded for the peasant and his urban counterpart, who could no longer rely on an honest means of local sustenance. Vagrancy and brigandage offered a solution, but as the war effort escalated, induction in military service seemed to provide an alternative. Yet, as Pérez de Herrera concedes, soldiers were subject to many more laws than civilians, endured all sorts of vicissitudes even when not in combat, and were discharged only at their superior's whim (*Amparo* 279). As we shall see in the soldiers' tales that stem initially from Lazarillo's localized narrative, the *pícaros* recruited into battle hold no illusions of articulating the 'rhetoric of honour' invoked in Foucault's depiction of seventeenth-century soldiers. Rather, in their strong criticism of Hapsburg military designs and of the treatment meted out to the recruits, these autobiographies ultimately sketch a far more realistic, if more cynical profile of Spanish soldiers.

The 'Other' and the Military Revolution

Most critics are disinclined to include soldiers' tales in the picaresque canon, and their position is valid if we take the picaresque solely as a literary development, with little regard to its social context or its historical base.[10] If, however, we consider that literary genres intersect not only with each other, but with contemporary non-literary discourses, and are affected by the material changes that occur at their inception, we gain a more profound understanding of generic change and development. Michael Murrin has cogently argued that the changes in military technology and their political and social consequences in turn caused a pivotal transformation in the production of literary genres. Charting the impact of what he calls the 'Gunpowder Revolution' on heroic literature, he states that poets faced a crisis that called into question both the code of heroic narrative and its future.[11] If traditional poets such as Boiardo overlooked or adapted to the early stages of this change, he claims, later military developments decisively affected the generic transformation from romance to epic. Appropriately, warriors in romances usually fought on horseback; in contrast, heroes of classical epics combatted on foot: 'Romance ... fits the old cavalry battles of the Middle Ages, while classical epic better accommodates the new styles of infantry fighting adopted by the English, Swiss, and Spanish. Tasso's heroes, accordingly, do most of their fighting on foot' (Murrin 13). Lepanto, fought on land and sea at close combat, inspired several epics, but because the Spanish fought on horseback in the New World, colonial poets like Alonso de Ercilla and Gaspar de Villagrá preferred the medieval code of chivalry, newly emphasizing the lone hero, but this time in his guise as military officer.[12] To Murrin's thesis, we should add that generic change was affected materially by the fluctuating numbers of soldiers available for recruitment. In Spain, conscription both contributed to and was influenced by the extensive depopulation caused by various plagues.[13] In the colonial period, then, soldiers fought on horseback not only because of the terrain, but also to make up for the lack of manpower. We can only speculate on the changes in literary production if whole armies had invaded the New World.

One significant similarity shared by the two genres, Murrin notes, is the increased preference for a historical approach, grounding both modes in recent military advancements to make the stories plausible, and blurring distinctions between strictly historical narratives and their own (14). When faced with the new technology of gunpowder, most poets of both genres responded negatively. Some, however, Camões and Ercilla among them, adopted what Murrin terms a 'modernist' position that combined the archaic chivalric code with a positive view of contemporary firearms (Murrin 124). For Cervantes, slated to be the last chronicler of romance fictions, the battle of Lepanto, in which he lost the use of a hand to a stray bullet, nevertheless remained the highlight of his military career. It should not surprise us, therefore, that, as Murrin claims, he would severely question the value of new military technology. Echoing Ariosto's sentiments in the *Orlando furioso*, Don Quixote fulminates against firearms, calling them the devil's own instruments:

Blessed were those ages that were without the dreadful fury of those diabolical engines of artillery, whose inventor, I truly believe, is now receiving in hell the reward for his devilish invention, by means of which a base and cowardly hand may deprive the most valiant knight of life.

[Bien hayan aquellos benditos siglos que carecieron de la espantable furia de aquestos endemoniados instrumentos de la artillería a cuyo inventor tengo para mí que en el infierno se le está dando el premio de su diabólica invención, con la cual dio causa que un infame y cobarde brazo quite la vida a un valeroso caballero. (*Don Quixote* I.38, 470–1)][14]

In one of his more lucid moments, the Don blames gunpowder for ruining his chances of achieving fame by dint of his valour and his sword:

I have a mind to say that I am grieved in my soul at having undertaken this profession of knight-errantry in so detestable an age as this we live in. For although no peril can daunt me, still it troubles me to think that powder and lead may deprive me of the chance of making myself famous and renowned for the strength of my arm and the edge of my sword over all the known earth.

[El alma me pesa de haber tomado este ejercicio de caballero andante en edad tan detestable como es ésta en que ahora vivimos; porque aunque a mí ningún peligro me pone miedo, todavía me pone recelo pensar si la pólvora y el estaño me han de quitar la ocasión de hacerme famoso y conocido por el valor de mi brazo y filos de mi espada. (*Don Quixote* I.38, 471)]

What we read between the lines, however, is his author's clever castigation of the chivalric code, mouthed by one of its most ardently erratic followers. Unlike Ariosto, who finds the gun 'unchivalric' in that it empowers evil men over good (Murrin 130), Cervantes's ironic criticism extends to warfare's elitist constellation – since Don Quixote articulates a soldier's complaint, not a commander's – and to the egotistical, self-serving motives behind men's military aspirations. By formulating the following rhetorical question, Cervantes, the inveterate soldier, has his ever-neophyte knight place the value of warfare seriously in doubt:

Now tell me, gentlemen, if you have ever considered it, how much fewer are those who have been rewarded by war than those who have perished in it? Without doubt you must answer that there is no comparison between them, for the dead are countless, whereas those who survive to win the rewards may be counted in numbers less than a thousand.

[Pero decidme, señores, si habéis mirado en ello: ¿cuán menos son los premiados por la guerra que los que han perecido en ella? Sin duda, habéis de responder, que no tienen comparación, ni se pueden reducir a cuenta los muertos, y que se podrán contar los premiados vivos con tres letras de guarismo. (*Don Quixote* I.38, 468)]

My brief synthesis of Murrin's complex and convincing arguments means only to draw attention to how profoundly historical changes influence generic development. It is not coincidental that heroic literature, whose major protagonists embody conventional military values, undergoes a radical transformation during the Renaissance; neither is it by chance that the picaresque, itself a new genre, also subsumes the discourses of soldiers who, for multiple reasons, desired to record their exploits. The Habsburg imperial expansion generated a vast and unprecedented paper trail, including eye-witness testimonies of voyages to and battles in both old and new worlds. As I proposed in the first chapter of this study, these narratives responded to more than the royal command for information. The sheer bulk of autobiographical writings reveal the authors' anxiety to inscribe themselves in history, to rehearse their experiences in a dauntingly and definitively changing world. Spain's encounters with its 'other' were reported in first-hand accounts by chroniclers ranging in rank from viceroys, ambassadors, and captains-general to missionaries and mercenaries.

The life of the *pícaro* thus gives way to soldiers' exploits in the military adventures of Jerónimo de Pasamonte (1605), Miguel de Castro (1613?), Captain Alonso de Contreras (1630), and Estebanillo González (1646).[15] Although Jerónimo de Pasamonte's *Vidas y trabajos* and Miguel de Castro's *Vida* are not, properly speaking, picaresque, at least two, the *Estebanillo González* and Alonso de Contreras's *Vida*, have been included in the canon. All these narratives, moreover, help us to formulate and compare the connections between soldiers' autobiographical narratives and the contemporary discourses of fictional rogue literature.[16] Even before these 'vidas y trabajos,' however, such episodes as Lazarillo's father's unwilling participation in the 'army against the Moors,' where he perishes along with his noble cavalry master, and Guzmán's sentence to the galleys forcefully confirm the correlation between soldiers' lives and the picaresque. One account in effect returns us to the mid-sixteenth century: the anonymous *Segunda parte del Lazarillo de Tormes*, published in Antwerp in 1555.

This 'second part' to the *Lazarillo* (reprinted in Milan in 1587 and 1615) cultivates the formal satirical tradition only alluded to by its more famous predecessor.[17] The text's disappearance from the canon may be due, not to the author's debatable talents as a writer, but to its fundamental structural differences with the narrative it purports to resume.[18] At a time when the *Lazarillo*'s protagonist exemplified the historical *pícaros* then deambulating from town to town, Lázaro's transformation from a complaisant cuckold to a sword-wielding tuna appears to deviate dramatically from the famished *pícaro*'s immediate materialist concerns as well as from any broader social satire. That his version was deemed an unacceptable continuation even by contemporaries is illustrated by Juan de Luna's 1620 continuation as a response to the first.[19] Yet the novel's curious plot, which narrates the story of Lázaro's undersea adventures with an army of tunafish, has been interpreted both as a cabalistic commentary on and a powerful critique of contemporary events.[20]

Although the *pícaro*'s satirical metamorphosis into a fish does not emulate any of the genre's conventional characteristics, it nonetheless adheres to the picaresque formula of distancing the protagonist from the reader's empathy. Indeed, the reader is twice distanced by the transformation: first, by the narrator's status as a poor soldier, then by his fabulous persona. The alienation that occurs thus doubly protects the reader from the unease felt at confronting the charges – however ironically formulated – brought forth for the first time and in the first person by a marginalized youth victimized by the very society now questioning his mode of survival. The *Segunda parte*'s interconnectedness with several picaresque motifs, therefore, is neither arbitrary nor far-fetched. Besides recalling the literary metamorphoses in Apuleius's *Golden Ass*, the allegorical depiction of the tuna-armies, aided by the soldier-fish Lázaro's contributions to their military prowess, advances a means of commenting on Hapsburg war strategies and military conduct.

One study assumes that Charles V's 1535 Tunisian expedition, where Lázaro's ship sinks, is also an allegory of both the battles fought in Argel in 1541 and Tripoli in 1551 (Saludo 29–30). The punning wordplay with Turks, Tunisia, the tuna-army, and *tunantes* would seem to confirm the allusion to the emperor's ongoing combat with the Ottoman Empire. Because these conflicts signalled Charles V's loss of Spanish North Africa (Elliott, *Imperial Spain*, 55), the *Segunda parte* has been posited as reflecting his mishandling of military tactics, and even as a direct attack on Charles V himself, who abdicated the same year the anonymous book was printed (Zwez 41). However, since the plot centres mainly on Lázaro's saviour, the tuna captain Licio, and the craven antics against him by the general Don Paver, the novel seems less a critique of the emperor than of those officers who treacherously abused their power and kept war spoils for themselves. When Lázaro rescues the school from certain death as they crowd into a cave, he rebukes the captain general for trying to save his own life above all others, contrasting his cowardice to the nobility of a Roman officer:

'Oh, captains!,' I said to myself, 'what little concern you have for others' lives in order to save yours! How many must behave in just such a way! ... And the first thing that [Roman commander Paulus Decius] did, when the battle started, was to place himself in the most dangerous part of the action so the others, and not he, could escape with their lives, and that is what happened. But not so with our captain tuna.'

[«¡Oh, capitanes!» dije yo entre mí, «qué poco caso hacen de las vidas ajenas por salvar las suyas! ¡Cúantos deben de hacer lo que éste hace! ... Y lo primero que procuró [Paulo Decio] comenzando la batalla, fue ponerse en parte tan peligrosa que no pudiese escapar con la vida, porque los suyos la hubiesen, y así la hubieron. Mas no le seguía en esto el nuestro general atún.» (*Segunda parte* 128)]

Yet, in this episode, and several others, the author laments the radical changes that, he believes, afflicted the Spanish military in its decline from an honourable tradition of military valour to a corrupt conduct driven by greed and the desire for power. The anonymous author's choice of topic, therefore, fully anticipates one of the major themes of seventeenth-century picaresque narratives: the role played by the Habsburg armies in the exploitation and destabilization of Spanish social groups.

The *Segunda parte*'s nostalgia for an idealized military code of ethics reminds us nevertheless that, while Charles V's *tercios* had deservedly gained a reputation as an international fighting force throughout Europe, the army had also been deployed closer to home at the beginning of his regime. Its control of local groups reaches as far back as the

1521 *comunero* rebellion, initially considered a response by traditionalist nobles against the European policies of the young Hapsburg monarch. Recently, the revolts have been assigned more complex causes: Cavillac, as we have seen, blamed their failure on the opposition between the local industrialists and the emperor's support of international capitalism. Other historians construe the rebellion as a defence by such disparate factions as *conversos*, the urban bourgeoisie, the lesser nobility, and the rural peasants against both the aristocracy and the establishment of an absolute monarchy.[21] Moreover, since the goals of the *comuneros* included more fiscal equality between privileged and unprivileged, and participation by the latter in municipal affairs, the nobility uneasily viewed the revolts as taking on a populist cause and encouraging rebellion.

According to Juan Ignacio Gutiérrez Nieto, one of the *comunero* movement's most perspicacious students, much of the historiography of the period reflects the views of the aristocracy then circulating as propaganda against the *comuneros*:

Attacks on the nobility, programs promulgating equality ... popular sovereignty, and larceny: these were the four themes that sixteenth-century historiographers made sure to emphasize. Their intent was clear: to instil a holy fear against any type of political turmoil led by the populace.

[Persecución de la nobleza, programa igualitario ... dictadura popular y robos: he ahí cuatro rasgos que la historiografía del siglo XVI puso empeño en remarcar. La intención era clara: hacer cobrar un santo temor a cualquier tipo de agitación política en que el pueblo pudiera ser el protagonista.][22]

In contrast, Vives, in line with his reformist ideology, considered the *comunero* revolts a popular uprising against the nobility, and blamed the increasing poverty on an unholy and unequal distribution of wealth: 'We in our wickedness have appropriated what a generous Nature gave to us in common. The things she openly laid forth we have enclosed and hidden away by means of doors, walls, locks, iron, arms, and finally laws. Thus our greed has brought want and hunger into the abundance of Nature, and poverty into the riches of God' (qtd. in Grice-Hutchinson, *Early Economic Thought in Spain*, 132).Yet the unprivileged poor's potential for social discord and violence was not the only menace the hegemonic powers saw themselves needing to defend against. As Spain's dominions extended from its borders to encompass much of

Europe and the New World, the country perceived itself, rightly or wrongly, as increasingly vulnerable to attack, both externally from the Turks and its European enemies and internally from its religious and cultural antagonists.

These fears created an atmosphere of hatred and suspicion that soon pervaded the treatment of all minority groups.[23] In effect, Domínguez Ortiz and Vincent perceptively observe that the 1526 document drafted in Granada at the emperor's instance, which prohibited the *moriscos* from publicly manifesting their ethnic differences, whether through their language, dress, eating habits, or rituals, changed their status, altering their susceptibilty from the specific accusation of 'infidel' to the far more menacing – because more inclusive – characterization of the 'other':

The conquering Christians, who in the beginning had shown concern only about religious matters and seemed inclined to tolerate cultural differences, ultimately came to realize the latter's importance, and drafted their inventory so as to completely eradicate them. At first, it was the Infidel who was rejected; later, it would simply be the Other.

[Los vencedores cristianos, que en un primer tiempo se interesaron sólo por el hecho religioso y parecían inclinados a tolerar las manifestaciones culturales, acaban descubriendo su importancia, y redactan su catálogo para extirparlas más completamente. En un primer momento había sido rechazado el infiel; en adelante lo sería simplemente el Otro. (22)][24]

Despite sporadic efforts at enforcement, the pragmatics against Muslim customs were seldom applied, as Charles V's assimilationist policies faltered before other, more pressing developments from outside the peninsula.[25] However, and notwithstanding the three years of peace from 1561 to 1564 that allowed Spain to rebuild its navy, the *moriscos* were seriously implicated in the loss of the African coastline, a military defeat alluded to by Lázaro's piscine conversion in the *Segunda parte*.

The *moriscos* were also blamed for taking part in the continuing attacks by the Barbary corsairs and the Turkish threat that continued well after Charles V's abdication:

When Philip II assumed the throne, Spain's possessions on the African coasts had been reduced to Melilla, Oran, Mers-el-Kebir, and La Goleta; the *moriscos* appear as an Islamic fifth column within Spain, liable to facilitate and support an enemy attack. The truth is that contacts between Constantinople, on the one hand, and the Granadan and Valencian *moriscos*, on the other, were a constant reality ... The *morisco* threat was not a mere fantasy. It was also manifested by means of banditry and piracy.

[Al comenzar el reinado de Felipe II, España sólo posee en las costas africanas Melilla, Orán, Mazalquivir y La Goleta; los moriscos aparecen como una quinta columna musulmana en el interior del territorio susceptible de facilitar y apoyar un ataque enemigo. Lo cierto es que los contactos entre Constantinopla de una parte y los granadinos y valencianos de otra fueron una realidad constante ... El peligro morisco no era pura utopía. Se expresaba también bajo la forma de bandidaje y piratería. (Domínguez Ortiz and Vincent, 28–9)]

Gravely concerned that, within Spain, Lutherans and *moriscos* endangered the faith and jeopardized national security, Philip II decided to impose severe restrictions against all heretics. Anticipating Andrew Hess's important revelation of the arrival, in 1570, of Ottoman troops in Granada to fight with the *moriscos* against the king's forces, Braudel had earlier made the connection:

Madrid was well aware of the contacts between the Moriscos and the rest of the Moslem world ... The request for military aid had been made to the Turks by the Morisco envoys, as well as on behalf of the kings of Morocco, Fez, and 'three or for others of Barbary' ... This news coincided with reports reaching Madrid almost simultaneously that the Sharif was preparing a military expedition against the *presidios* in Morocco; taken together they engendered fears that a concerted Moslem invasion of Spain was about to take place. (*Mediterranean* II: 1066)][26]

With the Council of Trent favouring a more aggressive approach to religious heterodoxy than that previously taken by the Emperor, the Inquisition and the state stepped up their repressive measures against New Christians.[27] Forbidden the possession of firearms, Valencian *moriscos'* houses were searched and any arms confiscated. Granadan *moriscos* were required to show title to their lands; if, as was often the case, they could not produce the documents or pay the fines, the land was expropriated. Increasingly taxed, the Granadan *morisco* silk industry now had to compete with Murcia.

To the beleaguered group, the episcopal synod convoked in Granada in 1566 proved the last straw. The bishops asked the king to again suppress all Muslim practices, to move Christian families to *morisco* lands, and to send the children of the leading *morisco* families, at their cost, to be raised in Old Castile so they would learn Christian habits and forget their own ('que a los hijos destos mas principales Vuestra Majestad los mandase llevar y criar en Castilla la Vieja a costa de sus padres para que cobrasen las costumbres y Christiandad de allá y olvidasen las de acá hasta que fuesen hombres' [Domínguez Ortiz and Vincent 31–2]). The king agreed to enforce the pragmatic, in part, Elliott remarks, because of a family feud between Pedro de Deza, president of the Granada *audiencia*, or central court, and Captain-General Iñigo López de Mendoza, Count of Tendilla, whose protectionist policies towards the *moriscos* were also opposed by Cardinal Diego de Espinosa, Inquisitor General and President of the Council of Castile (*Imperial Spain* 238–9). The *moriscos'* increased subjugation and the jealousies among the governing nobility pushed the desperate minority to the breaking point. First begun in the Alpujarras mountains on Christmas Eve, 1568, and described by Braudel as 'the inevitable clash of two civilizations' (*Mediterranean* II: 790), the rebellion that ensued only fuelled the fears of a Moslem invasion, since it resulted in the *moriscos'* massive deportation from their Granadan lands. Their resettlement generalized the problem over areas previously free of the 'infidel,' thus setting the stage for their later expulsion from Spain altogether.

With the rebels in disarray, and ultimately undermined by internecine factions, the Granada rebellion of the Alpujarras lasted only slightly more than two years. More than 50,000 *moriscos* were dispersed from Granada to Extremadura, Western Andalusia, and the two Castiles (Domínguez Ortiz and Vincent 35).[28] The spectacle of the *moriscos'* forced exile from their lands moved even the general in command, Don Juan de Austria, to lament their condition. One agent in charge of the deportation, Jerónimo de Fuentes, writes from Albacete to Cardinal Sigüenza:

[I]t is pitiful to see the large numbers of very small children and of women, and the never-ending poverty and misfortune with which they come.

[es tanta lástima ver la mucha cantidad de niños muy chiquitos y mujeres y la pobreza y desventura con que vienen. (Archivo del Instituto de Valencia de Don Juan, Madrid, envío 1, 49; qtd. in Domínguez Ortiz y Vincent 52)]

The battle, which underscored the phobia of the dominant classes towards minority groups, also proved a lesson in warfare, since it illustrated the military weakness of the area: 'The rebellion had been taken seriously from the start because the south of Spain had been inconsiderately deprived of manpower by [the Duke of Alba's] expedition. Here more than anywhere else recruitment had been heavy . . . At the same time the Spanish galleys were alerted to prevent the possible arrival of help from North Africa' (Braudel, *Mediterranean* II: 1061). The issue of conscription, at a time when Spain needed to maintain heavy army and naval forces at such distant posts as the Netherlands, the Atlantic, and the Mediterranean basin, represented another source of repression against the unprivileged. Pay was so poor in comparison with labourers' wages that the occasional scarcity of soldiers soon turned into a habitual shortage.[29] In 1567, the massive force assembled by Philip II under the Duke of Alba to intervene in Flanders was decimated by heavy desertions, at which time, Braudel claims, 'the recruiter's drum had to sound once more in Andalusia and elsewhere to fill these gaps' (*Mediterranean* II: 1053). During the Alpujarras conflict, Don Juan complained to the king that his troops, demoralized and undisciplined, often deserted immediately after they were levied (Braudel, *Mediterranean* II: 1069).

Once governments could no longer rely on individual volunteers for prolonged conflicts, they proceeded to raise men by recruiting entire units from other areas in Europe, enlisting foreign captured soldiers in their own army, and conscripting local men against their will (Parker, *Military Revolution*, 48). Following medieval military order, the lower nobility formed the officers' corps, with the high nobility, along with professional soldiers, comprising the high command. At the bottom ranks, the Spanish soldiers assigned to heavy combat came from Castile's lower strata, their recruitment carried out by officials appointed by the War Council mainly in the Castilian interior, which included the two Castilian *mesetas*, Extremadura, and western Andalusia. Transformed by three developments, classified by Parker as 'a new use of firepower, a new type of fortifications, and an increase in army size' (*Military Revolution* 43), warfare during the Renaissance also experienced a significant rise in cost.[30] In 1555, the expense of maintaining Spain's standing army of 15,000 to 20,000 soldiers did not exceed 8 per cent of the state budget. Military campaigns, however, required twice the number of soldiers and often depleted the treasury.[31] Since there were few periods during Charles V's and Philip II's reigns when armed conflicts were not waged at some point in the Hapsburg Empire, military costs – in both human and economic terms – were staggering.[32]

Ineffectual in establishing policy on military funding, the monarchy designated monies to guarantee the automatic payment of the military budget. However, this procedure, called *consignación*, was abandoned and funds diverted whenever other expenses were deemed more urgent (Thompson 83–5). As other methods, in particular, private financing, also failed to obtain regular revenues to ensure pay and provisions, recruitment became increasingly more difficult.[33] I.A.A. Thompson calls soldiering during this time a form of 'licensed extortion' or, at best, a 'part-time job,' since locals might be left for months, and even years, without pay, and most relied on their civilian trades between battles (74). While soldiers fighting outside Spain often mutinied or joined enemy armies, many stationed throughout the kingdoms died from deprivation:

The troops either took alternative employment where they were garrisoned or they deserted; if they could do neither they died. In despair starving soldiers fled to the Moors and surrendered themselves into slavery; virtual prisoners in their garrisons they threw themselves from the battlements or hanged themselves in their barrack-rooms. Even their enemies pitied them. (75)

Guaranteed little or no salary, clothes, or provisions, young men baulked at volunteering their services to the military. Captain Alonso de Contreras's pride in recruiting more than 300 soldiers in a call to arms at a Madrid plaza is understandable; few captains could count on their personal charisma alone to recruit soldiers.

Although Philip II could not levy taxes or troops at will, his bureaucracy, constituted by royal councils and their subcommittees, was empowered to contribute troops whenever necessary, and Castile especially had been the source of finances and men for the Imperial armies since Charles V (Domínguez Ortiz, *Antiguo régimen*, 298). By the end of the sixteenth century, Spain's resources had been drastically reduced, and not even the revenues from the Indies could support the war effort's spiralling debts. In fact, these same revenues, which had increased rapidly during Philip II's reign, were in actuality much less than the amount extorted from Castilian *pecheros*, or non-noble taxpayers.[34] R.A. Stradling comments that, similarly to the finances needed to maintain the armies, manpower had become a scarce commodity, in part due to the natural hardships of the times:

The conditions of general war in western Europe, which hampered supply and forced up prices, aggravated the internal problems of sharp increases in taxation and inflation. By 1599, when a potent virus of bubonic plague arrived in Spain, successive years of malnutrition had reduced the physiological resistance of the unprivileged masses to a low ebb ... The final aggregate death-toll of subsistence crises and disease was 600,000, in a population of less than 6 million – literally a decimation.[35]

The depopulation exhausted the supply of military personnel as well. Thompson calculates that, by 1600, the average company could recruit only one-third the numbers conscripted fifty years earlier (105). The Lepanto campaign, which fully engaged the Spanish forces, was also outfitted by the Italians, who paid about a third of its cost, and by the Holy League.[36] Not only did the battle result in an unparalleled military and psychological triumph for the Spaniards, since galleys required anywhere from 150 to 200 rowers, it supplied them with large numbers of much-needed slave oarsmen for their armada.[37]

According to both Elliott and Braudel, the ongoing insurrection in the Netherlands kept the Spanish forces so divided that no other single victory like Lepanto's was ever repeated (Elliott, *Imperial Spain*, 241–2; Braudel, *Mediterranean* II: 1106–42). In 1585, England aided the Dutch with one-fourth of its military budget and sent forces to the Caribbean, aggressions that would lead to Spanish efforts to contain England through the ill-fated Armada (Parker, *Philip II*, 129–30). As Spain fought to maintain and defend its European and New World hegemony, the country's demographic decline, which commenced in the second half of the sixteenth century, continued undeterred to the end of the seventeenth century. In his revisionary analysis of what has been termed, with reason, Europe's military revolution, Geoffrey Parker convincingly explains why Spain could no longer aspire to full naval mastery (*Military Revolution* 1–2). The Spanish tactics of 'grapple and board'– which preferred the employment of close-range cannonade, ramming, and boarding enemy ships over artillery bombardment and sinking – won the battle of Lepanto, but surrendered the Armada to the British. Both Spain and England continued to utilize these tactics, however; in point of fact, it would be the superior Dutch frigates of the Thirty Years War that finally took control of the seas.[38]

The relative peace during the first decades of the seventeenth century allowed Philip III the time and manpower to regroup the country's naval forces, which retained its strength until well into the seventeenth century.[39] The peace also allowed him to carry out the expulsion decree against the *moriscos* from 1609 to 1614: in order to save face over the

Twelve Years' Truce with the Netherlands obliged by Spain's bankruptcy, the monarchy orchestrated the expulsion on the same date, 9 April 1609, that it signed the pact (Elliott, *Imperial Spain*, 305). The Spanish forces stationed in Italy took part in the expulsion; Miguel de Castro mentions that galleys left Naples in August of 1609 'a lo de los moriscos' (*Vida* 597). Historians are still not agreed to the main reason behind the expulsion, whose seeds were sown by the Alpujarra war forty years earlier. Domínguez Ortiz and Vincent stipulate that not until a year before the first expulsions of 1609 were there any signs that either Philip III or his ministers concurred with the most vociferous of the *moriscos'* enemies, the Valencian archbishop, San Juan de Ribera.[40] In contrast to the expulsion of the Jews in 1492, which was based primarily on a perception of racial and religious differences whose consequences encroached on the political realm, the expulsion of the *moriscos* was attributable mainly to political motives that were then justified and defended through religious posturing.[41]

In effect, the many apologist discourses circulating at the time give the *moriscos'* apostasy of the Catholic faith as the reason for their support of the Turks. The Dominican Jaime Bleda, whose treatises *Defensio fidei* and *Corónica de los moros de España* reiterate Ribera's anti-*morisco* stance, stresses the cultural minority's heretical character:

That perverse nation was so incorrigible, that they were never seen to right their wrongs or learn from their punishments. Not one abandoned their false sect ... These evil, violent enemies conspired against the King's person and authority, and against the Christian religion ... the most infamous crimes of the Spanish moriscos known by all are, as I have said, heresy, apostasy, and dogmatism.

[Era tan incorregible esta perversa nación, que jamás se halló, que se enmendasen de sus delitos, ni escarmentasen por castigos. Ninguno dexó de guardar su falsa secta ... Conspiravan estos enemigos malvados rabiosos contra la persona y Corona Real, y contra la Religión Christiana ... Los delitos de los Moriscos de España mas sabidos, y conocidos de todos eran como se ha dicho, heregía, apostasía, y dogmatización.][42]

The increased threat of attacks by Turkish forces on the Mediterranean immediately provoked fears of a *morisco* fifth column. Although their so-called apostasy remained a strong concern for apologists, most of whom were members of religious groups, the more imperceptible rationale behind the expulsion rested on the *moriscos'* perceived refusal to assimilate culturally and their identification with the Turks. According to Elliott, unassimilated *moriscos* were a factor primarily in Valencia, where fully one-third of the population belonged to a tightly knit community of *moriscos* who also clung firmly to their customs (*Imperial Spain* 305–6). In 1606, the *letrado* Pedro de Valencia, representing the moderate faction among popular sentiment, insightfully placed the blame, not on the *moriscos* themselves, but on the church's poor catechizing and on state restrictions that confined the minority group to their communities. Since the *moriscos* were exempt from battle, forbidden to go to the New World, and, moreover, did not take any vows of chastity, consequently, he concluded, they reproduced in greater numbers than Christians; proximity to one another also encouraged them to continue in their customs. Instead, Valencia suggested, they should be distributed throughout the country in small groups (Domínguez Ortiz and Vincent 169).

It was the *moriscos'* cultural otherness and not their race, as was argued by nineteenth-century historians, that led finally to their expulsion from Spain, even to the point of irrevocably damaging the Valencian economy.[43] This fact is significant to my study, since it underscores how early modern Spanish hegemony first conceived of, and then reacted to the 'other,' whether that 'other' was *converso, morisco*, impoverished, or woman. In reality, *moriscos* were fully capable of integrating into the dominant Christian community; they had already assimilated in numerous parts of Spain, especially in Seville. Indeed, similarly to Miguel de Castro's suggestion that Turkish children be taken from their parents and baptized, *morisco* children were often stolen to be raised as Christians. As happens with Cervantes's Manchegan *morisco*, Ricote, the *pharmakos* in *Don Quixote* whose experiences emblematize the minority group's history, the assimilated *moriscos* were victimized along with those who steadfastly maintained their Moorish heritage.[44] In January 1610, the Sevillian archbishop, Pedro Vaca de Castro, implored Philip III's clemency in allowing the *moriscos* to remain in the city:

The *moriscos* who live in the city do not seem to present any danger, since they are few, most having left during the past rebellion ... There is no danger either among women of any age, nor in men over sixty to seventy years ... The children of *moriscas* married to Old Christians are themselves Old Christian, as are their fathers and grandfathers and grandsons. And their women, although *moriscas*, should rightfully enjoy their fathers' and husbands' privileges ... The same with the very young children, neither do they present any danger. Where are they to go?

[En los moriscos que habitan en esta ciudad parece que no ay peligro, porque son pocos, fueron sacados todos de aqui por la rebelión pasada ... No ay peligro tampoco en las mugeres de qualquier edad, ni en los hombres de mas de sesenta a setenta años ... En las mujeres moriscas casadas con christianos viejos y los hijos dellos, christianos viejos son ellos y sus padres y abuelos y nietos de tales. Y sus mujeres, aunque moriscas, deven gozar de los privilegios de sus maridos y padres ... Los niños criaturas infantes es lo mesmo, no ay peligro. ¿Adonde an de yr? (Qtd. in Domínguez Ortiz and Vincent, *Historia de los moriscos,* 281)]

The *moriscos'* exemption from military service reveals how dangerous they were deemed to the war effort. In 1599, fearful of a possible alliance with the French, the Council of State recommended that *moriscos* between the ages of sixteen and sixty be sent to the galleys, the women shipped to the Barbary Coast, and the children interned in seminaries to be catechized. In 1608, the council reiterated its proposal, this time supported by the Duke of Lerma, who at first had opposed the recommendation (Domínguez and Vincent 166, 171; Elliott, *Imperial Spain,* 306–7).

The expulsion thus began by equating the *moriscos* with *pícaros* and delinquents, as well as with the enemy soldiers captured in battle, all of whom were perceived as deleterious to the common good and condemned to the galleys. This perception was supported by several *arbitristas,* who theorized that *morisco* customs imperilled the economy. As early as 1596, pressing Philip II to accept his proposals, Pérez de Herrera insisted that, along with the poor unwilling to work, minorities such as the *moriscos* and the gypsies represented a continuous threat to society:

Because I believe that if [poverty] is not remedied rapidly, in twenty or thirty years, the major part of these kingdoms (save for some wealthy people of quality) will belong to beggars, Gascoigne migrants (the majority of whom are from that realm), *moriscos,* and gypsies, because these latter are constantly reproducing and growing, and we are decreasing swiftly through wars and religions.

[Porque pienso cierto que, si no se remedia esto con brevedad, dentro de veinte o treinta años, ha de ser la mayor parte destos reinos [fuera de alguna gente de calidad y rica] de mendigantes y gascones, por ser gran parte dellos desta nación, moriscos y gitanos, porque éstos van creciendo y multiplicándose mucho, y nosotros disminuyéndonos muy apriesa en guerras y religiones. (*Amparo de pobres* 177)][45]

The *morisco* 'other' was also designated a serious danger by González de Cellorigo; in 1597, he writes Philip II in favour of their expulsion. Reiterating Pérez de Herrera's concerns, Cellorigo complains that not only would the *moriscos* soon outnumber the Christians, they were hiding arms with which they could attack the country from within:

So [the *moriscos*] continue to increase, and the Christians decrease ... because Christians leave these kingdoms to take part in wars or other obligations, and the former remain always at home, among their kind. [While] many Christians become members of religious groups and remain celibate, [the *moriscos*] do not do so, but follow what their false prophet teaches them in his Koran, which is to multiply ... and thus their growth astounds everyone ... all the arms that they can find, they hoard and hide in secret ... And in the hands of these men, who belong to an opposing religion, arms are extremely dangerous.

[[S]egún se van aumentando, y los Christianos disminuyendo ... porque los Christianos salen fuera destos Reynos a guerras, o contrataciones que les son forcosas, y estos siempre perseveran en sus casas, y entre los de su nacion. Los Christianos muchos dellos se entran en religion y no se casan, estos como no tratan desto sino de su falso profeta en su Alcoran les ensenna que es que se den a la generacion ... y ansi espanta a todos lo que crecen ... todas las armas que pueden aver las recogen y tienen en secreto ... Y en hombres de contraria ley como estos, son peligrosas las armas.][46]

Ironically, despite their cautionary writings on the Spanish economy, both reformers seriously misjudged the expulsion's wide-ranging and long-lasting economic effects. Cavillac reasons that Pérez de Herrera backed the expulsion because, once reformed, the marginalized poor could take over the *moriscos*' vacated jobs ('Introducción,' *Amparo*, lxi). The *arbitrista*, who believed that the reformed poor offered an ideal solution to both the economy and the depleted Hapsburg armies, opposed the *moriscos*' presence mainly for economic reasons that he blamed on their 'otherness.' He argued that the *moriscos* contributed but slightly to taxable revenues because, in keeping with their cultural difference, they refused to buy wine, bacon, and other luxury items (Domínguez Ortiz and Vincent 201). The expulsion's negative repercussions on the economy proves that Spain's failed reform policies never succeeded in replacing the *moriscos* with the trained poor, as Pérez de Herrera had hoped. Again, however, this is as much a cultural issue as it is one of failed reform. Certain occupations, such as tailoring, muleteering, and construction, as well as jobs in agriculture and the silk industry, had traditionally been assigned to *moriscos*; as the trades became associated with a particular minority, they were scorned by the populace. The *moriscos'* withdrawal from their trades, therefore, would not necessarily warrant their replacement by another, culturally distinct, workforce.

Spain's continuing economic downslide, worsened by the halt of silver flow from the New World, forced the Duke of Lerma to form a *Junta de Reformación* in 1618 that, after the favourite's fall in 1619, led the king to confer with the Council of State (Elliott, *Imperial Spain*, 322). The famous *consulta*, or report, stipulating seven recommendations for economic reform, inspired Pedro Fernández de Navarrete's *Conservación de monarquías*, which, however, remained unpublished until 1626, several years after Philip III's death.[47] Clearly conflicted over the *morisco* expulsion, the *arbitrista* is among the first to criticize its results while acknowledging and supporting its motivation; his reasons, therefore, bear quoting at length:

The main reason for Castile's depopulation has been the many and numerous expulsions of Moors and Jews, enemies of our Holy Catholic faith ... But since Machiavellianist and Aretine reason of state has wished to censure this act ... so well executed by the glorious memory of our holy king, Philip III, I shall state only that despite the great importance of a large population to our kingdoms, the Spanish monarchs have always preferred that the monarchy's mystical body reduce its illustrious numbers than consent to harmful humours that by contagion may corrupt good blood ... For those with different customs and religion are not neighbours, but domestic enemies ... Despite all this, I am persuaded that if we had found a means of granting [the *moriscos*] some honour, without marking them with infamy, before their desperation led them to such evil thoughts, they might have entered through honour's door into the temple of virtue, and into the confederation and allegiance of the Catholic Church, without our bad opinion of them having incited their evil.

[La primera causa de la despoblación de España han sido las muchas y numerosas expulsiones de moros y judíos, enemigos de nuestra santa fe católica ... Pero porque la razón de Estado de los maquiavelistas y aretinos ... ha querido censurar esta acción ... tan felizmente ejecutada por la gloriosa memoria del santo Rey don Felipe III ... diré sólo que con ser la población de los reinos de tan grande importancia ... han querido siempre los reyes de España carecer de su lustrosa numerosidad, antes que consentir en el cuerpo místico de su monarquía los malos humores, que con su contagio podían corromper la buena sangre ...

porque los de diferentes costumbres y religión no son vecinos, sino enemigos domésticos ... con todo eso, me persuado a que si antes que [los moriscos] hubieran llegado a la desesperación que les puso en tan malos pensamientos, se hubiera buscado forma de admitirlos a alguna parte de honores, sin tenerlos en la nota y señal de infamia, fuera posible que por la puerta del honor hubieran entrado al templo de la virtud, y al gremio y obediencia de la Iglesia Católica, sin que los incitara a ser malos el tenerlos en mala opinión. (*Conservación* 67–8)]

The *arbitrista*'s ambivalent reasoning reflects the gradual change in public opinion in the wake of the expulsion. Before their exile, the *moriscos'* difference was constantly assailed as pernicious to the social body; deemed too treacherous to fight in the military, they were, however, often endorsed as galley slaves. The return to Spain of many of the *moriscos'* descendants during Philip IV's reign, surely sanctioned in the hope of improving the economy, confirms that the minority group was no longer considered socially injurious. The 'other,' then, did not signify an essentialized negative state of being; recurrently blamed for social ills, the group just as often served the needs of the majority. Like the *pícaros* and the poor, the *moriscos* formed an amorphous, permeable 'other' whose function as social *pharmakos* was determined by the dominant culture.

Pícaros' Lives, Soldiers' Tales

Soldiers' tales report the relation of poverty and war as one of interdependence: to the inducted, neither category would prove much of an improvement over the other. The soldiers who narrate their life stories appear, on the surface, to view the military as a means of escaping their penurious condition. The narratives' ambiguities, however, instead project the authors' difficulties in realizing their desires through the military's enforced discipline and institutionalized violence. Although few statistics are available on the numbers of army defectors, mutinies and desertion were common occurrences. Bartolomé and Lucile Bennassar trace 223 soldiers converted to Islam from 1573 to 1690 who appeared before different Inquisition tribunals in Spain, Portugal, and Venice.[48] As early as 1560, the Spanish garrisons on the *presidios* of the African coast were decimated by epidemics of desertion to the Turks, whose offerings of money and work prompted many Christian soldiers into reneging their faith (Braudel, *Mediterranean* II: 800).

The tensions created by this 'cultural rivalry,' as Braudel calls it, are registered in Pasamonte's autobiography, which the author dedicated to a Jesuit who helped him escape from the Turks, and to a Dominican, General of the Order in Rome. Pasamonte's *Vida y trabajos*, which was never published but written down by a Neapolitan friend of the author's in 1605, exemplifies the hardships awaiting soldiers and their attitude towards their military role. He first joins the army, he tells us, to 'honour' his family, yet he often falls ill before a voyage, leading us to believe that he suffered from an acute case of fear. A year after the 'felicísima victoria' of Lepanto, he is captured in La Goleta:

I was bought, along with others seriously wounded, for 15 ducats, and we traversed 700 miles to Turkey without my being cured, and I didn't die, crying out like a madman.

[Fuí comprado con otros heridos por muerto en 15 ducados, y fuimos 700 millas hasta Turquía cuasi sin curarme, y no pude morir, dando voces como loco. (9)]

The soldier has good reason to cry out: almost half the narrative is dedicated to the eighteen years he spends as galley slave in the Turkish navy.

Pasamonte is nonetheless careful to depict the leadership role he plays among the prisoners, and the numerous times he bravely tries to escape with other Christian slaves. Despite the many beatings he receives, life among the Turks teaches him that, unlike some of his fellow Christians, his captors are not averse to acting honourably. Once he is liberated, he travels from the northern Italian coast to Naples to collect his unpaid salary. He is asked to produce a billet authorizing his pay, but is nonetheless turned away from the court several times:

I walked out so disheartened I could hardly stand it, thinking that, if someone like me, who had been captured and had spilled so much blood, is made to sweat it out, how must they treat others! I concluded that there were more frauds among Christians than among Turks.

[Yo me bajé tan desconsolado que no lo podría encarecer, considerando si a un hombre como yo que viene de cautiverio y ha derramado tanta sangre le quitan su sudor, ¿qué harán a los demás! Juzgué que había más embustes entre cristianos que entre turcos. (31)]

Yet he insists that he was never tempted to renounce his Catholic faith, even when this would have saved him from torture by his captors. If we consider that he constantly laments not having honoured a youthful promise to join the Bernardines, it is not unreasonable to assume that Pasamonte hopes his addressees, both religious men of some importance, will support any hopes he may harbour of ending his days peacefully – and well taken care of – in a monastery.

Writing in simple, unlettered style, Pasamonte claims that he does not wish his narrative published, but composes it in order to serve notice on the 'bad angels' that have not only caused the fall of the 'Turks, Moors, Jews, and Greeks,' but also wreaked havoc among Christians:

And thus, by the wounds of the Son of God, I humbly plead that the harms afflicting Christians all be remedied, and I have written my life history for this reason alone, without aspiring to any vainglory.

[[Y] ansí suplico humilmente por las llagas del Hijo de Dios se dé remedio a tantos daños como hay entre católicos, y sólo por esto he escrito toda mi vida y mi intención, sin pretender ni haber ninguna vanagloria. (*Vida y trabajos* 5)]

The narrative's second part centres on his belief that evil spirits lurk everywhere: after he returns from captivity, he is blackmailed by his landlord's wife, who appears to him surrounded by demons. In a lengthy chapter, he documents the number of times his wife's parents attempt to bewitch him in their efforts to break up the match. Although, in the introduction to his edition, José María de Cossío interprets Pasamonte's obsession with the supernatural as a sign of his weak character ('Introducción' viii), it is evident that Pasamonte knows his beliefs place him at risk with the Inquisition. Despite several chapters which seek to confirm his orthodoxy by listing verbatim the prayers he learned from his grandmother, before its dedication to the Dominican general secured its permission, his book was accused by the Neapolitan archbishop of containing heretical thought.

In that Pasamonte intends a vigorous defence of his radical beliefs, his narrative lacks the ironic, double-voiced discourse we expect of the picaresque. Instead, his tale means to tell the truth as he perceives it, in order to explain how so much evil can exist in the world. Nonetheless, the autobiography's episodic structure, through which he relates his pitiable orphaned childhood, his many travels within Spain and in other countries, and his constant struggles to survive, recalls the formal ordering associated with the picaresque. Moreover, the very fact that

Pasamonte writes his life history as a means of justifying his behaviour and persuading his readers of his intentions, signifies that the narrative parallels the picaresque's rhetorical intent. Although Pasamonte's military life may not resemble that of the *pícaros*, and although his message is conveyed directly through his discourse while the picaresque makes use of a fictive narrator, in both its intention to convince and its social commentary Pasamonte's use of autobiography aspires to the same critical purpose as the picaresque genre.

Unlike Pasamonte's *Vida y trabajos*, which discloses no corrupt or immoral behaviour by its author, Miguel de Castro's incomplete *Vida* narrates several of his roguish escapades until it breaks off approximately around 1614. A soldier who fought against the Turks and spent his early years in the Italian garrisons, Castro states he was born in 1593 near Palencia. Abandoned by his father during his childhood and raised by several uncles in different towns, he joins the army as a young boy in 1604. Castro's detailed account of his soldierly exploits reads more like a journal daily written down than a reflective autobiography. However, it is evident that he does not rely on memory but reconstructs his life as he sees fit for narrative purposes. From the onset, Castro depicts the infantrymen's harsh experiences in graphic terms; their ordeal on board ship is so rough, he claims, that even the soldiers' bad treatment by their Italian hosts is welcome in comparison:

And then they would go to bed, finding it soft and good ... and since all or the majority were torn and in rags, and many shirtless, their hosts, pitying them, gave them what they could, and many gave their soldiers an old shirt, so they might freshen up and rid themselves of lice.

[Y luego se iban a la cama, que hallaban regalada y buena ... y como todos, o los más, iban tan rotos y desarrapados, y muchos sin camisas, los patrones, movidos de lástima, les daban lo que podían, que fueron muchos a sus soldados cada uno alguna camisa vieja, para que se refrescase y se limpiase el cuerpo de los piojos. (*Castro* 493)]

The narrative retraces the route taken by Castro along the Italian coastline as his company patrols the various towns, returning frequently to Naples for provisions. Although he gives the particulars of each voyage, Castro is obviously more interested in narrating his amatory conquests than his military victories. In effect, we read that his apparently uncontrollable sexual urge drives him to commit murder, to lie to and steal from his commanders, and to cheat on one of his closest friends. After slipping from his company with a lover, whom he conceals by disguising her as a soldier, he kills two men who attack the pair, then hides the woman in the barracks. The murder are found out, and when the woman is tortured to reveal the truth, Castro has her poisoned:

She drank the hidden poison, which went into effect without any indication; in less than eighteen hours, they found her dead, her colour normal and no signs of the kind of poison taken.

[Tomó el encubierto veneno, el cual hizo operación, sin que se echase de ver; antes de diez y ocho horas halláronla muerta sin ningún mal color, ni indicios de qué veneno hubiese sido. (*Castro* 498–9)]

His sexual pursuits lead him to form a strong and lasting bond with a Turkish woman captured and taken as slave by his commander, and to incur a passionate liaison with a Spanish courtesan living in Naples who first pairs up with his best friend, a soldier named Quevedo. Castro's feelings for his captain's slave corroborate the extensive fraternizing that went on between Turkish women and their captors, who often bid among themselves for the women's company. Like Cervantes in his 'Captive's Tale,' Castro lauds the Turkish woman's beauty and her emotional responsiveness to her captors; as in *Don Quixote*'s interpolated story, in which a Christianized Zoraida wishes to be renamed María, Mina, the woman admired by Castro, converts to Catholicism, assuming the Christian name Inés.

    As we have seen in the case of the *moriscos*, the Spaniard's concern for Turkish children demonstrates as well that the antagonism between Christians and their enemies was founded not so much on racial differences, but on what was perceived as cultural otherness. Ironically, despite often abusing his lovers himself, Castro is quick to criticize the soldiers' mistreatment of Turkish women and children:

There were some soldiers so merciless that however they found [the women], they would bury their pikes in them, and even their daggers ... I saw another act worthy of abomination as I walked along the castle wall, I came across a soldier from my same troop, who had found a little three-year-old boy ... and he took him by the arm and was going to throw him from the wall, if I didn't grab his arm in time, moved by pity and sorrow, and I begged him not to do so, since there was no advantage to this and it would be more worthwhile to take him as a slave, since he was worth five ducats alive and he could be baptized and brought up in the [Catholic] faith, which would gain a soul.

[Había algunos soldados tan sin piedad, que así como estaban [las mujeres] las escondían los chuzos en el cuerpo y aun las dagas ... Vi otra cosa harto digna de abominación, que yendo por la muralla del castillo, topé un soldado de la mesma compañía, que había hallado allí un chiquillo de tres años ... le tomó por el brazo y le iba a arrojar de la muralla abajo, si no llegara yo a tiempo que se le así del brazo, movido de lástima y piedad, y le rogué que no hiciera tal, pues que era de nengún provecho y más le sería llevalle esclavo, que valía el cuerpo vivo cinco ducados y era de edad que se podía bautizalle e instruille en la fe donde se ganaba una alma. (505)]

Castro's womanizing and swashbuckling while serving in the army have more in common with the archetypal *miles gloriosus* than with the *pícaro*, despite Cossío's statements to the contrary ('Introducción' xxvi). Notwithstanding his many escapades, he is proud of his ties to the Spanish army, and his autobiography serves as our guide, not only to the misogyny and bully tactics practised by the soldiers, but to the strict hierarchical relations that separated commanding officers from their recruits.

The narrative also illustrates the kingdom of Naples's dependence on Spain, which was formalized by the establishment, in 1559, of the Council of Italy, with representation from Milan, Naples, and Sicily. The city's strategic location, its wealth and natural beauty, and its population – greater even than Seville's – made Naples the most important city in the Mediterranean. Italian matters of state were usually handled, therefore, not by the council, but by Spain's Council of State and, save for few exceptions, Italy's highest government positions were assigned to Spaniards. Domínguez Ortiz suggests that the Italians were reconciled to Spanish control, judging it a lesser evil than the internecine feuds and attacks from outsiders that would be brought about by self-government; he believes this the reason why only about 5,000 Spanish soldiers were needed to control the expanse of the Italian kingdoms (Domínguez Ortiz, *El Antiguo Régimen*, 354–5). In effect, Italy served as a military school of sorts for recruits until they were sufficiently trained to be deployed to the various battlefields. Determining the soldier's Italian experience primarily a positive one, Domínguez Ortiz reminds us of the refrain 'My birthplace, Spain; my good fortune, Italy; Flanders, my burial ground' (España, mi natura, Italia, mi ventura, Flandes mi sepultura [*El Antiguo Régimen* 356]). Not coincidentally, the *pícaros* follow the path taken by their historical analogues. This road, which stretched across the breadth of the Spanish Empire and took the Hapsburg armies from Castile, through Italy, to Flanders, also traces the genre's development, from the *Lazarillo*'s Toledan adventures and the Italian manoeuvres described in Pasamonte and Castro's *Vida*s, to the *Estebanillo González*'s scenes of the Thirty Years War.

In relating his life, Castro not only depicts the soldiers' day-to-day activities while they patrol the Italian shoreline, but also renders a singular portrait of the Neapolitan viceregal court. After his appointment to the captain, he is asked by the Count of Benavente, then Neapolitan viceroy, to serve in his retinue, which totalled 263 servants.[49] As a member of the Viceroy's personal guard, Castro is eyewitness to the Count and Countess's daily protocol, describing in intimate detail the Viceroy's daily ablutions and the nightly dressing of their suppurating wounds (*Vida* 601–8).[50] Revealing his fascination with ostentation and spectacle, Castro seems most impressed by the Count's elaborate outfittings and the intricate dining etiquette required of the nobility. He reports not the food, but the ceremonial dinner services carried out by the major-domo and his entourage of waiters, pages, and cup bearers. What becomes apparent, from Castro's telling, is that these protracted rites, interspersed with long moments of prayer and reclusion, absorb most of the Viceroy's day, allowing him little time for affairs of state.

The Count of Benavente's serene Neapolitan viceregency served as an unlikely model for the Duke of Osuna's appointment, in 1611, as Viceroy of Sicily, a position whose many responsibilities outweighed its advantages. Osuna's strong rule in governing the island, far more oppressive than that wielded in Naples by Benavente and his successor, the Count of Lemos, was rationalized by the natural disasters that threatened the island such as earthquakes and storms, and the more menacing perils posed by pirates, bandits, and political uprisings. While nominally a kingdom, Sicily was in reality an amalgam of opposing factions and interests controlled and held together through Spanish governance (Domínguez Ortiz, *El Antiguo Régimen*, 358). When Castro accompanies Benavente to greet Osuna on his arrival at Palermo, he witnesses the sternness imposed on the court by the new viceroy; indeed, the Duke had already given signs of his rigour and power even prior to his official arrival. While at Messina, before he had been sworn into office, he was warned of several political activists known for their insubordination:

Three days after [the Duke] arrived, before assuming the Viceregency, he had
the case of the imprisoned delinquents brought before the judiciary for sentencing; nine were hanged and two burned at the stake that day. The city was none
too pleased over the matter.

[[A] tres días que estaba allí sin ser aún Virrey ni nada, hizo traer los procesos de
los delincuentes que estaban presos y los hizo ver de los jueces y sentenciarlos, y
ahorcaron aquel día a nueve y quemaron a dos. No se mostró la ciudad muy
agradable de esto. (*Vida* 620)]

Once he became viceroy, Osuna's persistence in maintaining Messina
under strict rule resulted in an uprising during Parliament, when he
addressed the city for the first time. Like other Italian cities, Messina contributed 500,000 ducats yearly in voluntary taxes from its silk industry to
support the Hapsburg war efforts and government expenses. Rather than
permit the Spanish government to collect the tax in perpetuity, the city
paid another 100,000 ducats for its right to administer the tax and to
review its possible repeal every five years. Osuna opposed the loophole,
forcing the city to accept Spanish management of the monies. Although
the Viceroy exercised sufficient power to quell the rebellion, Castro's
statement that the Sicilians held their country and their own laws above
the Hapsburg monarchy is instructive in that it demonstrates – even more
than Domínguez Ortiz is willing to concede – that the Italians viewed
themselves as a separate state under foreign domination:

And since the Duke is fearsome by nature, he is dreaded by most government
officials, and although they were more passionate for their country and its laws
than for their King, nonetheless, the Duke's nature and resolve held them in
check, at times with promises and entreatments and other times with threats, so
that the majority of the city courts agreed to it, as they say, more due to force
than desire.

[[Y] el Duque, como es temerario de condición, muchos de los del gobierno le
temían, y aunque ellos en sí son muy apasionados por la patria y sus fueros más
que por su Rey, con todo eso, la condición y determinación del Duque les hacía
estar a raya ya con ruegos y promesas, ya con amenazas, de suerte que la mayor
parte de los jurados de la ciudad había venido en ello, como dicen, más de
fuerza que de grado. (*Vida* 621–2)]

Political considerations inform a considerable part of these soldiers' autobiographies, necessarily incorporating their ideology as members of a particular national group. In comparing them to the picaresque, Cossío criticizes the narratives for focusing more on the author's individual desires and emotions, rendering them untrustworthy as to historical detail. However, their narrative displays, albeit unreflexively, the general convictions of the dominant patriarchal and political hierarchy. Through their treatment of women and the 'other,' we learn how the men, interpellated by the military apparatus, perceived themselves as integral components of the Spanish nation-state.

The soldiers' attitudes thus reflect and reproduce the belief systems of contemporary society: they admit to their guilt for eschewing their military responsibilities even while willingly satisfying their base urges. Despite Castro's truncated narration, we know from numerous comments that he will give up his 'lascivious' life to become a member of a religious order. Similarly, Jerónimo de Pasamonte and Diego Duque de Estrada propose their life stories, implicitly or explicitly, as confessions dedicated to their powerful addressees. In doing so, they attempt to explain away – all the while emphasizing – their bellicose and impious behaviour fostered by an opportunistic culture devoted to warfare and materialism. The soldiers' dubiously repentant attitudes instead seem aimed at convincing their readers, as they themselves are convinced, that they deserve the tangible benefits of a religious life after their travails in the military. In this, they concur with those *arbitristas* who, like Pérez de Herrera, believe veterans should be rewarded for their service, not only to help alleviate general poverty, but to encourage others to join the armies.[51] What is missing in these soldiers' tales, therefore, is the highly self-ironizing nature of the picaresque that allows for authorial critique.

Save for the *Vida del Capitán Alonso de Contreras*'s transitional narrative and the more ambiguously autobiographical *Estebanillo González: Hombre de buen humor*, soldiers' tales lack the double separation between author and fictional character – as well as that between protagonist and narrator – which in the picaresque provides an ironic critical perspective on the hypocritical values of society. Although the authors may promise a religious conversion, they experience no moral downfall because they aspire to no moral redemption in their message; Pasamonte and Castro do not question the values of society, since from the beginning they are inseparable from them. In the polyphonic picaresque novels, authorial and narrative discourses resonate separately, carefully counterposed and distinctly differentiated. In the monovalent soldiers' tales, these multiple discourses are instead merged into a single, driving will that compels the soldier/author not merely to survive, but to strive for the economic relief and enhanced social status that he, as author, narrator, and protagonist, ultimately wishes to obtain.

The Road to Flanders: *Alonso de Contreras, Estebanillo González*, and the End of the Picaresque

Although the beginning of the Thirty Years War seemed to promise Spain a quick victory, by 1629 a series of military manoeuvres in Flanders and Milan against the Spaniards had irrevocably weakened their position. According to Stradling, from the 1590s through the Thirty Years War, the Imperial armies and navies enjoyed an increase in manpower:

Spain's military establishment was exceptionally healthy during the opening campaigns of the war. Madrid was in control of four operational field armies, in Flanders, the Rhineland, central Europe and Italy, each around the optimum size of the period (20,000), in addition to twice as many garrison troops. Moreover, a virtually new navy had been created since about 1617, some fifty galleons being built, fitted and manned for service in the *armada del mar oceano*, not to mention other auxiliary squadrons such as that of Dunkirk. All in all, there seems little reason to doubt Philip IV's boast in 1626, that the monarchy had no less than 300,000 men under arms. (*Europe and the Decline of Spain* 62)

By increasing unemployment, Stradling speculates, the economic depression prior to the Thirty Years War had actually helped the war effort, at least in the short term, in that it released a larger number of men for military service. This hypothesis tends to be somewhat circular, since the previous wars were one of the causes of the depression, and the consequences of military expansion – more taxation and conscription – resulted in higher inflation and even less employment in the provinces. As *arbitristas* protested, the returning soldiers, either no longer physically fit for service or having deserted from the armies, added considerably to the numbers of impoverished and vagrants.

While departing from several of the conventions of the picaresque, the soldier's life nevertheless speaks to the *pícaro*'s in that both respond to issues of poverty, vagrancy, and truancy. The genre had always voiced a clear political message to its protagonist: that he had better heed the needs of society and serve its interests if he were to survive at all. During the seventeenth century, it was obvious that recruitment for the Imperial armies held the highest priority. Philip III's death in 1621 brought his pacifist reign to a close; the truce with the Netherlands expired the same year and was not renewed. The prospect of war accompanied Philip IV's monarchy, whose favourite, the Count-Duke of Olivares, had already wrested court power before the sixteen-year-old king assumed the throne (Elliott, *Imperial Spain*, 323).[52] During this period, which saw the beginnings of government reform and a renewed maritime strategy, Olivares's *Junta Grande de Reformación* urged that the provinces each support their share of naval vessels (Stradling, *Armada of Flanders*, 46 ff.). The military expenditures approved by Olivares more than doubled: the Atlantic fleet was allocated 1 million ducats yearly, while the Flanders army received 3.5 million ducats (Elliott, *Imperial Spain*, 326). The program's early efforts at recruitment led ultimately to Olivares's Union of Arms program that called for the pooling of fully equipped soldiers from each Spanish province. Such massive levies, however, finally ended in the depopulation of these same provinces, especially Castile.[53] Resistance from the different provinces, Stradling states, 'was, of course, fierce and unrelenting.'

Although the individual texts incorporate an indictment of the system, in that they offer the disenfranchised an opportunity to serve the Crown as an alternative to their poverty, picaresque narratives and soldiers' tales during this period affect the propagandistic tones of the Imperial military ideology. The nobility, perilously close to losing their immunity from service, could only approve of and delight in a discourse that would send the poor to war in their stead, resolving at the same time the problems of unemployment and delinquency at home. A partial solution to the problem of underpopulation, according to Stradling, was 'to encroach upon the legal immunities of the great nobility and their vassals.' He gives as an example the case of the Duke of Medina Sidonia, who, in 1634, was obliged to raise and maintain 3,000 men for service within the peninsula, while the less eminent 'were imposed upon *pro rata*' (*Europe and the Decline of Spain* 98).[54] Mateo Alemán had earlier drawn a pathetic portrait of the lesser nobility whose poverty forced them to request a military post:

[The captain] revealed his poverty and what his aspirations had cost, the length of time and the work it had taken him to achieve [his post], begging, putting up, flattering, serving, escorting, bowing, the head touching the floor, his hat in his hand, tiptoeing through the [court] corridors mornings and nights.

[Manifestóme su necesidad y lo que pretendiendo había gastado, el prolijo tiempo y excesivo trabajo con que lo había alcanzado rogando, pechando, adulando, sirviendo, acompañando, haciendo reverencias, postrada la cabeza por el suelo, el sombrero en la mano, el paso ligero, cursando los patios tardes y mañanas. (*GA* 1a, II, 10.342)]

Although the captain's servility scathingly depicts all those who solicited positions at court, the episode does not fail to criticize the changes in the military role of the nobility, which to Alemán, originated from an ethos of heroism and valour.[55]

In his study of the nobility's participation in war, Thompson asserts that, until the early seventeenth century, the feudal cavalry, supplied by the lesser and high nobility, needed to be 'uniformly armed, and reduced to company formations under experienced royal captains' (147). Olivares's insistence on military reform meant not only to develop a strong maritime policy and privatize the military, but to redistribute the pressure for fiscal and manpower contributions from Castile to the broader peninsula (Thompson 46–7). The difficulties in accruing revenues for the war effort, and Olivares's ultimate failure in revitalizing Spain's military units, are clearly evinced, whether consciously or not, in the soldiers' tales. It is no coincidence, then, that both soldiers and *pícaros* popularize their military exploits at a time when Spain's penurious military forces were again gearing up for battle.

Yet, unlike the circular plot common to the picaresque, these soldiers' lives strive for historical accuracy by structuring themselves around the developing events of the Mediterranean conflicts and the Thirty Years War. Although the soldiers' individual episodes may be taken as random occurrences, in the larger context of war they appear continuous and build up to a particular climax. The effect is one of narrative veracity: the contemporaneous reader is always aware that the theatre of action is the European battleground of the recent wars and that the participants, many still alive when the texts were written, are historical figures. The narrator also intends to capture the implied reader's benevolence by identifying with his beliefs. Conscious of the dominant hierarchy's rejection and fear of the 'other,' Alonso de Contreras stresses his honest, Old Christian heritage:

My parents were Old Christians, not of any Moorish or Jewish race, nor sentenced by the Holy Office ... They were poor and, as commanded by the Holy

Mother Church, lived twenty-four years in wedlock, in which time they had six-teen children.

[Fueron mis padres cristianos viejos, sin raza de moros, ni judíos, ni penitencia-dos por el Santo Oficio ... Fueron pobres y vivieron casados como lo manda la Santa Madre Iglesia veinticuatro años en los cuales tuvieron dieciséis hijos. (*Vida* 51–2)]

The narrator's assurances of his cleanliness of blood make sense when we later discover that he has applied for knighthood in the Order of Malta. As with picaresque narratives, however, his insistence only raises suspicions as to his true origins.

Estebanillo González also plays against the genre when he warns the reader that his life is not imaginary like the *pícaro's*:

And I warn you that mine is not fictional like the Guzmán de Alfarache, nor the fabled life of Lazarillo de Tormes, nor the imaginary life of the Caballero de la Tenaza [Pablos, the *buscón*], but a true account with eye-witnesses and those who attest to it.

[Y te advierto que no es la fingida de Guzmán de Alfarache, ni la fabulosa de Lazarillo de Tormes, ni la supuesta del Caballero de la Tenaza, sino una relación verdadera con parte presente y testigos de vista y contestes. (*Estebanillo Gonzalez* I: 13–14)]

The text's historicity lends credence to the narrative's purported mes-sage: that the life of a soldier, despite the risks and dangers, offers more of an option than the poverty and despair of the provinces. If, as we shall see, the message turns out to be true for Captain Contreras, it is promptly subverted by Estebanillo who, abandoning his military post early on, instead prefers the well-fed life of a military leader's buffoon.

These soldiers' lives measure the distance the picaresque has travelled from its first delimited point of departure in the *Lazarillo*. Contreras's *Vida* deviates more from Estebanillo's in that it avoids the puns, double meanings, asides, and visual imagery typical of the polysemic language of the picaresque. Moreover, its ungrammatical style lacks the genre's ironic ambiguities and contradictions by which the modern reader gains insight to the author's critical intent. Contreras's history instead gathers momentum by narrating in factual and unemotional terms his violent confrontations with Moors, Turks, and Spaniards alike. Begun in 1630 when, he claims, he wrote it in eleven days, the incomplete narrative details Contreras's life from his birth until it is interrupted in 1633:

I have surely forgotten many things, because in eleven days one can't recuperate thirty-three years' memory of happenings and events. This is written without design, as God disposed and as I remember, without verbosity or contrivances, only the truth as it occurred.

{[C]ierto se me olvidan muchas cosas, porque en once días no se puede recuperar la memoria y hechos y sucesos de treinta y tres años. Ello va seco y sin llover, como Dios lo crió y como a mí se me alcanza, sin retóricas ni discreterías, no más que el hecho de la verdad. (*Vida* 221)]

Nevertheless, if we believe him, the truth is a bitter one, as he strives constantly to defend himself against attacks from both his peers and superiors who, he claims, routinely harass and abuse him.

In contrast to Lázaro or Guzmán's childhood experiences, there is little in Contreras's tale that elicits our empathy. Indeed, his is a tale of intrigues and violence that shocks the reader in its contempt for the value of human life. From the first, when the schoolteacher whips Alonso at the instance of a rich schoolboy, his retaliation is quick, callous, and deadly:

I knocked the boy to the ground, face down, and I began to stab him with the old knife and as I thought I wasn't hurting him any, I turned him over and stabbed him in the guts; and since all the boys said that I had killed him, I fled and returned home that night as if I hadn't done a thing.

[[E]ché al muchacho en el suelo, boca abajo, y comencé a dar con el cuchillejo, y como me parecía no le hacía mal, le volví boca arriba y le di por las tripas, y diciendo todos los muchachos que le había muerto, me hui y a la noche me fui a mi casa como si no hubiera hecho nada. (*Vida* 52)]

Yet Contreras's early adventures could just as well have led him into a typical *pícaro*'s life. After stabbing his schoolmate, he flees from Madrid, serving first as cook's helper, then as a soldier in Flanders, Malta, Gibraltar, Rome, the Greek Islands, and even Puerto Rico.

Certainly, the resentment Contreras feels towards those in power might have provoked a cynical, hypocritical response like that of the fictional *pícaros*. Instead, he chooses to focus on the rewards he reaps from the military, where he is promoted first from soldier to ensign, then to captain. He prides himself on being one of the first to raise a company flag in Madrid's Antón Martín plaza, levying more than 300 soldiers for his post in Gibraltar. Stationed later at Nola, a town near Naples, Contreras bravely refuses to leave during an eruption by the Vesuvius volcano, ordering his soldiers to dig a ditch to deflect the lava flow and to bake bread to feed the townspeople, actions that saved numerous lives (*Vida* 222–5). On another occasion, he challenges the nobility's ruse of having the oldest son take minor orders and assume the family property in order to avoid quartering soldiers, who are placed with poor families. The Archbishop, who profited from the ploy, threatens Contreras with excommunication and urges the Viceroy to transfer him to another town. But in the interim, Contreras reports that 'the rich paid without the poor having to suffer, for no less a time than at least forty days' (en el ínter pagaron los ricos, sin que padeciese ningún pobre, que no fue tan poco que no duró más de cuarenta días [*Vida* 227]).

Once he arrives at L'Aquila, a remote lawless outpost to which he is assigned as governor and war captain, Contreras once more exercises his justice; he flogs and jails six local soldiers for failing to obey orders, decapitates a noble for criminal activities, and forces the town councilmen to lower food prices (*Vida* 231–2). Beverly Jacobs argues that his life narrative is motivated by his disillusionment at the social and military rejections he encounters due to his low caste and class standing.[56] On numerous occasions, however, Contreras is successful in fighting the system indirectly; similarly to the *pícaro*, he often dissembles, and even changes his identity. At one point, disenchanted by his mistreatment at Court, he becomes a hermit, taking the name of Alonso de la Madre de Dios and abandoning his ambitions to lead a saintly life. But he characteristically renounces his new-found virtue when pressed to join the hermitage's religious order (*Vida* 151–2). Unjustly accused of failing to report a large cache of arms found in a *morisco*'s house while stationed in Hornachos in 1608, he assumes a Christological position, emulating the *pícaro* as *pharmakos*:

Besetting me as I held a rosary in one hand and a shepherd's crook in the other, they grabbed and arrested me and immediately tied my hands behind my back and shackled both feet ... and seating me, bound and tied, on a donkey, they began to walk back to town. I then heard someone say 'this is the king of the Moors, see how devotedly he roamed the world.'

[[Ll]egandose a mí, que estaba con un rosario en la mano y un cayado en la otra, me agarraron y prendieron y al punto me ataron las manos atrás y pusieron un par de grillos en los pies ... y poniéndome encima de un pollino, asentado y atado, comenzaron a caminar la vuelta de la ciudad. Yo oía decir 'Este es el rey de los moriscos; miren con la devoción que andaba en la tierra.' (*Vida* 154–5)]

Despite suffering more than a few setbacks, Contreras manages to achieve considerable professional success. His efforts are repaid when he is finally inducted into the Order of the Knights of Malta for his 'notable deeds and exploits' (por mis notables hechos y hazañas [*Vida* 219]). While we need to remember that his *Vida* remained incomplete and thus cannot be presumed to have ended happily, it nonetheless portrays the best of what the soldier's life had to offer a *pícaro*. Contreras reaches his final triumph when he is promoted to cavalry captain. No longer a footsoldier, but literally entrusted with the equine symbol of chivalry, he displays his accomplishments at a military parade ordered by the Viceroy, where he recalls Foucault's description of the exalted soldier-hero. In gold-encrusted doublet and dashing plumed helmet, he rides proudly at the head of the Italian and Spanish cavalry comprising more than 2,500 horses (*Vida* 235).

Contreras's success, recapitulating the defeat of the Anglo-Dutch expedition to Cádiz and the Flanders armada's defeat of the Protestant alliance at Dunkirk, both cause for celebration throughout Spain (Stradling, *Armada of Flanders*, 44–5), is not to be repeated in the misadventures of Estebanillo González. While, in his dedication to the Duke of Amalfi, Estebanillo states he too wishes to become 'memorable,' he is driven not by the desire for fame and fortune, but by physical hunger. For this reason – and for the highly ironic and literate style he employs – his narrative more closely approximates the picaresque genre than the previous soldiers' tales that, however, also share Estebanillo's suspect beginnings and 'itinerant trans-Hispanism' (transhispanismo transhumante ['Introducción' xvi]). Just as there is no coming to terms with the text's literary value, there is no consensus as to the text's authenticity: some critics consider the story a true picaresque life, others reject the narrative's protagonist as its author, and still others prefer to ignore the authorial issue altogether.[57] The text's most recent editors, Antonio Carreira and Jesús Antonio Cid, convincingly attribute its authorship to Gabriel de la Vega, an Andalusian writer whose poetry, published in the Netherlands and chronicling the Thirty Years War, remarkably resembles the *Estebanillo*'s poetic language and style ('Introducción' lxxxviii–cxxxvi). While their comparative method may not provide absolute proof, we should note that, like *Lazarillo*'s anonymous author, *Estebanillo*'s creator displays a familiarity with literary texts far beyond that of a soldier-buffoon.

Whoever the author happens to be – and despite Estebanillo's admonition that his is not a 'fictional narrative'– he knowingly appropriates several of the characteristics assigned to the picaresque, even to the point of comparing himself with Lazarillo. Indeed, he begins with that most picaresque of openings, the address to an inquisitive – and gullible – reader:

Very dear or very cheap reader, or whoever you are, if, in your curiosity to know other people's lives, you come to read mine, I am called Estebanillo González, finest among ruffians.

[Carísimo o muy barato letor, o quien quiera que tú fueres, si, curioso de saber vidas ajenas, llegares a leer la mía, yo me llamo Estebanillo González, flor de la jacarandaina. (*EG* I: 13)]

The allusion to the inquisitorial phrase 'knowing other people's lives' immediately brings to mind another picaresque topos: the narrator's dubious origins.[58] A fortuitous baptism in Rome countermands his lowly birth in the Galician town of Salvatierra del Miño, making him, he tells us, a 'centaur, picaresque style, half-man and half-nag' (centauro a lo pícaro, medio hombre y medio rocín [*EG* I: 33]). Like Guzmán's boast of his parentage to a noble house, Estebanillo ironically lists his genealogy as descending patronymically from the legendary Count Fernán González. Following the *pícaro*'s tradition of subsuming all the cultural 'other,' however, he traces his degrading Galician origins through his wanton mother, who most probably was murdered for adultery by his Roman father, an inveterate gambler: 'My mother died from a craving for mushrooms, having gotten pregnant by my father, or so she said' (Murió mi madre de cierto antojo de hongos, estando preñada de mi padre, según ella decía [*EG* I: 39]). Strongly suggesting his *converso* origins, underlined as well by his father's ludicrous proof of an ancient title of nobility, Estebanillo is apprenticed to a barber to learn his suspect trade.[59]

Several critics have noted the narrative's division into two major cycles, the first reporting his picaresque adventures, and the second, his occupation as buffoon.[60] For them, this bipartite structure validates the narrative's nexus with the picaresque, as it demonstrates the author's conscious efforts to 'novelize' Estebanillo's life, thereby affecting the *pícaro*'s Protean guises (Talens 143; Estévez Molinero 144). In their endeavour to explain the link between the two conventions, however, critics nevertheless fail to note one of the text's most profound connections to the genre: Estebanillo's constant deprivation, which compels him both to join the army and become a buffoon. Running from his failure as a barber, he takes his first job as servant to two gambling cheats, whose incompetence leaves all three desperately hungry: 'And despite their considerable earnings by means of trickery, we were starving to death because what the Spaniard won at cards, he would lose in a crap shoot' (Y con hacer los dos muy grandes ganancias, cada uno en lo tocante a su flor, nos moríamos de hambre porque lo que ganaba el español a las cartas lo perdía a los dados [*EG* I: 57]). Estebanillo enters military service, therefore, solely as a means of satisfying his hunger. After sailing to Messina on a galley as cook's helper, he is hired as a standard-bearer's servant in a fleet chasing Turkish ships:

I went to this war so impartial as to ignore any plans or stratagems other than filling my belly; the hearth, my combat station; a spoon, my pike; and a bubbling cauldron, my deck cannon.

[Yo iba a esta guerra tan neutral que no me metía en debujos ni trataba de otra cosa sino de henchir mi barriga, siendo mi ballestera el fogón, mi cuchara mi pica, y mi cañón de crujía mi reverenda olla. (*EG* I: 70–1)]

A full belly remains his major concern while he takes on numerous servant's jobs; after a failed stint as surgeon at a Neapolitan hospital, he joins a *tercio* in Lombardy, where, fed and lodged by the townspeople, he concludes that a soldier's life 'is better than a surgeon's, if one can always take advantage of the locals' (aquella vida era mejor que la de cirujano, si durase siempre estar sobre el villano [*EG* I: 146]).

Although there will be no doubt of his cowardice as the prime motive for his desertions in Book II, in Book I Estebanillo has reason to blame his steady hunger for opportunistically joining the French army: 'Seeing that hunger was overtaking me, and that at the time, just to allay it, I'd join the Turk' (Yo, viendo que me apretaba la hambre y que en aquella ocasión, por sólo mitigarla, serviría al Mameluco [*EG* I: 255]). Already, however, his behaviour allegorizes the war's notoriously conflictive politics. As he soon rejoins the Spanish troops aiding the Duke of Saboya's army against the French army at Mantua, his turncoating anticipates the Duke's later alliance with the French.

Estebanillo's arduous military experiences not only illustrate the soldier's unremittingly harsh life, but also help to explain his increasing degradation. By the end of Book I, sentenced to hang for killing a comrade, Estebanillo has hardened into a swaggering braggart who saves himself by his waggery and wit. When, due to the army's chronic lack of funds, he is given to wear a dead soldier's uniform, he is finally convinced that the military offers no advancement over his previous picaresque occupations:

And, seeing that my being a soldier had left me more soldered than an old kettle, I tossed the military to one side and marching to the court's drum instead, I realized its benefits and got a good footing, reverting from death to life and from poor to rich.

[Y viéndome que por causa de ser soldado estaba con más soldaduras que una caldera vieja, arrimé a una parte, como a gigante, la milicia, y siguiendo la malicia de la corte reconocí su ventaja y asenté el pie, volviendo de muerte a vida y de pobre a rico. (*EG* I: 286–7)]

Estebanillo again bungles the opportunity to redeem himself when, during Spain's victorious battle against Sweden at Nordlingen, he hides under a horse's putrefying carcass, their two heads forming a grotesque version of the Habsburg *águila bicéfala*, or double-headed eagle (EG II: 308). The soldier's craven behaviour, the moment of the Imperial armies' greatest triumph, will set the tone for Book II. From this adventure forward, Estebanillo makes certain that his main connections with the military are restricted to the self-serving occupation of provisions supplier, what he exuberantly terms his 'mouthly commerce' (el comercio de la bucólica [*EG* II: 27]). In an allusion to his inconstancy, the untranslatable pun contrasts the Dutch penchant for commerce to Spanish military pursuits, but it no less seriously advances the soldiers' prerogative for daily sustenance. It is not coincidental, then, that Estebanillo again stresses how it was his hunger that impelled him to enter Count Ottavio Piccolomini, the Duke of Amalfi's service as a buffoon.[61] Hunger, then, induces both the turncoat soldiering and syncophantic posturing through which he comes to exemplify Hapsburg Spain's final demise.

Unlike Alonso de Contreras, who opts for dazzling military attire, Estebanillo trades his soldier's garb for a servant's uniform, rejecting the military as any possible solution to a *pícaro*'s life. Nicholas Spadaccini believes this choice encapsulates the *pícaro*'s need to survive:

While he was fully conscious that a servant's costume (librea) was nothing but a symbol of bondage, a garment of slavery ... he believed then, and continues to hold now, at the moment of narration, that he had no alternative but to accept the uniform ... The *pícaro*'s social situation is thus expressed unequivocally; any type of employment was preferable to idleness, which often meant starvation, or, at best, being forced to join an army. Playing the role of a clown, however humiliating or degrading, was a way of surviving the hardships of war, especially those inflicted on the common soldier who was often tricked or bullied into joining infantry regiments.[62]

But Estebanillo had long since abandoned his picaresque role; euphemized by the ironic epithet of 'good humour man,' he maintains only the *pícaro*'s cynicism while yielding to the humiliating position of clown. Moreover, as I hope to explain, surely for the contemporaneous reader, with little interest in Estebanillo's personal welfare, the soldier's donning a servant's uniform was a disappointing reversal of Contreras's military ambitions. Like his picaresque forerunners, Estebanillo, the clown, states one thing, while Estebanillo, the author, means another.

By incorporating several messages within its narrative, *Estebanillo* retains the ambiguity and irony inherent to the conventional picaresque genre. Referring to the text's language, Spadaccini quotes Bakhtin that a text has a 'plurality of discourses' whose polyphony 'cannot be reduced to the class participation of the authors.' In placing the text in its historical framework, he specifies its two discourses: the literal denotation, or 'burlas,' provoking the reader's mirth; and the 'veras,' or underlying social criticism, which to him is also evident at the literal level (Spadaccini, 'Imperial Spain' 60). Since *Estebanillo González* undeniably renders one of the darkest portraits of a society whose institutions impeded any social progress, Spadaccini is quite right in viewing it as an indictment of the system:

Through a pícaro-buffoon's mask the anonymous author portrays the common man's anguish, the result of the latter's inability to influence the course of politics and social life ... If Estebanillo is alienated from Spain's causes it is because he has no faith in its institutions – especially the Church and the Monarchy – and he is skeptical of its highly stratified social system. (Spadaccini, 'Imperial Spain' 61)

Estebanillo's alienation, then, is also the author's; yet Spadaccini has already pointed out that the text assumes more than the author's voice.

Through its duplicitous discourse, the text's social criticism is made perceptible to the modern reader. But even though this duplicity is expected of the genre, there is, nevertheless, a reticence in this particular text that suggests the author's awareness of the futility of his enterprise. Spadaccini has remarked upon the verse prologue's 'concern for the communication of a serious message' in its lines 'On God's behalf, I beg you / my friend and reader, that you read these jokes / through to the end / as they're mixed with truths. (de parte de Dios te pido / amigo lector, que leas / hasta el fin aquestas burlas / pues van mezcladas con veras [*EG* I: 23]). He cites them as proof that 'there appear weighty commentaries on contemporary history and social life' in the text (Spadaccini, 'Imperial Spain' 60).[63] Such a statement is perhaps too conclusive; as we know, hardly any medieval or Renaissance text fails to submit some version of *prodesse et delectare* as justification for its existence. In the narrative itself, Estebanillo instead recoils from the moral commentary so quickly proffered in earlier picaresque narratives:

Here, I'm tickled to say many things about what favours can attain and what moves our self-interest, and how interested parties are so quickly convinced, and the damage they cause, and the penalty they deserve; but as this amounts to mixing apples and oranges and has nothing to do with Estebanillo, I won't say a thing, since I know I'll be clamouring in the desert. So I turned instead to my work, motivated only by profit.

[Aquí me hacen coxquillas mil cosas que pudiera decir tocantes a lo que pueden las dádivas y a lo que mueve el interés, y lo presto que se convencen los interesados, y los daños que resultan por ellos y las penas que merecen; pero como es fruta de otro banasto y no perteneciente a Estebanillo no doy voces, porque sé que será darlas en desierto. Apliquéme de suerte a trabajar, cebado en la ganancia. (*EG* I: 183)]

In his edition of the text, Juan Millé y Giménez notes the lack of direct social satire, and attributes it to the uselessness of pointing out what was already so visible to the public:

Spain's inequities had been made abundantly manifest and were visible to all. There was no merit in pointing them out, nor any hope in a remedy that would cure them.

[Los males de España se habían manifestado demasiado y estaban ya a la vista de todos. No había mérito en señalarlos, ni tampoco esperanza de que pudiese sanarlo algún remedio. (*EG* I: 45)]

Rather than offering a cure for society's ills, Estebanillo González reflects them in the persona of the turncoat-soldier. In its reserve, his language marks the hopelessness of his situation, even while the polysemy of the text allows for social critique to be decoded from its literary discourse.

But if Estebanillo will not speak out, *Estebanillo González* gives expression to more than 'burlas' and 'veras'; that is to say, to a comic discourse and one of social concern. The comic discourse itself has a dual purpose: while making the public laugh at the soldier's buffoonery, it directs their attention towards the *pícaro*'s cowardly self-interest in abandoning the Imperialist cause. Clearly, Estebanillo's interests are at odds with the reader's, who nevertheless is quite willing to partake vicariously of the former's military exploits so long as the impoverished remain in the service.

There was need for this kind of entertainment: the continued demands for monetary support and manpower to maintain Spain's groundhold on the European front, along with the internal battles waged from 1640 on in Catalonia, Portugal, and Andalusia, contributed greatly to the erosion of the people's will.[64] In 1640, the English ambassador to Madrid reported:

[They are] taking tradesmen out of their shops and husbandmen from the plough, the most of them such as leave young women and children unprovided, which would cause general disconsolation but that they hope the business will be short, wherein they may be deceived. Nor will it secure these men from being sent to Italy in case they could be spared here, for I hear the Marquis of Leganes's army [in Milan] is much diminished, and that the kingdom of Naples is so exhausted as it grows unable to furnish any more men. (qtd. by Stradling, *Europe and the Decline of Spain* 98)

By Stradling's count, more than 100,000 military personnel were conscripted from Castile over the period 1628–43: indicating the 'prevailing levels of depopulation and disruption,' he adds that, in 1637, the War Council 'regarded as simply impossible a royal requisition for a fresh levy of 6,000 men in Castile' (*Europe and the Decline of Spain* 97). Favouring the Flanders armada over land armies, Olivares endeavoured to contain sailors' desertion, but by 1640 wages and provisions were again near depletion (Stradling, *Armada of Flanders*, 154). The shortage of men pressed numerous boatmen into service, from merchants to Irish rebels. Private Dutch ships signed up for a range of services, and it was as an alternative to these Flemish privateers, known as *armadores*, that in the mid-1640s, Spain turned to Dunkirk frigates to protect not only the Atlantic, but the Caribbean. To Stradling, the proposal, although rejected by the Council of War, proves that Spain's 'maritime war involved fighting piracy with piracy' (*Armada of Flanders* 124–35).

Sailing on a pirate ship in 1645, Estebanillo describes what Stradling calls 'the most fully-dimensional picture of a typical privateering voyage' (*Armada of Flanders* 210):

Mine sailed on Christmas Day, 1645, to pirateer against the Dutch, French, and Portuguese ... If we met up with a strong ship, we ran off like greyhounds, and everyone sad but me, who exploded with happiness ... [O]ther times we dealt blows to those weaker than ourselves, with the most cowardly transformed into invincible lions. At length, having sent several ships to the bottom and taken substantial prizes, we returned to Flanders ... As the wine had cost us nothing, we drank freely ... And by the afternoon we were all equal in drunkenness, falling on top of each other. When all is said and done, the life of the pirate is the death of the passenger.

[Salió la mía Día de Navidad del año de mil seiscientos cuarenta y cinco en corso contra holandeses, franceses y portugueses ... Si el bajel que encontrábamos era fuerte, huíamos como galgos, y todos muy tristes y yo reventando de alegría; otras veces dando alcances, por ser nosotros más fuertes, transformado el más cobarde en invincible león. Al fin, habiendo echado algunos bajeles a fondo y cogido presas de importancia, nos volvimos la vuelta de Flandes ... Como el vino no nos había costado nada bebíamos todos a discreción; ... Y a la tarde veníamos a estar todos iguales y caer unos sobre otros; en fin, vida de cosarios y muerte de pasajeros. (*EG* II:359–60)]

Estebanillo's degrading cowardice and drunken stupor aboard a predatory pirate ship emblematizes the utter amorality of Spain's military enterprise, as the country endorsed the privateers' plunder and ransoming in great part because such immoral actions benefited the state treasury. If, as Stradling ruefully remarks, in its barbarism piracy renders a strikingly apt image of the Thirty Years War (*Armada of Flanders* 228), then Estebanillo's sordid behaviour shamelessly symbolizes Spain's moral and economic insolvency.

Cynically claiming to have tired of 'labouring for peace' (fatigado de los trabajos de la paz [*EG* II: 367]), the buffoon is ready to abandon his participation in the war effort, but not until he exacts a ransom of his own. He first praises his master's, the Duke of Amalfi's, military exploits, then, blasphemously parodying the emperor's, Charles V's, retirement to Yuste, which he professes to emulate –'desiring to profit from such a great example' (quiriendo aprovecharme de tan grandioso ejemplar' (*EG* II: 367]) –,he asserts he writes his life to remind the Duke of his promise to grant him a pension. Despite the abundantly ironic turns of phrase, therefore, Estebanillo's reason for composing his auto-biography, he assures us, is meant not to justify his past or to serve as caveat to others, as previous picaresques had purported, but purely for economic benefit. His decision to gain further from his good humour, which had already rescued him from military service, amounts to a dou-ble sell-out: in exchanging his autobiography for a price, the *pícaro* duplicates his selling himself to the Duke as buffoon, and the text becomes the reification of his materialistic philosophy.

Like other picaresque novels, *Estebanillo González*'s polyphony incor-porates a comic discourse – the misadventures of a buffoon written as entertainment for the ruling classes – and one of social commentary in its oblique references to the Empire's moral bankruptcy.[65] But it also participates in a discourse formed beyond the individual text by the proliferation and consumption of the picaresque as a new genre. The picaresque's popularity domesticates its subversive nature; the reading public's rejection of the harsh realities faced by an ever-increasing poor, even as it consumes more and more picaresque novels detailing these realities, discloses yet another example of unintended complicity between literary texts and the dominant ideology. As discourses of pov-erty, soldiers' tales chronicle the social history of the marginalized sub-stratum of *pícaros*, all the while colluding with the system by positing their absorption into the Imperial war machine as an acceptable alterna-tive to their destitution.

Both strategies proffer the contemporaneous reader a release from moral and social responsibility. The *pícaro*'s portrayal as comic arche-type and incipient criminal, deservedly put upon for his anti-social behaviour, ensures his anonymity by separating his fictional self from his social reality. Further, his fictionalization into a literary nobody dis-tances the reader and desensitizes him to the historical problem of the marginalized poor. The *pícaro* is depicted as an alienated being who refuses to conform to society's norm. His punishment for this is to be ostracized from society; his redemption lies in the exchange of his own values for those of the privileged class. The literary solution offered by this discourse arises from a historical problem: the impoverished, like the *pícaro*, are interpellated by the state to acquiesce to its demands. The soldier's message and the picaresque narrative come full circle when we read that Estebanillo, in a sly parody of the *arbitrista*, Pérez de Herrera's treatise on poor soldiers, solicits a pension from the Duke. By doing so, the *Estebanillo González* recalls the *Lazarillo de Tormes*'s method of defence against the inquisitorial Vuestra merced: like Lázaro, Estebanillo asks to be remembered, not for his real–life adventures, whose sordidness he attributes to society's demands, but for his fictionalized 'life.'

Yet the picaresque is too deeply embedded in the social and economic conditions of its time to deny its origins by converting its anti-heroes into fictive clowns. It is surely significant that, as the last representative of the picaresque, Estebanillo fails both as *pícaro* and as soldier, as he paradoxically silences historical truth by selling his voice, and the power of his rhetoric, to the highest bidder. In Spain, the picaresque novel ceases to exist at the chaotic end of the Thirty Years War, when the increment of beggars and brigands is at its highest. With the *arbitristas'* concerns for social justice long silenced from public debate, and with the church's pious reclamation of its poor, the picaresque novel's unheeded message is instead made painfully manifest in the streets.[66]

The genre, however, embraces neither Estebanillo's silence nor his failure. Despite the picaresque's decline in Spain, new versions of the novels continued to appear in more critically receptive environments as poverty and poor relief prompted attempts at corrective measures.[67] In the less insular political arenas of France, England, and Germany, as well as post-colonial Mexico and the United States, despite the persisting historical conditions of economic deprivation and human suffering, the desire for social reform stimulated and ensured the circulation of its discourses.

Notes

1. Charity, Poverty, and Liminality in the *Lazarillo*

1 *Lazarillo de Tormes*. Ed. Francisco Rico (Madrid: Cátedra, 1987), 71. All citations are from this edition. I have slightly altered Michael Alpert's translation, *Two Spanish Novels* (New York: Penguin Books, 1980). Unless otherwise noted, all translations in this study are my own.

2 The *Lazarillo*'s 'reality' was first seriously questioned by Angel González Palencia, *Del Lazarillo a Quevedo: Estudios históricos literarios*, 3–39. Marcel Bataillon notes the text's inclusion of several well-known themes in European and Oriental folklore in his *Novedad y fecundidad del 'Lazarillo de Tormes'*. Cf. María Rosa Lida de Malkiel, 'Función del cuento popular en el *Lazarillo de Tormes*.' For a valuable structuralist analysis of the picaresque that, however, denies the genre's connection to concrete historical events, see Aldo Ruffinatto, *Struttura e significazione del 'Lazarillo de Tormes,' I, La costruzione del modelo operativo. Dall'intreccio alla fabula; II, La 'fabula', il modello transformazionale*.

3 A 1525 date of composition has been proposed by Manuel J. Asensio, 'La intención religiosa del *Lazarillo de Tormes* y Juan de Valdés'; and Albert A. Sicroff, 'Sobre el estilo del *Lazarillo de Tormes*.' As Bataillon has shown, however, the *Lazarillo* makes mention of the laws against the 'foreign' poor in Toledo, which were published in 1540 in Madrid and in 1544 in Medina del Campo (*Novedad y fecundidad*). See also Francisco Márquez Villanueva, *Espiritualidad y literatura en el siglo XVI*, 115–21. Recently, Aldo Ruffinatto has given 1551 as the probable date of composition (Private communication with the author).

4 By realism, I do not refer to the text's 'naturalism' or verisimilitude, which has generated an extensive bibliography, but rather to studies situating the narrative within the actual social conditions of Renaissance Spain. Among

the most important are Javier Herrero, 'Renaissance Poverty and Lazarillo's Family: The Birth of the Picaresque Genre'; Márquez Villanueva, *Espiritualidad y literatura*; Augustin Redondo, 'Pauperismo y mendicidad en Toledo en época del *Lazarillo*'; Francisco Rico, 'Resolutorio de cambios de Lázaro de Tormes (hacia 1552)'; Julio Rodríguez Puértolas, '*Lazarillo de Tormes* o la desmitificación del imperio'; Georgina Sabat-Rivers, 'La moral que Lázaro nos propone'; and Harry Sieber, *Language and Society in the 'Lazarillo de Tormes'*.

5 For arguably the best, and certainly the most extensive, discussion of generic theories applied to the picaresque, see Ulrich Wicks, *Picaresque Narrative, Picaresque Fictions: A Theory and Research Guide*.

6 Gómez-Mariana proposes that the picaresque text's 'social nature' must nonetheless also integrate its specificity, and that the critic's task is precisely one of meeting the challenge to bring together the 'four elements ... of the literary fact: context, author, text, reader,' without fetishizing any single element. See his 'Epilogue,' *Discourse Analysis as Sociocriticism: The Spanish Golden Age*, 145–50.

7 I do not mean to imply here that the picaresque genre or its protagonists 'evolve' in a positivist manner; rather, that the *pícaro*'s agency cannot be separated from his authors' determinate historical circumstances. For an early critique of formalist readings of the picaresque, see Enrique Tierno Galván, *Sobre la novela picaresca y otros escritos*, 11 ff.

8 See Joseph Ricapito's listings in 'Estudios sobre el origen de la palabra "Pícaro"' in *Bibliografía razonada y anotada de las obras maestras de la novela picaresque española*, 118. According to Wicks, Corominas documents the term's first appearance in 1525 in the neutral sense of *pícaro de cocina*, but in Eugenio de Salazar's *Carta del Bachiller de Arcadia* (1548), it is counterposed to courtier, and by the *Guzmán de Alfarache*'s 1604 second part, Guzmán laments the epithet (Wicks, *Picaresque Narrative*, 7).

9 For bibliography on the picaresque's literary origins, see Ricapito and Joseph L. Laurenti, *Bibliografía de la literatura picaresca. Desde sus orígenes hasta el presente*; also, Joseph L. Laurenti, *Catálogo bibliográfico de la literatura picaresca, siglos XVI–XX*.

10 Peter N. Dunn, *Spanish Picaresque Fiction: A New Literary History*. See also his *The Spanish Picaresque Novel*.

11 Ian Watt, *The Birth of the Novel*, 12–35. Cited by Dunn: *Spanish Picaresque Fiction*, 37.

12 For a different view of narrative closure and continuity that reflects on the phenomenology of historicized time and the emergence of subjectivity, and which considers the *Lazarillo* a 'closed' text, see Hans U. Gumbrecht,

'Cosmological Time and the Impossibility of Closure: A Structural Element in Spanish Golden Age Narratives.'

13 In his 'Introducción,' Francisco Rico cites Antonio Llull's *De oratione libri septem* as already noting the resemblance in 1556 (55–7). Modern critics comparing the *Golden Ass* to the *Lazarillo* include Alexander Blackburn, *The Myth of the Pícaro: Continuity and Transformation of the Picaresque Novel, 1554–1954*; Fernando Lázaro Carreter, '*Lazarillo de Tormes*' *en la picaresca*; Jean Molino, '*Lazarillo de Tormes* et les *Metamorphoses* d'Apulée'; Antonio Vilanova, L'*Ane d'Or* d'Apulée, source et modele du *Lazarillo de Tormes*'; and Michael Zappala, 'The *Lazarillo* Source – Apuleius or Lucian? – and Recreation.'

14 For Michel Foucault, Europe's social disintegration in the early modern period may be gauged not solely through language's inherently internal divisions, which constantly elude any approximation at transparency of meaning, but by its epistemic break with resemblance to the external world. Foucault's epistemic shifts thus accord historicity to language as an area of knowledge, despite its fragmented nature. See *The Order of Things: An Archaeology of the Human Sciences*, 35–6.

15 Although conceding that he employs 'individualism,' for want of a better term, Maravall cites numerous contemporary texts to defend its definition as the desire for social freedom. See especially his ch. 7, 'Individualismo y soledad radical del pícaro. La libertad picaresca,' in Maravall, *La literatura picaresca desde la historia social (Siglos XVI y XVII)*. For a critique of an idealist interpretation of individualism as 'subjectivity' see George Mariscal, *Contradictory Subjects: Quevedo, Cervantes, and Seventeenth-Century Spanish Culture*.

16 One such category, in fact, would be the autobiographies of women religious written mainly at the behest of their confessors; see, among others, Electa Arenal and Stacey Schlau, *Untold Sisters: Hispanic Nuns in Their Own Writings*; Kathleen A. Myers, '"Miraba las cosas que desía": Writing, Picaresque Tales, and the *Relación autobiográfica* by Ursula Suárez (1666–1749)'; and Ruth Anthony El Saffar, *Rapture Encaged: The Suppression of the Feminine in Western Culture*.

17 Stephen Greenblatt, *Renaissance Self-Fashioning: From More to Shakespeare*. For self-fashioning's implications as an exclusively male exercise, see Ruth El Saffar, 'Literary Reflections on the "New Man": Changes in Consciousness in Early Modern Europe.' Also, see Judith Newton, 'History as Usual? Feminism and the "New Historicism."'

18 For the ideological affinities between the *relaciones* and the picaresque, see Roberto González Echevarría, 'The Law of the Letter: Garcilaso's *Commentaries* and the Origins of the Latin American Narrative.' I thank Diana de Armas Wilson for this reference.

19 For a Neo-marxian critique of the idealist ideology supporting individual-ism, see Mariscal; cf. my review in *Revista de Estudios Modernos* 27 (1993): 154–7.

20 See the anonymous French translation *L'Historie plaisante et facétieuse du Lazar de Tormes Espagnol* (Paris, 1561) and *The Pleasaunt Historie of Lazarillo de Tormes*, trans. David Rowland (London, 1586). Both translations underscore the text's cultural difference.

21 Barry Jordan, *British Hispanism and the Challenge of Literary Theory*, 27.

22 Michel Foucault, *The Archaeology of Knowledge*, 55.

23 As an example, see Ruffinatto's perceptive essay on Lazarillo's choice of direction towards Toledo, '"En Torrijos cría tus hijos; en Maqueda tenla queda" (A proposito di strani percorsi del *tontilisto* Lazarillo).'

24 Although I disagree with his reasons, I concur with M.J. Woods's admoni-tion that we should not moralize about Lazaro's behaviour: 'Pitfalls for the Moralizer in "Lazarillo de Tormes."'

25 For a study of child abandonment that documents the historical prevalence of Lazarillo's predicament, see John Boswell, *The Kindness of Strangers: The Abandonment of Children in Western Europe from Late Antiquity to the Renais-sance.*

26 In the chapter 'Stereotypes of Persecution,' René Girard posits that persecu-tion is triggered by extreme loss of social order: *The Scapegoat*, 15–23. For a Jungian interpretation of the scapegoat, see Sylvia Brinton Perera, *The Scape-goat Complex: Toward a Mythology of Shadow and Guilt.*

27 I take the term liminality from Arnold Van Gennep, whose French term *marge* has been translated as 'liminal': *The Rites of Passage*. See also Victor Turner, *The Ritual Process: Structure and Antistructure*; and Victor Turner, 'Variations on a Theme of Liminality.'

28 My views of leprosy and liminality in Spain are indebted to Michel Fou-cault's *Madness and Civilization: A History of Insanity in the Age of Reason*. I have also benefited from Steven Mullaney's excellent study of theatrical space and marginality, *The Place of the Stage: License, Play, and Power in Renais-sance England.*

29 Francisco Rico has pointed out that, along with the chapter headings, the title of the Burgos edition was the brainchild of Juan de Junta to elicit reader sym-pathy. Rico believes that Junta based himself on *La vida de San Amaro y de los peligros que pasó*, which had been recently published in 1552: 'La transmisión de la novela picaresca.'

30 See also Bruce Wardropper, 'The Strange Case of Lázaro González Pérez'; and Alan Deyermond, 'Lazarus and *Lazarillo*.'

31 Alan Deyermond, *Lazarillo de Tormes: A Critical Guide*, 28 ff.

32 Peter Richards, *The Medieval Leper and His Northern Heirs*, 8. See also Charles
    A. Mercier, *Leper Houses and Medieval Hospitals*.

33 According to Robert Ian Moore's studies of European leper hospitals, in
    England and Wales alone, sixteen were built during the period 1150–75, for a
    total of forty-five; four more constructed in the period 1175–1200. By 1275–
    1300, surviving records show, only eighteen hospitals remained. In the Paris
    region, the period 1225–50 records the highest number, twenty-nine, in
    comparison with thirteen by the beginning of the fourteenth century. See his
    *The Formation of a Persecuting Society: Power and Deviance in Western Europe,
    950–1250*, 52. For construction of lazarhouses in France, see also Jean Louis
    Goglin, *Les misérables de l'Occident Médiévale*; and Albert Bourgeois, *Lépreux et
    Maladreries du Pas-de-Calais (x-xviii siècles, Mémoires de la Commission Départ-
    mentale des Monuments Historiques du Pas-de-Calais*.

34 Saul Nathaniel Brody, *The Disease of the Soul: Leprosy in Medieval Literature*,
    136.

35 Among other stories, Brody gives as examples Hartmann von Aue's *Der
    Arme Heinrich* (ca 1195); the Middle English poem *Amis and Amiloun*; the
    legend of Constantine; and Robert Henryson's The Testament of Cresseid,
    the sequel to Chaucer's *Troilus and Criseyde*.

36 Turner has identified these activities as liminal instead of 'liminoid' only
    when they have not yet become secularized or fragmented: 'Liminal
    phenomena are centrally integrated into the total social process, forming
    with all its other aspects a complete whole ... *liminoid phenomena* develop
    most characteristically *outside* the central economic and political processes'
    ('Variations' 44); see also Turner, *The Ritual Process*, 102 ff.

37 Félix Contreras Dueñas and Ramón Miquel y Suárez de Inclán, *Historia de la
    lepra en España*.

38 Linda Martz, *Poverty and Welfare in Hapsburg Spain: The Example of Toledo*, 46.

39 Moore notes that the difficulties in determining how widely containment
    policies were followed result from the fact that, despite the Lateran Council's
    restatement that lepers should be segregated from their communities,
    infringement of lazarhouse rules resulted in expulsion (R.I. Moore 54–5).

40 R.I. Moore cites from S.C. Mesmin, 'The Leper Hospital of St. Gilles de Pont-
    Auderner,' 36.

41 Augustin Redondo calls attention to the belief during the sixteenth century
    that plagues were divine retribution for the evils brought on by leprosy.
    Redondo admits, however, that they were considered punishment for all
    sinners, not only for the sacralized figure of the leper. See his 'Le pestiféré ou
    divers aspects du refus de l'autre au XVIe siècle.'

42 Mullaney mentions that, while the disappearance of the disease in London

went unaccounted for due to the city's penchant for novel events, other European towns ritually celebrated its passing (32).

43 Like the lepers, *pícaros* would later become associated with *conversos* and witches, figures accused of child-murders. See Stephen Haliczer, 'The Jew as Witch: Displaced Aggression and the Myth of the Santo Niño de la Guardia.'

44 Sanford Shepard, *Lost Lexicon: Secret Meanings of Spanish Literature during the Inquisition*, 97. That the word was also used to refer to *conversos* by medieval and early modern Jewish writers in Spain demonstrates that the former were not distinguished so much by their 'race' as such, but by their Christianized behaviour. See chapter 3 for a fuller discussion of *conversos'* social role.

45 Derek W. Lomax, 'On Re-Reading the *Lazarillo de Tormes*,' 376.

46 Likewise, in the sixteenth century, the Crown of Aragón incorporated Navarra, Aragón, Catalonia, and Valencia. All future references to the Crown of Castile will be 'Castile.'

47 Marjorie Grice-Hutchinson, *Early Economic Thought in Spain: 1170–1740*, 125.

48 Henry Kamen, *European Society 1500–1700*, 52–5; and H.G. Koenigsberger and George L. Mosse, *Europe in the Sixteenth Century*. For information on the price revolution in Spain, see Earl J. Hamilton's classic study, *American Treasure and the Price Revolution in Spain, 1501–1650*; Ramón Carande, *Carlos V y sus banqueros*; Marjorie Grice-Hutchinson, *The School of Salamanca. Readings in Spanish Monetary Theory, 1544–1605*; and her *Early Economic Thought in Spain, 1177–1740*; and John H. Elliott, *Imperial Spain 1469–1716*, 181–208.

49 Woods cites the *Ordenanças reales de Castilla, recopiladas por Alonso Díaz de Montalvo* (1560) to corroborate his thesis that, as Lázaro's wife did not live with the archpriest, their liaison was unlikely to cause them serious problems; only 'blatantly public concubinage' was frowned upon by legal authorities (592).

50 'Nuevos apuntes sobre la carta de Lázaro.' Rico notes, however, that in a 1577 *pragmática* the wilful pandering of a wife is punishable by law (*Lazarillo* 130, note 18).

51 For admonishments against fraudulent pilgrims, see the citations in Augustin Redondo, 'Folklore, referencias histórico-sociales y trayectoria narrativa en la prosa castellana del Renacimiento,' 83, n.14.

52 That Tavera's decrees failed to move the clergy to abandon concubinage is made clear by the *Ordenanzas reales*, which mandated concubines to identify themselves by means of a scarlet cloth visibly pinned to their veil.

53 Although there is no modern biography of Tavera, see Pedro de Salazar y Mendoza, *Chronica de el cardenal Juan Tavera* (Toledo, 1603); for additional information, see Hayward Keniston, *Francisco de los Cobos, Secretary to Charles V*.

54 Albert Sicroff cites Salazar y Mendoza that Tavera was the first archbishop to consider imposing statutes against *conversos* in the Toledo church: *Los estatutos de limpieza de sangre: controversias entre los siglos XV y XVII*, 126. Notwithstanding his chronicler's arguments that Tavera's indecision was due to strong opposition (212), given what we know of his professional and personal integrity, it is more likely that, despite equally strong pressure in support of the statutes, he did not wish to take such deleterious action against his parishoners. Instead, it was by order of Juan Martínez Silíceo, Archbishop of Toledo from 1546 to 1557, that the statutes were enacted, Sicroff suggests, due to an 'obstinate' Silíceo's hardened attitude towards *conversos* and his desire to avenge Francisco de los Cobos's opposition to his nomination (Sicroff 127–8). For these reasons, I cannot agree with the early identification by Fonger de Haan or Fred Abrams's more recent statement that Martínez Silíceo might be the addressee of Lázaro's letter: see Fonger de Haan, *An Outline of the History of the 'Novela Picaresca' in Spain*; and Fred Abrams, 'To Whom was the Anonymous *Lazarillo de Tormes* Dedicated?'

55 Francisco de Osuna, *Norte de los estados en que se da regla de vivir a los ma[n]cebos y a los casados* (Burgos, 1541), fol.iii. Osuna's treatise, although first published in 1531, was written on occasion of the marriage of his benefactor, Diego López Pacheco, Marquis of Villena and Duke of Escalona – the same duke whose village Lazarillo and the blind man visited, and where the young boy exchanges the turnip for the sausage. Manuel J. Asensio has seen in the reference to the town an allusion to the group of Illuminists led by the Duke and often joined by Juan de Valdés, to whom he attributes the authorship of the *Lazarillo* ('La intención religiosa del *Lazarillo de Tormes*'). See also Manuel J. Asensio, 'Más sobre el *Lazarillo de Tormes*.' For Osuna, see Fidéle Ros, *Un Maître de Sainte Thérèse. Le père François d'Osuna. Sa vie, son oeuvre, sa doctrine spirituelle.*

56 George Shipley's witty articles putting Lazarillo on trial rightly condemn his hypocritical stance, but in doing so the critic falls victim to the author's fiction. See his 'The Critic as Witness for the Prosecution: Making the Case against Lázaro de Tormes'; 'The Critic as Witness for the Prosecution: Resting the Case against Lázaro de Tormes'; and 'Lazarillo de Tormes Was Not a Hardworking, Clean-Living Water Carrier.'

57 For poverty in early modern Europe besides studies cited previously, see J.C.K. Cornwall, *Wealth and Society in Early Sixteenth Century England*; Peter Kroedte, *Peasants, Landlords, and Merchant Capitalists: Europe and the World Economy*; and Brian Pullan, *Rich and Poor in Renaissance Venice: The Social Institutions of a Catholic State, to 1620.*

58 Martz estimates the percentage of poor in Toledo as 20 per cent in 1558, but

the year saw much famine and sickness. The poor in the parish of San Salvador accounted for less than 12 per cent, and ranked eighteenth of the twenty-one parishes, indicating that Lázaro lived in a very good neighbourhood (113–14). She gives the following percentages for other Castilian cities: Medina del Campo, 8.89; Valladolid, 9.54; Segovia, 15.74; Málaga, 22.60; and Trujillo, 50 (118).

59 See Elena Maza Zorrilla, *Pobreza y asistencia social en España, Siglos XVI al XX*, 82.

60 Vives's *De subventionem pauperum* was not translated into Spanish until 1781 by Juan de Gonzalo Nieto e Ivarra as *Tratado del socorro de los pobres*. I cite from the undated Clásicos Españoles edition, published in Valencia by Prometeo, which reproduces Nieto's translation. See also Abel Athougia Alves, 'The Christian Social Organism and Social Welfare: The Case of Vives, Calvin and Loyola.'

61 See, in particular, Michel Mollat's ch. 6, 'The Urgency of Charity,' in *The Poor in the Middle Ages: An Essay in Social History*, 87–117.

62 For Maravall, one reason for charity towards the poor was the very real threat of rebellion; see his 'Pobres y pobreza del medioevo a la primera modernidad,' 193–4.

63 Soto's treatise was published in 1556; the modern translation is *De iustitia et iure libre decem. De la justicia y del derecho*. Trans. M. González Ordóñez, 4 vols. (Madrid: Instituto de Estudios Políticos, 1967–8). See also J.I. Tellechea Idígoras, *El obispo ideal en el siglo de la reforma*.

64 I cite from the modern edition, Fray Domingo de Soto, O.P., *Deliberación en la causa de los pobres (y réplica de Fray Juan de Robles, O.S.B.)* (Madrid: Instituto de Estudios Políticos, 1965), 15–17.

65 Law vi of the 1640 *Recopilación* –'That the poor should not beg outside their place of origin' (que los pobres no anden a pedir fuera de sus naturalezas) – contains in the margins the history of some of these laws: 'Emperor Charles V and d. Juana [his mother] in Valladolid, 1524, petition 66; and in Toledo, 1525, petition 47, ordained all the following laws; and decreed they be following in Madrid, 24 August, 1540' (El Emperador don Carlos y D. Juana en Valladolid, año 24, pet. 66; y en Toledo año de 1525, pet. 47, mandó ordenar todas las leyes siguie[n]tes; y despues en Madrid, año 40. a 24 de Agosto las ma[n]dó guardar]. *Recopilación de las leyes destos reynos*, Libro Primero, Título XII. [Madrid, 1640], 53v). The laws promulgated in 1525 lend credence to those critics who believe this the year of Charles V's entry into Toledo remarked on by Lazarillo, although this would not necessarily date the text's composition.

66 The two orders, however, were understandably rivals: as early as the thir-

teenth century, Dominicans vied with Franciscans over land space for convents, prospective members, and sermon material. Franciscans, who upheld *usus pauper*, the restricted use of goods in such areas as food and clothing, criticized the Dominicans for accepting monies. In Oxford, a Dominican accused the Franciscans of hiding behind a subterfuge in receiving money through middlemen: David Burr, *Olivi and Franciscan Poverty: The Origins of the Usus Pauper Controversy*. See also Lester Little, *Religious Poverty and the Profit Economy in Medieval Europe*.

67 For Márquez Villanueva, the short timespan between the publication of the two treatises confirms the passionate interest aroused by the debates. To my knowledge, he is the first to associate the Soto–Robles debate with the *Lazarillo* (*Espiritualidad y literatura* 121, n.88). I am grateful to him for referring me to the writings of Francisco de Osuna.

68 Francisco de Osuna, *Quinta Parte: del abecedario espiritual ... que es Consuelo de pobres y Aviso de ricos* (Burgos, 1542).

69 Redondo asserts that Tavera spent part of 1544 with Prince Philip at the *cortes* in Valladolid, where he queries Soto as to the advisability of the orders against almsgiving currently being applied in Zamora ('Pauperismo' 706). Soto documents his disapproval in his introduction ('Having asked me about this in Valladolid the Most Reverend Cardinal of Toledo, I answered that I could not reasonably agree with all that was being done. [Habiéndome preguntado el Revendísimo Cardenal de Toledo en Valladolid sobre esta razón, dije que no me cabía bien en el entendimiento todo lo que se hacía (20)]). In the introduction to his response to Soto, Robles specifically invokes Tavera: 'Last November, when in Valladolid I kissed Your Highness's hands, speaking with the Most Reverend Cardinal of Toledo [Tavera] on the order regarding almsgiving currently in place at several localities in the kingdom, [Tavera] asked that I put in writing my reasons for suggesting such an order, since he knew that it was due to my advice and preaching that the order had been implemented in Zamora' (El mes de noviembre próximo pasado, cuando estando en Valladolid besé las manos a Vuestra Alteza, hablando con el Reverendísimo Cardenal de Toledo sobre esta orden de la limosna que se ha tomado en algunos lugares del reino, me encargó que pusiese en escrito los fundamentos que había tenido para aconsejar que se tomase esta orden, porque estaba informado que por mi consejo y predicación se había comenzado en la ciudad de Zamora [147]).

70 Colbert Nepaulsingh, *Apples of Gold in Filigrees of Silver: Jewish Writing in the Eye of the Spanish Inquisition*. To posit Lazarillo as a *converso* does not make the author one: Nepaulsingh's argument (44) that 'confesso' is a coded term for *converso* only decipherable by *conversos* belies its use in Quevedo's *Buscón*.

I believe it is critically more fruitful to assign the *pícaro* the non-essentialized role of alienated 'other,' which subsumes all marginalized groups in that their scapegoating fills a societal need at specific historical moments.

71 Here, I modify Sieber's illuminating reference to the Lazarillo's construction of the self through the Lacanian mirror stage by suggesting that it is in Lázaro's fragmented reflection on the waters of the River Tormes, as son of both a miller and a thief, that his 'natural' and 'literary' births take place and coincide, a 'birth' that is then repeated when he views his younger brother as an alienated other (*Language and Society* 2 n.5).

72 Augustin Redondo, 'Folklore y literatura en el *Lazarillo de Tormes*: Un planteamiento nuevo (el 'caso' de los tres primeros tratados).'

73 Augustin Redondo, 'De molinos, molineros y molineras. Tradiciones folklóricas y literatura en la España del Siglo de Oro.'

74 Both for its colour and its generative qualities, Redondo gives semen as one of the meanings of flour ('Molino' 107).

75 Claudio Guillén views the relationship between Zaide and Lazarillo's mother as one fuelled by his 'pequeña familia clandestina': 'Los silencios de Lázaro de Tormes.'

76 In his *El niño pícaro literario de los siglos de oro*, Antonio Gómez Yebra contrasts Lazarillo's mother's parting words with Luis de Granada's admonishment to mothers: 'See how much a good and wise mother loves her child; how she warns him of any dangers; how she fulfils his every need; how she counsels him on his faults ... with what devotion she always prays for him to God; and, finally, how she cares far more for him than for herself and how cruelly she treats herself in order to lovingly nurture him. (Mira de la manera que una buena y cuerda madre ama a su hijo: cómo le avisa en sus peligros, cómo le acude en sus necesidades, cómo lleva todas sus faltas ... con qué devoción ruega siempre a Dios por él; y, finalmente, cuánto tiene dél que de sí misma, y cómo es cruel para sí por ser piadosa para con él (62; cited from *Guía de pecadores* [Madrid: Apostolado de la Prensa, 1948], 527).

77 Francisco Rico notes the possibility that this expression is modeled after the myth of Astraea, the maiden goddess of justice who abandoned earth due to human corruption (*Lazarillo* 72, n.4). Such a conflation with charity would also serve to underscore Lazarillo's ambivalence regarding his right to beg for alms, and proffers a veiled critique of Charles V's expansionist policies that were resulting in increasing unemployment and poverty.

78 Although there is no indication that Poor Laws were established in Toledo in 1540, as they were in Madrid, Linda Martz notes that the date of 1541 is substantiated by a manuscript written by the Franciscan Luis de Scala, who defended the rights of the poor to beg (120). The most active year for

welform reform, however, was 1543, when Cardinal Tavera visited Toledo to initiate another welfare reform that prohibited public begging and recorded all the needy of the city parishes and their allotted bread rations in the 'Book of the Poor' (121–2).

79 See Augustin Redondo, 'Historia y literatura: el personaje del escudero de *El Lazarillo*.'

80 See John Beverley, 'Lazarillo and Primitive Accumulation: Spain, Capitalism, and the Modern Novel.'

2. The Poor in Spain: Confinement and Control

1 As I comment in my following chapter, this was only one way in which reason formed part of the 'practical politics' fostered by late-sixteenth century treatises on reason of state such as Giovanni Botero's *Ragione di stato*.

2 For the classic study on price inflation, see Hamilton, *American Treasure*; also, his 'The Decline of Spain.' For other views, see M. Morineau, 'D'Amsterdam a Séville: De quelle réalité l'histoire des prix est-elle la miroir?'; and *Inflation: Causes, Consequences, Cures*, a debate between Lord Robbins et al. (London: Institute of Economic Affairs, 1974), 14–15 (cited in Grice-Hutchinson, *Early Economic Thought*, 8); and J.H. Elliott, 'The Decline of Spain,' in *Spain and Its World, 1500–1700: Selected Essays*, 217-40; see especially his 'Introduction' to Part IV, 213–16.

3 Joseph Pérez asserts that, by 1515, Segovia's textile industry alone supported more than 20,000 workers: *La Révolution des 'Comunidades' de Castille (1520–1521)*, 36–9.

4 Jan De Vries, *The Economy of Europe in an Age of Crisis: 1600–1750*, 48-9. See also Julius Klein, *The Mesta,* and Carla Rahn Phillips and William D. Phillips, Jr, *Spain's Golden Fleece: Wool Production and the Wool Trade from the Middle Ages to the Nineteenth Century*.

5 See José Antonio Maravall, *La cultura del Barroco*.

6 Cavillac's suggestion ('Introducción' lxxxvi–lxxxviii) that the loss of a bourgeois nationalist conscience redirected economic focus from Castile to the Burgos–Antwerp axis might explain the *Lazarillo*'s publication in these two cities.

7 Castile and Valencia's grain prices rose by 376 index points in the sixteenth century (Kroedte 48–9).

8 The 1540 law was of special import; for the first time, the poor were forbidden to beg freely within the cities, and the legitimate poor assigned to hospitals. It was against this law, which deprived the poor of free movement, that Soto wrote his *Deliberación en causa de los pobres* five years later.

9 See Marcel Bataillon, 'Juan Luis Vives, réformateur de la bienfaissance.'

10 *Memorial al rey para que no salgan dineros de estos reinos de España* (1558). Cited in Michel Cavillac, 'Introducción,' *Cristóbal Pérez de Herrera. Amparo de Pobres.* Ed. Michel Cavillac (Madrid: Espasa-Calpe, 1975), cv. See also the modern edition by J. Larraz, published by Instituto de España (Madrid, 1970).

11 A previously unknown edition of the *Lazarillo de Tormes* printed in Medina del Campo on 1 March 1554, was found in 1992 in a small clandestine library hidden between the walls of a house in the town of Barcarrota, Extremadura. The library's contents, currently housed in the Museo Extremeño e Iberoamericano de Arte Contemporáneo in Cáceres, were all placed on the Inquisition's 1559 index of forbidden books and point to an owner who was interested in chiromancy, and Hebraic and Erasmian writings.

12 John Lynch, *Spain under the Hapsburgs: Empire and Absolutism, 1516–1598,* 248 ff. Richard Kagan notes that Toledo's textile industry, which in 1575 employed a third of the population as workers and artisans, protected the city from economic stagnation, although by the 1580s it already gave signs of the crisis affecting the broader national economy: lack of investment capital, high taxes on industry and trade, rising labour costs, and competition from foreign textiles. See his chapter 'The Toledo of El Greco,' *El Greco de Toledo: Exhibition of El Greco at the Toledo Museum of Art.*

13 Despite Lynch's excellent point, David Vassberg has rightly noted that the term 'peasant' is problematic; for an important discussion of its many applications, see his *Land and Society in Golden Age Castile,* 141–7.

14 Michel Foucault, *Discipline and Punish: The Birth of the Prison,* 198.

15 Philip's reign oversaw approximately 1,000 Inquisition cases yearly; while most concerned religious deviancy, approximately 15 per cent dealt with such social crimes as bigamy, homosexuality, and fornication: see Geoffrey Parker, *Philip II,* 100–2.

16 The same rigorous divisions between rogues and the populace occurred in England. See my 'Sonnes of the Rogue: Picaresque Relations in England and Spain.'

17 José Antonio Maravall, 'Trabajo y exclusión: El trabajador manual en el sistema social español de la primera modernidad.' Maravall speaks solely of *estamentos,* or estates, based on a religious world order, although he acknowledges that these often clashed and blurred with caste divisions. See chapter 3 for discussion of caste and ethnic distinctions.

18 Peter Russell makes a strong case for the final compatibility of arms and letters in Spain in the figure of Garcilaso de la Vega. See his 'Arms versus Letters: Towards a Definition of Spanish Fifteenth-Century Humanism.' Garcilaso's idealized positioning as a 'soldier poet' should nonetheless be

reconsidered in light of the social tensions between him and Charles V. See my 'Self-Fashioning in Spain: Garcilaso de la Vega.' See also José Antonio Maravall, *Utopía y contrautopía en el 'Quijote'*.

19 The phrase's ironic turn has been pointed out by Rico (*Lazarillo* 14, n.9). It follows Lázaro's hilarious misapplication of the beatitude (Mat. 5: 10): 'Blessed are they who suffer persecution for justice's sake' (y padesció persecución por justicia [14]).

20 Foucault's thesis on control during the classical age may be extended to include the *pícaros* who were inducted into service by the Hapsburg regime (*Discipline and Punish* 136).

21 This section owes much of its information on Toledo hospitals to Linda Martz's excellent study, *Poverty and Welfare in Habsburg Spain: The Example of Toledo*.

22 The childless couple left all their possessions to the hospital: 'e después de nuestras vidas, como dicho es, todo el remanente de los dichos nuestros bienes, e herencia ... sea del Dicho Hospital de la Misericordia, nuestro universal heredero' (clause no. 50, *Testamento de los Señores Don Luis de Antezana y Doña Isabel de Guzmán su muger fundadores del Hospital de Nuestra Señora de la Misericordia en Alcalá de Henares otorgado el 18 de octubre de 1483*; cited by Jesús Fernández Majolero, *Hospital de Nuestra Señora de la Misericordia de Alcalá de Henares: Datos previos para un estudio histórico, siglos XV y XVI*, 59).

23 In 1523, Adrian VI issued another bull granting indulgences to those who contributed to the hospital or helped in its rebuilding and conservation (Fernández Majolero 62–3).

24 Juan de Dios's mentor, Juan de Avila, warned him to 'guard against dealing too much with females because you should know that they are a trap sent by the devil so that the servants of God should fall': *Obras completas del beato Juan de Avila*, Eds. L. Sala Balust and F. Martín Hernández, vol. 1, carta 45 (Madrid, 1952–71), 501 (qtd. in Martz 41). See also Grace Goldin, 'Juan de Dios and the Hospital of Christian Charity.'

25 Toledo counted with twenty-one hospitals in 1549, including one dedicated to repentant prostitutes: Blas de Ortiz, *Summi templi toletani* (1549) fols. 143 ff.; cited in Rosario Díez del Corral Garnica, *Arquitectura y mecenazgo: La imagen de Toledo en el Renacimiento*, 187. Garnica cites Pedro Salazar de Mendoza in stipulating that of these, only eight were devoted to the sick; the rest took in beggars and the poor (186).

26 According to Martz, the Hospital del Rey treated contagious and incurable diseases, with a probable mortality rate of 100 per cent (177). This chapter relies on Martz for information on hospital ordinances and relief; see especially 125–227.

27 According to Mary Elizabeth Perry, the hospital cared for women of all ages, most of whom were indigent: *Gender and Disorder in Early Modern Seville*, 153–7.

28 See Enrique Rodríguez Solís, *Historia de la prostitución en España y América*, 270.

29 The manuscript, titled 'Que los hospitales generales es buen medio para el remedio de los pobres, si la Republica en comun se encarga del sustento dellos,' was discovered by Jacques Soubeyroux in the Biblioteca del Real Monasterio del Escorial, ms. L-I-12. An excerpt appears in his article 'Sur un projet original d'organisation de la bienfaisance en Espagne au XVIe siècle.'

30 See Maureen Flynn, *Sacred Charity: Confraternities and Social Welfare in Spain, 1400–1700*. See also José Sánchez Herrero, 'Cofradías, hospitales y beneficencia en algunas diócesis del Valle del Duero, siglos XIV y XV'; and Antonio Rumeu de Armas, *Historia de la previsión social en España*. For a study of a Madrid confraternity, see William J. Callahan, *La Santa y Real Hermandad del Refugio y Piedad de Madrid, 1618–1832*.

31 In 1454, Enrique IV forbade the founding of confraternities not specifically under a prelate that regulated their spirituality; nonetheless, his 1473 mandate that confraternities also receive royal approval went unheeded (Fernández Majolero 72).

32 Hilario Casado Alonso, *Señores, mercaderes y campesinos. La comarca de Burgos a fines de la Edad Media*, 550–4.

33 The claim dragged on from Isabel de Guzmán's death in 1503 to 1515, when Cardinal Cisneros ruled that the church chapter owed the hospital confraternity 100,000 *maravedís* ('[E]l ilustre e muy reverendísimo señor don fray Francisco Ximénez de Cisneros, cardenal dEspaña, arzobispo de Toledo, nuestro señor, ovo dado e pronunciado e dio e pronunció ... de los quales dichos cient mil maravedís nos damos e otorgamos por bien contentos e pagados, entregados a toda nuestra voluntad en nombre de la dicha yglesia' [quoted in Fernández Majolero 132]).

34 The confraternity had an interesting history; founded in 1085 to ransom Christians held captive by the Moors and to provide the *mozárabes* of Toledo with Christian burial, by the sixteenth century it included some of the most illustrious nobles of the city, but allowed only thirty female members, who should be *beatas* and widows (Martz 189).

35 The literary thieves' groups no doubt also have as their models the criminal associations formed throughout Europe. Julio Caro Baroja proposes the Sevillian prisoners' organization *Germanía*, whose language is also called by that name, as the source for Cervantes's *Rinconete y Cortadillo*, stating that this term is etymologically related to *hermandad*: Julio Caro Baroja, *Realidad y fantasía en el mundo criminal*, 30–40.

36 Lynch (96–100) notes Philip II's religious zeal in evangelizing the New World, convening the Council of Trent, in which more than 100 Spanish priests and theologians took a prominent part in its deliberations from 1562 to 1563, and fighting heresy in the Netherlands. Nonetheless, the King did not balk at making alliances with non-Catholic monarchs (Parker, *Philip II*, 53).

37 See Chaves's *Relación*, most likely written in 1599, for a description of the Sevillian jail's physical plant and the prisoners' organization: *Relación de lo que pasa en la Cárcel de Sevilla*, edited by Aureliano Fernández Guerra, in B.J. Gallardo, *Ensayo de una biblioteca española de libros raros y curiosos*, vol. I (Madrid, 1863), cols. 1,341–71.

38 In his *Microcosmía y govierno universal del hombre cristiano* (Barcelona, 1592, re-edited Madrid, 1595), the Augustinian theologian Marco Antonio de Camós states that, due to the wealthy's cruel lack of charity, the poor are forced to beg and vagabonds unwilling to work take up begging as their profession, maiming their children and serving as negative example to them (cited in Caro Baroja, *Realidad y fantasía*, 67 n.138). It would not be until Cristóbal Pérez de Herrera's *Amparo de pobres*, however, that Philip II heeds the warnings to improve the lot of the poor through secular means.

39 See Elena Maza Zorrilla, *Pobreza y asistencia social en España, siglos XVI al XX*, 87 n.123. She quotes from Marcel Bataillon, *Erasmo y el erasmismo*, 193.

40 *Nueva Orden para el recogimiento de los pobres y socorro de los verdaderos*, in *Novísima recopilación* (lib. VII, tít. XXXIX, law XIV). Cited in Cavillac, 'Introducción,' *Cristóbal Pérez de Herrera: Amparo de pobres*, cxv–cxvi.

41 Miguel de Giginta, *Tractado de remedio de pobres* (Coimbra, 1578).

42 Chapter 25 of Giginta's *Tractado*, cited by Maza Zorrilla, 88, n.125.

43 Miguel de Giginta, *Del amparo de los pobres* (Biblioteca Nacional, Madrid, MS 18653/12). The memorial develops four principal points: 1 / that the poor should be organized in houses built in all the larger towns; 2 / that pairs of poor be allowed to beg mornings to obtain food; 3 / that the poor be taught trades such as weaving reeds, wool, or silk; and 4 / that the buildings should either be donated by the towns or paid for by the poor's work or with alms collected (65–66v).

44 On the reasons Giginta dedicated his treatise to Pazos, see Martz 70 ff.

45 Giginta may thus be placed towards the centre of the stratum that leads from the 'enclosed disciplines' of social control to the indefinitely generalizable 'panopticism' described by Foucault (*Discipline* 216). As I argue, however, in Spain, the insistence that the poor circulate more or less freely among society remained a strong imperative.

46 See my 'The Abjected Feminine in the *Lazarillo de Tormes*.'

47 Written in 1589, Botero's treatise was translated and published several times

in Spanish, including the Barcelona 1599 edition and the Burgos 1603 edition addressed to the Condestable de Castilla y León. Two Italian editions are addressed besides to Spanish nobles Diego Fernández de Cabrera and Bobadilla, Major-domo of the Supreme Councils of Aragón and Castile (Rome, 1598), and Antonio de Córdoba y Cardona, Duke of Sessa and Spanish Ambassador to Rome (Pavia, 1598). I quote from Giovanni Botero, *Practical Politics*, trans. G.A. Moore.

48 According to Elliott, by 1540, the year of the Poor Laws, the textile industry was in dire need of labour (*Imperial Spain* 190). See, besides, Antonio Domínguez Ortiz, *El Antiguo Régimen: los Reyes Católicos y los Austrias*, 298. Also, the Duke of Alba's expedition to the Netherlands in 1568 had depleted the south of Spain of manpower, seriously weakening the armed response to the *morisco* rebellion in Granada that same year: Fernand Braudel, *The Mediterranean and the Mediterranean World in the Age of Philip II*, vol. II: 1961. See also Jan de Vries, *The Economy of Europe in an Age of Crisis: 1600–1750*, 148–9.

49 See Juan de Tavera, *Constituciones sinodales del Arzobispado de Toledo* (Alcalá, 1636); and Jean-Pierre Dedieu, '"Christianization" in New Castile: Catechism, Communion, Mass, and Confirmation in the Toledo Archbishopric, 1540–1650.'

50 Although he lived mainly in Madrid, Cardinal Gaspar de Quiroga, the Toledan archbishop from 1577 to 1594, was known for his support of charitable acts; however, the city's success in combating the effects of disease and famine, according to Richard Kagan, was due to its strong economy: see 'The Toledo of El Greco,' 38–40.

51 Williams does not assign a chronological value to 'residual,' but intends instead the mediation of the traditional by novel alternative movements; see his *Marxism and Literature*, 121–7. For a broader application of Williams's theory to poverty, see Darlene Múzquiz, 'Charity, Punishment, and Labor: The Textualization of Poverty in XVII and XVIII Century Spain.'

52 According to Adrian Shubert, the view that eighteenth-century Spain, unlike other European countries, maintained a high degree of tolerance for the poor is inaccurate; see his '"Charity Properly Understood": Changing Ideas about Poor Relief in Liberal Spain.'

53 Flinn points out that, although infectious diseases struck randomly, their cycles at times peaked with those of irregular harvests, bringing on severe crises as those in Spain in 1597–1603 (51). See also Bartolomé Bennassar, *Recherches sur les Grandes Epidémies dans le Nord de l'Espagne à la fin du XVIe siècle*, 68.

54 For biographical information on Pérez de Herrera, I have relied on Michel Cavillac's indispensable introduction to his edition of the *Amparo de pobres*.

55 Michel Cavillac notes that Pérez de Herrera's ideas were also enthusiastically approved by religious reformers, in particular, the Jesuits, who were eager to apply more rational approaches to the problem of poor relief. See his 'L'enfermement des pauvres, en Espagne, à la fin du XVIème siècle.'

56 The *Diccionario de Autoridades* defines 'arbitrista' as 'he who offers means to augment state finances or the prince's income ... [they are] taken as negative and universally rejected, since their proposals and projects have been injurious to monarchs and damaging to the common good' (el que discurre medios para acrecentar el erario público o las rentas del príncipe ... se toma en mala parte y con universal aversión, respecto de que han sido mui perjudiciales a los Príncipes y mui gravosas al comun sus trazas y arbitrios). For Grice-Hutchinson, sixteenth-century political economists such as Pérez de Herrera portended the *arbitristas*, whom she defines as '"projectors" who, called up by the plight of their country, were to proliferate throughout the seventeenth century' (*Early Economic Thought* 132–3). For literature on *arbitrismo*, see J.H. Elliott, *The Revolt of the Catalans: A Study in the Decline of Spain, 1598–1640*; Jean Vilar, *Literatura y economía: La figura satírica del arbitrista en el Siglo de Oro*; Michael D. Gordon, 'The Arbitristas: An Historiographical and Bibliographical Survey'; and Juan Ignacio Gutiérrez Nieto, 'El pensamiento económico, político y social de los arbitristas.'

57 As I discuss in chapter 4, Quevedo opposes those he considers Machiavellian. Cervantes satirizes their schemes by having Don Quixote compare himself to one (*Don Quixote* II: 1). In Luis Vélez de Guevara's *Diablo cojuelo*, the *arbitrista*'s recommendations serve as a veiled critique of the Count Duke of Olivares's policies: see Francisco Rodríguez Marín, ed., *El diablo cojuelo*, 80.

58 See Gwendolyn Barnes-Karol, 'Religious Oratory in a Culture of Control.'

59 Vallés, called 'el divino' for his extensive medical knowledge, was professor of medicine at the Universidad Complutense. In 1548, he brought Pedro Jimeno, a student of Vessalius in Padua, to Alcalá de Henares where, in 1559, they published the commentaries to Galen's *De locis patientibus* (Fernández Majolero 81). Pérez de Herrera himself referred to Vallés as 'celeberrimus inter medicos regios primus magister meus et vere Mecenas' in his dedication to the *Compendium Totius Medicinae* (Madrid, 1614), although there is no is proof that he studied at Alcalá with Vallés (Cavillac, 'Introducción,' xvi–xvii). See also Luis S. Granjel, *Los médicos humanistas españoles*, VIII: 273–84.

60 Philip's awareness of the insufficient military equipment of the Armada, according to Geoffrey Parker, prompted the change in the enterprise's original plan from attacking England directly to detouring to the Netherlands for more troops and equipment (Parker, *Philip II*, 151–2). See also Garrett Mattingly, *The Armada*, 208–10.

61 Supported by Pérez de Herrera's admirer Rodrigo Vázquez Arce, who allocated city tax funds for the project, the Madrid hospital exceeded its initial cost of 80,000 ducats; see Cavillac, *Amparo*, xxxix.

62 Lope's interest in social reform has been little studied, although he wrote the play *Juan de Dios y Antón Martín* about the founder of the Hermanos Hospitallers, deemed by Caro Baroja 'an exaltation of Charity' (*Realidad* 74). See also Manuel Fernández Alvarez, who quotes from the play the following maxim by Antón Martín: ' ... La moneda / en que ha de pagar un pobre, / es de rogar a Dios por quien / le hace el bien' (The coin paid by the poor / is to pray to God for those / who have been good to him [Act III, scene 13]): *La sociedad española en el Siglo de Oro*, 866–88. The *Amparo* also includes poems by Félix Arias Girón and Bartolomé López de Enciso, both mentioned in Cervantes's *Viage del Parnaso*; the Viceroy of Mexico, Juan de Mendoza y Luna, Marqués de Montesclaros; fray Prudencio de Luzón; Luis Fernández de Portocarrero, Conde de Palma; Enrique de Araíz y Verrasoeta, Philip III's accountant; the Franciscan biographer Antonio Daza de Madrigal; Bernabé de la Serna Ramírez; and Pérez de Herrera's son, Juan Antonio de Herrera.

63 '[W]hose greatness but yours, so full of courage, prudence and admirable maturity, fulfilling and promising, despite your youth, great happiness and hope to these kingdoms, should give needed relief to the true poor, banish the false poor from this kingdom, and constrain the vagabond from acting as a drone among bees? And, since this task is worthy of a sovereign prince, approved and begun by the prudence and Christian efforts of the King, our Lord (whose most fortunate reign decreed the laws ensuring the good government and reformation desired by all to preserve their lives and customs), it behooves Your Highness, as his successor, emulator of his achievements, and son of such a Christian and clement father, to continue, protect, and support his work in order to sustain its conservancy; since the paramount concern of the true reason of state is that princes serve and please God through their works, and endeavour to rid their kingdom of the vicious and vagabond sorts threatening to destroy its good customs' (¿[A] quién sino a su grandeza, llena de valor, prudencia y madurez admirable, que en tan tiernos años da y promete grandes felicidades y esperanzas en estos reinos, pertenece dar al verdadero pobre el remedio que ha menester, y echar destos reinos al fingido, y disponerlo de manera que el vagabundo no lo sea, ni sirva de lo que los zánganos en el reino de las abejas? Y porque, siendo esta obra digna de príncipe soberano, y como tal aprobada y comenzada por la prudencia y cristiandad del Rey, Nuestro Señor [pues en sus felicísimos días han salido y fundádose todas las órdenes de buen gobierno y reformación que pueden los hombres desear para conservación

de vidas y costumbres], es necesario también que V.A., como sucesor suyo, imitador de sus obras, y hijo de padre de tan gran cristiandad y clemencia, lo prosiga, ampare y favorezca, como tanta parte de su conservación; pues el punto mayor de la verdadera razón de Estado consiste en hacer los príncipes obras con que sirvan, y agraden a Dios, y procurar limpiar sus reinos de gente vagabunda y viciosa que estraga las buenas costumbres dellos [*Amparo de pobres* 9–10]).

64 For the various surcharges collected from theatre rates and their distribution to hospitals, see John J. Allen, 'Los corrales y la sociedad,' in J.M. Ruano de la Haza and John J. Allen, *Los teatros comerciales del siglo XVII y la escenificación de la comedia*, 190–3. See also Charles Davis and John Varey, *Los corrales de comedias y los hospitales de Madrid. 1574–1615. Estudio y documentos.*

65 Quoting Bentham, Foucault draws attention to the system's totalizing effects, as Bentham's preface to *Panopticon* opens with a list of the benefits to be obtained from his 'inspection-house': '*Morals reformed – health preserved – industry invigorated – instruction diffused – Public burthens lightened –* Economy seated, as it were, upon a rock – the gordian knot of the Poor-Laws not cut, but untied – all by a simple idea in architecture!' (*Discipline* 207; quoted from Jeremy Bentham, *Works*. Ed. Bowring, IV, 1843. 39).

66 Cavillac cites Burgos *procurador* Jerónimo de Salamanca, who in 1597 proposed to the *Cortes* that artillery and the marine ropes currently imported from Germany be manufactured in Spain: *Amparo de pobres* 106, n.1 (quoted from *Actas de las Cortes*, t. XV, 484).

67 I am grateful to Sara T. Nalle for providing me a list of these *artes* and *tratados*: Fray Juan de Ortega, *Siguese vna compusicion de la arte de la arismetica y juntamente de geometria* (Leon, 1512); Juan Andrés, *Sumario breue de la practica de la arithmetica* (Valencia, 1515); Juan Gutiérrez, *Arte breue y muy prouechoso de cuenta Castellana y Arismetica* (Toledo, 1539); Cristóbal de Villalón, *Prouechoso tratado de cambios, y contrataciones de mercaderes, y reprouacion de vsura* (Valladolid, 1541); Gaspar de Texeda, *Suma de Arithmetica practica y de toas Mercadrias con la horden de contadores* (Valladolid, 1546).

68 For education in Spain, see Richard Kagan, *Students and Society in Early Modern Spain*; and Alfonso Capitán Díaz, *Historia de la educación en España*.

69 Common practice in sixteenth-century Spain, Kagan informs us, was for children to enter a 'training period' soon after the age of six. Poor children were often sent out as servants, domestics, or apprentices (*Students and Society* 8–9). The picaresque reflects the custom: Lazarillo is given up for adoption, while Guzmán and Pablos, the *buscón*, are sent to school. See also Boswell. Education for the poor continued through the eighteenth century in royal orphanages; Valentina Tikoff documents the case of Francisco de

Cáceres Martínez, affiliated with the Real Colegio Seminario de San Telmo in Seville from 1788 to 1802, an association that demonstrates the beneficial interaction that often ensued between the poor and providers of poor relief.

70 See Jean Bodin, *Response to the Paradoxes of Malestroit*, 37.

71 '[E]verything is included in this science, founded on its principles: proof, reason, geometry, and arithmetic' (todo se incluye en esta ciencia, fundada en sus principios demostración, razón, geométrica y arismétrica [*Amparo de pobres* 108]).

72 In France, it was not until the revolution that education began to be considered an ideal means of preparing children for mechanical work as disciplines came to function as techniques for creating useful individuals: see Foucault, *Discipline*, 211.

73 According to R.I. Moore, the medieval period blurred distinctions between lepers, the poor, and heretics: 'If leprosy and heresy were the same disease it was to be expected that their carriers should have the same characteristics. The leper's tattered and filthy clothing, staring eyes and hoarse voice are also part of the standard depiction of the wandering preacher and the wandering heretic– all, as it were, *paupers Christi*, or claiming to be' (R.I. Moore 63).

3. The Picaresque as *Pharmakos*

1 Before the *Guzmán*'s success in 1599, which inspired the publication of nine separate editions of the *Lazarillo* by 1603, only the castigated 1573 edition remains extant: Harry Sieber, *The Picaresque*, 11. For discussion of the *Lazarillo*'s popularity, see Claudio Guillén, 'Luis Sánchez, Ginés de Pasamonte y el descubrimiento del género picaresco.'

2 Vásquez Arce was replaced as president of the Council of Castile by Lerma's brother-in-law, the Count of Miranda, and Diego de Yepes, Philip II's confessor, exiled to Tarazona as bishop. Although Pérez de Herrera remained in Madrid, his pleas to the king to subsidize the city and not transfer the court to Valladolid fell on deaf ears. For the role Philip III's aunt, the Empress María, played in the court's move from Madrid, see Magdalena S. Sánchez, 'Empress María and the Making of Political Policy in the Early Years of Philip III's Reign.' The perception that Philip III depended solely on the Duke of Lerma has been challenged by Antonio Feros, 'The King's Favorite, the Duke of Lerma: Power, Wealth, and Court Culture in the Reign of Philip II of Spain, 1598–1621.'

3 *Del amparo de los verdaderos pobres de los Reynos y Reduccion de los vagabundos dellos*. Borrador de la cédula de Felipe 30., 1599. Biblioteca Nacional, R-18728.26.

4 Martín González de Cellorigo makes mention of a law, passed by Philip II in 1577, that specifically converts convicts sent to the galleys into the king's 'slaves': *Memorial de la política necesaria y útil restauración a la República de España y estados de ella y del desempeño universal de estos Reinos (1600)*, 74.

5 See Américo Castro, *Cervantes y los casticismos españoles*, 43; Donald McGrady, *Mateo Alemán*, 80; and Joseph Silverman, 'Plineo, Pedro Mejía y Mateo Alemán: La enemistad entre las especies hecha símbolo visual.' Peter Dunn attributes Alemán's pessimism instead to the tradition of *contemptus mundi* (*Spanish Picaresque* 59, n.28). Critics rejecting Guzmán's conversion as hypocritical also implicitly or explicitly attribute his negativity to his *converso* origins. For the most convincing anti-conversion advocates, see Joan Arias, *Guzmán de Alfarache: The Unrepentant Narrator*; Carroll Johnson, *Inside Guzman de Alfarache*; Benito Brancaforte, *Guzmán de Alfarache: ¿conversión o proceso de degradación?*; and Judith Whitenack, *The Impenitent Confession of Guzmán de Alfarache*.

6 Explaining the reaction in terms of Alemán's social status, Guillén takes fully at face value the jailer's accusations against the author, describing his outrage as 'furious, passionate, impulsive, and leaning more toward quixotic than picaresque' ([i]racundo, fogoso, impulsivo y acaso más quijotesco que picaresco). See Guillén's chapter 'Los pleitos extremeños de Mateo Alemán' (*El primer Siglo de Oro* 195). This is an expanded version of the article that appeared in *Archivo Hispalense* 32 (1960): 387–407.

7 See Germán Bleiberg, *El 'Informe secreto' de Mateo Alemán sobre el trabajo forzoso en las minas de Almadén*.

8 'And this witness has seen many prisoners attend to the ovens where metals are heated to extract the mercury, the most dangerous work of all, since the daily contact with the smoke from the metal ruins men's health as many lose their minds and others become poisoned. And from carrying buckets of mercury ... and sifting the ashes, as these imperceptively enter the mouth, eyes and nose, this witness has seen many become poisoned and some lose their minds and has heard say that many have died from this. And being very hot, the ashes burn their feet and hands besides' (Y a visto este testigo que muchos forçados de asistir al cozimyento de los metales de donde se saca el azogue de los hornos que es el trauajo de mayor peligro que ay para la salud porque con el humo del dicho metal y la hordinaria asistencia haze notable daño a la salud de los hombres porque muchos bienen a perder el juizio y otros a quedar azogados y de la dicha ocasion de llevar los cubos del azogue dende donde los lauan ... y de cerner las cenyzas porque se les entran syn sentir por la boca los ojos y narizes este testigo a uisto a muchos quedar azogados y algunos perder el juicio y a oydo dezir que an muerto muchos

dello demas de que por estar como estanlas dichas cenyzas muy calientes se les abrasan los pies y las manos [Bleiberg 55–6]).

9 For confirmation of Alemán's *converso* origins, McGrady relies mainly on Francisco Rodríguez Marín, *Discursos leídos ante la Real Academia Española*, 2d ed. (Seville: Francisco de P. Díaz, 1907). See also Guillén, 'Los pleitos extremeños,' 179.

10 Michel Cavillac expands on this in his perceptive contextual studies of Alemán's novel, *Gueux et marchands dans le 'Guzmán de Alfarache' (1599–1604)* and 'Para una relectura del *Guzmán de Alfarache* y de su entorno sociopolítico.' Although best suited to the *Guzmán de Alfarache*, Cavillac's thesis has been central to my own argument on the picaresque in general.

11 Bleiberg believes that Alemán's rents and property allowed him to live comfortably (*El 'informe'* 12).

12 However, see Eugenio Asensio, *La España imaginada de Américo Castro*. Francisco Rico cites Edmond Cros's *Protée et les gueux* that Alemán had been granted permission to emigrate to Peru before presenting proof of his *limpieza de sangre* ('Apendices,' in Mateo Alemán, *Guzmán de Alfarache* (Barcelona: Planeta, 1983), 944. All my quotations are from this edition.

13 Although not all *arbitristas* were *conversos*, biographical data point to Pérez de Herrera's *converso* origins despite his claim to Old Christian ascendance. See Cavillac, 'Introducción,' in *Amparo de pobres*, xiv–xv; and José Antonio Domínguez Ortiz, *Los judeoconversos en España y América*, 185–86. Alonso de Barros served at court until his death in 1604. His letter in support of the *Amparo de pobres*, included by Pérez de Herrera in his final edition (255–61), was also published separately. Alemán wrote the prologue to Barros's *Proverbios morales* (1598), which he reciprocated by composing a eulogy for the *Guzmán*'s Part One. As mentioned earlier, Lope de Vega, who dedicated a sonnet to Alemán's *San Antonio de Padua*, also formed part of this group.

14 See Edmond Cros, *Protée et les gueux: Recherches sur les origines et la nature du récit picaresque dans 'Guzmán de Alfarache'*, 433–44; and by the same author, *Mateo Alemán: Introducción a su vida y a su obra*, 95–6. That this danger was perceived by a majority may be seen in Sayavedra's apocryphal *Guzmán*; Caro Baroja cites the passage from Part Two, book II, chapter 3 (*Realidad y fantasía* 69–7).

15 Caro Baroja (*Realidad y fantasía* 30–1) notes that the Sevillian jail, which housed more than 1,000 inmates, tolerated an organization run by *jermanes*, as described by Chaves (*Relación de lo que pasa en la Cárcel de Sevilla*, I, cols. 1.341–1371). Caro Baroja makes the case for the linguistic connection between *germanía* – thieves' language and customs – and *hermanía* (38). For Carroll Johnson, the Monipodio episode in *Rinconete y Cortadillo* represents

all the exclusivist corporations of early modern Spain, while the *pícaros* stand for the new order of 'entrepreneurial capitalism'; see his 'The Old Order Passeth, or Does It? Some Thoughts on Community, Commerce, and Alienation in *Rinconete y Cortadillo*.'

16 'The *pícaro* is not the same as the poor to whom the organizers of poverty and unemployment relief do not address their essays. He remains an outsider, an inconformist, unadaptable' (El pícaro no es el pobre al que se dirigen los ensayos de los organizadores de ayuda al menesteroso y al desempleado. Es el que queda fuera de esto, disconforme, inadaptable [Maravall, *La literatura picaresca* 370]). Maravall seems here to base his view only on literary examples; what he misses, I believe, is that the treatment of poverty often encouraged delinquent behaviour among both literary and historical *pícaros*.

17 See Germán Bleiberg, 'Mateo Alemán y los galeotes,' 363.

18 Although translations of the text are my own, I have consulted James Mabbe, *The Rogue or the Life of Guzman de Alfarache*.

19 Maravall describes individualism mainly as resulting from the reaction against the social barriers imposed by social divisions (*Literatura picaresca* 304); he agrees with Lawrence Stone's use of the term to characterize the impulse to promote internal social changes, which Maravall translates as *medrar*. See Lawrence Stone, *The Crisis of the British Aristocracy, 1558–1641* (654). Nevertheless, Stone has also pointed out that the movement by those on the 'bottom rung' of the social ladder, which included dependents on charity, apprentices, and live-in servants, was restricted to their geographical displacement from farms to towns: 'Social Mobility in England, 1500–1700.'

20 At least four years elapsed between the composition of the *Guzmán*'s Part One (finished in 1598) and its Part Two, which countered Juan Martí's apocryphal *Segunda parte de la vida del pícaro Guzmán de Alfarache* (published in Valencia in 1602). During this time, Spain suffered considerable economic and political upheavals as Philip III came into power.

21 As is well known, Báñez and Molina held a central role in the theological controversy over divine grace and free will. Molina accused Báñez of Calvinistic tendencies for believing that man's free will was compromised by Original sin: see 'Báñezianism,' in *Encyclopedic Dictionary of Religion*, eds. P.K. Meagher et al. (Washington: Corpus, 1979), 1: 355–6.

22 Michel Cavillac summarizes the discussions on free will in the *Guzmán de Alfarache* in the section titled 'Les coordonnées augustiniennes du discours de Guzmán sur la grace' (*Gueux et marchands* 70–102). His conclusion that, through his conversion, Guzmán regenerates into a 'new man' in service to the state, is, I believe, flawed by his acceptance of the dubious conversion narrative, which he deems an act of divine providence, and his interpretation

of the *pícaro* as personifying the merchant class, rather than serving as an ironic rhetorical vehicle for Alemán's defence of mercantilism ('L'Homme Nouveau et l'*homo hispanus* régénéré au service de la république ne faisaient qu'un. Cette consubstantialité de la religion et du civisme impregne la totalité de l'énoncé' [*Gueux* 109]).

23 It is likely that the urge to accumulate silver *reales*, or *patacones*, comments also on the impending switch to copper coins, or *vellones* (Elliott, *Imperial Spain*, 304).

24 For a subtle deconstruction of Guzmán's discourse through its 'burlas' and 'veras,' see Nina Cox Davis, *Autobiography as 'burla' in the 'Guzmán de Alfarache'*.

25 See Michel Cavillac, 'Para una relectura del *Guzmán de Alfarache* y de su entorno sociopolítico.'

26 Martín González de Cellorigo, *Memorial de la política necesaria y útil restauración a la república de España y estados de ella y del desempeño universal de estos reinos (1600)*. Ed. José Pérez de Ayala (Madrid: Instituto de Estudios Fiscales, 1991). Born in Valladolid, Cellorigo was a member of the Royal Chancellery and an Inquisition lawyer; he wrote two other treatises, both supporting the expulsion of the *moriscos*: (*Memorial dirigido a S.A. el Príncipe D. Felipe, hijo de Felipe 2° ... en que por segunda vez se avisan los daños que los nuevos convertidos de Moros a estos Reinos causan* [Valladolid, 1597]).

27 Among these, Pérez de Ayala lists Domingo de Soto, Luis de Molina, and Tomás de Mercado as proposing fair rates; and Luis Ortiz as protectionist ('Estudio preliminar,' *Memorial*, xxv–xvi). See his article 'Un teórico español de la política financiera: D. Martín González de Cellorigo,' *Revista de Derecho Financiero y Hacienda Pública* 36 (December 1959): 711–47. For a broader treatment of early modern Spanish economy, see José Luis Sureda Carrión, *La Hacienda castellana y los economistas del siglo XVII*; Jean Vilar, *Literatura y economía*; and José Ignacio Gutiérrez Nieto, 'El pensamiento económico, político y social de los arbitristas,' 250 and 293.

28 Maravall explains this historical process as one brought on by 'the weakening and abandonment of the bourgeoisie ... , due not to a crisis or disclaiming its role, but to the intentional strengthening of the power of the nobility who, for its own protection, drew the newly wealthy along with them and curbed other ascendent groups' (la pérdida de fuerza y abandono de la burguesía ... más que a una crisis de ella misma, más que a una retracción de su papel, se debió a un intencionado fortalecimiento del poder de la nobleza, que para ayudarse arrastró consigo a los enriquecidos y otros grupos ascendentes se vieron frenados [Maravall, *La cultura del Barroco*, 86]).

29 *Juros* represented a contract between the Crown and an individual or group

for an annual pension for various services rendered and confiscation or indemnization of property. Derived from specific Crown income, they could be assigned for life, bequeathed to heirs, or redeemed by the Crown. *Censos* functioned as mortgage loans, usually against agricultural lands; their interest was lower and affected farmers and labourers, for which reason these loans were blamed for the demise in agriculture: 'those who have money do not work the land and they who work and reap the land, lack the funds to do so' (tienen el dinero los que no labran la tierra y carecen de ello los que la labran y hacen que dé fruto [quoted in Alfredo Alvar Ezquerra, *La economía europea en el siglo XVI*, 144]). For the above, I utilize Alvar's helpful discussion of instruments of exchange (132–45).

30 Although Pérez de Ayala notes that Cellorigo does not use the moderm term 'investment,' he believes that this is what the economist means when he states that Spain's troubles are due to the imbalance between 'querer y poder,' what people desire economically and what they are able to accomplish; the wealthy do not wish to invest in agriculture, and the poor have no money with which to do so (*Memorial* xxxiv; 77).

31 Américo Castro, in fact, called the *Memorial* 'a book that today would be considered subversive, as it effectively states that the payment "poor people" make to God should be stopped, without having, on top of it, to pay even more to land owners (libro que hoy se consideraría subversivo, en el que se dice: que ya basta que la "gente pobre" pague el dinero debido a Dios, sin tener que pagar, además, otro muy mayor a los dueños de la heredad' [*La realidad histórica de España*, 242]).

32 A virulent supporter of the Catholic monarchs' earlier efforts to achieve religious homogeneity, Cellorigo not only urged expulsion of the *moriscos* who had not truly converted, but proposed restricting all *moriscos* to agricultural field labour, both because its 'rustic' nature best suited their condition and to keep them from stirring up trouble: 'since their work (for which they are earmarked) not only benefits the state where most needed, this kind of occupation, in itself so strenuous, would leave them dependent and exhausted, therefore reducing the dangers everyone warns about' (así como con su trabajo [a que son aplicados] aprovecharían a esta República en cosa tan necesaria, con semejante ocupación, que de suyo es trabajosa, quedarían más sujetos y rendidos y el peligro que todos dicen más asegurados [*Memorial* 84]).

33 Castro notes that Alemán's allegory of Creation in Part Two (2a,II.3.515–18) goes so far as to insist on its failure, attributing the world and the human race to a divine initial error (*Cervantes y los casticismos* 47–8).

34 Enrique Moreno Báez, *Lección y sentido del 'Guzmán de Alfarache'*, 56–9.

35 Two decades later, the state apologist, Andrés de Almansa y Mendoza, would observe that the only 'true practical reason of state takes care to benefit vassals so that they will not wish to change their lord or their fate. In applying equal justice, it sees to it that the nobility's benefits are what most tie them to their obligations' (La verdadera razón de Estado práctica es tener los vasallos beneficiados de suerte que no deseen mudar señor ni fortuna, en la justicia distributiva se tiene gran cuidado que el beneficiar la nobleza es el vínculo que más la obliga [Cartas de Andrés de Almansa y Mendoza. Novedades de esta Corte y avisos recibidos de otras partes (1621–1626). Cartas XIV (28 noviembre 1623) y XV (3 febrero 1624), in Libros raros y curiosos (Madrid, 1886), 234 and 261; quoted in Maravall, Cultura, 86]). Maravall adds: 'The system's reason and logic, then, is to privilege the great with all sorts of advantages so as to jointly maintain order' (Tal es, pues, la razón y sentido del sistema: privilegiar, con toda suerta de ventajas, a los distinguidos, para sustentar juntos el orden [Cultura 86]).

36 'And [kings] must love and honour their citizens, for they are the kingdom's treasurers and resources, and treat merchants in like manner, since they bring to their domains what is needed there, and [kings] should also love and help artisans and labourers, as their kings are aided and governed by their work and toil, as are all others in their domains, and no one can live without them' (E aun deben amar e honrar a los ciudadanos, porque ellos son como tesoreros e raiz de los Reinos, e esto mesmo deben facer a los mercaders que traen de otras partes a sus señorios las cosas que son y menester; e amar, e amparar deben otro si a los menestrales, e a los labradores, porque de sus menesteres e de sus labranzas se ayudan e se gobiernan los Reyes, e todos los otros de sus señorios, e ninguno non puede sin ellos vivir [Segunda Partida, III.10, quoted in Memorial 80]).

37 See Geoffrey Parker, Valor actual del humanismo español, 15–17; and Rico, 'Introduction,' 33–5.

38 Deeming Guzmán's conversion an 'aesthetic necessity,' Cavillac instead believes that its suddenness can only be explained through the pícaro's 'extreme Augustinianism,' the opposition of man's fundamental helplessness to God's omnipotence (Gueux 72).

39 In contrast, Peter Dunn ascribes Guzmán's disclosure of Soto's sedition to a 'civic act' that symbolizes Alemán's efforts to save the 'ship of state' and confirms the pícaro's conversion, which presumably has taken place immediately before (142). The act also releases him from his father's legacy, in that he 'betray[s] the betrayer' and is therefore 'free to enter into new relations with the figures of legitimate authority' (144). While I agree that Alemán has the state's welfare in mind, it seems more likely that the passage, besides sub-

stantiating Guzmán's failure to redeem himself, blames the sedition on the galley slaves' mistreatment.

40 For a discussion of various critical interpretations of Guzmán's closing words, see Brancaforte's first chapter, 'El ritmo de Sísifo y la estructura de *Guzmán de Alfarache*,' 1–26; also Whitenack 42–8; and Davis 104–7. In an otherwise tightly reasoned study, Dunn blames Guzmán's ambiguously narrated redemption on Alemán's immature writing skills: '[T]he work was also Alemán's first attempt at writing. Not surprisingly, it has some rough places and some technical maladroitness. Some readers find in these places not the faltering hand of the author but evidence of the narrator's irredeemable rottenness and bad faith. I cannot agree with them' (*Spanish Picaresque* 180).

41 'En fait, au début du xviie. siècle, le judéo-chrétien cesse de faire figure d'ennemi prioritaire: c'est aux dépens du Morisque et de l'étranger en général (la xénophobie monte alors en fleche) que s'exerce maintenant le refus de l'Autre' (Cavillac, *Gueux et marchands*, 32). In Seville especially, many foreigners (particularly Genoese, Germans, Flemings, and Portuguese) came to take advantage of the New World trade. See Ruth Pike, *Aristocrats and Traders: Sevillian Society in the Sixteenth Century*, 17, n.28.

42 One might make an analogy between the latter part of the fifteenth and that of the sixteenth century in that, at both times, *conversos* and *moriscos* were thrust into the Old Christian mainstream. In his lengthy book on the Spanish Inquisition, Benzion Netanyahu, disregarding the *moriscos*, maintains that the *conversos'* extraordinary success provoked the founding of the Inquisition. See his *The Origins of the Inquisition in Fifteenth Century Spain*.

43 Thus, the initial date given by Parker in his book's title: *Literature and the Delinquent: The Picaresque Novel in Spain and Europe, 1599–1753*.

44 See also Carlos Blanco Aguinaga, 'Cervantes y la picaresca: Notas sobre dos tipos de realismo.'

45 For two important studies on the picaresque as literary genre besides Wicks's, see Fernando Lázaro Carreter, 'Para una revisión del concepto 'novela picaresca,' and Claudio Guillén, 'Toward a Definition of the Picaresque.' Wicks has best phrased the problems of establishing the generic repertoire of the picaresque: 'It sometimes seems that in the process of clarifying some particular aspect of the picaresque, each new critical work contributes simultaneously to the theoretical disarray of the concept as a whole, until at one extreme the very existence of a historical picaresque genre is called into question, while at the other extreme the term *picaresque* is so diminished from its historical origins that it becomes critically meaningless' (18).

46 According to Miguel San Angel, the Arabic root f-r-g signifies 'to enjoy or console one's self'; the Arab word *farag*, 'to be free from worries or cares;

happiness, tranquility; pleasure': *Sentido y estructura del 'Guzmán de Alfarache' de Mateo Alemán*, 55.

47 My use of the term 'other' is prompted by the protracted arguments over the various designations by those who wish to categorize social groups by their difference. The term's identificatory force, however, stems not from what a group is – since groups may interconnect and reform according to specific interests – but to what a group is *not*. Recently the term 'queer' has been applied to disparate groups outside hegemonies of power, beyond its initial essentialized distinction delimited by homosexuality. Since the term still serves to refer primarily to homosocial relations as well as to homosexual activities and preferences, I do not believe that its application in this study would equally serve my purpose, although *conversos* and *moriscos* were often accused of homosexual tendencies as a means of further denigration. See Jonathan Goldberg, ed., *Queering the Renaissance*. For a compendium of essays that address the duality of the term as applied to Spanish culture, see Josiah Blackmore and Gregory S. Hutcheson, *Queer Iberia: Crossing Cultures, Crossing Sexualities*.

48 In his *La realidad histórica de España* and in *Cervantes y los casticimos españoles*, Castro defends his use of the term 'caste' to designate *conversos*, asserting that, as the *conversos* were not Jews but Spaniards, they did not belong to an ethnic or religious group, but to a caste system, since 'race' denoted shared physical characteristics: 'The Spanish problem was one of Moorish and Jewish caste (not race!)'; El problema español era de castas (¡no razas!) mora y judía [*Cervantes* 108 and 147]). To this purpose, however, he cites numerous contemporary writings that speak to the *converso*'s *linaje*, or lineage, a tag that clearly denotes biological affiliation.

49 Castro, *La realidad histórica*; Marcel Bataillon, 'Les nouveaux chrétiens dans l'essor du roman picaresque'; and McGrady 100–1.

50 On other occasions, Maravall's comments are much closer to the mark, as when he cautions against focusing too narrowly on only one aspect of the social estates, or *estamentos*; yet, he seems to fall prey to the same narrow judgment when he asserts that wealth is what most distinguished a group. His thoughts on the complexities of social hierarchy are included in several of his works; see especially *Honor, poder y élites en el siglo XVII*, 13–15.

51 While it is true that the *moriscos* were far less desirous of, and successful in assimilating with the Old Christian hegemony, the notion that they formed a completely 'unassimilated' class, as Pike states, is currently under revision (Pike, *Aristocrats*, 154–70). See Mary Elizabeth Perry, 'The Politics of Race, Ethnicity, and Gender in the Making of the Spanish State.'

52 In defining the structure of what he calls 'stereotypes of persecution' and the

patterns of collective violence, René Girard explains that social and cultural differences are obliterated in moments of institutional crisis, paradoxically creating a 'negative reciprocity' that then allows for a sameness whereby confusion results and all take on a monstrous aspect. 'The signs that indicate a victim's selection result not from the difference within the system but from the difference outside the system, the potential for the system to differ from its own difference, *in other words not to be different at all, to cease to exist as a system*' (my emphasis): *The Scapegoat*, 12 ff.

53 Although offering a corrective to the extreme views generated by the *limpieza de sangre* controversies, Kamen nevertheless trivializes the consequences of racism when not institutionalized by the state. See his 'Limpieza and the Ghost of Américo Castro: Racism as a Tool of Literary Analysis.'

54 See Jaime Contreras, 'Aldermen and Judaizers: Cryptojudaism, Counter-Reformation, and Local Power.'

55 See Ruth Pike, *Enterprise and Adventure: The Genoese in Seville and the Opening of the New World*. Genoese merchants first formed colonies in Seville, Lisbon, Medina del Campo, Valladolid, Antwerp, and the New World. Fernand Braudel explains that the Sevillian founding chapter was signed by the Catholic Monarchs in 1493, recognizing its right to elect and change consuls: *The Mediterranean and the Mediterranean World in the Age of Philip II*, vol. 1: 342–3.

56 See also John Lynch, *Spain 1516–1598*, 148–9.

57 Pike translates from the *Actas capitulares* of the Seville Cabildo, 8 April 1598.

58 Exasperated by the inflated interest rates of the *asientos*, the royal letters of credit issued by Genoese banks, Philip II delayed payments to consolidate the state's floating debt, incurring the 'bankruptcies' of 1557, 1560, and 1575. The withholding of funds by the Genoese in 1576, which prompted Antwerp's sacking by unpaid soldiers, forced Philip II to concede extremely favourable conditions in exchange for a 5-million-ducat loan (Alvar 1328–39); 154–5). See also Felipe Ruiz Martín, *Pequeño capitalismo, gran capitalismo. Simón Ruiz y sus negocios en Florencia*, 16 ff.

59 *Memoriales y discursos de Francisco Martínez de Mata* 60); and Cristóbal Suárez de Figueroa, in *El Passagero* (Madrid, 1914), 20; quoted by Mary Elizabeth Perry, *Crime and Society in Early Modern Seville*, 437. n.31.

60 See Ruth Pike, 'The Image of the Genoese in Golden Age Literature.'

61 *La Isla de los Menopantes* (1639); cited in Braudel, *The Mediterranean and the Mediterranean World*, II: 825–6.

62 In distinguishing the role played by trade in various contemporary cultures, Cellorigo implicitly gives us a biased psychological portrayal of the people. The Romans hold agriculture to be a more noble occupation; the Neapolitans

accept leisure only as noble and honourable, and hate work so much they consider theft more honourable than any occupation; while the Genoese and Venetians place trade above all else, granting merchants every possible honour, even that of Great Duce (86–7).

63 Lynch calculates that over half of Spain's Atlantic fleet was lost (*Spain* 248). According to Kevin Ingram, there were no fleet sailings between Drake's raid of April 1587 and March 1589, causing a rise in freight rates; the *averia* increased from 1.7 per cent in 1585 to 8 per cent in 1591. I am grateful to him for making available his unpublished paper 'The Ineluctable Decline of the Seville Merchant Community, 1503–1621,' read at the Society for Spanish and Portuguese Historical Studies Conference, Toronto, Canada, 20–3 April 1995.

64 While I am fully aware of the various theories of reader-response aesthetics, it is not my purpose here to address the narrator's ideal inferred, or informed readers, but the actual seventeenth-century consumers of picaresque narratives. In this regard, my intention of positing an unmanipulated reader remains closer to that of Judith Fetterley in *The Resisting Reader: A Feminist Approach to American Fiction* than to the readers alluded to in, among others, Stanley Fish, *Is There a Text in This Class? The Authority of Interpretive Communities*; Wolfgang Iser, *The Implied Reader: Patterns of Communication in Prose Fiction from Bunyan to Beckett*; Norman N. Holland, *The Dynamics of Literary Response*; and in the essays collected in *Reader-Response Criticism from Formalism to Post-Structuralism*, ed. Jane P. Tompkins.

65 For Rico, since the *Guzmán* aspires to create a 'perfect man,' everything that relates to him becomes a target for the novel's didacticism ('Introducción' 45, n.52).

66 The Laurenti and Ricapito bibliographies list the main studies on the *Guzmán*. Recent books include Brancaforte, *Guzmán de Alfarache: ¿Conversión o proceso de degradación?*; Carlos Antonio Rodríguez Matos, *El narrador pícaro: Guzmán de Alfarache*; Whitenack, *The Impenitent Confession*; and Davis, *Autobiography as 'burla'*.

67 'If the *Guzmán* seems contradictory and discontinuous it may be not because it betrays the deceit of the character it represents (or alternatively the subtle, ironic design of the author who produced it), but because it reproduces contradictions in the practice of writing which are both general to that practice and specific to a historical instance of it' (*Writing in the Margin* 102).

68 The lack of critical unity is reflected in Maurice Molho's inspired view of the text as a dialogue between the *pícaro* and the reader who, like his addressor, takes on several roles: Maurice Molho, *Introducción al pensamiento picaresco*, 68.

69 See Walter J. Ong, 'The Writer's Audience Is Always a Fiction.'

70 B.F. Ife, *Reading and Fiction in Golden-Age Spain: A Platonist Critique and Some Picaresque Replies*, 92. Ife's study remains an indispensable guide to the communicative function of literature in early modern Spain.

71 The expression is from Hans Robert Jauss's influential 'Levels of Identification of Hero and Audience,' See also his 'Literary History as a Challenge to Literary Theory.' For a useful introduction to modes of reader response to the genre, see Helen H. Reed, *The Reader in the Picaresque Novel.*

72 For a reader-response theory that problematizes the social dimension of art, see Hans Robert Jauss, *Toward an Aesthetic of Reception.*

73 Harry Sieber, 'Literary Continuity, Social Order, and the Picaresque' (Brownlee and Gumbrecht, eds., *Cultural Authority in Golden Age Spain* 143–64). Sieber states that other editions of the expurgated *Lazarillo* appeared in 1586 and, with Lucas Gracián Dantisco's *Galateo español*, in 1603 and possibly earlier (162, n. 25). See also Enrique Macaya Lahmann, *Bibliografía del Lazarillo de Tormes.*

74 Claudio Guillén, 'Toward a Definition of the Picaresque,' 144.

75 Maxime Chevalier, *Lectura y lectores en la España de los Siglos XVI y XVII*, 20 ff.

76 'En cambio, parece ser que los mercaderes, la clase propiamente burguesa de la España del Siglo de Oro, no manifiesta gran interés por la literatura de ficción' (27). Chevalier summarizes the contemporaneous readership as: 1 / a fraction of the cultured *hidalgos* and *caballeros*, especially the latter; 2 / a portion of the *letrados*, university professors, and intellectuals; 3 / those clerics who had sufficient economic resources, intellectual curiosity, and interest in fiction; and 4 / servants to the great noble houses who were educated, engaged in literature, and had access to their masters' libraries (29–30).

77 Sara T. Nalle, 'Literacy and Culture in Early Modern Castile,' *Past and Present* 125 / 1–2 (1989): 65–95. Nalle corrects Kagan's statement that only 10 to 15 per cent of the population could read and write (Kagan 23). To account for the contradictions that have stymied scholars when confronted by the low book-ownership figures in testaments despite the 'revolution' in literacy, Nalle's study also reviews the inventories of various publishing houses and Inquisition records that queried reading knowledge and book ownership.

78 Keith Whinnom, 'The Problem of the "Best-Seller" in Spanish Golden-Age Literature,' *BHS* 57 (1980): 189–98. According to Whinnom, early modern printing was 'dominated by prose non-fiction, devotional, moralizing and historical works' (Whinnom 194). Nonetheless, Whinnom confirms that, in the category of fiction, the *Guzmán de Alfarache*'s thirty-nine editions places it second only to the *Celestina* (Whinnom 193).

79 Of Ayala's 'staggering' inventory of 33,324 books and 135,575 ephemera,

more than one-third were devotional and another one-third 'well-known titles from late medieval and Renaissance Spanish imaginative literature: chivalric novels, proverbs, ballads and early examples of Spanish dramaturgy' (Nalle 83).

80 Umberto Eco has identified this change in interpretation as a 'principle' in mass communication media: 'the message which has been evolved by an educated elite ... is expressed at the outset in terms of a fixed code, but is caught by divers groups of receivers and deciphered on the basis of other codes. The sense of the message often undergoes a kind of filtration or distortion in the process, which completely alters its "pragmatic" function' (*The Role of the Reader: Explorations in the Semiotics of Texts* 141).

81 Arguments proposing Cervantes's *Don Quixote* as a 'funny book' exemplify the preference of some modern readers to privilege contemporaneous interpretations over an ambiguous text's more serious concerns; see Peter Russell, '*Don Quixote* as a Funny Book.' This phenomenon also often occurs in modern popular entertainment when serious social messages are inserted. In Norman Lear's 1970s television series *All in the Family*, the exaggerated right-wing opinions of arch-conservative Archie Bunker were perceived by conservative viewers to defend American middle-class family values against the radical railings of his anti-establishment son-in-law, Meathead, despite the producer's claims for the series' liberal stance.

82 Carlos Blanco Aguinaga, Julio Rodríguez Puértolas, and Iris M. Zavala, *Historia social de la literatura española*, I: 308.

83 See Anthony Zahareas, 'El género picaresco y las autobiografías de criminales.'

84 William Nelson, *Fact or Fiction: The Dilemma of the Renaissance Storyteller.*

4. Textualizing the Other's Body

1 After arguing unsuccessfully to keep the court in Madrid, Pérez de Herrera moves to Valladolid, where his salary goes unpaid. Almost bankrupt, he finally writes the king that he has dedicated twenty-eight years of his life to the state (Cavillac, 'Introducción,' l–lviii).

2 Henry Kamen, *Una sociedad conflictiva: 1469–1714*, 320.

3 Significantly, the *arbitristas*' concerns for economic renovation gave way to anti-Machiavellian analyses of statecraft, which appealed to ethical idealism and constitutional legalism against absolutism and reason of state: R.A. Stradling, *Philip IV and the Government of Spain, 1621–1665*, 14. That these treatises held little sway over Spain's decline is evinced by the Council's 1619 *consulta*, in response to Philip III's consultation with the Council in 1618,

which then prompted Pedro Fernández de Navarrete's *Conservación de monarquías*.

4 After the 1600 decree transferring the court to Valladolid, Pérez de Herrera reissues his 1597 treatise, 'Las grandes partes y calidades desta villa de Madrid,' adding a section on the means by which the city could remedy its food supply by establishing a central warehouse to control the price of wheat, and build a trading house and an underground sewer system. These urban improvements would put to work and eliminate as many 'idle *pícaros* as are now detrimental to the state' (agotar y ocupar tantos pícaros ociosos como andan en gran detrimento de la república [Cavillac, 'Introducción,' liii).

5 Citing Umberto Eco's *Opera aperta: Forma e indeterminazione nelle poetiche contemporeanee*, Benito Brancaforte offers an 'open' versus 'closed' reading of the narrative's structure. See his edition, *Guzmán de Alfarache*, vol. 1 (Madrid: Cátedra, 1981), 23–4.

6 Francisco de Quevedo, *El buscón*. Ed. Pablo Jauralde Pou (Madrid: Clásicos Castalia, 1990). For all citations, I rely on the Jauralde edition. Translations are my own, although I have consulted Alpert, *Two Spanish Picaresque Novels*.

7 There seems to be good reason for Quevedo's having rejected his novel's authorship. When the *Buscón* is first printed in Zaragoza, Quevedo was striving to ingratiate himself with the Count-Duke of Olivares; in 1631, the novel was placed on the Inquisition's Index: see Fernando Cabo Aseguinolaza's 'Prólogo' to his edition of the *Buscón*, Biblioteca Clásica, vol. 63 (Barcelona: Crítica, 1993), 3.

8 Paul Julian Smith, *Quevedo: El Buscón*.

9 Pablo Jauralde Pou, *Quevedo: Leyenda e historia*; and Gonzalo Díaz Migoyo, *La estructura de la novela: Anatomía de 'El Buscón'*.

10 For possible composition dates, see also Fernando Lázaro Carreter, 'La originalidad del *Buscón*.'

11 Lázaro Carreter's critical edition, based on the three extant manuscripts (Bueno, Santander [S], and Córdoba [C]) and the 1626 Zaragoza printed edition (E), conserves the masculine addressee, since he considers the B manuscript 'primitive' and relies on a second 'definitive' redaction reworked by a more mature Quevedo: see Fernando Lázaro Carreter, 'Estudio preliminar,' in Francisco de Quevedo, *La vida del Buscón llamado don Pablos*.

12 Francisco Rico denies the novel's parodic intent, viewing it as Quevedo's desire to copy the latest literary style: 'Puntos de vista. Postdata a unos ensayos sobre la novela picaresca.'

13 Quevedo writes the *España defendida* at about the same time, an anti-Machiavellian tract that will lead to his more mature work, the *Política de Dios*. See

España defendida y los tiempos de ahora, ed. R. Selden Rose, and *Política de Dios. Gobierno de Cristo*, ed. James O. Crosby.

14 *Historia de la vida del buscón*, ed. Edmond Cros (Madrid: Taurus, 1988).

15 Although Cabo Aguinolaza mentions Alfonso Rey's suggestion that Quevedo might have sent the book in 1630 to the Duchess, neither he nor, for that matter, Jauralde Pou comments on the gender distinction in the *Buscón*'s address ('Revisión del *Buscón*,' *Insula* 531 [1991]: 5–6; cited in Cabo 50). Edmond Cros's 1988 edition, also based entirely on the Bueno manuscript, likewise transcribes 'Yo, *señora*, soy de Segovia' (my emphasis), without, however, commenting on the address.

16 On Quevedo's misogyny, see Amédée Mas, *La caricature de la femme, du mariage et de l'amour dans l'oeuvre de Quevedo.*

17 Mariscal concurs with Amédée Mas's assessment that marginal figures exerted a strong attraction over Quevedo, although both critics attribute this interest to the exaggerated freedom represented by the *pícaro*. For Mariscal in particular, Quevedo's picaresque poetry articulates 'an alternative form of subjectivity produced from within an anti-aristocratic language linked to a concrete and subordinate social group' (Mariscal, *Contradictory Subjects*, 137–49).

18 According to Lía Schwartz Lerner, Quevedo's comparison, in his satirical poems and prose, of such practitioners of liberal professions as judges and *escribanos* to merchants for enriching themselves and purchasing titles of nobility, reveals his adherence to the traditional aristocratic hierarchy: *Quevedo: Discurso y representación*, 108–14.

19 According to James Crosby, the *letrilla* is one of some seventeen poems written by Quevedo before his twenty-third birthday, and published by Pedro Espinosa in *Flores de poetas ilustres de España*. Crosby publishes both the early and the revised version; see his *Francisco de Quevedo: Poesía varia*, 87–93.

20 Francisco Rico, *La novela picaresca y el punto de vista*, 114–29.

21 For Ettinghausen, Pablos's 'sordid' narrative linguistically conveys his condemnation by the author: 'Quevedo's *converso pícaro*.' See also James Iffland, 'Pablos' Voice: His Master's? A Freudian Approach to Wit in *El buscón*.'

22 Mariscal states that the 'so-called freedom of the picaresque, although it is marked as immoral and mad by aristocratic discourse, nonethless makes visible in writing a form of subjectivity completely at odds with those authorized by the dominant ideologies' (*Contradictory Subjects* 147).

23 Some critics note in the *Buscón* an indirect attack on Rodrigo Calderón; see Augustin Redondo, 'Del personaje de don Diego Coronel a una nueva

interpretación del *Buscón'*; and Antonio Rey Hazas, ed., *Historia de la vida del Buscón*, 82.

24 Pablo's feelings towards Don Toribio recall Lazarillo's initial sympathy towards his third master, the squire. Despite his assertions that he is a *montañés* of noble origins, Don Toribio reveals his *converso* status by adding the toponym 'Jordán' to his string of names. See Redondo, 'Del personaje de don Diego Coronel,' 707.

25 Besides the 'estudio preliminar' to his edition of *El buscón*, Cros's studies include *L'aristocrate et le carnaval des gueux. Etude sur le 'Buscón' de Quevedo*; *Ideología y genética textual. El caso del 'Buscón'*; and 'Lectura sacrificial de la muerte de Cristo y rivalidad mimética en el *Buscón*.'

26 Obviously siding with those who considered street beggars a nuisance to society, Quevedo paints them as tricksters who make a good living from charitable donations: 'I sewed sixty *reales*, which I had left over, into my gown, and with this, I took to being poor, trusting my good style. I pounded the pavement eight days, whining and crying out prayers: "Good Christian and the Lord's servant, give to the mangled and lacerated poor like me, I beg of you".' (Cosíme sesenta reales, que me sobraron, en el jubón, y con esto me metí a pobre, fiado en mi buena prosa. Anduve ocho días por las calles, aullando en esta forma, con voz dolorida y realzamiento de plegarias: – '¡Dalde, buen cristiano, siervo del Señor, al pobre lisiado y llagado, que me veo y me deseo!' [236–37]).

27 See, for instance, Molho's dismissal of a scatological episode as a 'citation ... répugnante' in his 'Introduction,' *Romans picaresques espagnols*, lxxxix.

28 Mikhail Bakhtin, *Rabelais and His World*, 149.

29 Julia Kristeva, *Powers of Horror: An Essay on Abjecton*.

30 Malcolm K. Read, *Visions in Exile: The Body in Spanish Literature and Linguistics: 1500–1800*, 65.

31 'The sovereign exercised his right of life only by exercising his right to kill, or by refraining from killing; he evidenced his power over life only through the death he was capable of requiring. The right which was formulated as the "power of life and death" was in reality the right to *take* life or *let* live ... Power in this instance was essentially a right of seizure: of things, time, bodies, and ultimately life itself; it culminated in the privilege to seize hold of life in order to suppress it': Michel Foucault, *The History of Sexuality. Volume I: An Introduction*, 136.

32 The expulsion, an abstract 'murdering' of an entire people and a seizing of their belongings, reverts to what Foucault calls a 'subtraction mechanism, a right to appropriate a portion of the wealth, a tax of products, goods and services, labor and blood, levied on the subjects' (*History of Sexuality* 136).

33 What María Grazia Profeti asserts of the ' poetry of corporeal disgust' (poesia del disgusto del corpo) may also be said of the *Buscón*'s scatological excess: 'the obscene, in fact, constitutes an explosion of what is not said: condemned and negated, sexuality and the body will find their own means of affirmation through condemnation and negation–repulsion; and the more violently they are negated, the more violently they express and make themselves felt' (l'osceno costituisce infatti una esplosione del non detto: il corpo e il sesso condannati e negati troveranno lo loro vie di affermazione proprio attraverso la condanna e la negazione-repulsione; e tanto più violentemente si nega quanto più violentemente ci si sente attratti e si dice [*Quevedo: La scrittura e il corpo*, 173]).

34 Maravall has emphasized that *vileza*, or humble origins, was feared more than the taint of non-Christian lineage. However, he does not seem to be aware of Don Diegos's *converso* status, since he gives the character's rejection of Pablos as main evidence of his hypothesis (*Poder, honor y élites en el siglo XVII* 113–16).

35 Francisco de Quevedo, *Execración contra los Judíos*. Ed. Fernando Cabo Aseguinolaza and Santiago Fernández Mosquera. Anejos de Biblioteca Clásica (Barcelona: Crítica, 1996). The manuscript's full title, *Execración por la fe católica contra la blasfema obstinación de los judíos que hablan portugués y en Madrid fijaron los carteles sacrílegos y heréticos, aconsejando el remedio que ataje lo que, sucedido en este mundo, con todos los tormentos aun no se puede empezar a castigar*, demonstrates that Quevedo made use of the anti-Christian pamphlets posted anonymously in Madrid to attack Spain's growing reliance on loans subsidized by Portuguese Jews.

36 'Just as this contact with feces will mark an entry into a new stage of his existence, so will his various other contacts with it and other excreta of the human body signal the beginning of further stages in his career toward nowhere': James Iffland, *Quevedo and the Grotesque, II*, 89.

37 Carroll Johnson and Augustin Redondo have both written on Don Diego's *converso* ancestry: see Carroll B. Johnson,'*El buscón*: D. Pablos, D. Diego y D. Francisco,' and Redondo, 'Del personaje.'

38 Edward Friedman notes perceptively that the *buscón*'s ultimate inability to change identities conforms to the text's circular structure: 'Trials of Discourse: Narrative Space in Quevedo's *Buscón*.'

39 The child's death at the hands of Cabra recalls the demonological myth of the Santo Niño de la Guardia that circulated widely in Toledo, copied by the *converso* Sebastián de Horozco, and which fanned the fears of *conversos* as childkillers: see Stephen Haliczer, 'The Jew as Witch: Displaced Aggression and the Myth of the Santo Niño de La Guardia.'

40 For a psychoanalytical reading of the passage's Oedipal significance, see Maurice Molho, 'Cinco lecciones sobre el *Buscón*.'

41 The anti-Machiavellian stance behind Quevedo's early attacks on the *arbitristas*' ineffectual solutions is echoed in his 1609 *España defendida i los tiempos de aora de las calumnias de los noveleros i sediziosos*, ed. Selden Rose, *Boletín de la Real Academia de la Historia* 68 (1916). See also his 'Arbitristas en Dinamarca,' 204.

42 For an analysis of Quevedo's social commentary throughout his writings, which compares him to an *arbitrista*, see René Querillacq, 'Ensayo de una lectura socioeconómica de la obra de Quevedo.'

43 See *Feminism and Foucault: Reflections on Resistance*, ed. Irene Diamond and Lee Quinby, especially, Sandra Lee Bartky's 'Foucault, Femininity, and Patriarchal Power,' 61–86.

44 Peter Dunn situates them, along with Cervantes's 'quasi-picaresque narratives' and the *Estebanillo González*, 'beyond the canon' (*Spanish Picaresque Fiction* 218; 232 ff.).

45 See Thomas Hanrahan, *La mujer en la novela picaresca española*; and Sieber, *The Picaresque*. Both consider *La pícara Justina* to be the first female picaresque novel; the latter rejects Alonso de Salas Barbadillo's *La hija de la Celestina* for not conforming to the conventions of the male picaresque (Sieber 32). See also Carlos Blanco Aguinaga, 'Picaresca española, picaresca inglesa: Sobre las determinaciones del género.' While a useful compendium of narratives, Pablo J. Ronquillo, *Retrato de la pícara: La protagonista de la picaresca española del Siglo XVII*, ignores the genre's inherent irony when, for instance, it takes seriously the descriptions of the *pícaras* as great beauties (19). His characterization of the *pícara* as socially mobile and easily metamorphosed into noble women (13 ff.) further overlooks the inglorious endings of the narratives and their condemnation – explicit and implicit – of the protagonists' so-called independent lives.

46 Edward H. Friedman, *The Antiheroine's Voice: Narrative Discourse and Transformations of the Picaresque*, 72.

47 Although the autobiography of the nun-ensign Catalina de Erauso may be considered picaresque, the fact that she lived undetected as a man justifies my not including it among female picaresque narratives. Her exploits in the New World approximate far more the bravado and criminality typical of soldiers' tales.

48 Anne Kaler's *The Pícara: From Hera to Fantasy Heroine* also comments on this literary lineage; her numerous misreadings of Spanish literature, however, render the book unserviceable.

49 Peter N. Dunn, *Castillo Solórzano and the Decline of the Spanish Novel*, 55.

Recently, however, he seems to have moderated his position: '[T]he sex that functions as a lure is never more than a lure ... [The *pícara*] has no sexual role except one that is legitimized by the institutional order' (*Spanish Picaresque Fiction* 249). See also Marcia Welles, 'The *Pícara*: Towards Female Autonomy, or the Vanity of Virtue.'

50 For all quotations, I have used the following editions: *La Lozana andaluza*, ed. Claude Allaigre (Madrid: Cátedra, 1985); *La pícara Justina*, ed. Antonio Rey Hazas, 2 vols. (Madrid: Editora Nacional, 1977); *La hija de la Celestina*, ed. José Fradejas Lebrero (Madrid: Instituto de Estudios Madrileños, 1983).

51 For prostitution in early modern Spain, see Enrique Rodríguez Solís, *Historia de la prostitución en España y América*; Vicente Graullera Sanz, 'Un grupo social marginado: las mujeres públicas (el burdel de Valencia en los siglos XVI y XVII)'; and P. Herrera Puga, 'La mala vida en tiempo de los Austria.' See also Perry, ch. 6, 'Sexual Rebels,' and ch. 7, 'Prostitutes, Penitents, and Brothel Padres' (*Gender and Disorder*); and her articles 'Deviant Insiders: Legalized Prostitutes and a Consciousness of Women in Early Modern Seville' and '"Lost Women" in Early Modern Seville: The Politics of Prostitution.' Francisco Núñez Roldán's *Mujeres públicas: Historia de la prostitución en España* offers only a lurid collection of undocumented facts.

52 Angel Galán Sánchez and María Teresa López Beltrán, 'El "status" teórico de las prostitutas del Reino de Granada en la primera mitad del siglo XVI (Las Ordenanzas de 1538),' 162.

53 Law II, Title XXII, *Las Siete Partidas*, 1429–30.

54 Manuel Carboneres, *Picaronas y alcahuetes o la mancebía en Valencia*, 16 ff.

55 See also Fernando Henríques, *Prostitution in Europe and the New World*, 52–3.

56 See Angel Caffarena, *Apuntes para la historia de las mancebías de Málaga*, and María Teresa López Beltrán, *La prostitución en el Reino de Granada en época de los Reyes Católicos: El caso de Málaga*, 27–33.

57 Mary Elizabeth Perry, *Crime and Society in Early Modern Seville*, 227–8.

58 See José Deleito y Piñuela, *La mujer, la casa y la moda (en la España del Rey Poeta)*, 64. He cites Antonio de León Pinelo, *Velos antiguos y modernos en los rostros de las mujeres. Sus conveniencias y daños. Ilustración de la Real Pramática de las Tapadas* (Madrid, 1641).

59 See Edward H. Friedman, 'Man's Space, Woman's Place: Discourse and Design in *La pícara Justina*.'

60 Mary Douglas, *Purity and Danger: An Analysis of Concepts of Pollution and Taboo*, 162.

61 María Isabel Barbeito cites a request dated 1593 to Philip II, signed and approved by the monarch, for establishing a reformatory for 'lost women': *Cárceles y mujeres en el siglo XVII*, 9.

62 Mary Elizabeth Perry, 'Magdalens and Jezebels in Counter-Reformation Spain' (Perry and Cruz, *Culture and Control*, 9).

63 'De la forma de reclusión y castigo para las mujeres vagabundas y delincuentes destos reinos,' in *Amparo de pobres*, 62–132.

64 The court chronicler, Luis Cabrera de Córdoba, writes: 'they have given the name of "Galley" to a house enclosing young girls who do not want to serve and others living with men, exchanging their dress for a coarse gown, trimming their hair and eyebrows, and making them do needlework, weaving, and other labor they know or have been taught' (han puesto el nombre de Galera á una casa donde recogen las mozas que no quieren servir, y otras amancebadas, y las mudan de vestido con un saco de sayal, y las quitan el cabello y las cejas, y las hacen traabajar a la labor, hilar, coser, y otras cosas que saben ó las enseñan): *Relaciones de las cosas sucedidas en la Corte de España desde 1599 hasta 1614* (Madrid, 1857); quoted in María Dolores Pérez Baltasar, *Mujeres marginadas: Las casas de recogidas en Madrid*, 30 n.36.

65 This reformatory was probably the same 'Hospital of Lost Women' located on a street called 'Santa Isabel' which consolidated with the 'Escogidas de Santa María Magdalena de la Penitencia' and moved in 1623 to the street called 'Hortaleza' (Barbeito 10–12). Sor Magdalena, whose family name was Zamudio (Barbeito 37–9), travelled with the Archduchess Isabel Clara Eugenia to Belgium, where she spent several years as her confidante. She was a close friend of the religious poet Luisa de Carvajal y Mendoza, who wrote her copious letters asking for her support in encouraging the Archduchess to claim the English throne after Elizabeth I's death. See my 'Willing Desire: Luisa de Carvajal y Mendoza and Female Subjectivity.'

66 For the myths on Mary Magdalen that conflate these figures, see Raymond Willis, 'Mary Magdalene, Mary of Bethany, and the Unnamed Woman Sinner. Another Instance of Their Conflation in Old Spanish Literature'; J.K. Walsh and B. Bussell Thompson, *The Myth of the Magdalen in Early Spanish Literature*; and Susan Haskins, *Mary Magdalen: Myth and Metaphor*. For the many references to the Magdalen in Golden Age literature, see Elizabeth Davis, '"Woman, Why Weepest Thou?" Re-visioning the Golden Age Magdalen.'

67 Sor Magdalena de San Jerónimo, *Razón y forma de la galera y Casa Real* (edited in Barbeito 61–95), 65.

68 A sign above the door, displaying the royal arms and an unsheathed sword, should read: 'This is the Galley that His Majesty the King has built to punish women vagrants, thieves, witches, and procuresses' (Esta es la Galera que su Magestad del Rey nuestro Señor ha mandado hacer para castigo de las mujeres vagantes, ladronas, hechiceras y alcahuetas, donde serán castigadas conforme a su culpa y delito [*Galera* 77]).

69 José Antonio Maravall, *El mundo social de 'La Celestina'*, 71.

70 Alan Deyermond, 'Divisiones socio-económicas, nexos sexuales: La sociedad de Celestina,' 8.

71 See in particular, Bruce Wardropper, 'La novela como retrato: el arte de Francisco Delicado,' and José A. Hernández Ortiz, *La génesis artística de la 'Lozana andaluza.' El realismo literario de Francisco Delicado*. For a Bakhtinian reading of the novel's use of *retrato*, see Tatiana Bubnova, *F. Delicado puesto en diálogo: Las claves bajtinianas de 'La Lozana andaluza'*, 153–87.

72 Delicado translates the island's name as 'the couples,' stating that he sends Lozana and Rampín there because it had previously served as a prison for dangerous criminals, who were sent there without mates (487). However, he may also have had in mind Boccaccio's *Decameron*, whose second story of the fifth day ends with its lovers reunited on the island.

73 See Umberto Gnoli, *Cortigiane Romane: Note e Bibliografia* , 11–14. Paul Larivaille confirms that Gnoli's estimated ratio is accurate, at least in the decades preceding the Counter-Reformation: *La vie quotidienne des courtisanes en Italie au temps de la Renaissance: Rome at Venise, XVe et XVIe siècles*, 32.

74 Allaigre often makes note of Delicado's anti-Semitism (179, n.17; see also the Trigo episode, *mamotreto* XVI). For the relevance of Lozana's Jewish heritage and the novel's realistic portrayal of prostitution, see Angus MacKay, 'Averroístas y marginadas.' See also Francisco Márquez Villanueva, *El mundo converso de 'La Lozana andaluza'*.

75 Bruno Damiani, *Francisco López de Ubeda*, 135–49. Ubeda might also have read Aretino's *Ragionamenti*, acknowledged to have been influenced by *La Lozana andaluza*.

76 Marcel Bataillón, *Pícaros y picaresca: La pícara Justina*, 44 ff.

77 See Francisco Márquez Villanueva, 'La identidad de Perlícaro.' While Oltra ascribes the parody to López de Ubeda's desire to outdo Alemán's *Guzmán de Alfarache*, he cannot come up with any reason why the author should be opposed to Pérez de Herrera and Francisco de Vallés, who he claims are denounced under false names in the novel. Oltra also challenges Bataillon's belief that the novel, dedicated to Calderón, meant to celebrate the favourite's recent accession to power: see José Miguel Oltra Tomás, *La parodia como referente en 'La Pícara Justina'*.

78 Luis de León, *La perfecta casada y poesías selectas*, 110.

79 Recently, Nina Cox Davis has claimed the *pícara*'s language as the medium through which Justina elides male control: 'in the offering of both story and body she proves to be neither an object they can domesticate nor a force they may dismiss.' See her 'Breaking the Barriers: The Birth of Lopez de Ubeda's "Pícara Justina".'

5. From *Pícaro* to Soldier

1 Foucault's analysis of a modern disciplinary society, first presented in his
   Surveiller et Punir: Naissance de la prison, is developed further in the last chapter of his *La volonté du savoir*, translated into English as 'Right of Death and
   Power Over Life.' For a discussion of how these new systems of power functioned, see Barry Smart, *Foucault, Marxism and Critique*, 108-9.
2 Geoffrey Parker notes that the Scottish government, in 1605, sentenced 150
   members of the Graham clan, known for its lawlessness, to the wars in the
   Netherlands. Demonstrating the range of 'other' recruited into European
   armies, in 1627, the Lord of Spynie included in his regiment all 'strong, able,
   and counterfeit limmers called Egyptians [sc. gypsies],' as well as all 'strong
   and sturdy beggars and vagabonds, masterless men and idle loiterers, who
   want ... trades and calling and competent means to live upon': Quoted in
   Parker, *The Military Revolution: Military Innovation and the Rise of the West,
   1500–1800*, 49.
3 See Manuel Fernández Alvarez and Ana Díaz Medina, *Historia de España 8:
   Los Austrias mayores y la culminación del Imperio (1516–1598)*, 247.
4 Piero Pieri, *Il rinascimento e la crisi militare italiana*, 543-4.
5 Fernand Braudel, *Capitalism and Material Life, 1400–1800*, 290-1.
6 Lucas Gracián Dantisco's *El Galateo español* counsels soldiers to remove their
   flamboyant plumes, brocades, and gilded trappings when in cities or at court
   so as not to offend the conservatively dressed citizenry (181).
7 L. Lalanne, ed., *Oeuvres completes de Bourdeille, seigneur de Brantôme*, I (Paris,
   1974), 103 f.; quoted in Parker, *Military Revolution*, 174, n.14.
8 Archives de l'Etat, Geneva, P.H. 2651, unfol., Dr Isaac Wake to the council of
   Geneva, 4 July 1620. Cited in Parker, *Military Revolution*, 174-5, n.14.
9 Cavillac ('Introducción,' *Amparo de pobres*, clxv) cites the following treatises
   that, along with Pérez de Herrera's *Amparo de pobres*, discuss the changes
   obtaining in the military from its medieval tradition of individual heroism to
   one relying on technology: Francisco de Valdés, *Espejo y disciplina militar*
   (1589); Cristóbal Mosquera de Figueroa, *Comentarios de disciplina militar*
   (1596); and Cristóbal de Rojas, *Teoría y práctica de fortificación* (1598).
10 Peter Dunn's comment that readers might suspect ulterior motives in the
   Estebanillo González's classification as picaresque ('to swell the genre to
   respectable size') projects rather his own reaction against the connection
   between this text and the traditional canon (*Spanish Picaresque Fiction* 283).
11 Michael Murrin, *History and Warfare in Renaissance Epic*, 12.
12 Murrin (138) cites the three epics written to celebrate Lepanto: Juan Latino,
   Austriadis libri duo (1573); Jerónimo Corte Real, *Felicissima victoria* (1578); and

Juan Rufo, *Austriada* (1582). The latter, a military biography of Don Juan de Austria, includes both the war of Granada and that of Lepanto.

13 The most virulent plagues occurred in 1596 and 1637. See Vicente Pérez Moreda, *La crisis de mortalidad en la España interior (siglos XVI–XIX).*

14 All passages in English translation from *Don Quixote* are from the William Starkie edition (New York: Signet Classics, 1979).

15 For soldier's narratives, I have used the following editions: Jerónimo de Pasamonte and Miguel de Castro, *Autobiografías de soldados (Siglo XVII)*. Ed. José María de Cossío (Madrid: Biblioteca de Autores Españoles, 1956); *Alonso de Contreras: Vida, nacimiento, padres y crianza del capitán Alonso de Contreras.* Ed. Fernando Reigosa (Madrid: Alianza, 1967); and *La vida y hechos de Estebanillo González.* Ed. Antonio Carreira and Jesús Antonio Cid (Madrid: Cátedra, 1990).

16 Mention should also be made of two very different soldiers' accounts: Diego Duque de Estrada's *Memorias* and Gonzalo de Céspedes y Meneses's *Varia fortuna del soldado Píndaro* (1626). As the literate exploits of a young nobleman-playwright first fallen from grace, fighting in Italy and Germany, then professing as Fray Justo Duque de Estrada, Duque de Estrada's *Memorias* differ considerably from the low-born soldier's adventures. Although, like Miguel de Castro, he spent time at the Neapolitan court, his elegant lifestyle there, where he took part in the Academia's plays and *saraos*, could not have been more dissimilar. De Céspedes y Meneses's *Píndaro* is a fictive account of a soldier who metamorphosizes into an ass, incorporating aspects of Apuleius's *Golden Ass* and the picaresque: see Frederick de Armas, 'Evoking Apuleius' Mysteries: Myth and Witchcraft in Céspedes y Meneses' *El soldado Píndaro.'*

17 See Robert Fiore, *Lazarillo de Tormes*, 16; and Marina Scordilis Brownlee, 'Generic Expansion and Generic Subversion: The Two Continuations of the *Lazarillo de Tormes.'*

18 With few exceptions, critics have been unduly hard on the *Second Part*. While it lacks the masterful irony of its precursor, this fish fable, which reveals the author's keen perception of military and courtly behaviour through the *pícaro*'s manoeuvres in an aquatic environment, manages to be both delightfully humorous and instructive. Further, the last chapter, when Lázaro reverts to his original human self, offers another picaresque connection, anticipating Quevedo and Vélez de Guevara, by subtly introducing the possibility that the dream-like tale might be just another instance of Lázaro's self-aggrandizement.

19 For the *Lazarillo*'s two 'continuations,' the anonymous *Segunda parte* (1555) and Juan de Luna's *Segunda parte del Lazarillo*, published in Paris in 1620, see

Josep Sola-Solé, *Los tres Lazarillos*, vol. 1. See also Judith Whitenack, 'Juan de Luna's *Lazarillo*: Continuation or Subversion?' For information on Luna, who as a Protestant fled Spain to settle in France, see Sabina Collet Sedola, 'Juan de Luna et la première edition de l'*Arte breve*.'

20 Bataillon believes the textual allegory alludes to the Jews who fled Spain and joined the Turkish armies: see his introduction to A. Morel Fatio's translation, *La vie de Lazarillo de Tormés* , 62–8. In a fascinating study, Máximo Saludo Stephan interprets part of the adventures through Christian symbolism, associating Lázaro's entry in the island cave with Christ, Jonas, Truth, and the Knights of Malta: *Misteriosas andanzas atunescas de 'Lazaro de Tormes' descifradas de los seudo-jeroglíficos del Renacimiento*. Despite Saludo's often excessive insistence on esoteric connections, the correlations suggested between the text and the Knighthood of Malta and the Duke of Medina Sidonia bear further study. Cavillac has drawn attention to the relation between the exploitation by the Duke of the rogues he employed as tuna fishers and the Fuggers' exploitation of the Almadén mine workers ('Introducción,' *Amparo de pobres*, cxc). For another political interpretation, see Richard E. Zwez, *Hacia la revalorización de la 'Segunda Parte del Lazarillo' (1555)*. Robert S. Rudder, 'Lazarillo de Tormes y los peces: La continuación anónima de 1555,' seeks thematic analogies among the original, its anonymous continuation, and Juan de Luna's Second Part.

21 Antonio Domínguez Ortiz, *El Antiguo Régimen: Los Reyes Católicos y los Austrias*, 246–7.

22 Juan Ignacio Gutiérrez Nieto, *Las comunidades como movimiento antiseñorial (La formación del bando realista en la guerra civil castellana de 1520–1521)*, 42.

23 For treatment of minority groups in Spain, see Domínguez Ortiz, ch. 9, 'Los elementos sociales exteriores al sistema,' *Antiguo régimen*, 175–93.

24 While the Moors were forcibly converted under the reign of the Catholic Monarchs, their integration into Old Christian society varied considerably, depending on place of origin, whether Castilian or Aragonese. The bibliography on *moriscos* is extensive. Miguel Angel de Bunes, *Los moriscos en el pensamiento histórico*, offers a concise and reasoned historiography. For an objective overview of the history of the *moriscos*, see Julio Caro Baroja, *Los moriscos del Reino de Granada (Ensayo de historia social)*; Antonio Domínguez Ortiz and Bernard Vincent, *Historia de los morisco: vida y tragedia de una minoría*; and Braudel, ch. 3, 'Origins of the Holy League: 1566–1570' (*The Mediterranean and the Mediterranean World of Philip II*, II: 1027–87).

25 Elliott notes that, in his forty years as king, Charles V spent just under sixteen in Spain; after 1543, he did not return until his abdication in 1556 (*Imperial Spain* 164).

26 See Andrew C. Hess, 'The Moriscos: An Ottoman Fifth Column in XVIth-Century Spain.' See also his *The Forgotten Frontier: A History of the Sixteenth-Century Ibero-African Frontier.*

27 Inquisition records show that from 1520 to 1569 the numbers of *moriscos* condemned increased from 3 to 368, the majority imprisoned, tortured, and deprived of their property: see Parker, *Philip II,* 103.

28 Domínguez Ortiz and Vincent (51) rely on an expulsion agent's figures of slightly more than 50,000 *moriscos* (Archivo del Instituto de Valencia de Don Juan, Madrid, envío 62, 515). However, Parker estimates the deportation at between 80,000 and 100,000, with as many as 20 per cent of the *moriscos* perishing en route (Philip II 107); and Michael W. Flinn gives 80,000 as an approximate number in his *The European Demographic System 1500–1820.*

29 Thompson notes that the average daily salary of a Castilian labourer, who often received foodstuffs besides, rose from 38 *maravedíes* in the 1550s to 83 in 1581–1600, while the common soldier's pay remained at 34 *maravedíes,* plus a small bonus if piker or harquebusier, from which he fed, clothed, and equipped himself. 'If he were lucky enough to be paid one month in three, he would not uncommonly find himself either cheated out of his earnings by captain and victualler or so heavily indebted to them for food and equpment that little remained for his own enjoyment' (106–7).

30 For early modern warfare, see especially John R. Hale, *Renaissance War Studies* and *War and Society in Renaissance Europe, 1450–1620;* J. Black, ed., *The Origins of War in Early Modern Europe;* and Bert S. Hall, *Weapons and Warfare in Renaissance Europe.*

31 According to Fernández Alvarez and Díaz Medina (249–50), Charles V's military campaigns of 1536 and 1546–7 each averaged, in ducats, 400,000 for 4 *tercios;* 936,000 for 18,000 mercenary soldiers; 1,066,666 for 10,000 cavalry; and 405,280 for auxiliary artillery, a total expenditure of 2,807,946 ducats. Since the Crown's budget did not quite reach 3 million ducats, any of the numerous battles fought by the Emperor quickly exhausted the treasury.

32 I.A.A. Thompson states that, although revenues had increased since 1562 by a half, war expenditures had doubled by the early 1570s, and 'in some years Philip II was spending 10 million ducats, more than half as much as he received.' He adds that these costs fell mainly on Castile: *War and Government in Habsburg Spain: 1560–1620,* 69.

33 Thompson notes, however, that private financing remained a permanent part of the military economy; the effect was to 'move the royal administration one step further away from direct management of the financing and, at the same time, to increase the hold of foreign business interests over the government of the country and in the counsels of the state' (99). How this

affected conscription is, I believe, evident in the ease with which Estebanillo González switches armies.

34 John Lynch, *Empire and Absolutism: 1516–1598*, 136–7.

35 R.A. Stradling, *Europe and the Decline of Spain: A Study of the Spanish System, 1580–1720*, 30.

36 According to Thompson (70), the battle cost 1,100,000 ducats. Renaissance historian Ambrosio de Morales gives the numbers of ships and their place of origin. He notes that Spain's Venetian and Genoese allies seemed reluctant to do battle, which prompted Don Juan to exclaim 'I nonetheless understand that the affairs of war are such that they should not be dealt with by merchants or depend on their opinions' (entiendo, sin embargo, que los asuntos de la guerra son de tal naturaleza que no deben andar en manos de mercaderes ni depender de sus opiniones). Apparently in a self-censoring gesture, Morales crosses out the sentence and adds in the margins 'although true, this should not be stated (aunque es verdad no se ha de dezir': *Descriptio Belli Nautici et Expugnatio Lepanti per D. Ioannem de Austria*, 45.

37 See Michael Mallett and J.R. Hale, *The Military Organization of a Renaissance State: Venice, c. 1400 to 1617*, 237.

38 In a brilliant analysis of the Armada débâcle, Parker explains that the resultant tactical change was not easily adopted by either fleet: 'It was in fact the Dutch, not the English, who first created a high-seas fleet capable of operating at long range ... The critical element was the change in ship-design, for only frigates could operate effectively for long periods at long range' (*Military Revolution* 95–104). See also Colin Martin and Geoffrey Parker, *The Spanish Armada*, and Carla Rahn Phillips, *Six Galleons for the King of Spain: Imperial Defense in the Early Seventeenth Century*, 216. For information on Flemish frigates, see Stradling's ch. 8, 'Men and Ships – The Cutting Edge,' in *The Armada of Flanders: Spanish Maritime Policy and European War, 1568–1668*, 153–75.

39 For Spain's naval power, see R.A. Stradling, *The Armada of Flanders*.

40 According to Domínguez Ortiz and Vincent, Ribera's strident attacks were due to his failure at catechizing the Valencian *moriscos*, who were repulsed by his repeated threats. For precedents for the expulsion, see their ch. 8 in *Historia de los moriscos*, 159–76.

41 While it is not within the scope of this study to enter into the irresolvable debates on this issue, critics who attribute primarily political motivations to the expulsion unaccountably disregard any religious factors on similar occasions, such as the Catholic Monarchs' staunch religious convictions – as well as those of the post-1391 New Christians – in Christianizing their subjects, as well as the Granada reconquest's significance as a fundamentally spiritual crusade. They also overlook the fact that the notion of a unified Spain, as a

nation-state, did not come into being until a century later. For a thoughtful discussion of the Jews as a civilization, see Braudel, 'One Civilization Against the Rest: The Destiny of the Jews' (*Mediterranean* II: 802–26). For recent debates on Medieval Spanish *conversos*, see the Critical Cluster 'Inflecting the Converso Voice,' Gregory Hutcheson, guest editor, in *La Corónica* 25.1 (Fall 1996): 3–68.

42 Jaime Bleda, *Corónica de los moros de España* (Valencia, 1618), 883; cited in Bunes, *Los moriscos*, 34. Other anti-*morisco* treatises include Damián Fonseca, *Iusta expulsión de los moriscos de España* (Valencia, 1611); Pedro Aznar Cardona, *Expulsión justificada de los moriscos españoles* (Huesca, 1612); Marcos de Guadalajara y Javier, *Prodición y destierro de los moriscos de Castilla hasta el valle de Ricote* (Pamplona, 1514). Bunes's historiography synthesizes these works.

43 Domínguez Ortiz and Vincent do not believe that popular opinion influenced the *moriscos'* expulsion in any way; the blame, they insist, should fall on the Duke of Lerma for convincing Philip III to sign the decree (*Historia de los moriscos* 171). For nineteenth-century historiography, see Bunes's ch. 2, 'El nacimiento de una polémica: La historiografía liberal y conservadora,' in *Los moriscos*, 57–102.

44 On the symbolism of Ricote as a *morisco* place name, see Francisco Márquez Villanueva, 'Parte cuarta: el morisco Ricote.' Similarly, Diane Sieber has recently argued that Ana Félix's patronymic refers to a town in the Alpujarras where *morisco* women and children were murdered by Spanish soldiers (Personal communication with the author).

45 Although incorporated in the *Amparo de pobres* published in 1598, his reasoning was initially included in the 1596 *última y undécima duda a que responde ... para acabar de facilitar la ejecución, y perpetuar el discurso que escribió al Rey Nuestro Señor, en la materia de la reducción y amparo de los pobres mendigantes de sus reinos*: see Cavillac, 'Bibliografía,' *Amparo de pobres*, cxcvii.

46 Martín González de Cellorigo, *Memorial encareciendo la obligación de los vasallos en avisar a su Rey y Señor los daños que causan los nuevamente convertidos de Moros a estos Reinos* (Valladolid, 1597) cited in Bunes 50. In his autobiography, Alonso de Contreras narrates how, when passing through the town of Hornachos in 1603, he comes across a cache of arms hidden in a cave by the local *moriscos* (*Vida* 127–9).

47 Pedro Fernández de Navarrete, *Conservación de monarquías y discursos políticos*.

48 Bartolomé Bennassar and Lucile Bennassar, *Los cristianos de Alá. La fascinante aventura de los renegados*, 257.

49 Castro enumerates the Viceroy's retinue, from his major-domo, Juan

Velázquez, through his secretaries of state, and finance, accountants, stable lords, chamber lords and servants, to servants' servants. Besides a governess, the Countess's attendants included her chambermaid, ten duennas, fourteen ladies, eight female slaves, seven servant's servants, and two dwarfs (*Vida de Miguel de Castro* 606–7).

50 Demonstrating the absence of any sense of privacy during the Renaissance, Castro also describes how the Count continues to be dressed by his servants while sitting on the toilet. Once the Count finishes and the container is removed by a bathroom servant, he cleans himself with a folded cloth dampened by the aide, who then hands the soiled cloth to the servant: 'Después de puesto el cuello, se levanta del útil, el cual toma el mozo de retrete y le saca fuera. El ayuda de cámara da el paño de servicio doblado en cuatro dobleces al Conde, y él le toma en la mano y le pone, sobre el cual echa el ayuda de cámara un poco de agua con el jarro, y el Conde se limpia, y después le toma el ayuda de cámara y le da al mozo de retrete' (*Vida* 604).

51 Pérez de Herrera, for instance, recommends that a house be built in Madrid for sick and disabled veterans, and a 'restitution' of room, board, and 12,000 *maravedís* for clothing allowance. These ordinary soldiers could be sent overseas as military advisers, or teach orphaned youths military skills at the seminary of Santa Isabel at court. Officers and other military 'of quality' could receive monetary rewards (*Amparo de pobres* 267–301).

52 For an excellent biography of Olivares, see John H. Elliott, *The Count-Duke of Olivares: The Statesman in an Age of Decline*.

53 Olivares's plan was for each province to maintain an auxiliary force of 140,000 fully equipped men as follows (in thousands): Castile, 44; Catalonia, 16; Portugal, 16; Naples, 16; Flanders, 12; Aragón, 10; Milan, 8; Valencia, 6; Sicily, 6; The Islands, 6. According to Stradling, 'the figures stipulated may have been unrealistic, as much for Castile itself as in the much more celebrated case of Catalonia ... On balance, the question of the numbers envisaged as performing "national service" was less critical than that of the local financial effort demanded by their support ... For this reason, in his search for regular recruits, Olivares was obliged to turn to the nobility as well as to the regional authorities' (Stradling, *Europe and the Decline of Spain*, 96).

54 Accepting the situation as an example of 'refeudalization,' Thompson warns that the nobility often exploited this power, as Medina Sidonia's conspiracy to rule Andalusia as a separate nation proves (Thompson 158). Cf. Antonio Domínguez Ortiz, 'Algunas consideraciones sobre la refeudalización del siglo XVII.'

55 Although he comments on the military's difficult life, Alemán refuses to make his *pícaro* Guzmán a soldier: see Monique Joly, 'Guzmán y el capitán.'

56 Beverly S. Jacobs, 'Social Provocation and Self-Justification in the "Vida" of Captain Alonso de Contreras.'

57 Earlier critics have assumed the existence of an Esteban González who wrote his autobiography; others, while acknowledging his existence, doubt his authorship. See Willis Knapp Jones, 'Estebanillo González'; and Franco Meregalli, 'La existencia de Estebanillo González.' In his *Novela picaresca y práctica de la transgresión*, Jenaro Talens calls the book 'explícitamente testimonial' (141). For Reinaldo Ayerbe-Chaux, it is the text, and not the author's authenticity, that matters: '*Estebanillo González*: La picaresca y la corte.'

58 In an essay addressing the expression's historical and literary significance, Joseph Silverman noted that, while it exposed the Inquisition's mode of scrutiny, the expression was subverted by Cervantes: see his 'On Knowing Other People's Lives, Inquisitorially and Artistically' (Perry and Cruz, *Cultural Encounters*, 157–75). Although Silverman does not refer to the *Estebanillo González*'s use of the term, its author emulates Cervantes on this, as on numerous occasions.

59 His father's title of nobility is so ancient, Estebanillo says, that it is illegible and untouchable, and makes sterile even the mice that nibble on it (*EG* I: 38). On Estebanillo's possible *converso* background, repudiated by Carreira and Cid (*EG* I: 249, n.139), see Willis Knapp Jones, 'Estebanillo González,' and Maria Giovanna Chiesa, 'Estebanillo González e gli ebrei.'

60 See, among others, Talens 143; Ayerbe-Chaux 741; Nicholas Spaddacini, 'Las vidas picarescas en *Estebanillo González*'; and, in particular, Angel Estévez Molinero, *El (Libro de) Buen Humor de Estebanillo González (Compostura de pícaro y chanza de bufón)*, 144–5.

61 Having been introduced to the Count by a captain, Estebanillo is invited to sit at the Count's table on a chair, however, turned around by a servant. Punning on the chair's reversal, he describes his overindulgence at dinner: 'And since I hadn't come to discuss the follies of seating arrangements, but to swell my saddlebags, although ill-saddled, I galloped past more than thirty stops on the road to Brindis [Toast], What began as repast and ended in a banquet finally concluded ... [T]he only ones left were myself, His Excellency, and the captain who had brought me there to save my gut from a bad year's harvest. (Y como no iba yo a atratar de vanidades de asientos, sino de henchir la talega, corrí más de treinta postas camino de Brindis, con estar mal ensillado. Dio fin lo que empezó en comida y acabó en banquete ... [Q]uedamos solos yo y su Excelencia y el capitán que me había conducido a que sacase la tripa de mal año [*EG* I: 47].

62 'Imperial Spain and the Secularization of the Picaresque Novel,' 59.

63 See also Spadaccini; 'History and Fiction: The Thirty Years' War in *Estebanillo González.'*

64 See Antonio Domínguez Ortiz, *Política y hacienda de Felipe IV*, for public reaction to the excessive taxes and loans solicited by the government.

65 Juan Carlos Rodríguez compares the text's duplicitous discourse to a 'tapestry' that narrates the 'Spanish/Imperial truth,' over which is 'scratched' the buffoon's 'degraded truth': see his *La literatura del pobre*, 259–61.

66 Nalle's statement that education as a social solution began to be doubted at the end of the sixteenth century corroborates our view that the *arbitistas* were no longer heeded. She notes that the closing of schools in turn meant the end of popular literacy, which compounded the depression of the book trade: '[o]ne indication of the extent of the disaster in Cuenca, a diocese hard hit by plague and depression in the wool industry, is that not a single book was published in the capital between 1675 and 1800' (Nalle 94).

67 Inspired by the Spanish picaresque, in the seventeenth century the genre continued its development with, in England, Richard Head's *The English Rogue* (1665); in France, Charles Sorel's *Francion* (1623–33); and, in Germany, with Hans Jakob Christoffel von Grimmelshausen's *Simplicius Simplicissimus* (1688) and his *Die Landstörtzerin Courasche* (1670). Eighteenth-century picaresque novels include Alain-René Lesage's *Gil Blas de Santillane* (France, 1715); Daniel Defoe's *Moll Flanders* (England, 1722) and his *Roxana* (1724); and Tobias Smollett's *Roderick Random* (England, 1748). Mexico published its own picaresque novel, José Joaquín Fernández de Lizardi's *El periquillo sarniento*, in 1815, and the United States, Herman Melville's *The Confidence Man*, in 1857. For other examples of picaresque texts, see Wicks.

Works Cited

Abrams, Fred. 'To Whom Was the Anonymous *Lazarillo de Tormes* Dedicated?' *Romance Notes* 8 (1967): 273–7.

Alemán, Mateo. *Guzmán de Alfarache*. Ed. Benito Brancaforte. 2 vols. Madrid: Cátedra, 1979.

– *Guzmán de Alfarache*. Ed. Francisco Rico. Barcelona: Planeta, 1983.

– *The Rogue or the Life of Guzman de Alfarache. Written in Spanish by Matheo Aleman and done into English by James Mabbe, Anno 1621*. 4 vols. New York: AMS, 1967.

– *San Antonio de Padua*. Seville, 1604.

Almansa y Mendoza, Andrés de. *Cartas de Andrés de Almansa y Mendoza. Novedades de esta Corte y avisos recibidos de otras partes (1621–1626)*. In *Libros raros y curiosos*. Madrid, 1886.

Alonso Hernández, José Luis, ed. *Literatura y folklore: Problemas de intertextualidad*. Salamanca; Groningen: Ediciones de la U de Salamanca, 1983.

Alpert, Michael, trans. *Two Spanish Picaresque Novels. Lazarillo de Tormes; The Swindler*. Harmondsworth: Penguin, 1969.

Alvar Ezquerra, Alfredo. *La economía europea en el siglo XVI*. Madrid: Síntesis, 1991.

Alves, Abel Athougia. 'The Christian Social Organism and Social Welfare: The Case of Vives, Calvin and Loyola.' *Sixteenth Century Journal* 20 (1989): 3–21.

Del amparo de los verdaderos pobres de los Reynos y Reduccion de los vagabundos dellos. Borrador de la cédula de Felipe 3°., 1599. Ms. R-18728.26, Biblioteca Nacional, Madrid.

Andrés, Juan. *Sumario breue de la practica de la arithmetica*. Valencia, 1515.

Arenal, Electa, and Stacey Schlau. *Untold Sisters: Hispanic Nuns in Their Own Writings*. Albuquerque: U of New Mexico P, 1989.

Arias, Joan. *Guzmán de Alfarache: The Unrepentant Narrator*. London: Tamesis, 1977.

Armas, Frederick de. 'Evoking Apuleius' Mysteries: Myth and Witchcraft in Céspedes y Meneses' *El soldado Píndaro.*' Galván, Stoll, and Brown 1–16.

Asensio, Eugenio. *La España imaginada de Américo Castro.* Barcelona: El Albir, 1976.

Asensio, Manuel J. 'La intención religiosa del *Lazarillo de Tormes* y Juan de Valdés.' *Hispanic Review* 27 (1959): 78–83.

– 'Más sobre el *Lazarillo de Tormes.*' *Hispanic Review* 28 (1960): 245–50.

Autobiografías de soldados (Siglo XVII). Ed. José María de Cossío. Madrid: Biblioteca de Autores Españoles, 1956.

Avila, Beato Juan de. *Obras completas.* Ed. L. Sala Balust and F. Martín Hernández. Vol. 1. Madrid: Biblioteca de Autores Cristianos, 1952–71.

Ayerbe-Chaux, Reinaldo. '*Estebanillo González*: la picaresca y la corte.' Criado de Val 739–47.

Aznar Cardona, Pedro. *Expulsión justificada de los moriscos españoles.* Huesca, 1612.

Bakhtin, Mikhail. *Rabelais and His World.* Trans. H. Iswolsky. Bloomington: Indiana UP, 1984.

'Bañezianism.' *Encyclopedic Dictionary of Religion.* Ed. P.K. Meagher, Thomas C. O'Brien, and Sister Consuelo María Aherne, SSJ. Washington, DC: Corpus, 1979. 1: 355–6.

Barbeito, María Isabel. *Cárceles y mujeres en el siglo XVII.* Madrid: Castalia, 1991.

Barnes-Karol, Gwendolyn. 'Religious Oratory in a Culture of Control.' Cruz and Perry 51–77.

Barros, Alonso de. *Proverbios morales.* Madrid, 1598.

Barry, Norman. *Welfare: Concepts in Social Thought.* Minneapolis: U of Minnesota P, 1990.

Bartky, Sandra Lee. 'Foucault, Femininity, and Patriarchal Power.' Diamond and Quinby 61–86.

Bataillon, Marcel. *Erasmo y el erasmismo.* Barcelona: Edición Crítica, 1977.

– 'Introduction.' *La vie de Lazarillo de Tormés.* Trans. A. Morel Fatio. Paris: Editions Montaigne, 1958.

– 'Juan Luis Vives, réformateur de la bienfaissance.' *Bibliotheque d'Humanisme et Renaissance* 16 (1952): 141–58.

– 'Les nouveaux chrétiens dans l'essor du roman picaresque.' *Neophilologus* 48 (1964): 283–98.

– *Novedad y fecundidad del 'Lazarillo de Tormes'.* Madrid: Anaya, 1968.

– *Pícaros y picaresca: La pícara Justina.* Madrid: Taurus, 1969.

Bennassar, Bartolomé. *Recherches sur les Grandes Epidémies dans le Nord de l'Espagne a la fin du XVIe Siècle.* Paris: Ecole Practique des Hautes Etudes, 1969.

Bennassar, Bartolomé, and Lucile Bennassar. *Los cristianos de Alá. La fascinante aventura de los renegados*. Trans. José Luis Gil Aristu. Barcelona: Nerea, 1989.

Bentham, Jeremy. *Works*. Ed. Bowring. Vol. 4. 1843. Rpt. New York: Russell and Russell, 1962.

Beverley, John. 'Lazarillo and Primitive Accumulation: Spain, Capitalism, and the Modern Novel.' *Bulletin of the Midwest Modern Language Association* 15 (1982): 29–42.

Black, Jeremy, ed. *The Origins of War in Early Modern Europe*. Edinburgh: J. Donald, 1987.

Blackburn, Alexander. *The Myth of the Picaro: Continuity and Transformation of the Picaresque Novel, 1554–1954*. Chapel Hill: U of North Carolina P, 1979.

Blackmore, Josiah, and Gregory S. Hutcheson, eds. *Queer Iberia: Sexualities, Cultures, and Crossings from the Middle Ages to the Renaissance*. Durham, NC: Duke UP, 1999.

Blanco Aguinaga, Carlos. 'Cervantes y la picaresca: Notas sobre dos tipos de realismo.' *Nueva Revista de Filología Hispánica* 22 (1957): 314–42.

– 'Picaresca española, picaresca inglesa: Sobre las determinaciones del género.' *Edad de Oro* 2 (1983): 49–65.

Blanco Aguinaga, Carlos, Julio Rodríguez Puértolas, and Iris M. Zavala. *Historia social de la literatura española*. Vol. 1. Madrid: Taurus, 1969.

Bleda, Jaime. *Corónica de los moros de España*. Valencia, 1618.

Bleiberg, Germán. *El 'Informe secreto' de Mateo Alemán sobre el trabajo forzoso en las minas de Almadén*. London: Tamesis, 1985.

– 'Mateo Alemán y los galeotes.' *Revista de Occidente* 39 (1976): 330–63.

Bodin, Jean. *Response to the Paradoxes of Malestroit*. Trans. G.A. Moore. Washington, DC: Country Dollar Press, 1947.

Bonneville, Henri, ed. *Hommage des hispanistes français a Noël Salomon*. Barcelona: Laia, 1978.

Boswell, John. *The Kindness of Strangers: The Abandonment of Children in Western Europe from Late Antiquity to the Renaissance*. New York: Pantheon, 1988.

Botero, Giovanni. *Practical Politics*. Trans. G.A. Moore. Washington, DC: Country Dollar Press, 1948.

Bourdeille, Pierre de, Seigneur de Brantôme. *Oeuvres complètes*. Ed. Ludovic Lalanne. Vol. 1. Paris: Mme ve. J. Renourd, 1864–72.

Bourgeois, Albert. *Lépreux et Maladreries du Pas-de-Calais (X–XVIII siècles) Mémoires de la Commission Départmentale des Monuments Historiques du Pas-de-Calais*, vol. 14,2. Arras: Commission Départmentale des Monuments Historiques du Pas-de-Calais, 1972.

Brancaforte, Benito. *Guzmán de Alfarache: ¿Conversión o proceso de degradación?* Madison, WI: Hispanic Seminary of Medieval Studies, 1980.

Braudel, Fernand. *Capitalism and Material Life, 1400–1800*. Trans. Miriam Kocham. New York: Harper Colophon, 1975.

– *The Mediterranean and the Mediterranean World in the Age of Philip II*. Trans. Siän Reynolds. Vol. 2. New York: Harper & Row, 1973.

Brody, Saul Nathaniel. *The Disease of the Soul: Leprosy in Medieval Literature*. Ithaca, NY: Cornell UP, 1974.

Brownlee, Marina Scordilis. 'Generic Expansion and Generic Subversion: The Two Continuations of the *Lazarillo de Tormes*.' *Philological Quarterly* 61 (1982): 317–27.

Brownlee, Marina Scordilis, and Hans U. Gumbrecht, eds. *Cultural Authority in Golden Age Spain*. Baltimore, MD: Johns Hopkins UP, 1995.

Bunes, Miguel Angel de. *Los moriscos en el pensamiento histórico*. Madrid: Cátedra, 1992.

Bubnova, Tatiana. *F. Delicado puesto en diálogo: Las claves bajtinianas de 'La lozana andaluza'*. México: U Nacional Autónoma de México, 1987.

Burr, David. *Olivi and Franciscan Poverty: The Origins of the Usus Pauper Controversy*. Philadelphia: U of Pennsylvania P, 1989.

Cabrera de Córdoba, Luis. *Relaciones de las cosas sucedidas en la Corte de España desde 1599 hasta 1614*. Madrid, 1857.

Caffarena, Angel. *Apuntes para la historia de las mancebías de Málaga*. Málaga: Juan Such, 1968.

Callahan, William J. *La Santa y Real Hermandad del Refugio y Piedad de Madrid, 1618–1832*. Biblioteca de Estudios Madrileños. Vol. 25. Madrid: Consejo Superior de Investigaciones Científicas, 1980.

Camós, Marco Antonio de. *Microcosmía y govierno universal del hombre cristiano*. Barcelona, 1592; Madrid, 1595.

Carande, Ramón. *Carlos V y sus banqueros*. 2 vols. Madrid: Sociedad de Estudios y Publicaciones, 1943–9.

Carboneres, Manuel. *Picaronas y alcahuetes o la mancebía en Valencia*. Valencia: Librería de Pascual Aguilar, 1876.

Caro Baroja, Julio. *Los moriscos del Reino de Granada (Ensayo de historia social)*. Madrid: Instituto de Estudios Políticos, 1976.

– *Realidad y fantasía en el mundo criminal*. Madrid: Consejo Superior de Investigaciones Científicas, 1986.

Casado Alonso, Hilario. *Señores, mercaderes y campesinos. La comarca de Burgos a fines de la Edad Media*. Valladolid: Junta de Castilla y León, 1987.

Castillo Solórzano, Alonso de. *La garduña de Sevilla y anzuelo de las bolsas*. Madrid: Espasa-Calpe, 1972.

– *La niña de los embustes. Teresa de Manzanares, natural de Madrid*. Mexico: Aguilar, 1964.

Castro, Américo. *Cervantes y los casticismos españoles*. Madrid: Alianza, 1974.
– *La realidad histórica de España*. Mexico: Porrúa, 1966.
Cavillac, Michel. 'L'enfermement des pauvres, en Espagne, à la fin du XVIème siècle.' *Picaresque Européene: Actes du Colloque International du Centre d'Etudes et de Recherches Sociocritiques. Montpellier. Mars 1976*. Montpellier: Etudes Sociocritiques, 1976. 45-82.
– *Gueux et marchands dans le 'Guzmán de Alfarache' (1599–1604): Roman picaresque et mentalité bourgeoise dans l'Espagne du Siècle d'Or*. Bordeaux: Institut d'Etudes Ibériques et Ibéro-Américains de l'Université de Bordeaux, 1983.
– 'Para una relectura del *Guzmán de Alfarache* y de su entorno sociopolítico.' Iglesias et al. 397–411.
Certeau, Michel de. *Heterologies: Discourse on the Other*. Trans. Brian Massumi. Minneapolis: U Minnesota P, 1956.
Cervantes, Miguel de. *Don Quixote de la Mancha*. Ed. Luis Andrés Murillo. 2 vols. Madrid: Castalia, 1982.
– *Don Quixote*. Trans. Walter Starkie. New York: Signet Classics, 1979.
– *Novelas ejemplares*. Ed. Harry Sieber. 2 vols. Madrid: Cátedra, 1985.
Céspedes y Meneses, Gonzalo de. *Varia fortuna del soldado Píndaro*. Ed. A. Pacheco. Clásicos Castellanos 202, 203. Madrid: Espasa-Calpe, 1975.
Chandler, Frank W. *The Literature of Roguery*. 2 vols. New York: Burt Franklin, 1958.
– *Romances of Roguery. An Episode in the History of the Novel. Part I: The Picaresque Novel in Spain*. New York: Burt Franklin, 1961.
Chaves, Cristóbal de. *Relación de lo que pasa en la Cárcel de Sevilla*. Ed. Aureliano Fernández Guerra. In B.J. Gallardo, ed., *Ensayo de una biblioteca española de libros raros y curiosos*. Vol. 1. Madrid, 1863. Cols. 1341-70.
Chevalier, Maxime. *Lectura y lectores en la España de los Siglos XVI y XVII*. Madrid: Turner, 1976.
Chiesa, Maria Giovanna. 'Estebanillo González e gli ebrei.' *Rassegna Iberistica* 11 (1981): 3–20.
Compendium totius medicinae. Madrid, 1614.
Contreras, Alonso de. *Vida, nacimiento, padres y crianza del capitán Alonso de Contreras*. Ed. Fernando Reigosa. Madrid: Alianza, 1967.
Contreras Dueñas, Félix, and Ramón Miquel y Suárez de Inclán. *Historia de la lepra en España*. Madrid: Gráficas Hergon, 1973.
Cornwall, J.C.K. *Wealth and Society in Early Sixteenth-Century England*. London: Routledge & Kegan Paul, 1988.
Contreras, Jaime. 'Aldermen and Judaizers: Cryptojudaism, Counter-Reformation, and Local Power.' Cruz and Perry 93–123.
Corte Real, Jerónimo. *Felicissima victoria*. Lisbon, 1578.

Criado de Val, Manuel, ed. *La Picaresca: Orígenes, textos, estructuras. Actas del I Congreso Internacional sobre la Picaresca*. Madrid: Fundación Universitaria Española, 1979.

Cros, Edmond. *L'aristocrate et le carnaval des gueux. Etude sur le 'Buscón' de Quevedo*. Montpellier: CERS, 1975.

– *Ideología y genética textual. El caso del 'Buscón.'* Madrid: Planeta, 1980.

– 'Lectura sacrificial de la muerte de Cristo y rivalidad mimética en el *Buscón.*' In *Homenaje a Quevedo. Actas de la II Academia Literaria Renacentista*. Salamanca: Universidad de Salamanca, 1980.

– *Mateo Alemán: Introducción a su vida y a su obra*. Salamanca: Anaya, 1971.

– *Protée et les gueux. Recherches sur les origines et la nature du récit picaresque dans 'Guzmán de Alfarache'*. Paris: Didier, 1967.

Crosby, James O. *Francisco de Quevedo: Poesía varia*. Madrid: Cátedra, 1987.

Cruz, Anne J. 'The Abjected Feminine in the *Lazarillo de Tormes.*' *Crítica Hispánica* 19 (1997): 99–109.

– Review of Mariscal, *Contradictory Subjects*. *Revista de Estudios Hispánicos* 27 (1993): 164–57.

– 'Self-Fashioning in Spain: Garcilaso de la Vega.' *Romanic Review* 83 (1992): 517–38.

– 'Sonnes of the Rogue: Picaresque Relations in England and Spain.' Maiorino 248–72.

– 'Willing Desire: Luisa de Carvajal y Mendoza and Female Subjectivity.' *The Mendoza Women: Gender and Power in Early Modern Spain*, Helen Nader, ed. Forthcoming.

Cruz, Anne J., and Mary Elizabeth Perry, eds. *Culture and Control in Counter-Reformation Spain*. Hispanic Issues. Vol. 7. Minneapolis: U of Minnesota P, 1992.

Damiani, Bruno. *Francisco López de Ubeda*. Boston: Twayne; G.K. Hall and Co., 1977.

Davis, Charles, and John Varey. *Los corrales de comedias y los hospitales de Madrid. 1574–1615. Estudio y documentos*. London: Tamesis, 1997.

Davis, Elizabeth. '"Woman, Why Weepest Thou?" Re-visioning the Golden Age Magdalen.' *Hispania* 76 (March 1993): 38–48.

Davis, Nina Cox. *Autobiography as 'burla' in the 'Guzman de Alfarache'*. Lewisburg, PA: Bucknell UP, 1991.

– 'Breaking the Barriers: The Birth of López de Ubeda's "Pícara Justina".' Maiorino 137–58.

Dedieu, Jean Pierre. '"Christianization" in New Castile: Catechism, Communion, Mass, and Confirmation in the Toledo Archbishopric, 1540–1650.' Cruz and Perry 1–24.

Deleito y Piñuela, José. *La mujer, la casa y la moda (en la España del Rey Poeta)*. Madrid: Espasa-Calpe, 1966.

Delicado, Francisco. *La lozana andaluza*. Ed. Claude Allaigre. Madrid: Cátedra, 1985.

Derrida, Jacques. *Dissemination*. Trans. Barbara Johnson. Chicago: U of Chicago P, 1981.

Deyermond, Alan. 'Divisiones socio-económicas, nexos sexuales: La sociedad de Celestina.' *Celestinesca* 8 (1984): 3–10.

– *Lazarillo de Tormes: A Critical Guide*. London: Tamesis, 1975.

– 'Lazarus and *Lazarillo*.' *Studies in Short Fiction* 2 (1965): 351–7.

Diamond, Irene, and Lee Quinby, eds. *Feminism and Foucault: Reflections on Resistance*. Boston: Northeastern UP, 1988.

Díaz Migoyo, Gonzalo. *La estructura de la novela: Anatomía de 'El buscón'*. Madrid: Fundamentos, 1978.

Díaz de Montalvo, Alonso. *Ordenanças reales de Castilla, recopiladas por ...* Madrid, 1560.

Díez del Corral Garnica, Rosario. *Arquitectura y mecenazgo: La imagen de Toledo en el Renacimiento*. Madrid: Alianza, 1987.

Domínguez Ortiz, Antonio. 'Algunas consideraciones sobre la refeudalización del siglo XVII.' Iglesias et al. 1: 499–507.

– *El Antiguo Régimen: Los Reyes Católicos y los Austrias*. Madrid: Alianza, 1981.

– *Los judeoconversos en España y América*. Madrid: Istmo, 1971.

– *Política y hacienda de Felipe IV*. Madrid: Editorial de Derecho Financiero, 1960.

Domínguez Ortiz, Antonio, and Bernard Vincent. *Historia de los moriscos: Vida y tragedia de una minoría*. Madrid: Alianza, 1978.

Douglas, Mary. *Purity and Danger: An Analysis of Concepts of Pollution and Taboo*. New York: Praeger, 1966.

Dunn, Peter N. *Castillo Solórzano and the Decline of the Spanish Novel*. Oxford: Blackwell, 1952.

– *Spanish Picaresque Fiction: A New Literary History*. Ithaca, NY: Cornell UP, 1993.

– *The Spanish Picaresque Novel*. Boston: Twayne, 1979.

Eco, Umberto. *Opera aperta: Forma e indeterminazione nelle poetiche contemporanee*. Milan: Bompiani, 1963.

– *The Role of the Reader: Explorations in the Semiotics of Texts*. Bloomington: Indiana UP, 1984.

Elliott, John H. *The Count-Duke of Olivares: The Statesman in an Age of Decline*. New Haven; London: Yale UP, 1986.

– *Imperial Spain, 1469–1716*. Harmondsworth: Penguin, 1990.

– *The Revolt of the Catalans: A Study in the Decline of Spain, 1598–1640*. Cambridge: Cambridge UP, 1963.

– *Spain and Its World, 1500–1700: Selected Essays*. New Haven; London: Yale UP, 1989.

El Saffar, Ruth. 'Literary Reflections on the "New Man": Changes in Consciousness in Early Modern Europe.' *Revista de Estudios Hispánicos* 22 (1988): 1–23.

– *Rapture Encaged: The Suppression of the Feminine in Western Culture.* London: Routledge, 1994.

Estebanillo González, La vida y hechos de. Ed. Antonio Carreira and Jesús Antonio Cid. Madrid: Cátedra, 1990.

La vida de Estebanillo González. Vol. 1. Ed. Juan Millé y Giménez. Madrid: Espasa Calpe, 1956.

Estévez Molinero, Angel. *El (Libro de) Buen Humor de Estebanillo González (Compostura de pícaro y chanza de bufón).* Córdoba: U de Córdoba, 1995.

Ettinghausen, Henry. 'Quevedo's *converso pícaro.' MLN* 102 (March 1987): 241–54.

Fernández Alvarez, Manuel. *La sociedad española en el Siglo de Oro.* Madrid: Editorial Nacional, 1983.

Fernández Alvarez, Manuel, and Ana Díaz Medina. *Historia de España 8. Los Austrias mayores y la culminación del Imperio (1516–1598).* Madrid: Gredos, 1987.

Fernández Majolero, Jesús. *Hospital de Nuestra Señora de la Misericordia de Alcalá de Henares: Datos previos para un estudio histórico, siglos XV y XVI.* Torrejón de Ardoz: Grafisanz, 1985.

Fernández de Navarrete, Pedro. *Conservación de monarquías y discursos políticos.* Ed. Michael D. Gordon. Madrid: Instituto de Estudios Fiscales, Ministerio de Hacienda, 1982.

Feros, Antonio. 'The King's Favorite, the Duke of Lerma: Power, Wealth, and Court Culture in the Reign of Philip III.' PhD diss., Baltimore: Johns Hopkins U, 1994.

Fetterley, Judith. *The Resisting Reader: A Feminist Approach to American Fiction.* Bloomington: Indiana UP, 1979.

Fiore, Robert. *Lazarillo de Tormes.* Boston: G.K. Hall, 1984.

Fish, Stanley. *Is There a Text in This Class? The Authority of Interpretive Communities.* Cambridge, MA: Harvard UP, 1980.

Flinn, Michael C. *The European Demographic System, 1500–1820.* Sussex: Harvester, 1981.

Flynn, Maureen. *Sacred Charity: Confraternities and Social Welfare in Spain, 1400–1700.* Ithaca, NY: Cornell UP, 1988.

Fonseca, Damián. *Iusta expulsion de los moriscos de España.* Valencia, 1611.

Foucault, Michel. *The Archaeology of Knowledge.* Trans. A.M. Sheridan Smith. New York: Harper Torchbooks, 1973. Originally published as *La volonté du savoir.* Paris: Gallimard, 1976.

– *Discipline and Punish: The Birth of the Prison.* Trans. Alan Sheridan. New York: Vintage, 1979. Originally published as *Surveiller et Punir: Naissance de la prison.* Paris: Gallimard, 1975.

– *Madness and Civilization: A History of Insanity in the Age of Reason.* Trans. Richard Howard. New York: Vintage, 1973. Originally published as *L'Histoire de la folie.* Paris: Librairie Plon, 1961.

– *The Order of Things: An Archaeology of the Human Sciences.* New York: Vintage, 1975. Originally published as *Les mots et les choses.* Paris: Gallimard, 1971.

Friedman, Edward H. *The Antiheroine's Voice: Narrative Discourse and Transformations of the Picaresque.* Columbia: U of Missouri P, 1987.

– 'Man's Space, Woman's Place: Discourse and Design in *La pícara Justina.*' *La Chispa '85 Selected Proceedings.* Ed. Gilberto Paolini. The Sixth Louisiana Conference on Hispanic Languages and Literatures. New Orleans, LA: Tulane UP, 1985. 115–23.

– 'Trials of Discourse: Narrative Space in Quevedo's *Buscón.*' Maiorino 183–225.

Galán Sánchez, Angel, and María Tresa López Beltrán. 'El "status" teórico de las prostitutas del Reino de Granada en la primera mitad del siglo XVI (Las Ordenanzas de 1538).' *Las mujeres en las ciudades medievales: Actas de las Terceras Jornadas de Investigación Interdisciplinaria.* Ed. Cristina Segura Graiño. Seminario de Estudios de la Mujer. Madrid: U Autónoma de Madrid, 1984.

Galván, Delia G., Anita K. Stoll, and Phillipa Brown Yin, eds. *Studies in Honor of Donald W. Bleznick.* Delaware, NJ: Juan de la Cuesta, 1995..

Giginta, Miguel de. *Del amparo de los pobres.* 1579. Ms. 18653/12, Biblioteca Nacional, Madrid.

Girard René. *The Scapegoat.* Trans. Yvonne Freccero. Baltimore, MD: Johns Hopkins UP, 1986.

Gnoli, Umberto. *Cortigiane Romane: Note e Bibliografia.* Arezzo: Edizioni della Rivista Il Vasari, 1941.

Goglin, Jean Louis. *Les misérables de l'Occident Mediévale.* Paris: Editions du Seuil, 1976.

Golden, Grace. 'Juan de Dios and the Hospital of Christian Charity.' *Journal of the History of Medicine and Allied Sciences* 33 (1978): 6–34.

Gómez-Mariana, Antonio. *Discourse Analysis as Sociocriticism: The Spanish Golden Age.* Minneapolis: U of Minnesota P, 1993.

Gómez Yebra, Antonio. *El niño pícaro literario de los siglos de oro.* Barcelona: Anthropos, 1988.

González de Cellorigo, Martín. *Memorial de la política necesaria y útil restauración a la República de España y estados de ella y del desempeño universal de estos Reinos (1600).* Ed. José Luis Pérez de Ayala. Madrid: Instituto de Estudios Fiscales, 1991.

– *Memorial dirigido a S.A. el Principe D. Felipe, hijo de Felipe 2°...en que por segunda vez se avisan los daños que los nuevos convertidos de Moros a estos Reinos causan.* Valladolid, 1597.

– *Memorial encareciendo la obligación de los vasallos en avisar a su Rey y Señor los daños que causan los nuevamente convertidos de Moros a estos Reinos.* Valladolid, 1597.

González Echevarría, Roberto. "The Law of the Letter: Garcilaso's *Commentaries* and the Origins of the Latin American Narrative.' *Yale Journal of Criticism* 1 (Fall 1987): 107–31.

González Palencia, Angel. *Del Lazarillo a Quevedo: Estudios históricos literarios.* Madrid: Consejo Superior de Investigaciones Científicas, 1946.

Gordon, Michael D. 'The Arbitristas: An Historiographical and Bibliographical Survey.' *Newsletter of the Society for Spanish and Portuguese Historical Studies* 2 (1974): 7–23.

Gracián Dantisco, Lucas. *El Galateo español.* Ed. Margherita Morreale. Madrid: Consejo Superior de Investigaciones Científicas, 1968.

Granada, Luis de. *Guía de pecadores.* Madrid: Apostolado de la Prensa, 1948.

Granjel, Luis. *Los médicos humanistas españoles.* Vol. 8. Madrid: AIAHM, 1956.

Graullera Sanz, Vicente. 'Un grupo social marginado: Las mujeres públicas (el Burdel de Valencia en los siglos XVI y XVII).' *Coloquio de Pau sobre Historia de Valencia* (1978): 75–98.

Greenblatt, Stephen. *Renaissance Self-Fashioning: From More to Shakespeare.* Chicago: U of Chicago P, 1980.

Grice-Hutchinson, Marjorie. *Early Economic Thought in Spain: 1170–1740.* London: Allen & Unwin, 1978.

– *The School of Salamanca. Readings in Spanish Monetary Theory, 1544–1605.* Oxford: Clarendon Press, 1952.

Guadalajara y Javier, Marcos de. *Prodicion y destierro de los moriscos de Castilla hasta el valle de Ricote.* Pamplona, 1614.

Guillén, Claudio. 'Luis Sánchez, Ginés de Pasamonte y el descubrimiento del género picaresco.' *El primer Siglo de Oro.* 197–211.

– *El primer Siglo de Oro: Estudios sobre géneros y modelos.* Barcelona: Editorial Crítica, 1988.

– 'Los pleitos extremeños de Mateo Alemán.' *El primer Siglo de Oro.* 177–96. Expansion of article published in *Archivo Hispalense* 32 (1960): 387–407.

– 'Los silencios de Lázaro de Tormes.' *El primer Siglo de Oro.* 66–108.

– 'Toward a Definition of the Picaresque.' *Literature as System: Essays Toward a Theory of Literary History.* Princeton, NJ: Princeton UP, 1971. 71–106.

Gumbrecht, Hans U. 'Cosmological Time and the Impossibility of Closure: A Structural Element in Spanish Golden Age Narratives.' Brownlee and Gumbrecht 304–21.

Gutiérrez, Juan. *Arte breue y muy prouechoso de cuenta Castellana y Arismetica.* Toledo, 1539.

Gutiérrez Nieto, Juan Ignacio. *Las comunidades como movimiento antiseñorial (La formación del bando realista en la guerra civil castellana de 1520–1521)*. Barcelona: Planeta, 1973.
– 'El pensamiento económico, político y social de los arbitristas.' Jover 235–51.
Haan, Fonger de. *An Outline of the History of the 'Novela Picaresca' in Spain*. New York; The Hague: Martinus Nijhoff, 1903.
Hale, John R. *Renaissance War Studies*. London: Hambledon Press, 1983.
– *War and Society in Renaissance Europe, 1450–1620*. Leicester: Leicester UP, in association with Fontana Paperbacks, 1985.
Haliczer, Stephen. 'The Jew as Witch: Displaced Aggression and the Myth of the Santo Niño de la Guardia.' Perry and Cruz 146–56.
Hall, Bert S. *Weapons and Warfare in Renaissance Europe*. Baltimore, MD: Johns Hopkins UP, 1997.
Hamilton, Earl J. *American Treasure and the Price Revolution in Spain, 1501–1650*. Cambridge, MA: Harvard UP, 1934.
– 'The Decline of Spain.' *Economic History Review* 8 (1938): 168–79. Rpt. in John H. Elliott, *Spain and Its World*, 217–40.
Hanrahan, Thomas. *La mujer en la novela picaresca española*. 2 vols. Madrid: Ediciones Porrúa Turanzas, 1967.
Haskins, Susan. *Mary Magdalen: Myth and Metaphor*. New York: Harcourt Brace, 1993.
Henríques, Fernando. *Prostitution in Europe and the New World*. London: MacGibbon & Kee, 1963.
Henríquez de Villegas, Diego. *Lenas de la gente de guerra. Su empleo en todas las facciones militares*. Madrid, 1647.
Hernández Ortíz, A. *La génesis artística de la 'Lozana andaluza'. El realismo literario de Francisco Delicado*. Madrid: Ricardo Aguilera, 1974.
Herrero, Javier. 'Renaissance Poverty and Lazarillo's Family: The Birth of the Picaresque Genre.' *PMLA* 94 (1979): 876–86.
Hess, Andrew C. *The Forgotten Frontier: A History of the Sixteenth-Century Ibero-African Frontier*. Chicago: U of Chicago P, 1978.
– 'The Moriscos: An Ottoman Fifth Column in XVI-Century Spain.' *The American Historical Review* 74 (1968): 1–25.
Holland, Norman N. *The Dynamics of Literary Response*. New York: Oxford UP, 1968. Rpt. New York: Norton, 1975.
Hospitales generales. Que los hospitales generales es buen medio para el remedio de los pobres, si la Republica en comun se encarga del sustento dellos. Ms. L-I-12, Biblioteca Real Monasterio del Escorial.
Hutcheson, Gregory S., guest ed. 'Inflecting the Converso Voice.' Critical Cluster. *La Corónica* 25.1 (Fall 1996): 3–68.

Ife, B.F. *Reading and Fiction in Golden-Age Spain: A Platonist Critique and Some Picaresque Replies.* Cambridge: Cambridge UP, 1985.

Iffland, James. 'Pablos' Voice: His Master's? A Freudian Approach to Wit in *El buscón.' Romanische Forschungen* 91 (1979): 213–43.

– *Quevedo and the Grotesque.* Vol. 2. London: Tamesis, 1983.

Iglesias, María Carmen, Carlos Moya, and Luis Rodriguez, eds. *Homenaje a José Antonio Maravall.* Vol. I. Madrid: Centro de Investigaciones Sociológicas, 1985.

Ingram, Kevin. 'The Ineluctable Decline of the Seville Merchant Community, 1503–1621.' Unpublished paper read at the Society for Spanish and Portuguese Historical Studies Conference, Toronto, Canada, 20–22 April 1995.

Iser, Wolfgang. *The Implied Reader: Patterns of Communication in Prose Fiction from Bunyan to Beckett.* Baltimore, MD: Johns Hopkins UP, 1974.

La Isla de los Monopantos. Madrid, 1639. Quevado, *Obras,* 414–19.

Jacobs, Beverly S. 'Social Provocation and Self-Justification in the *Vida* of Captain Alonso de Contreras.' *Hispanic Review* 51 (Summer 1983): 303–19.

Jameson, Fredric. *The Political Unconscious: Narrative as a Socially Symbolic Act.* Ithaca, NY: Cornell UP, 1981.

Jauralde Pou, Pablo. *Quevedo: Leyenda e historia.* Granada: U de Granada, 1980.

– 'Revisión del *Buscón.' Insula* 531 (1991): 5–6.

Jauss, Hans Robert. 'Levels of Identification of Hero and Audience.' *New Literary History* 5 (1974): 283–317.

– 'Literary History as a Challenge to Literary Theory.' *New Literary History* 2 (1970–1): 7–31.

– *Toward an Aesthetic of Reception.* Trans. Timothy Bahti. Minneapolis: U of Minnesota P, 1982.

Johnson, Carroll B. '*El buscón*: D. Pablos, D. Diego y D. Francisco.' *Hispanófila* 51 (1974): 1–26.

– *Inside Guzmán de Alfarache.* Berkeley: U of California P, 1978.

– 'The Old Order Passeth, Or Does It? Some Thoughts on Community, Commerce, and Alienation in *Rinconete y Cortadillo.*' Parr 85–104.

Joly, Monique. 'Guzmán y el capitán.' Bonneville 431–45.

Jordan, Barry. *British Hispanism and the Challenge of Literary Theory.* Warminster: Aris and Phillips, 1990.

Jover, J.M. *El siglo del Quijote (1580–1680).* Series *Historia de España Menéndez Pidal.* Vol. 26. Madrid: Espasa-Calpe, 1986.

Kagan, Richard. *Students and Society in Early Modern Spain.* Baltimore, MD: Johns Hopkins UP, 1977.

– 'The Toledo of El Greco.' *El Greco de Toledo. Exhibition of El Greco at the Toledo*

Museum of Art. A New York Graphic Society Book. Boston: Little, Brown, 1988. 35–73.

Kaler, Anne. *The Pícara: From Hera to Fantasy Heroine.* Bowling Green, OH: Bowling Green State U Popular P, 1991.

Kamen, Henry. *European Society, 1500–1700.* London: Hutchinson, 1984.

– 'Limpieza and the Ghost of Américo Castro: Racism as a Tool of Literary Analysis.' *Hispanic Review* 64 (1996): 19–29.

– *Una sociedad conflictiva: 1469–1714.* Madrid: Alianza, 1984.

Keniston, Hayward. *Francisco de los Cobos, Secretary of Emperor Charles V.* Pittsburgh: U of Pittsburgh P, 1960.

Koenigsberger, H.G., and George L. Mosse. *Europe in the Sixteenth Century.* New York: Holt, Rinehart & Winston, 1968.

Kroedte, Peter. *Peasants, Landlords, and Merchant Capitalists: Europe and the World Economy.* Cambridge: Cambridge UP, 1983.

Kristeva, Julia. *Powers of Horror. An Essay on Abjection.* Trans. Leon Roudiez. New York: Columbia UP, 1982.

Larivaille, Paul. *La vie quotidienne des courtisanes en Italie au temps de la Renaissance. Rome et Venise, XVe et XVIe. siècles.* Paris: Librairie Hachettte, 1975.

Latino, Juan. *Austriadis libri duo.* Granada, 1573.

Laurenti, Joseph L. *Bibliografía de la literatura picaresca. Desde sus orígenes hasta el presente.* Metuchen, NJ: Scarecrow, 1973; New York: AMS, 1981.

– *Catálogo bibliográfico de la literatura picaresca, siglos XVI–XX.* Kassel: Reichenberger, 1988.

– 'De la imagen de las mujeres en la *Segunda parte de la vida de Lazarillo de Tormes ... (1620)* de Juan de Luna.' *La Torre, Nueva Epoca* 14 (April–June 1990): 181–95.

Lázaro Carreter, Fernando. – *'Lazarillo de Tormes' en la picaresca.* Barcelona: Ariel, 1972.

– 'La originalidad del *Buscón.' Studia Philologica: Homenaje ofrecido a Dámaso Alonso por sus amigos y discípulos con ocasión de su 60 aniversario.* Vol. 2. Madrid: Gredos, 1960–3. 319–38.

– 'Para una revisión del concepto "novela picaresca".' *Actas del Tercer Congreso de Hispanistas.* Mexico: El Colegio de México, 1970. 27–45.

Lazar du Tormes Espagnol, L'Histoire plaisante et facétieuse de. Paris, 1561.

Lazarillo de Tormes. Medina del Campo, 1554.

Lazarillo de Tormes. Ed. Francisco Rico. Madrid: Catedra, 1971.

Lazarillo de Tormes, The Pleasaunt Historie of. Trans. David Rowland, London, 1586.

Lazarillo. Segunda Parte. 1555. See Sola-Solé.

León Pinelo, Antonio de. *Velos antiguos y modernos en los rostros de las mujeres. Sus conveniencias y daños. Ilustración de la Real Pramática de las Tapadas.* Madrid, 1641.

Lerner, Lía Schwartz. *Quevedo: Discurso y representación.* Pamplona: Ediciones U de Navarra, 1986.

Lewis, Archibald R., ed. *Aspects of the Renaissance: A Symposium.* Austin: U of Texas P, 1967.

Lewis, Thomas E., and Francisco J. Sánchez, eds. *Subjectivity and the Modern State in Spain, 1550–1850.* Hispanic Issues, vol. 20. New York: Garland, 1999.

León, Luis de. *La perfecta casada y poesías selectas.* Ed. Florencia Grau. Barcelona: Obras Maestras, n.d.

Little, Lester. *Religious Poverty and the Profit Economy in Medieval Europe.* Ithaca, NY: Cornell UP, 1978.

Lomax, Derek. W. 'On Re-Reading the *Lazarillo de Tormes.' Studia Iberica: Festshrift für Hans Flasche.* Ed. Karl-Hermann Korner and Klaus Ruhl. Bern: Francke Verlag, 1973. 271–381.

López Beltrán, María Teresa. *La prostitución en el Reino de Granada en época de los Reyes Católicos: El caso de Málaga.* Málaga: Biblioteca Popular Malagueña, 1985.

López de Ubeda, Francisco. *La pícara Justina.* Ed. Antonio Rey Hazas. 2 vols. Madrid: Editora Nacional, 1977.

Luis de Granada, Fray. *Guía de pecadores.* Madrid: Apostolado de la Prensa, 1948.

Luna, Juan de. *Segunda parte de la vida de Lazarillo de Tormes.* Ed. Joseph L. Laurenti. Madrid: Espasa-Calpe, 1979.

Lynch, John. *Empire and Absolutism: 1516–1598.* Vol. I of *Spain under the Hapsburgs,* 2d ed., 1964. Oxford: Blackwell, 1981.

– *Spain, 1516–1598: From Nation-State to World Empire.* Oxford: Blackwell, 1992. Rev. ed. of *Spain under the Hapsburgs.* Vol. 1, 2d ed., 1981.

Macaya Lahmann, Enrique. *Bibliografía del Lazarillo de Tormes.* San José, Costa Rica: Ediciones del Convivio, 1935.

MacKay, Angus. 'Averroistas y marginadas.' *Actas del IIIer. Coloquio de Historia Medieval Andaluza; La Sociedad Medieval Andaluza, Grupos No Privilegiados.* Jaén: Diputación Provincial de Jaén, Instituto de Cultura, 1984. 247–61.

Magdalena de San Jerónimo, Sor. *Razón y forma de la galera y Casa Real.* Barbeito 61–95.

Maiorino, Giancarlo, ed. *The Picaresque: Tradition and Displacement.* Hispanic Issues 12. Minneapolis: U of Minnesota P, 1996.

Malkiel, María Rosa Lida de. 'Función del cuento popular en el *Lazarillo de Tormes.' Actas del Primer Congreso Internacional de Hispanistas.* Ed. Frank Pierce and Cyril A. Jones. Vol. 1. Oxford: Dolphin, 1964. 349–59.

Mallet, Michael, and J.R. Hale. *The Military Organization of a Renaissance State: Venice, c. 1400 to 1617.* Cambridge: Cambridge UP, 1984.

Maravall, José Antonio. *La cultura del Barroco: Análisis de una estructura histórica.* Barcelona: Ariel, 1981.

– *Honor, poder y élites en el siglo XVII.* Madrid: Siglo Veintiuno, 1984.

– *La literatura picaresca desde la historia social (Siglos XVI y XVII).* Madrid: Taurus, 1986.

– *El mundo social de 'La Celestina'.* Madrid: Gredos, 1964.

– 'Pobres y pobreza del medioevo a la primera modernidad: Para un estudio histórico-social de la picaresca.' *Cuadernos Hispano Americanos* 367–8 (1981): 189–242.

– 'Trabajo y exclusión: El trabajador manual en el sistema social español de la primera modernidad.' Redondo 135–59.

– *Utopía y contrautopía en el 'Quijote'.* Santiago de Compostela: Pico Sacro, 1976.

Mariscal, George. *Contradictory Subjects: Quevedo, Cervantes, and Seventeenth-Century Spanish Culture.* Ithaca, NY: Cornell UP, 1991.

Márquez Villanueva, Francisco. *Espiritualidad y literatura en el siglo XVI.* Madrid: Alfaguara, 1969.

– 'La identidad de Perlícaro.' *Homenaje a José Manuel Blecua.* Madrid: Gredos, 1984. 423–32.

– *El mundo converso de 'La lozana andaluza'.* Seville: Archivo Hispalense, 1973.

Martí, Juan [pseud]. *Segunda parte de la vida del pícaro Guzmán de Alfarache.* Valencia, 1602.

Martin, Colin, and Geoffrey Parker. *The Spanish Armada.* New York: Norton, 1988.

Martínez de Mata, Francisco. *Memoriales y discursos de Francisco Martínez de Mata.* Ed. Gonzalo Anes Alvarez. Madrid: Moneda y Crédito, 1971.

Martz, Linda. *Poverty and Welfare in Hapsburg Spain: The Example of Toledo.* Cambridge: Cambridge UP, 1983.

Mattingly, Garrett. *The Armada.* Boston: Houghton Mifflin, 1959.

Mas, Amedée. *La caricature de la femme, du mariage et d l'amour dans l'oeuvre de Quevedo.* Paris: Ediciones Hispanoamericanas, 1957.

Mauss, Marcel. *The Gift: The Form and Reason for Exchange in Archaic Societies.* Trans. W.D. Halls. London; New York: Routledge, 1990.

Maza Zorrilla, Elena. *Pobreza y asistencia social en España. Siglos XVI al XX.* Valladolid: U de Valladolid, 1987.

Memorial al rey para que no salgan dineros de estos reinos de España. Madrid, 1558.

McGrady, Donald. *Mateo Alemán.* New York: Twayne, 1978.

Mercier, Charles A. *Leper Houses and Medieval Hospitals.* London: Lewis, 1915.

Meregalli, Franco. 'La existencia de Estebanillo González.' *Revista de Literatura* 61 (1979): 55–67.

Mesmin, S.C. 'The Leper Hospital of St. Gilles de Pont-Auderner.' Diss., University of Reading, 1978.

Miletich, John, ed. *Hispanic Studies in Honor of Alan D. Deyermond: A North American Tribute*. Madison, WI: Hispanic Seminary of Medieval Studies, 1986.

Molho, Maurice. 'Cinco lecciones sobre el *Buscón*.' *Semántica y poética (Góngora y Quevedo)*. Barcelona: Crítica, 1977. 89–131.

– *Introducción al pensamiento picaresco*. Salamanca: Anaya, 1973.

– *Romans picaresques espagnols*. Paris: Gallimard, 1968.

Molino, Jean. '*Lazarillo de Tormes* et les *Metamorphoses* d'Apulée.' *Bulletin Hispanique* 67 (1965): 332–3.

Mollat, Michel. *The Poor in the Middle Ages: An Essay in Social History*. Trans. Arthur Goldhammer. New Haven; London: Yale UP, 1986.

Moore, Robert I. *The Formation of a Persecuting Society: Power and Deviance in Western Europe, 950–1250*. Oxford: Blackwell, 1986.

Moore, Sally F., and Barbara G. Myerhoff, eds. *Secular Ritual*. Amsterdam: Van Gorcum, Assen, 1977.

Morales, Ambrosio de. *Descriptio Belli Nautici et Expugnatio Lepanti per D. Ioannem de Austria*. Trans. Jenaro Costas Rodríguez. Madrid: Cuadernos de la UNED, 1987.

Moreno Báez, Enrique. *Lección y sentido del 'Guzmán de Alfarache'*. Anejo 40. Madrid: Revista de Filología Española, 1943.

Mosquera de Figueroa, Cristóbal. *Comentarios de disciplina militar*. Madrid, 1596.

Mullaney, Steven. *The Place of the Stage: License, Play, and Power in Renaissance England*. Chicago: U of Chicago P, 1988.

Murrin, Michael. *History and Warfare in Renaissance Epic*. Chicago: U of Chicago P, 1994.

Múzquiz, Darlene. 'Charity, Punishment, and Labor: The Textualization of Poverty in XVII and XVIII-Century Spain.' Diss., University of California, San Diego, 1994.

Myers, Kathleen A. '"Miraba las cosas que desia": Writing, Picaresque Tales, and the *Relación autobiográfica* by Ursula Suárez (1666–1749).' *Romance Quarterly* 3 (1993): 156–72.

Nalle, Sara T. 'Literacy and Culture in Early Modern Castile.' *Past and Present* 125/1–2 (1989): 65–95.

Nelson, William. *Fact or Fiction: The Dilemma of the Renaissance Storyteller*. Cambridge, MA: Harvard UP, 1973.

Nepaulsingh, Colbert. *Apples of Gold in Filigrees of Silver: Jewish Writing in the Eye of the Spanish Inquisition*. New York: Holmes & Maier, 1995.

Netanyahu, Benzion. *The Origins of the Inquisition in Fifteenth-Century Spain*. New York: Random House, 1994.

Newton, Judith. 'History as Usual? Feminism and the "New Historicism".' *Cultural Critique* 9 (1988): 87–121.

Nueva orden para el recogimiento de los pobres y socorro de los verdaderos. In *Novisima recopilación*. Libro VII, Titulo XXXIX, Law XIV.

Núñez Roldán, Francisco. *Mujeres públicas: Historia de la prostitución en España*. Madrid: Temas de Hoy, 1995.

Oltra Tomás, José Miguel. *La parodia como referente en 'La pícara Justina'*. León: Instituto 'Fray Bernardino de Sahagún,' Consejo Superior de Investigaciones Científicas, 1985.

Ong, Walter J. 'The Writer's Audience Is Always a Fiction.' *PMLA* 90 (1975): 9–21.

Ortega, Juan de. *Sigue vna compusicion de la arte de la arismetica y iuntamente de geometria*. Leon, 1512.

Osuna, Francisco de. *Norte de los estados en que se da regla de vivir a los ma[n]cebos y a los casados*. Burgos, 1541.

– *Quinta Parte: del abecedario espiritual ... que es Consuelo de pobres y Aviso de ricos*. Burgos, 1542.

Parker, Alexander A. *Literature and the Delinquent: The Picaresque Novel in Spain and Europe, 1599–1753*. Edinburgh: Edinburgh UP, 1967.

– *Valor actual del humanismo español*. Madrid: Ateneo, 1956.

Parker, Geoffrey. *The Military Revolution: Military Innovation and the Rise of the West, 1500–1800*. Cambridge: Cambridge UP, 1988.

– *Philip II*. London: Hutchinson, 1979.

Parr, James A., ed. *On Cervantes: Essays for L.A. Murillo*. Newark, DL: Juan de la Cuesta, 1994.

Perera, Sylvia Brinton. *The Scapegoat Complex: Toward a Mythology of Shadow and Guilt*. Studies in Jungian Psychology by Jungian Analysts 23. Toronto: Inner City, 1986.

Pérez Baltasar, María Dolores. *Mujeres marginadas: Las casas de recogidas en Madrid*. Madrid: Gráficas Lormo, 1984.

Pérez de Ayala, José. 'Un teórico español de la política financiera: D. Martín González de Cellorigo.' *Revista de Derecho Financiero y Hacienda Pública* 36 (December 1959): 711–47.

Pérez de Herrera, Cristóbal. Amparo de pobres. Ed. Michel Cavillac. Madrid: Espasa-Calpe, 1975. Also edited by J. Larraz. Madrid: Instituto de España, 1970.

Pérez, Joseph. *La Révolution des 'Comunidades' de Castille (1520–1521)*. Bordeaux: Institut d'Études Ibériques et Ibéro-Americaines de l'Université, 1970.

Pérez Moreda, Vicente. *La crisis de mortalidad en la España interior (siglos XVI–XIX)*. Madrid: Siglo XXI, 1980.

Perry, Mary Elizabeth. *Crime and Society in Early Modern Seville*. Hanover, NH: UP of New England, 1980.

- 'Deviant Insiders: Legalized Prostitutes and a Consciousness of Women in Early Modern Seville.' *Journal for Comparative Study of Society and History* (1985): 238–58.
- *Gender and Disorder in Early Modern Seville*. Princeton, NJ: Princeton UP, 1990.
- '"Lost Women" in Early Modern Seville: The Politics of Prostitution.' *Feminist Studies* 4 (1978): 195–214.
- 'Magdalens and Jezebels in Counter-Reformation Spain.' Cruz and Perry 124–44.
- 'The Politics of Race, Ethnicity, and Gender in the Making of the Spanish State.' Lewis and Sánchez, 34–53.
Perry, Mary Elizabeth, and Anne J. Cruz, eds. *Cultural Encounters: The Impact of the Inquisition in Spain and the New World*. Berkeley: U of California P, 1991.
Phillips, Carla Rahn. *Six Galleons for the King of Spain: Imperial Defense in the Early Seventeenth Century*. Baltimore, MD: Johns Hopkins UP, 1986.
Phillips, Carla Rahn, and William D. Phillips, Jr, *Spain's Golden Fleece: Wool Production and the Wool Trade from the Middle Ages to the Nineteenth Century*. Baltimore, MD: Johns Hopkins UP, 1997.
Pieri, Piero. *Il rinascimento e la crisi militare italiana*. Turin: Einaudi, 1952.
Pike, Ruth. *Aristocrats and Traders: Sevillian Society in the Sixteenth Century*. Ithaca, NY: Cornell UP, 1973.
- *Enterprise and Adventure: The Genoese in Seville and the Opening of the New World*. Ithaca, NY: Cornell UP, 1966.
- 'The Image of the Genoese in Golden Age Literature.' *Hispania* 46 (1963): 705–14.
Profeti, Maria Grazia. *Quevedo: La scrittura e il corpo*. Rome: Bulzoni Editore, 1984.
Pullan, Brian. *Rich and Poor in Renaissance Venice: The Social Institutions of a Catholic State, to 1620*. Cambridge, MA: Harvard UP, 1971.
Querillacq, René. 'Ensayo de una lectura socioeconómica de la obra de Quevedo.' *Criticón* 27 (1982): 13–66.
Quevedo, Francisco de. 'Arbitristas en Dinamarca.' *La hora de todos y la fortuna con seso*. Ed. Jean Bourg, Pierre Dupont, and Pierre Geneste. Madrid: Cátedra, 1987.
- *El buscón*. Ed. Fernando Cabo Aseguinolaza. Biblioteca Clásica. Vol. 23. Barcelona: Crítica, 1993.
- *El buscón*. Ed. Pablo Jauralde Pou. Madrid: Clásicos Castalia, 1990.
- *España defendida y los tiempos de ahora*. Ed. R. Selden Rose, *Boletín de la Real Academia de la Historia* 68 (1916): 529–43; 69 (1916): 140–82.
- *Execración contra los Judíos*. Ed. Fernanco Cabo Aseguinolaza and Santiago Fernández Mosquera. Anejos de Biblioteca Clásica. Barcelona: Crítica, 1996.

- *Historia de la vida del buscón.* Ed. Edmond Cros. Madrid: Taurus, 1988.
- *Historia de la vida del Buscón.* Madrid: Sociedad General Española de Librería, 1983.
- *Obras.* Ed. Aureliano Fernández-Guerra. Vol. 23. Madrid: Biblioteca de Autores Españoles, 1946
- *Política de Dios. Gobierno de Cristo.* Ed. James O. Crosby. Urbana: U of Illinois P, 1966.
- *La vida del buscón llamado don Pablos.* Ed. Fernando Lázaro Carreter. 2d rpt. Salamanca: Ediciones U de Salamanca, 1980.
Read, Malcolm K. *Visions in Exile: The Body in Spanish Literature and Linguistics, 1500–1800.* Purdue University Monographs in Romance Languages. Amsterdam: John Benjamins, 1990.
Recopilación de las leyes destos reynos. Libro Primero, Título XII. Madrid, 1640.
Redondo, Augustin. 'Del personaje de don Diego Coronel a una nueva interpretación del *Buscón*.' In *Actas del V Congreso Internacional de Hispanistas.* Vol. 2. Instituto de Estudios Ibéricos e Iberoamericanos. Burdeos: U de Bordeaux III, 1977. 699–711.
- 'De molinos, molineros y molineras. Tradiciones folklóricas y literatura en la España del Siglo de Oro.' *Literatura y folklore: Problemas de intertextualidad.* Ed. Alonso Hernández. 101–15.
- 'Folklore, referencias histórico-sociales y trayectoria narrativa en la prosa castellana del Renacimiento.' *Actas de la Asociación Internacional de Hispanistas. 23–28 agosto 1986. Berlin.* Frankfurt: Ibero-Amerikanisches Institut Preussischer Kulturbesitz, 1989. 65–88.
- 'Folklore y literatura en el *Lazarillo de Tormes*: Un planteamiento nuevo (el "caso" de los tres primeros tratados).' Redondo *Mitos* 81–110.
- 'Historia y literatura: El personaje del escudero de *El Lazarillo*.' Criado de Val 421–35.
- 'Pauperismo y mendicidad en Toledo en época del *Lazarillo*.' Bonneville 703–24.
- 'Le pestiféré ou divers aspects du refus de l'autre au XVIe siècle.' Redondo 121–37.
- ed. *Mitos, folklore y literatura.* Zaragoza: Caja de Ahorros y Monte de Piedad de Zaragoza, Aragón y Rioja, 1987.
- ed. *Les problèmes de l'exclusion en Espagne (XVIe–XVIIe Siècles).* Travaux des Centre de Recherche en Espagne des XVIe et XVIIe Siècles. Paris: U de la Sorbonne Nouvelle-Paris III, 1983.
- ed. *Les representations de l'Autre dans l'espace iberique et ibéroaméricain.* No. 8. Paris: Cahiers de l'UFR d'Etudes Ibériques et Latino-Americains, 1991.
Reed, Helen H. *The Reader in the Picaresque Novel.* London: Tamesis, 1984.

Ricapito, Joseph. *Bibliografía razonada y anotada de las obras maestras de la novela picaresca española*. Madrid: Castalia, 1980.

Richards, Peter. *The Medieval Leper and His Northern Heirs*. Cambridge: D.S. Brewer, 1977.

Rico, Francisco. *La novela picaresca y el punto de vista*. Barcelona: Seix Barral, 1970.

– 'Nuevos apuntes sobre la carta de Lázaro.' *Serta Philologica Fernando Lázaro Carreter*. Vol. 2. Madrid: Cátedra: 1983. 413–25. Rpt. in Rico, *Problemas del Lazarillo*.

– *Problemas del Lazarillo*. Madrid: Cátedra, 1988.

– 'Puntos de vista. Postdata a unos ensayos sobre la novela picaresca.' *Edad de Oro* 3 (1984): 227–40.

– 'Resolutorio de cambios de Lázaro de Tormes (hacia 1552).' *Problemas del Lazarillo*. Madrid: Cátedra, 1988. 93–112.

– 'La transmisión de la novela picaresca.' Paper read at the Primer Congreso de la Asociación Siglo de Oro, Madrid and Córdoba, Spain, 29 June–3 July 1987.

Rodríguez, Juan Carlos. *La literatura del pobre*. Granada: De Guante Blanco, 1994.

Rodríguez-Luis, Julio. 'Pícaras: The Modal Approach to the Picaresque.' *Comparative Literature* 31 (1979): 32–46.

Rodríguez Matos, Antonio. *El narrador pícaro: Guzmán de Alfarache*. Madison, WI: Hispanic Seminary of Medieval Studies, 1985.

Rodríguez Puértolas, Julio. 'Lazarillo de Tormes o la desmitificación del imperio.' *Literatura, historia, alienación*. Barcelona: Ed. Labor, 1976. 349–57.

Rodríguez Solís, Enrique. *Historia de la prostitución en España y América*. Madrid: Biblioteca Nueva, 1921.

Rojas, Cristóbal de. *Teoría y práctica de fortificación*. Madrid, 1598.

Ronquillo, Pablo J. *Retrato de la pícara: la protagonista de la picaresca española del Siglo XVII*. Madrid: Playor, 1980.

Ros, Fidéle. *Un maître de Sainte Thérèse. Le père François d'Osuna. Sa vie, son oeuvre, sa doctrine spirituelle*. Paris: Gabriel Beauchesne, 1936.

Ruano de la Haza, J.M., and John J. Allen. *Los teatros comerciales del siglo XVII y la escenificación de la comedia*. Madrid: Castalia, 1994.

Rudder, Robert S. 'Lazarillo de Tormes y los peces: La continuación anónima de 1555.' *Explicación de Textos Literarios* 3 (1974): 157–66.

Ruffinatto, Aldo. '"En Torrijos cría tus hijos; en Maqueda tenla queda' (A proposito di strani percorsi del *tontilisto* Lazarillo).' *Symbolae Pisanae: Studi in onore di Guido Mancini*. Ed. Blanca Periñán and Francesco Guazzelli. Vol. 2. Pisa: Giardini Editori, 1989. 539–52.

– *Struttura e significazione del 'Lazarillo de Tormes'. I. La costruzione del modello operativo. Dall'intreccio alla fabula; II. La 'fabula'. Il modello transformazionale*. Turin: Giappichelli Editore, 1975; 1977.

Rufo, Juan. *Austriada*. Madrid, 1584.

Ruiz Martín, Felipe. *Pequeño capitalismo, gran capitalismo. Simón Ruiz y sus negocios en Florencia*. Barcelona: Crítica, 1990.

Rumeo de Armas, Antonio. *Historia de la previsión social de España*. Barcelona: El Albir, 1983.

Russell, Peter. 'Arms versus Letters: Towards a Definition of Spanish Fifteenth-Century Humanism.' Lewis 47–58.

– '*Don Quixote* as a Funny Book.' *Modern Language Review* 64 (1969): 312–26.

Sabat-Rivers, Georgina. 'La moral que Lázaro nos propone.' *MLN* 95 (1980): 233–51.

Saint-Saëns, Alain, ed. *Religion, Body, and Gender in Early Modern Spain*. San Francisco: Mellen Research UP, 1991.

Salas Barbadillo, Alonso de. *La hija de Celestina y la Ingeniosa Elena*. Ed. José Pradejas Lebrero. Madrid: Instituto de Estudios Madrileños, 1983.

Salazar y Mendoza, Pedro de. *Chronica de el cardenal Juan Tavera*. Toledo, 1603.

Saludo Stephan, Máximo. *Misteriosas andanzas atunescas de 'Lázaro de Tormes' descifradas de los seudo-jeroglíficos del Renacimiento*. San Sebastián: Izarra, 1969.

San Angel, Miguel. *Sentido y estructura del 'Guzmán de Alfarache'*. Madrid: Gredos, 1971.

Sánchez Herrero, José. 'Cofradías, hospitales y beneficencia en algunas diócesis del Valle del Duero, siglos XIV y XV.' *Hispania* 34 (1974): 5–51.

Sánchez, Magdalena S. 'Empress María and the Making of Political Policy in the Early Years of Philip III's Reign.' Saint-Saëns 139–47.

Seaver, Paul S., ed. *Seventeenth-Century England: Society in an Age of Revolution*. New York; London: New Viewpoints, 1976.

Sedola, Sabina Collet. 'Juan de Luna et la première edition de l'*Arte Breve*.' *Bulletin Hispanique* 79 (Ja.–June 1977): 147–54.

Shepard, Sanford. *Lost Lexicon: Secret Meanings of Spanish Literature during the Inquisition*. Miami: Ediciones Universal, 1982.

Shipley, George. 'The Critic as Witness for the Prosecution: Making the Case against Lázaro de Tormes.' *PMLA* 97 (1982): 179–94.

– 'The Critic as Witness for the Prosecution: Resting the Case against Lázaro de Tormes.' Surtz and Weinerth 105–24.

– 'Lazarillo de Tormes Was Not a Hardworking, Clean-Living Water Carrier.' Miletich 247–55.

Shubert, Adrian. '"Charity Properly Understood": Changing Ideas about Poor Relief in Liberal Spain.' *Comparative Studies in Society and History* 33 (January 1991): 36–55.

Sicroff, Albert A. *Los estatutos de limpieza de sangre: Controversias entre los siglos XV y XVII*. Madrid: Taurus, 1985.

- 'Sobre el estilo del *Lazarillo de Tormes*.' *Nueva Revista de Filología Hispánica* 11 (1957): 157–70.
Sieber, Harry. *Language and Society in the 'Lazarillo de Tormes'*. Baltimore, MD: Johns Hopkins UP, 1977.
- 'Literary Continuity, Social Order, and the Picaresque.' Brownlee and Gumbrecht 143–64.
- *The Picaresque*. The Critical Idiom. London: Methuen, 1977.
Siete Partidas, Las. Trans. Samuel Parsons Scott. New York: The Comparative Law Bureau of the American Bar Association, Commerce Clearing House, Loose Leaf Service Division of the Corporation Trust Company, 1931.
Silverman, Joseph. 'On Knowing Other People's Lives, Inquisitorially and Artistically.' Perry and Cruz 157–75.
- 'Plineo, Pedro Mejía y Mateo Alemán: La enemistad entre las especies hecha símbolo visual.' *PSA* 53 (1969): 30–8.
Smart, Barry. *Foucault, Marxism and Critique*. London; New York: Routledge, 1983. Rpt. 1989.
Smith, Paul Julian. *Quevedo: El Buscón*. Critical Guides to Spanish Texts 51. London: Grant & Cutler in association with Tamesis Books, 1991.
- *Writing in the Margin*. Oxford: Clarendon Press, 1988.
Sola-Solé, Josep. *Los tres Lazarillos*. Vol. 1. Barcelona: Puvill, 1987.
Soto, Domingo de. *De iustitia et iure libre decem. De la justicia y del derecho*. Trans. M. González Ordóñez. 4 vols. Madrid: Instituto de Estudios Políticos, 1967–8.
- *Deliberación en la causa de los pobres (Y réplica de Fray Juan de Robles, O.S.B.)*. Madrid: Instituto de Estudios Políticos, 1965.
Soubeyroux, Jacques. 'Sur un projet original d'organisation de la bienfaisance en Espagne au XVIe siècle.' *Bulletin Hispanique* 74 (1972): 118-24.
Spadaccini, Nicholas. 'History and Fiction: The Thirty Years' War in *Estebanillo González*.' *Kentucky Romance Quarterly* 24 (1977): 37–87.
- 'Imperial Spain and the Secularization of the Picaresque Novel.' *Ideologies & Literature* 1 (December 1976–January 1977): 59–62.
- 'Las vidas picarescas en *Estebanillo González*.' Criado de Val 749–63.
Stone, Lawrence. *The Crisis of the Aristocracy, 1558–1641*. Oxford: Clarendon Press, 1965.
- 'Social Mobility in England, 1500–1700.' Seaver 25–70.
Stradling, R.A. *The Armada of Flanders: Spanish Maritime Policy and European War. 1568–1668*. Cambridge: Cambridge UP, 1992.
- *Europe and the Decline of Spain: A Study of the Spanish System, 1580–1720*. London: George Allen & Unwin, 1981.
- *Philip IV and the Government of Spain, 1621–1665*. Cambridge: Cambridge UP, 1988.

Suárez de Figueroa, Cristóbal. *El pasajero: Advertencias utilísimas a la vida humana.* Ed. Francisco Rodríguez Marín. Madrid: Renacimiento, 1913.

– *El Passagero.* Madrid, 1614.

Sureda Carrión, Jose Luis. *La Hacienda castellana y los economistas del siglo XVII.* Madrid: Consejo Superior de Investigaciones Científicas, 1949.

Surtz, Ronald E., and Nora Wienerth, eds. *Creation and Recreation: Experiments in Literary Form in Early Modern Spain.* Newark, DE: Juan de la Cuesta, 1983.

Talens, Jenaro. *Novela picaresca y práctica de la transgresión.* Madrid: Ediciones Júcar, 1975.

Tavera, Juan de. *Constituciones sinodales del Arzobispado de Toledo.* Alcalá, 1536.

Tellechea Idígoras, J.I. *El obispo ideal en el siglo de la reforma.* Rome: Iglesia Nacional, 1963.

Texeda, Gaspar de. *Suma de Arithmetica practica y de toas Mercadrias con la horden de contadores.* Valladolid, 1546.

Thompson, I.A.A. *War and Government in Habsburg Spain: 1560–1620.* London: University of London, Athlons Press, 1976.

Tierno Galván, Enrique. *Sobre la novela picaresca y otros escritos.* Madrid: Tecnos, 1971.

Tikoff, Valentina. 'Life in an Old Regime Orphanage: The Case of Francisco de Cáceres Martinez.' Paper read at the Society for Spanish and Portuguese Studies Conference, St Louis, MO, 24–6 April 1998.

Tompkins, Jane P., ed. *Reader-Response Criticism from Formalism to Post-Structuralism.* Baltimore, MD: Johns Hopkins UP, 1980.

Turner, Victor. *The Ritual Process: Structure and Antistructure.* Chicago: Aldine, 1969.

– 'Variations on a Theme of Liminality.' Moore and Myerhoff 36–52.

Two Spanish Picaresque Novels. 'Lazarillo de Tormes'; 'The Swindler'. Trans. Michael Alpert. Harmonsdworth: Penguin, 1980.

Valdés, Francisco de. *Espejo y disciplina militar.* Brussels, 1589.

Van Gennep, Arnold. *The Rites of Passage.* Trans. Monika B. Vizedom and Gabrielle L. Caffee. London: Routledge & Kegan Paul, 1960.

Vassberg, David. *Land and Society in Golden Age Castile.* Cambridge: Cambridge UP, 1984.

Vega, Lope de. *Juan de Dios y Antón Martín,* vol. 186. Madrid: Biblioteca de Autores Españoles, 1963. 273–336.

Vélez de Guevara, Luis. *El diablo cojuelo.* Ed. Francisco Rodríguez Marín. Madrid: Clásicos Castellanos, 1918.

– *Vida i sucesos de la Monja Alférez.* Ed. Rima de Vallbona. Tempe: Arizona State UP, 1992.

Vilanova, Antonio. 'L'Ane d'Or d'Apulée, source et modele du *Lazarillo de*

Tormes.' L'Humanisme dans les lettres espagnoles (Actes du XIX. Colloque International d'Etudes Humanistes. Tours, 1976). Paris: Vrin, 1979. 267–85.

Vilar, Jean. *Literatura y economía: La figura satírica del arbitrista en el Siglo de Oro.* Madrid: Revista de Occidente, 1973.

Villalón, Cristóbal. *Prouechoso tratado de cambios, y contrataciones de mercaderes, y reprouacion de vsura.* Valladolid, 1541.

Villavicencio, Lorenzo de. *De aeconomia sacra circa pauperum curam a Christo institutam.* Paris, 1564.

Vives, Juan Luis. *Tratado del socorro de los pobres.* Trans. Juan de González Nieto e Ivarra. Valencia: Clásicos Españoles, n.d.

Vries, Jan De. *The Economy of Europe in an Age of Crisis: 1600–1750.* Cambridge: Cambridge UP, 1976. Rpt. 1978.

Walsh, John K., and B. Bussell Thompson. *The Myth of the Magdalen in Early Spanish Literature.* New York: Lorenzo Clemente, 1986.

Wardropper, Bruce. 'La novela como retrato: El arte de Francisco Delicado.' *Nueva Revista de Filología Hispánica* 7 (1953): 475–88.

– 'The Strange Case of Lázaro González Pérez.' *MLN* 92 (1977): 202–12.

Watt, Ian. *The Birth of the Novel.* Berkeley: U of California P, 1962.

Welles, Marcia. 'The *Pícara*: Towards Female Autonomy, or the Vanity of Virtue.' *Kentucky Romance Quarterly* 33 (1986): 63–70.

Whinnom, Keith. 'The Problem of the "Best-Seller" in Spanish Golden-Age Literature.' *BHS* 57 (1980): 189–98.

Whitenack, Judith. *The Impenitent Confession of Guzmán de Alfarache.* Madison, WI: Hispanic Seminary of Medieval Studies, 1985.

– 'Juan de Luna's *Lazarillo*: Continuation or Subversion?' *Philological Quarterly* 67 (1988): 177–94.

Wicks, Ulrich. *Picaresque Narrative, Picaresque Fictions: A Theory and Research Guide.* New York: Greenwood, 1989.

Williams, Raymond. *Marxism and Literature.* Oxford: Oxford UP, 1977.

Willis, Raymond. 'Mary Magdalene, Mary of Bethany, and the Unnamed Woman Sinner. Another Instance of Their Conflation in Old Spanish Literature.' *Romance Philology* 24 (1970–1): 89–90.

Woods, M.J. 'Pitfalls for the Moralizer in Lazarillo de Tormes.' *Modern Language Review* 74 (1979): 50–98.

Zahareas, Anthony. 'El género picaresco y las autobiografías de criminales.' Criado de Val 79–111.

Zappala, Michael. 'The *Lazarillo* Source – Apuleius or Lucian? – and Recreation.' *Hispanófila* 33 (1971): 1–16.

Zwez, Richard E. *Hacia la revalorizacíon de la 'Segunda Parte del Lazarillo' (1555).* Valencia: Albatros Ediciones, 1970.

Index

Page numbers in parentheses indicate the text page on which the note appears.

and clergy reform, 4, 28, 61; closure
of, 54; and Domingo de Soto, 23;
and heretics, 172; and women's
prisons, 143
Counter-Reformation, 53–4, 61, 97,
149, 150, 155
Count of Tendilla, 173
Cros, Edmond, 82, 107–9, 118–19,
121–5, 228n. 12 (81), 228n. 14 (81)
Crosby, James, 240n. 19 (120)

Damiani, Bruno, 150–1
damnosa heritas, 107–8
Davis, Charles, 225n. 64 (65), 233n. 40
(96), 236n. 66 (106)
Davis, Elizabeth, 245n. 66 (143)
Davis, Nina Cox, 230n. 24 (90), 246n.
79 (154)
Daza de Madrigal, Antonio, 224n. 62
(64)
debates, Soto-Robles, xii, xv, 4, 21,
23–9, 33, 41; *see also* Robles, Juan
de; Soto, Domingo de
Dedieu, Jean-Pierre, 222n. 49 (60)
Defensio fidei (Bleda), 177
Defoe, Daniel, 255n. 67 (206)
Deleito y Piñuela, José, 244n. 58 (139)
Deliberación en la causa de los pobres
(Soto), 23
Delicado, Francisco, xvi, 11, 146–50,
151–2
Derrida, Jacques, xi, 75
desengaño, 95
De Sully, Maurice, 13
Deyermond, Alan, 11–12, 145, 210n.
30 (11)
Deza, Pedro de, 173
Díaz Medina, Ana, 247n. 3 (161),
250n. 31 (174)
Díaz Migoyo, Gonzalo, 118

Díez del Corral Garnica, Rosario,
219n. 25 (49)
Dios, Juan de, 49, 50, 84
Discipline and Punish (Foucault), 3,
116, 160
discourses, in response to increase of
marginalized poor, xi, 8
discurso, 8
*Discursos del amparo de los legítimos
pobres y reducción de los fingidos*
(Pérez de Herrera). *See Amparo de
pobres*
Dissemination (Derrida), 75
domandores, 53
Domínguez Ortiz, José Antonio, 171,
222n. 48 (59), 228n. 13 (81), 249n.
21 (170), 253n. 54 (192), 255n. 64
(203)
Dominicans, 24
Don Quixote de la Mancha (Cervantes),
75, 80, 85, 114, 160, 178, 186
Douglas, Mary, 141
Dunn, Peter N.: on Alemán, 227n. 5
(80), 232n. 39 (96), 233n. 40 (96); on
Estebanillo González, 247n. 10 (164);
on female picaresque, 136, 243n. 44
(135), 244n. 49 (136); studies of
picaresque by, 6–7, 8, 20
Duque de Estrada, Diego, 190, 248n.
16 (167)

Eco, Umberto, 238n. 80 (113), 239n. 5
(117)
El Saffar, Ruth Anthony, 209n. 16 (7),
209n. 17 (7)
Eleazar, 11, 12
Elliott, John H., 121; on Charles V,
249n. 25 (171); on economic
situation, 212n. 48 (17), 217n. 2
(40), 222n. 48 (59), 223n. 56 (62); on

secularized proposals for, 21–2, 26–7, 55–61, 64–73
Relación de lo que pasa en la Cárcel de Sevilla (Chaves), 54
relaciones de Indias, 7
Renaissance: authors of, 115; and 'discourse,' xi; and *discurso*, 8; heroic literature during, 167; and madness, 39; and reader-response theorists, 110–11; rhetorical strategies of, 56–8; and Spain's army, 161–2; texts of the, 7, 45, 96, 202; warfare during, 174
Restauración de Estado (González de Cellorigo), 79
retablo, 56
Revolution, Gunpowder, 165
revolution, military, 164–82
rey de gallos, 122, 127–8, 129
Rey Hazas, Antonio, 241n. 23 (121)
rhetoric, 106–15
Ribagorza, Count of, 52–3
Ribera, Catalina de, 50
Ribera, San Juan de, 177
Ricapito, Joseph, 208n. 8 (6), 208n. 9 (6)
Richards, Peter, 12–13, 14
Rico, Francisco: on *El buscón*, 120, 239n. 12 (118); on *Guzmán de Alfarache*, 87, 95, 228n. 12 (81), 236n. 65 (106); on *Lazarillo de Tormes*, 18, 37, 46, 208n. 4 (4), 209n. 13 (7), 210n. 29 (11), 216n. 77 (36)
Rinconete y Cortadillo (Cervantes), 53, 82, 114
Rise of the Novel (Watt), 6
Robles, Juan de: and Cardinal Silíceo, 50; and Cardinal Tavera, 29; debates with Soto (*see* debates, Soto-

Robles); *De la orden que en algunos pueblos de España se ha puesto en la limosna para remedio de los verdaderos pobres*, 25–9; and ideas in Giginta's treatise, 56; and Peréz de Herrera, 62; as proponent of containment, 47, 60
Rodríguez, Juan Carlos, 255n. 65 (205)
Rodríguez Marín, Francisco, 223n. 57 (62), 228n. 9 (81)
Rodríguez Matos, Carlos Antonio, 236n. 66 (106)
Rodríguez Puértolas, Julio, 208n. 4 (4), 238n. 82 (114)
Rodríguez Solís, Enrique, 220n. 28 (50), 244n. 51 (136)
Rojas, Cristóbal de, 247n. 9 (163)
Rojas, Fernando de, 135
Roman Catholic Church. *See* Catholic Church
Romances of Roguery (Chandler), xiii
Ronquillo, Pablo J., 243n. 45 (135)
Ros, Fidéle, 213n. 55 (19)
Rudder, Robert S., 249n. 20 (168)
Ruffinatto, Aldo, 207n. 2 (4), 207n. 3 (4), 210n. 23 (8)
Ruiz Martín, Felipe, 235n. 58 (102)
Rumeu de Armas, Antonio, 220n. 30 (52)
Russell, Peter, 218n. 18 (45), 238n. 81 (113)

Sabat-Rivers, Georgina, 208n. 4 (4)
Saboya, Duke of, 199
Sala Balust, L., 219n. 24 (49)
Salamanca, Jerónimo de, 225n. 66 (70)
Salas Barbadillo, Alonso Jerónimo de, xvi, 155–7